READINGS IN STRATEGIC MANAGEMENT

This reader is one part of an Open University integrated teaching system and the selection is therefore related to other material available to students. It is designed to evoke the critical understanding of students. Opinions expressed in it are not necessarily those of the course team or of the University.

classical

READINGS IN STRATEGIC MANAGEMENT

Edited by

David Asch
School of Management
Open University

and

Cliff Bowman
School of Management
Cranfield Institute of Technology

 in association with
THE OPEN UNIVERSITY

First published 1989 by
THE MACMILLAN PRESS LTD
Houndmills, Basingstoke, Hampshire RG21 2XS
and London
Companies and representatives
throughout the world

ISBN 0–333–51809–8 paperback
ISBN 0–333–51793–8 hardcover

A catalogue record for this book is available
from the British Library.

12   11   10   9   8
01   00

Printed in Great Britain by
Antony Rowe Ltd
Chippenham, Wiltshire

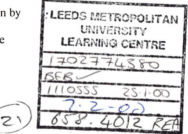

Contents

List of figures   ix
List of tables   xi
Preface   xiii
Acknowledgements   xvii

PART I   STRATEGIC MANAGEMENT PROCESSES

Introduction   2

1 Of Strategies, Deliberate and Emergent   4
   Henry Mintzberg and James A. Waters

2 Managing Strategic Change   20
   James Brian Quinn

3 Rethinking Incrementalism   37
   Gerry Johnson

4 Paralysis by Analysis: Is Your Planning System
   Becoming Too Rational?   57
   R. T. Lenz and Marjorie A. Lyles

5 Strategic Planning for the World Wildlife Fund   71
   G. J. Medley

6 Corporate Strategy and the Small Firm   78
   Sue Birley

PART II   STRATEGY FORMULATION

Introduction   84

7 Does Strategic Planning Improve Company
   Performance?   86
   Gordon E. Greenley

v

8   **Business Policy Formulation: Understanding the
    Process**   102
    Ron McLellan and Graham Kelly

9   **Whatever Happened to Environmental Analysis?**   113
    Jack L. Engledow and R. T. Lenz

10 **How Competitive Forces Shape Strategy**   133
    Michael E. Porter

11 **Portfolio Planning: Uses and Limits**   144
    Philippe Haspeslagh

12 **Defining Corporate Strengths and Weaknesses**   162
    Howard H. Stevenson

13 **The Risky Business of Diversification**   177
    Ralph Biggadike

14 **Assessing Opportunities for Diversification:
    An Analytical Approach**   191
    Michael Younger

15 **An Introduction to Divestment: The Conceptual
    Issues**   201
    John Coyne and Mike Wright

16 **End-game Strategies for Declining Industries**   219
    Kathryn Rudie Harrigan and Michael E. Porter

17 **From Competitive Advantage to Corporate Strategy**   234
    Michael E. Porter

18 **The Use of Corporate Planning Models: Past,
    Present and Future**   256
    Jae K. Shim and Randy McGlade

19 **Business Ethics: Two Introductory Questions**   270
    Tom Sorell

20 **Strategy and Ethics: Pilkington PLC**   280
    Tom Sorell

PART III   MANAGING STRATEGIC CHANGE   291

Introduction   292

21 **Choosing Strategies for Change**   294
    John P. Kotter and Leonard A. Schlesinger

22   Strategy Implementation versus Middle Management
      Self-interest   307
      William D. Guth and Ian C. MacMillan

23   The Structuring of Organizations   322
      Henry Mintzberg

24   Configurations of Strategy and Structure:
      Towards a Synthesis   353
      Danny Miller

25   Evolution and Revolution as Organizations Grow   373
      Larry E. Greiner

26   Successfully Implementing Strategic Decisions   388
      Larry D. Alexander

27   Strategic Control: An Overview of the Issues   397
      David Asch

28   The Nature and Use of Formal Control Systems
      for Management Control and Strategy
      Implementation   409
      Richard L. Daft and Norman B. Macintosh

Index   428

List of figures

1.1	Types of strategies	5
1.2	Strategic learning	18
3.1	A pattern of strategy development	39
3.2	The cultural web of an organization	46
3.3	A pattern of problem resolution and strategy formulation	49
3.4	A notional pattern of incremental change	50
3.5	Incremental change and 'strategic drift'	51
4.1	Organizational and technical forces contributing to over-rationalized planning	59
5.1	WWF UK net funds	76
5.2	WWF UK income per employee – productivity	76
8.1	Alpha process	104
8.2	Beta process	105
8.3	Gamma process	106
8.4	Delta process	107
9.1	Summary of role and form changes	122
10.1	Forces governing competition in an industry	134
12.1	Factors which influence a manager in defining strengths and weaknesses	167
12.2	Criteria used to judge an attribute	173
14.1	Analytical system for selecting sectors	193
14.2	System for appropriateness of a sector to a company's strengths-mesh	197
14.3	System for overall assessment of sectors	198
14.4	Selection of sectors based on alternative strategies for business development	199
15.1	Route to adaptation through ownership change	212
16.1	Strategies for declining businesses	230
18.1	Typical structure of a corporate planning model	263
23.1	The six basic parts of the organization	323
23.2	The basic mechanisms of co-ordination	325
23.3	Structures to deal with residual interdependencies	333

23.4	A permanent matrix structure in an international firm	334
23.5	Shifting matrix structure in the NASA weather satellite program	335
23.6	Six types of decentralization	337
23.7	Six pulls on the organization	346
23.8	The simple structure	346
23.9	The machine bureaucracy	347
23.10	The professional bureaucracy	348
23.11	The divisionalized form	349
23.12	The adhocracy	350
23.13	The missionary	351
24.1	Five successful configurations of strategy	360
25.1	Model of organization development	375
25.2	The five phases of growth	378
27.1	A simple control model	397
28.1	Average managerial ranking of management control subsystem use for five control functions	416
28.2	Model of vertical linkage among control systems for strategy implementation	422

List of tables

1.1	Summary description of types of strategies	16
5.1	WWF UK key areas 1978	73
7.1	Comparison of surveys (i)	89
7.2	Comparison of surveys (ii)	97
9.1	Organizational roles of environmental analysis units	118
9.2	Changes in role and form in ten environmental analysis units	120
12.1	Steps in the process of assessing strengths and weaknesses	164
12.2	Categories for assessing strengths and weaknesses	165
12.3	The relative importance of attributes identified as strengths and weaknesses (all managers)	166
12.4	The attributes examined in relation to the companies studied	167
12.5	Attributes of common concern to the companies studied	168
12.6	The relationship between the category of attribute examined and the manager's organizational level	170
12.7	Percentage of responses identifying category as a strength at each organizational level	171
12.8	The association of specific criteria with identification of strengths and weaknesses	172
13.1	Financial performance in the first four years of operations	179
13.2	Operating and capital ratios in the first four years of operations	180
13.3	Median performance in start-up, adolescent, and mature stages	182
13.4	Relationship between financial and market performance	185
13.5	Financial performance and change in relative share, first four years	186
13.6	Distribution of sample on entry scale, first two years	187
13.7	Performance by index of entry scale, first two years	188

14.2 System for classifying sectors according to degree of
      maturity   194
14.3 Scoring system for sector maturity   195
15.1 Spectrum of divestment   203
15.2 Divestment change and breakdown in key areas   207
16.1 Structural factors that influence the attractiveness of
      declining industry environments   226
17.1 Concepts of corporate strategy   242
18.1 Results of surveys for the use of corporate planning
      models   259
18.2 Applications of corporate planning models   259
18.3 Reasons for discontinuing models   262
18.4 Success factors in modelling   265
21.1 Methods for dealing with resistance to change   302
21.2 Strategic continuum   303
23.1 Basic dimensions of the six configurations   344
24.1 Representative strategic variables within each dimension   357
24.2 Structure, environments and strategies   362
24.3 Matching strategy and structure   364
25.1 Organization practices during evolution in the five
      phases of growth   384
26.1 Types of strategic decisions implemer.ted   389
26.2 Ten most frequent strategy implementation problems   390
28.1 Management control system frequency size and cycles   415
28.2 Relationship of management control cycle to MCS
      and personal control   424

Preface

'Strategic management is the process of making and implementing strategic decisions ... (it) is about the process of strategic change' (Bowman and Asch, 1987, p. 4). This general definition of strategic management conforms with that of most texts in the field (for example, Jauch and Glueck, 1988, p. 5, and Johnson and Scholes, 1988, p. 10). The task of strategic management involves both top management and managers at all levels in the organization. Readers will probably be aware that strategic management is sometimes referred to as corporate strategy, business policy, management policy and organizational policy, which all deal with the same general area of study.

Strategic management affects all parts of the organization. Strategic decisions concern the scope of an organization's activities. That is, should the organization focus on one type of activity, or should it encompass many different types? Strategic management is also concerned with matching of the organization to the environment in which it operates. Accordingly, management will need to consider what threats or opportunities exist, or may exist in the future, in order to position the entity appropriately. Linked closely with this is the need to understand the organization's own capabilities. The availability of resources (people, technology and finance for example) to meet environmental discontinuities and change is fundamental to the organization's strategic development. Strategic decisions are, therefore, likely to have a significant impact on the organization's resources. This may involve disposal or acquisition of resources, or it may involve major changes to the financial structure of the organization. Then again strategic decisions could have a major influence on working patterns and the skills and abilities required of the employees. The way in which an organization develops will also be a function of how managers view their world, the power relationships within the organization, and how the organization is structured and controlled.

The Bradford studies of decision making identified a number of issues concerning strategic decisions (Hickson *et al.*, 1986). They found that strategic decisions themselves tend to be less frequent and more nonroutine than most other decisions, and are, therefore, comparatively novel (pp. 26–54). There will be few if any precedents for them, yet they are likely to set precedents for subsequent decisions. Strategic decisions commit substantial resources and are organization-wide in their consequences. The most frequent decision topics were those concerning technologies (to re-equip, rebuild), reorganizations, followed by controls (making of plans, the fixing of budgets, commitments on data processing equipment), and domain or market type decisions (price, distribution, image).

The challenge of strategic management is in the involvement of managers in guiding the future direction of the organization. They need, therefore, to understand the complexity deriving from the need both to adopt a strategic perspective, as opposed to a functional or specialist or technical view, and to understand and appreciate the subtlety, inconsistency, bureaucracy, political machinations and the imperatives of the world in which the organization operates. Realistically, we should recognize this complexity and avoid a simplistic approach. Consequently, our selection of readings is intended to illustrate the complex world of the strategic development of organizations so that readers can develop and enhance their own approach to the subject. In conclusion, a single paradigm is not appropriate. We need to recognize that different skills and techniques are required in a dynamic and innovative organization as opposed to those required in a bureaucracy. Strategic management deals with both the uncertain and the unknowable. So, in addition to analysis, managers rely on accumulated experience – a 'feel' for the situation, or intuition. As a result, the paramount indispensable attribute is good judgment which should underlie every decision and action (see, for example, Quinn *et al.*, 1988).

We have selected and structured this collection of readings to reflect the broad and diverse nature of the developing field of strategic management. The wide variety of issues associated with both the theoretical and the practical development of the subject are presented through this range of articles. By virtue of the nature of the subject, some of the papers offer contradictory views. We believe this to be a strength in that it enables a critical examination to be made of the different perspectives arising from differing contexts. Each of the three parts contains papers which develop the conceptual framework of strategic management as well as pieces reporting on the findings of empirical research. We have included some papers with a very prescriptive or normative view of strategic management and some which seek to describe strategic management in practice. There is no one best way in management, so no prescription works for all organizations. Normative concepts have been included where we believe they offer some understanding of the complexity of organizational strategy and where they are associated with other readings or empirical evidence of their use.

We have selected these articles because we believe that they contribute to our understanding of strategic management, or some aspect thereof, better than other articles. Some articles are new, some are older, three have been written specifically for this collection. In order to present a wide variety of good ideas we have edited each of the previously published papers. This has often involved the elimination of interesting examples and/or the detailed methodologies used. In so doing, we have endeavoured to ensure that the key messages have been retained in as concise a manner as possible.

Part I is concerned with strategic management processes. Inherent in it is the view that strategic management is more than corporate or strategic planning. Indeed, corporate planning may be a part of, or element in, the strategy process. In these articles we seek to reflect the differing approaches to the subject as a management process. We believe that an appreciation of the process by which strategic decisions are made is fundamental to understanding why and how such decisions are arrived at. Some knowledge of the process may also help us to grapple with the realities and complexities involved in formulating policy and managing strategic change. Because strategic management is relevant to all types of organization, this part of the collection includes an article on small firms and another on a non-profit-making organization. Part I provides an important perspective on our view of both strategy formulation and the management of strategic change and is crucial to our understanding of the contexts in which these activities take place.

Strategy formulation, Part II, focuses on strategic analysis. The readings concentrate on analysis of the organization in terms of internal and external features, a consideration of strategic options plus a view of the issues involved in the selection of an appropriate strategic alternative. Also included in Part II are two papers on business ethics which we believe raise some interesting issues for the reader to consider as part of developing an understanding of strategy formulation. The number of contributions in this section reflects the fact that it is arguably the most developed part of the literature. Its size also reflects the breadth of the subject matter.

The final section, Part III, is concerned with managing strategic change. This part has contributions on strategy implementation, strategic control and strategy and structure. The management of strategic change concerns issues involved in translating the formulated, often well articulated, strategies into action plans. The articles span a range of interrelated topics from strategic control to power relationships to the stages of growth in organizations. Given the iterative nature of what can be a very complex process, it may not always be appropriate to distinguish formulation and implementation of strategy quite so neatly. Reality is likely to be much more confused, complex and messy.

References

Bowman, C. and Asch, D. (1987) *Strategic Management* (London: Macmillan).

Hickson, D. J., Butler, R. J., Cray, D., Mallory, G. R. and Wilson, D. C. (1986) *Top Decisions: Strategic Decision-Making in Organizations* (Oxford: Blackwell).

Jauch, L R. and Glueck, W. F. (1988) *Business Policy and Strategic Management* (New York: McGraw Hill) 5th edn.

Johnson, G. and Scholes, K. (1988) *Exploring Corporate Strategy* (London: Prentice Hall) 2nd edn.

Quinn, J. B., Mintzberg, H. and James, R. M. (1988) *The Strategy Process: Concepts, Contexts, and Cases* (Englewood Cliffs, NJ: Prentice Hall).

Acknowledgements

The authors and publishers wish to thank the following who have kindly given permission for the use of copyright material.

Harvard Business Review for excerpts from articles from various issues of *Harvard Business Review*.

Journal of General Management for articles extracted from S. Birley, 'Corporate Strategy and the Small Firm', *Journal of General Management*, vol. 8, no. 2, Winter 1982–3, pp. 82–6; and R. McLellan and G. Kelly, 'Business Policy Formulation: Understanding the Process', *Journal of General Management*, Autumn 1980, pp. 38–47.

The Open University for article by D. Asch, 'Strategic Control: An Overview of the Issues', 1988.

Pergamon Press plc for articles extracted from R. T. Lenz and M. A. Lyles, 'Paralysis by Analysis: Is Your Planning System Becoming too Rational?', *Long Range Planning*, vol. 18, no. 4, 1985, pp. 64–72; G. J. Medley, 'Strategic Planning for the World Wildlife Fund', *Long Range Planning*, vol. 21, no. 1, 1988, pp. 46–54; G. Greenley, 'Does Strategic Planning Improve Company Performance?', *Long Range Planning*, vol. 19, no. 2, 1986, pp. 101–9; J. Engledow and R. T. Lenz, 'Whatever Happened to Environmental Analysis?', *Long Range Planning*, vol. 18, no. 2, 1985, pp. 93–106; M. Younger, 'Assessing Opportunities for Diversification', *Long Range Planning*, vol. 17, no. 4, 1984, pp. 10–15; L. D. Alexander, 'Successfully Implementing Strategic Decisions', *Long Range Planning*, vol. 18, no. 3, 1985, pp. 91–7; J. K. Shim and R. Glade, 'The Use of Corporate Planning Models: Past, Present and Future', *Journal of the Operational Research Society*, vol. 35, no. 10, 1984, pp. 885–93.

Philip Allan Publishers Ltd for J. Coyne and M. Wright, 'An Introduction to Divestment: The Conceptual Issues', from Coyne and Wright (eds), *Divestment and Strategic Change*, 1985, ch. 1, pp. 1–26.

Prentice Hall, Inc. for material extracted from H. Mintzberg, *The Structuring of Organisations*, 1979.

Sloan Management Review for articles extracted from J. B. Quinn, 'Managing Strategic Change', *Sloan Management Review*, Summer 1980, pp. 3–20; and H. H. Stevens, 'Defining Corporate Strengths and Weaknesses', *Sloan Management Review*, Spring 1976, pp. 51–68.

Tom Sorell for papers 'Business Ethics': Two Introductory Questions', 1988, and 'Strategy and Ethics: Pilkington PLC', 1988.

Southern Management Association for article extracted from R. E. Daft and N. B. Macintosh, 'The Nature and Use of Formal Central Systems for Management Control and Strategy Implementation', *Journal of Management*, vol. 10, no. 1, 1984, pp. 43–66.

John Wiley & Sons Ltd for articles extracted from H. Mintzberg and J. H. Waters, 'Of Strategies Deliberate and Emergent', *Strategic Management Journal*, vol. 6, 1985, pp. 257–72; G. Johnson, 'Rethinking Incrementalism', *Strategic Management Journal*, vol. 9, 1988, pp. 75–91; W. D. Guth and I. C. MacMillan, 'Strategy Implementation versus Middle Management Self Interest', *Strategic Management Journal*, vol. 7, 1986, pp. 313–27; D. Miller, 'Configurations of Strategy and Structure: Towards a Synthesis', *Strategic Management Journal*, vol. 7, 1986, pp. 233–49.

Every effort has been made to trace all the copyright-holders, but if any have been inadvertently overlooked the publishers will be pleased to make the necessary arrangement at the first opportunity.

PART I

STRATEGIC MANAGEMENT PROCESSES

Introduction

The article by Mintzberg and Waters that opens Part I provides a basic framework of types of strategy making processes. At one end of the continuum they propose the planned strategy. Here the strategy makers clearly formulate their intentions which are subsequently translated into action. Moving along the continuum through entrepreneurial, ideological and umbrella strategies, the authors gradually relax the requirement for precise articulation of the content of the strategy, so that in the case of umbrella strategies only broad guidelines are set centrally. At the other end of this continuum are the emergent strategies. For example, the consensus strategy evolves through a process whereby the results of many individual actions come together to form a consistent pattern.

This framework recognizes that there is no 'one best way' of formulating strategy: the strategy making process appropriate for one organization facing a particular type of task and environment may well be inappropriate for another organization in a different setting. They take, then, a 'contingency' approach to the subject.

In the second article Quinn develops in some depth a particular type of strategy formulation process he labels 'logical incrementalism'. This describes a purposeful blending of deliberate and emergent processes to achieve viable and acceptable strategic changes. His findings are based on processes he observed at work in a small sample of large, relatively complex organizations, hence we should be wary of translating his conclusions directly into dissimilar organizations.

The themes of strategic change and incrementalism are developed further in Johnson's article. He introduces two very useful concepts which can help us understand why some organizations are so slow to adapt to changing environmental conditions. He suggests that some organizations have strong systems of beliefs and assumptions shared by the management group, which he describes as a 'paradigm'. The 'paradigm' is preserved and legitimized by a 'cultural web' of control systems, rituals, myths, power structures and symbols. The paradigm can be so powerful that the managers resist or reinterpret strong signals from the environment, indicating that a change in strategy is called for. The second contribution he makes is the notion of 'strategic drift'. Here, because of the strength of the paradigm, managers make only incremental adjustments to strategy, meanwhile the environment is drifting further away from the organization.

The Quinn and Johnson articles explore the more emergent, incremental end of Mintzberg and Waters' continuum of strategy processes. The next two articles concentrate on deliberate, planned strategy making processes. Lenz and Lyles highlight some of the problems that can occur if organizations look for excessive rationality and quantification in their planning processes. Inflexibility and an absence of entrepreneurial creativity can result if the planning system 'takes over'. They suggest some measures that can be taken to avoid these pitfalls.

In his article Medley demonstrates the benefits that can accrue if strategic planning is correctly introduced into an organization. Interestingly, his organization is a non-profit-making charity, illustrating that sound management principles are applicable to many types of organization. In her article Birley reintroduces the contingency approach to strategy making processes highlighted by Mintzberg and Waters. She points out that as the goals, product/market choices, resources and structures of the small firm are likely to differ significantly from those of larger organizations, we need to understand how the small entrepreneur goes about making strategy. In this way we can improve the help and advice provided for the small firms sector.

CHAPTER 1

Of Strategies, Deliberate and Emergent

HENRY MINTZBERG and JAMES A. WATERS

Introduction

How do strategies form in organizations? Research into the question is necessarily shaped by the underlying conception of the term. Since strategy has almost inevitably been conceived in terms of what the leaders of an organization 'plan' to do in the future, strategy formation has, not surprisingly, tended to be treated as an analytic process for establishing long-range goals and action plans for an organization; that is, as one of formulation followed by implementation. As important as this emphasis may be, we would argue that it is seriously limited, that the process needs to be viewed from a wider perspective so that the variety of ways in which strategies actually take shape can be considered.

For over 10 years now, we have been researching the process of strategy formation based on the definition of strategy as 'a pattern in a stream of decisions' (Mintzberg, 1972, 1978; Mintzberg and Waters, 1982, 1984; Mintzberg et al., 1986; Mintzberg and McHugh, 1985; Brunet, Mintzberg and Waters, 1986). This definition was developed to 'operationalize' the concept of strategy, namely to provide a tangible basis on which to conduct research into how it forms in organizations. Streams of behaviour could be isolated and strategies identified as patterns or consistencies in such streams. The origins of these strategies could then be investigated, with particular attention paid to exploring the relationship between leadership plans and intentions and what the organizations actually did. Using the label strategy for both of these phenomena – one called *intended*, the other *realized* – encouraged that exploration.

[...]

Comparing intended strategy with realized strategy, as shown in Figure 1.1, has allowed us to distinguish *deliberate* strategies – realized as

4

FIGURE 1.1   **Types of strategies**

intended – from *emergent* strategies – patterns or consistencies realized despite, or in the absence of, intentions.
[. . .]
   This paper sets out to explore the complexity and variety of strategy formation processes by refining and elaborating the concepts of deliberate and emergent strategy. We begin by specifying more precisely what pure deliberate and pure emergent strategies might mean in the context of organization, describing the conditions under which each can be said to exist. What does it mean for an 'organization' – a collection of people joined together to pursue some mission in common – to act deliberately? What does it mean for a strategy to emerge in an organization, not guided by intentions? We then identify various types of strategies that have appeared in our empirical studies, each embodying differing degrees of what might be called deliberateness or emergentness. The paper concludes with a discussion of the implications of this perspective on strategy formation for research and practice.

Pure deliberate and pure emergent strategies

For a strategy to be perfectly deliberate – that is, for the realized strategy (pattern in actions) to form exactly as intended – at least three conditions would seem to have to be satisfied. First, there must have existed precise intentions in the organization, articulated in a relatively concrete level of detail, so that there can be no doubt about what was desired before any actions were taken. Secondly, because organization means collective action, to dispel any possible doubt about whether or not the intentions were organizational, they must have been common to virtually all the actors: either shared as their own or else accepted from leaders, probably in response to some sort of controls. Thirdly, these collective intentions must have been realized exactly as intended, which means that no external force (market, technological, political, etc.) could have interfered with them. The environment, in other words, must have been either perfectly predictable, totally benign, or else under the full control of the organization. These three conditions constitute a tall order, so that we are unlikely to find any perfectly deliberate strategies in organizations. Nevertheless, some strategies do come rather close, in some dimensions if not all.

For a strategy to be perfectly emergent, there must be order – consistency in action over time – in the absence of intention about it. (No consistency means no strategy or at least unrealized strategy – intentions not met.) It is difficult to imagine action in the *total* absence of intention – in some pocket of the organization if not from the leadership itself – such that we would expect the purely emergent strategy to be as rare as the purely deliberate one. But again, our research suggests that some patterns come rather close, as when an environment directly imposes a pattern of action on an organization.

Thus, we would expect to find tendencies in the directions of deliberate and emergent strategies rather than perfect forms of either. In effect, these two form the poles of a continuum along which we would expect real-world strategies to fall. Such strategies would combine various states of the dimensions we have discussed above: leadership intentions would be more or less precise, concrete and explicit, and more or less shared, as would intentions existing elsewhere in the organization; central control over organizational actions would be more or less firm and more or less pervasive; and the environment would be more or less benign, more or less controllable and more or less predictable.

Below we introduce a variety of types of strategies that fall along this continuum, beginning with those closest to the deliberate pole and ending with those most reflective of the characteristics of emergent strategy. We present these types, not as any firm or exhaustive typology (although one may eventually emerge), but simply to explore this continuum of emergentness of strategy and to try to gain some insights into the notions of intention, choice and pattern formation in the collective context we call organization.

The planned strategy

Planning suggests clear and articulated intentions, backed up by formal controls to ensure their pursuit, in an environment that is acquiescent. In other words, here (and only here) does the classic distinction between 'formulation' and 'implementation' hold up.

In this first type, called *planned strategy*, leaders at the centre of authority formulate their intentions as precisely as possible and then strive for their implementation – their translation into collective action – with a minimum of distortion, 'surprise-free'. To ensure this, the leaders must first articulate their intentions in the form of a plan, to minimize confusion, and then elaborate this plan in as much detail as possible, in the form of budgets, schedules and so on, to pre-empt discretion that might impede its realization. Those outside the planning process may act, but to the extent possible they are not allowed to decide. Programmes that guide their behaviour are built into the plan, and formal controls are instituted to ensure pursuit of the plan and the programmes.

But the plan is of no use if it cannot be applied as formulated in the environment surrounding the organization so the planned strategy is found in an environment that is, if not benign or controllable, then at least rather predictable. Some organizations, as Galbraith (1967) describes the 'new industrial states', are powerful enough to impose their plans on their environments. Others are able to predict their environments with enough accuracy to pursue rather deliberate, planned strategies. We suspect, however, that many planned strategies are found in organizations that simply extrapolate established patterns in environments that they assume will remain stable. In fact, we have argued elsewhere (Mintzberg and Waters, 1982) that strategies appear not to be *conceived* in planning processes so much as elaborated from existing visions or copied from standard industry recipes (see Grinyer and Spender, 1979); planning thus becomes programming, and the planned strategy finds its origins in one of the other types of strategies described below.

Although few strategies can be planned to the degree described above, some do come rather close, particularly in organizations that must commit large quantities of resources to particular missions and so cannot tolerate unstable environments. They may spend years considering their actions, but once they decide to act, they commit themselves firmly. In effect, they deliberate so that their strategies can be rather deliberate. Thus, we studied a mining company that had to engage in a most detailed form of planning to exploit a new ore body in an extremely remote part of Quebec. Likewise, we found a very strong planning orientation in our study of Air Canada, necessary to co-ordinate the purchase of new, expensive jet aircraft with a relatively fixed route structure.
[...]

The entrepreneurial strategy

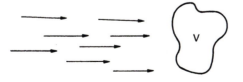

In this second type of strategy, we relax the condition of precise, articulated intentions. Here, one individual in personal control of an organization is able to impose his or her vision of direction on it. Because such strategies are rather common in entrepreneurial firms, tightly controlled by their owners, they can be called *entrepreneurial strategies*.

In this case, the force for pattern or consistency in action is individual vision, the central actor's *concept* of his or her organization's place in its world. This is coupled with an ability to impose that vision on the organization through his or her personal control of its actions (e.g. through giving direct orders to its operating personnel). Of course, the environment must again be co-operative. But entrepreneurial strategies most commonly appear in young and/or small organizations (where personal control is feasible), which are able to find relatively safe niches in their environments. Indeed, the selection of such niches is an integral part of the vision. These strategies can, however, sometimes be found in larger organizations as well, particularly under conditions of crisis where all the actors are willing to follow the direction of a single leader who has vision and will.

Is the entrepreneurial strategy deliberate? Intentions do exist. But they derive from one individual who need not articulate or elaborate them. Indeed, for reasons discussed below, he or she is typically unlikely to want to do so. Thus, the intentions are both more difficult to identify and less specific than those of the planned strategy. Moreover, there is less overt acceptance of these intentions on the part of other actors in the organization. Nevertheless, so long as those actors respond to the personal will of the leader, the strategy would appear to be rather deliberate.

In two important respects, however, that strategy can have emergent characteristics as well. First, as indicated in the previous diagram, vision provides only a general sense of direction. Within it, there is room for adaptation: the details of the vision can emerge *en route*. Secondly, because the leader's vision is personal, it can also be changed completely. To put this another way, since here the formulator is the implementor, step by step, that person can react quickly to feedback on past actions or to new opportunities or threats in the environment. He or she can thus reformulate vision, as shown in the figure below.

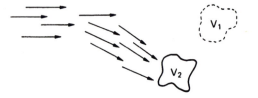

It is this adaptability that distinguishes the entrepreneurial strategy from the planned one. Visions contained in single brains would appear to be more flexible, assuming the individual's willingness to learn, than plans articulated through hierarchies, which are comprised of many brains. Adaptation (and emergentness) of planned strategies are discouraged by the articulation of intentions and by the separation between formulation and implementation. Psychologists have shown that the articulation of a strategy locks it into place, impeding willingness to change it (e.g. Kiesler, 1971). The separation of implementation from formulation gives rise to a whole system of commitments and procedures, in the form of plans, programmes and controls elaborated down a hierarchy. Instead of one individual being able to change his or her mind, the whole system must be redesigned. Thus, despite the claims of flexible planning, the fact is that organizations plan not to be flexible but to realize specific intentions. It is the entrepreneurial strategy that provides flexibility, at the expense of the specificity and articulation of intentions. [...]

The ideological strategy

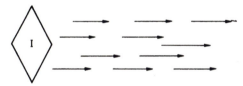

Vision can be collective as well as individual. When the members of an organization share a vision and identify so strongly with it that they pursue it as an ideology, then they are bound to exhibit patterns in their behaviour, so that clear realized strategies can be identified. These may be called *ideological strategies*.

Can an ideological strategy be considered deliberate? Since the ideology is likely to be somewhat overt (e.g. in programmes of indoctrination), and perhaps even articulated (in rough, inspirational form, such as a credo), intentions can usually be identified. The question thus revolves around whether these intentions can be considered organizational and whether they are likely to be realized as intended. In an important sense, these intentions would seem to be most clearly organizational. Whereas the intentions of the planned and entrepreneurial strategies emanate from one centre and are accepted passively by everyone else, those of the ideological strategy are positively embraced by the members of the organization.

As for their realization, because the intentions exist as a rough vision, they can presumably be adapted or changed. But collective vision is far more immutable than individual vision. All who share it must agree to change their 'collective mind'. Moreover, ideology is rooted in the past, in traditions and precedents (often the institutionalization of the vision of a departed, charismatic leader: one person's vision has become everyone's ideology). People, therefore, resist changing it. The object is to interpret 'the word', not to defy it. Finally, the environment is unlikely to impose change: the purpose of ideology, after all, is to change the environment or else to insulate the organization from it. For all these reasons, therefore, ideological strategy would normally be highly deliberate, perhaps more so than any type of strategy except the planned one. [...]

The umbrella strategy

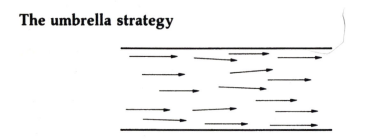

Now we begin to relax the condition of tight control (whether bureaucratic, personal or ideological) over the mass of actors in the organization and, in some cases, the condition of tight control over the environment as well. Leaders who have only partial control over other actors in an organization may design what can be called *umbrella strategies*. They set general guidelines for behaviour – define the boundaries – and then let other actors manoeuvre within them. In effect, these leaders establish kinds of umbrellas under which organizational actions are expected to fall – for example that all products should be designed for the high-priced end of the market (no matter what those products might be).

When an environment is complex, and perhaps somewhat uncontrollable and unpredictable as well, a variety of actors in the organization must be able to respond to it. In other words, the patterns in organizational actions cannot be set deliberately in one central place, although the boundaries may be established there to constrain them. From the perspective of the leadership (if not, perhaps, the individual actors), therefore, strategies are allowed to emerge, at least within these boundaries. In fact, we can label the umbrella strategy not only deliberate and emergent (intended at the centre in its broad outlines but not in its specific details), but also 'deliberately emergent' (in the sense that the central leadership intentionally creates the conditions under which strategies can emerge).
[...]
We have so far described the umbrella strategy as one among a

number of types that are possible. But, in some sense, virtually all real-world strategies have umbrella characteristics. That is to say, in no organization can the central leadership totally pre-empt the discretion of others (as was assumed in the planned and entrepreneurial strategies) and, by the same token, in none does a central leadership defer totally to others (unless it has ceased to lead). Almost all strategy making behaviour involves, therefore, to some degree at least, a central leadership with some sort of intentions trying to direct, guide, cajole or nudge others with ideas of their own. When the leadership is able to direct, we move towards the realm of the planned or entrepreneurial strategies; when it can hardly nudge, we move toward the realm of the more emergent strategies. But in the broad range between these two can always be found strategies with umbrella characteristics.

In its pursuit of an umbrella strategy – which means, in essence, defining general direction subject to varied interpretation – the central leadership must monitor the behaviour of other actors to assess whether or not the boundaries are being respected. In essence, like us, it searches for patterns in streams of actions. When actors are found to stray outside the boundaries (whether inadvertently or intentionally), the central leadership has three choices: to stop them, ignore them (perhaps for a time, to see what will happen), or adjust to them. In other words, when an arm pokes outside the umbrella, you either pull it in, leave it there (although it might get wet), or move the umbrella over to cover it.

In this last case, the leadership exercises the option of altering its own vision in response to the behaviour of others. Indeed, this would appear to be the place where much effective strategic learning takes place – through leadership response to the initiatives of others. The leadership that is never willing to alter its vision in such a way forgoes important opportunities and tends to lose touch with its environment (although, of course, the one too willing to do so may be unable to sustain any central direction). The umbrella strategy thus requires a light touch, maintaining a subtle balance between proaction and reaction.

The process strategy

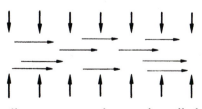

Similar to the umbrella strategy is what can be called the *process strategy*. Again, the leadership functions in an organization in which other actors must have considerable discretion to determine outcomes, because of an environment that is complex and perhaps also unpredictable and uncontrollable. But instead of trying to control strategy content at a general level, through boundaries or targets, the leadership instead needs to exercise influence indirectly. Specifically, it controls the *process* of strategy making while leaving the *content* of strategy to other actors. Again, the resulting behaviour would be deliberate in one respect and emergent in others: the central leadership designs the system that allows others the flexibility to evolve patterns within it.

The leadership may, for example, control the staffing of the organization, thereby determining who gets to make strategy if not what that strategy will be (all the while knowing that control of the former constitutes considerable influence over the latter). Or it may design the structure of the organization to determine the working context of those who get to make strategy.
[...]

Divisionalized organizations of a conglomerate nature commonly use process strategies: the central headquarters creates the basic structure, establishes the control systems and appoints the division managers, who are then expected to develop strategies for their own businesses (typically planned ones for reasons outlined by Mintzberg, 1979: 384–392); note that techniques such as those introduced by the Boston Consulting Group to manage the business portfolios of divisionalized companies, by involving headquarters in the business strategies to some extent, bring their strategies back into the realm of umbrella ones.

The unconnected strategies

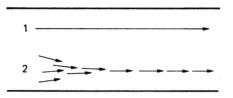

The *unconnected strategy* is perhaps the most straightforward one of all. One part of the organization with considerable discretion – a subunit, sometimes even a single individual – because it is only loosely coupled to the rest, is able to realize its own pattern in its stream of actions.
[...]

Unconnected strategies tend to proliferate in organizations of experts, reflecting the complexity of the environments that they face and the

resulting need for considerable control by the experts over their own work, providing freedom not only from administrators but sometimes from their own peers as well. Thus, many hospitals and universities appear to be little more than collections of personal strategies, with hardly any discernible central vision or umbrella, let alone plan, linking them together. Each expert pursues his or her own strategies – method of patient care, subject of research, style of teaching. On the other hand, in organizations that do pursue central, rather deliberate strategies, even planned ones, unconnected strategies can sometimes be found in remote enclaves, either tolerated by the system or lost within it.
[...]

The consensus strategy

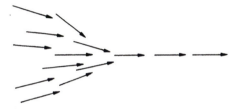

In no strategy so far discussed have we totally dropped the condition of prior intention. The next type is rather more clearly emergent. Here many different actors naturally converge on the same theme, or pattern, so that it becomes pervasive in the organization, without the need for any central direction or control. We call it the *consensus strategy*. Unlike the ideological strategy, in which a consensus forms around a system of beliefs (thus reflecting intentions widely accepted in the organization), the consensus strategy grows out of the mutual adjustment among different actors, as they learn from each other and from their various responses to the environment and thereby find a common, and probably unexpected, pattern that works for them.

In other words, the convergence is not driven by any intentions of a central management, nor even by prior intentions widely shared among the other actors. It just evolves through the results of a host of individual actions. Of course, certain actors may actively promote the consensus, perhaps even negotiate with their colleagues to attain it (as in the congressional form of government). But the point is that it derives more from collective action than from collective intention.
[...]

The imposed strategies

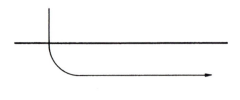

All the strategies so far discussed have derived in part at least from the will (if not the intentions) of actors within the organization. The environment has been considered, if not benign, then at least acquiescent. But strategies can be *imposed* from outside as well; that is, the environment can directly force the organization into a pattern in its stream of actions, regardless of the presence of central controls. The clearest case of this occurs when an external individual or group with a great deal of influence over the organization imposes a strategy on it. We saw this in our study of the state-owned Air Canada, when the minister who created and controlled the airline in its early years forced it to buy and fly a particular type of aircraft. Here the imposed strategy was clearly deliberate, but not by anyone in the organization. However, given its inability to resist, the organization had to resign itself to the pursuit of the strategy, so that it became, in effect, deliberate.

Sometimes, the 'environment' rather than people *per se* impose strategies on organizations, simply by severely restricting the options open to them. Air Canada chose to fly jet aeroplanes and later wide-body aeroplanes. But did it? Could any 'world class' airline have decided otherwise? Again the organization has internalized the imperative so that strategic choice becomes a moot point.
[...]

Reality, however, seems to bring organizations closer to a compromise position between determinism and free choice. Environments seldom pre-empt all choice, just as they seldom offer unlimited choice. That is why purely determined strategies are probably as rare as purely planned ones. Alternatively, just as the umbrella strategy may be the most realistic reflection of leadership intention, so too might the partially imposed strategy be the most realistic reflection of environmental influence. As shown in the figure below, the environment bounds what the organization can do, in this illustration determining under what part of the umbrella the organization can feasibly operate.
[...]

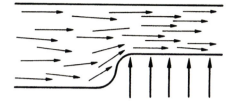

This completes our discussion of various types of strategies. Table 1.1 summarizes some of their major features.

Emerging conclusions

This chapter has been written to open up thinking about strategy formation, to broaden perspectives that may remain framed in the image of it as an *a priori*, analytic process or even as a sharp dichotomy between strategies as either deliberate or emergent. We believe that more research is required on the process of strategy formation to complement the extensive work currently taking place on the content of strategies; indeed, we believe that research on the former can significantly influence the direction taken by research on the latter (and vice versa).

One promising line of research is investigation of the strategy formation process and of the types of strategies realized as a function of the structure and context of organizations. Do the various propositions suggested in this chapter, based on our own limited research, in fact hold up in broader samples, for example, that strategies will tend to be more deliberate in tightly coupled, centrally controlled organizations and more emergent in decentralized, loosely coupled ones?

It would also be interesting to know how different types of strategies perform in various contexts and also how these strategies relate to those defined in terms of specific content. Using Porter's (1980) categories, for example, will cost leadership strategies prove more deliberate (specifically, more often planned), differentiation strategies more emergent (perhaps umbrella in nature), or perhaps entrepreneurial? Or using Miles and Snow's (1978) typology, will defenders prove more deliberate in orientation and inclined to use planned strategies, whereas prospectors tend to be more emergent and more prone to rely on umbrella or process, or even unconnected, strategies? It may even be possible that highly deliberate strategy making processes will be found to drive organizations away from prospecting activities and towards cost leadership strategies whereas emergent ones may encourage the opposite postures.

The interplay of the different types of strategies we have described can

TABLE 1.1   Summary description of types of strategies

Strategy	Major features
Planned	Strategies originate in formal plans: precise intentions exist, formulated and articulated by central leadership, backed up by formal controls to ensure surprise-free implementation in benign, controllable or predictable environment; strategies most deliberate
Entrepreneurial	Strategies originate in central vision: intentions exist as personal, unarticulated vision of single leader, and so adaptable to new opportunities; organization under personal control of leader and located in protected niche in environment; strategies relatively deliberate but can emerge
Ideological	Strategies originate in shared beliefs: intentions exist as collective vision of all actors, in inspirational form and relatively immutable, controlled normatively through indoctrination and/or socialization; organization often proactive *vis-à-vis* environment; strategies rather deliberate
Umbrella	Strategies originate in constraints: leadership, in partial control of organizational actions, defines strategic boundaries or targets within which other actors respond to own forces or to complex, perhaps also unpredictable environment; strategies partly deliberate, partly emergent and deliberately emergent
Process	Strategies originate in process: leadership controls process aspects of strategy (hiring, structure, etc.), leaving content aspects to other actors; strategies partly deliberate, partly emergent (and, again, deliberately emergent)
Unconnected	Strategies originate in enclaves: actor(s) loosely coupled to rest of organization produce(s) patterns in own actions in absence of, or in direct contradiction to, central or common intentions; strategies organizationally emergent whether or not deliberate for actor(s)
Consensus	Strategies originate in consensus: through mutual adjustment, actors converge on patterns that become pervasive in absence of central or common intentions; strategies rather emergent
Imposed	Strategies originate in environment: environment dictates patterns in actions either through direct imposition or through implicitly pre-empting or bounding organizational choice; strategies most emergent, although may be internalized by organization and made deliberate

be another avenue of inquiry: the nesting of personal strategies within umbrella ones or their departure in clandestine form from centrally imposed umbrellas; the capacity of unconnected strategies to evoke organizational ones of a consensus or even a planned nature as peripheral patterns that succeed pervade the organization; the conversion of entrepreneurial strategies into ideological or planned ones as vision becomes institutionalized one way or another; the possible propensity of imposed strategies to become deliberate as they are internalized within the organization; and so on. An understanding of how these different types of strategies blend into each other and tend to sequence themselves over time in different contexts could reveal a good deal about the strategy formation process.

At a more general level, the whole question of how managers learn from the experiences of their own organizations seems to be fertile ground for research. In our view, the fundamental difference between deliberate and emergent strategy is that whereas the former focuses on direction and control — getting desired things done — the latter opens up this notion of 'strategic learning'. Defining strategy as intended and conceiving it as deliberate, as has traditionally been done, effectively precludes the notion of strategic learning. Once the intentions have been set, attention is riveted on realizing them, not on adapting them. Messages from the environment tend to get blocked out. Adding the concept of emergent strategy, based on the definition of strategy as realized, opens the process of strategy making up to the notion of learning.

Emergent strategy itself implies learning what works — taking one action at a time in search for that viable pattern or consistency. It is important to remember that emergent strategy means, not chaos, but, in essence, *unintended order*. It is also frequently the means by which deliberate strategies change. As shown in Figure 1.2, in the feedback loop added to our basic diagram, it is often through the identification of emergent strategies — its patterns never intended — that managers and others in the organization come to change their intentions. This is another way of saying that not a few deliberate strategies are simply emergent ones that have been uncovered and subsequently formalized. Of course, unrealized strategies are also a source of learning, as managers find out which of their intentions do not work, rejected either by their organizations themselves or else by environments that are less than acquiescent.

We wish to emphasize that emergent strategy does not have to mean that management is out of control, only — in some cases at least — that it is open, flexible and responsive, in other words, willing to learn. Such behaviour is especially important when an environment is too unstable or complex to comprehend, or too imposing to defy. Openness to such

Strategic learning

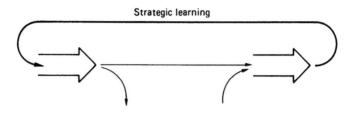

FIGURE 1.2   Strategic learning

emergent strategy enables management to act before everything is fully understood – to respond to an evolving reality rather than having to focus on a stable fantasy. For example, distinctive competence cannot always be assessed on paper *a priori*; often, perhaps usually, it has to be discovered empirically, by taking actions that test where strengths and weaknesses really lie. Emergent strategy also enables a management that cannot be close enough to a situation, or to know enough about the varied activities of its organization, to surrender control to those who have the information current and detailed enough to shape realistic strategies. Whereas the more deliberate strategies tend to emphasize central direction and hierarchy, the more emergent ones open the way for collective action and convergent behaviour.

Of course, by the same token, deliberate strategy is hardly dysfunctional either. Managers need to manage too, sometimes to impose intentions on their organizations – to provide a sense of direction. That can be partial, as in the cases of umbrella and process strategies, or it can be rather comprehensive, as in the cases of planned and entrepreneurial strategies. When the necessary information can be brought to a central place and environments can be largely understood and predicted (or at least controlled), then it may be appropriate to suspend strategic learning for a time to pursue intentions with as much determination as possible (see Mintzberg and Waters, 1984).

Our conclusion is that strategy formation walks on two feet, one deliberate, the other emergent. As noted earlier, managing requires a light deft touch – to direct in order to realize intentions while at the same time responding to an unfolding pattern of action. The relative emphasis may shift from time to time but not the requirement to attend to both sides of this phenomenon.

[...]

References

Brunet, J. P., Mintzberg, H. and Waters, J. (1986) 'Does Planning Impede Strategic Thinking? The Strategy of Air Canada 1937–1976,' in Lamb, R. (ed.) *Advances in Strategic Management* (Englewood Cliffs, NJ): Prentice Hall) vol. 4.

Galbraith, J. K. (1967) *The New Industrial State* (Boston: Houghton Mifflin).

Grinyer, P. H. and Spender, J. C. (1979) *Turnaround: the Fall and Rise of the Newton Chambers Group* (London: Association Business Press)

Kiesler, C. H. (1971) *The Psychology of Commitment: Experiments Linking Behaviour to Belief* (New York: Academic Press).

Miles, R. and Snow, C. (1978) *Organizational Strategy, Structure, and Process* (New York: McGraw-Hill)

Mintzberg, H. (1972) 'Research on Strategy-making', *Proceedings of the 32nd Annual Meeting of the Academy of Management*, Minneapolis.

Mintzberg, H. (1978) 'Patterns in Strategy Formation', *Management Science*, pp. 934–48.

Mintzberg, H. (1979) *The Structuring of Organizations* (Englewood Cliffs, NJ: Prentice-Hall).

Mintzberg, H. and McHugh, A. (1985) 'Strategy Formation in Adhocracy', *Administrative Science Quarterly*.

Mintzberg, H. and Waters, J. A. (1982) 'Tracking Strategy in an Entrepreneurial Firm', *Academy of Management Journal*, pp. 465–99.

Mintzberg, H. and Waters, J. A. (1984) 'Researching the Formation of Strategies: The History of Canadian Lady, 1939–1976', in Lamb, R. (ed.) *Competitive Strategic Management* (Englewood Cliffs, NJ: Prentice Hall).

Mintzberg, H., Otis, S., Shamsie, J. and Waters, J. A. (1986) 'Strategy of Design: A Study of "Architects in Co-partnership"', in Grant, John (ed.) *Strategic Management Frontiers* (Greenwich, CT: JAI Press).

Porter, M. E. (1980) *Competitive Strategy: Techniques for Analyzing Industries and Competitors* (New York: Free Press).

CHAPTER 2

Managing Strategic Change

JAMES BRIAN QUINN

Introduction

[...]
Executives managing strategic change in large organizations should not
– and do not – follow highly formalized textbook approaches in long-
range planning, goal generation, and strategy formulation.[1] Instead, they
artfully blend formal analysis, behavioral techniques, and power politics
to bring about cohesive, step-by-step movement toward ends which
initially are broadly conceived, but which are then constantly refined and
reshaped as new information appears.[2] Their integrating methodology
can best be described as 'logical incrementalism'.
[...]
Managers *consciously* and *proactively* move forward *incrementally*:

- To improve the quality of information utilized in corporate strategic
  decisions.
- To cope with the varying lead times, pacing parameters, and sequencing needs of the 'subsystems' through which such decisions tend to be
  made.
- To deal with the personal resistance and political pressures any
  important strategic change encounters.
- To build the organizational awareness, understanding, and psychological commitment needed for effective implementation.
- To decrease the uncertainty surrounding such decisions by allowing
  for interactive learning between the enterprise and its various impinging environments.
- To improve the quality of the strategic decisions themselves by
  (1) systematically involving those with most specific knowledge,
  (2) obtaining the participation of those who must carry out the

decisions, and (3) avoiding premature momenta or closure which could lead the decision in improper directions.

How does one manage the complex incremental processes which can achieve these goals? The following is perhaps the most articulate short statement on how executives proactively manage incrementalism in the development of corporate strategies:

> Typically you start with general concerns, vaguely felt. Next you roll an issue around in your mind till you think you have a conclusion that makes sense for the company. You then go out and sort of post the idea without being too wedded to its details. You then start hearing the arguments pro and con, and some very good refinements of the idea usually emerge. Then you pull the idea in and put some resources together to study it so it can be put forward as more of a formal presentation. You wait for 'stimuli occurrences' or 'crises', and launch pieces of the idea to help in these situations. But they lead toward your ultimate aim. You know where you want to get. You'd like to get there in six months. But it may take three years, or you may not get there. And when you do get there, you don't know whether it was originally your own idea – or somebody else had reached the same conclusion before you and just got you on board for it. You never know. The president would follow the same basic process, but he could drive it much faster than an executive lower in the organization.[3]

Because of differences in organizational form, management style, or the content of individual decisions, no single paradigm can hold for all strategic decisions.[4] However, very complex strategic decisions in my sample of large organizations tended to evoke certain kinds of broad process steps. These are briefly outlined below. While these process steps occur generally in the order presented, stages are by no means orderly or discrete. Executives do consciously manage individual steps proactively, but it is doubtful that any one person guides a major strategic change sequentially through all the steps. Developing most strategies requires numerous loops back to earlier stages as unexpected issues or new data dictate. Or decision times can become compressed and require short-circuiting leaps forward as crises occur.[5] Nevertheless, certain patterns are clearly dominant in the successful management of strategic change in large organizations.

Creating awareness and commitment – incrementally

Although many of the sample companies had elaborate formal environmental scanning procedures, most major strategic issues first emerged in vague or undefined terms, such as 'organizational overlap', 'product proliferation', 'excessive exposure in one market', or 'lack of focus and motivation'.[6] Some appeared as 'inconsistencies' in internal action patterns or 'anomalies' between the enterprise's current posture and some perception of its future environment.[7] Early signals may come from anywhere and may be difficult to distinguish from the background 'noise' of ordinary communications. Crises, of course, announce themselves with strident urgency in operations control systems. But, if organizations wait until signals reach amplitudes high enough to be sensed by formal measurement systems, smooth, efficient transitions may be impossible.[8]

Need-sensing: leading the formal information system

Effective change managers actively develop informal networks to get objective information − from other staff and line executives, workers, customers, board members, suppliers, politicians, technologists, educators, outside professionals, government groups, and so on − to sense possible needs for change. They purposely use these networks to short-circuit all the careful screens[9] their organizations build up to 'tell the top only what it wants to hear'.
[...]
    To avoid undercutting intermediate managers, such bypassing has to be limited to information gathering, with no implication that orders or approvals are given to lower levels. Properly handled, this practice actually improves formal communications and motivational systems as well. Line managers are less tempted to screen information and lower levels are flattered to be able 'to talk to the very top'. Since people sift signals about threats and opportunities through perceptual screens defined by their own values, careful executives make sure their sensing networks include people who look at the world very differently than do those in the enterprise's dominating culture. Effective executives consciously seek options and threat signals beyond the *status quo*.
[...]

Amplifying understanding and awareness

In some cases executives quickly perceive the broad dimensions of needed change. But they still may seek amplifying data, wider executive understanding of issues, or greater organizational support before initiating action. Far from accepting the first satisfactory (satisficing) solution − as some have suggested they do − successful managers seem to consciously generate and consider a broad array of alternatives.[10] Why? They want to stimulate and choose from the most creative solutions offered by the best minds in their organizations. They wish to have colleagues knowledgeable enough about issues to help them think through all the ramifications. They seek data and arguments sufficiently strong to dislodge preconceived ideas or blindly followed past practices. They do not want to be the prime supporters of losing ideas or to have their organizations slavishly adopt 'the boss's solution'. Nor do they want – through announcing decisions too early – to prematurely threaten existing power centres which could kill any changes aborning.

Even when executives do not have in mind specific solutions to emerging problems, they can still proactively guide actions in intuitively desired directions – by defining what issues staffs should investigate, by selecting principal investigators, and by controlling reporting processes. They can selectively 'tap the collective wit' of their organizations, generating more awareness of critical issues and forcing initial thinking down to lower levels to achieve greater involvement. Yet they can also avoid irreconcilable opposition, emotional overcommitment,[11] or organizational momenta beyond their control by regarding all proposals as 'strictly advisory' at this early stage.

As issues are clarified and options are narrowed, executives may systematically alert ever wider audiences. They may first 'shop' key ideas among trusted colleagues to test responses. Then they may commission a few studies to illuminate emerging alternatives, contingencies, or opportunities. But key players might still not be ready to change their past action patterns or even be able to investigate options creatively. Only when persuasive data are in hand and enough people are alerted and 'on board' to make a particular solution work, might key executives finally commit themselves to it. Building awareness, concern, and interest to attention-getting levels is often a vital – and slowly achieved – step in the process of managing basic changes.
[. . .]

Changing symbols: building credibility

As awareness of the need for change grows managers often want to signal the organization that certain types of changes are coming, even if specific solutions are not in hand. Knowing they cannot communicate directly with the thousands who would carry out the strategy, some executives purposely undertake highly visible actions which wordlessly convey complex messages that could never be communicated as well – or as credibly – in verbal terms.[12] Some use symbolic moves to preview or verify intended changes in direction. At other times, such moves confirm the intention of top management to back a thrust already partially begun – as Peter McColough's relocation of Xerox headquarters to Connecticut (away from the company's Rochester reprographics base) underscored that company's developing commitment to product diversification, organizational decentralization, and international operations. Organizations often need such symbolic moves – or decisions they regard as symbolic – to build credibility behind a new strategy. Without such actions even forceful verbiage might be interpreted as mere rhetoric. [...]

Legitimizing new viewpoints

Often before reaching specific strategic decisions, it is necessary to legitimize new options which have been acknowledged as possibilities, but which still entail an undue aura of uncertainty or concern. Because of their familiarity, older options are usually perceived as having lower risks (or potential costs) than newer alternatives. Therefore, top managers seeking change often consciously create forums and allow slack time for their organizations to talk through threatening issues, work out the implications of new solutions, or gain an improved information base that will permit new options to be evaluated objectively in comparison with more familiar alternatives.[13] In many cases, strategic concepts which are at first strongly resisted gain acceptance and support simply by the passage of time, if executives do not exacerbate hostility by pushing them too fast from the top. [...]

Tactical shifts and partial solutions

At this stage in the process guiding executives might share a fairly clear vision of the general directions for movement. But rarely does a total new corporate posture emerge full grown – like Minerva from the brow of Jupiter – from any one source. Instead, early resolutions are likely to be partial, tentative, or experimental.[14] Beginning moves often appear as mere tactical adjustments in the enterprise's existing posture. As such, they encounter little opposition, yet each partial solution adds momentum in new directions. Guiding executives try carefully to maintain the enterprise's ongoing strengths while shifting its total posture incrementally – at the margin – toward new needs. Such executives themselves might not yet perceive the full nature of the strategic shifts they have begun. They can still experiment with partial new approaches and learn without risking the viability of the total enterprise. Their broad early steps can still legitimately lead to a variety of different success scenarios. Yet logic might dictate that they wait before committing themselves to a total new strategy.[15] As events unfurl, solutions to several interrelated problems might well flow together in a not-yet-perceived synthesis. [...]

Broadening political support

Often these broad emerging strategic thrusts need expanded political support and understanding to achieve sufficient momentum to survive.[16] Committees, task forces, and retreats tend to be favoured mechanisms for accomplishing this. If carefully managed, these do not become the 'garbage cans' of emerging ideas, as some observers have noted.[17] By selecting the committee's chairman, membership, timing, and agenda, guiding executives can largely influence and predict a desired outcome, and can force other executives toward a consensus. Such groups can be balanced to educate, evaluate, neutralize, or overwhelm opponents. They can be used to legitimize new options or to generate broad cohesion among diverse thrusts, or they can be narrowly focused to build momentum. Guiding executives can constantly maintain complete control over these 'advisory processes' through their various influences and veto potentials.
[...]

Overcoming opposition: 'zones of indifference' and 'no lose' situations

Executives of basically healthy companies in the sample realized that any attempt to introduce a new strategy would have to deal with the support its predecessor had. Barring a major crisis, a frontal attack on an old strategy could be regarded as an attack on those who espoused it – perhaps properly – and brought the enterprise to its present levels of success. There often exists a variety of legitimate views on what could and should be done in the new circumstances that a company faces. And wise executives do not want to alienate people who would otherwise be supporters. Consequently, they try to get key people behind their concepts whenever possible, to co-opt or neutralize serious opposition if necessary, or to find 'zones of indifference' where the proposition would not be disastrously opposed.[18] Most of all they seek 'no lose' situations which will motivate all the important players toward a common goal.
[...]

Structuring flexibility: buffers, slacks, and activists

Typically there are too many uncertainties in the total environment for managers to program or control all the events involved in effecting a major change in strategic direction. Logic dictates, therefore, that managers purposely design flexibility into their organizations and have resources ready to deploy incrementally as events demand. Planned flexibility requires: (1) proactive horizon scanning to identify the general nature and potential impact of opportunities and threats the firm is most likely to encounter, (2) creating sufficient resource buffers – or slacks – to respond effectively as events actually unfurl, (3) developing and positioning 'credible activists' with a psychological commitment to move quickly and flexibly to exploit specific opportunities as they occur, and (4) shortening decision lines from such people (and key operating managers) to the top for the most rapid system response. These – rather than pre-capsuled (and shelved) programmes to respond to stimuli which never quite occur as expected – are the keys to real contingency planning.

The concept of resource buffers requires special amplification. Quick access to resources is needed to cushion the impact of random events, to offset opponents' sudden attacks, or to build momentum for new strategic shifts.
[. . .]

Systematic waiting and trial concepts

The prepared strategist may have to wait for events, as Roosevelt awaited a trauma like Pearl Harbor. The availability of desired acquisitions or real estate might depend on a death, divorce, fiscal crisis, management change, or an erratic stock market break.[19] Technological advances may have to await new knowledge, inventions, or lucky accidents. Despite otherwise complete preparations, a planned market entry might not be wise until new legislation, trade agreements, or competitive shake-outs occur. Organizational moves have to be timed to retirements, promotions, management failures, and so on. Very often the specific strategy adopted depends on the timing or sequence of such random events.[20]
[. . .]

Solidifying progress – incrementally

As events move forward, executives can more clearly perceive the specific directions in which their organizations should – and realistically can – move. They can seek more aggressive movement and commitment to their new perceptions, without undermining important ongoing activities or creating unnecessary reactions to their purposes. Until this point, new strategic goals might remain broad, relatively unrefined, or even unstated except as philosophic concepts. More specific dimensions might be incrementally announced as key pieces of information fall into place, specific unanswered issues approach resolution, or significant resources have to be formally committed.

Creating pockets of commitment

Early in this stage, guiding executives may need to actively implant support in the organization for new thrusts. They may encourage an array of exploratory projects for each of several possible options. Initial projects can be kept small, partial, or ad hoc, neither forming a comprehensive program nor seeming to be integrated into a cohesive strategy. Executives often provide stimulating goals, a proper climate for imaginative proposals, and flexible resource support, rather than being personally identified with specific projects. In this way they can achieve organizational involvement and early commitment without focusing attention on any one solution too soon or losing personal credibility if it fails.

Once under way, project teams on the more successful programs in the sample became ever more committed to their particular areas of exploration. They became pockets of support for new strategies deep within the organization. Yet, if necessary, top managers could delay until the last moment their final decisions blending individual projects into a total strategy. Thus, they were able to obtain the best possible match among the company's technical abilities, its psychological commitments, and its changing market needs. By making final choices more effectively – as late as possible with better data, more conscientiously investigated options, and the expert critiques competitive projects allowed – these executives actually increased technical and market efficiencies of their enterprises, despite the apparent added costs of parallel efforts.[21]

In order to maintain their own objectivity and future flexibility, some executives choose to keep their own political profiles low as they build a new consensus. If they seem committed to a strategy too soon, they might discourage others from pursuing key issues which should be raised.[22] By stimulating detailed investigations several levels down, top executives can seem detached yet still shape both progress and ultimate outcomes – by reviewing interim results and specifying the timing, format, and forums for the release of data. When reports come forward, these executives can stand above the battle and review proposals objectively, without being personally on the defensive for having committed themselves to a particular solution too soon. From this position they can more easily orchestrate a high-level consensus on a new strategic thrust. As an added benefit, negative decisions on proposals often come from a group consensus that top executives can simply confirm to lower levels, thereby preserving their personal veto for more crucial moments. In many well-made decisions people at all levels contribute to the generation, amplification, and interpretation of options and information to the extent that it is often difficult to say who really makes the decision.[23]

Focusing the organization

In spite of their apparent detachment, top executives do focus their organizations on developing strategies at critical points in the process. While adhering to the rhetoric of specific goal setting, most executives are careful not to state new goals in concrete terms before they have built a consensus among key players. They fear that they will prematurely centralize the organization, pre-empt interesting options, provide a common focus for otherwise fragmented opposition, or cause the organization to act prematurely to carry out a specified commitment. Guiding executives may quietly shape the many alternatives flowing upward by using what Wrapp refers to as 'a hidden hand'. Through their information networks they can encourage concepts they favour, let weakly supported options die through inaction, and establish hurdles or tests for strongly supported ideas with which they do not agree but which they do not wish to oppose openly.

Since opportunities for such focusing generally develop unexpectedly, the timing of key moves is often unpredictable. A crisis, a rash of reassignments, a reorganization, or a key appointment may allow an executive to focus attention on particular thrusts, add momentum to some, and perhaps quietly phase out others.[24] Most managers surveyed seemed well aware of the notion that 'if there are no other options, mine wins'. Without being Machiavellian, they did not want misdirected options to gain strong political momentum and later have to be terminated in an open bloodbath. They also did not want to send false signals that stimulated other segments of their organizations to make proposals in undesirable directions. They sensed very clearly that the patterns in which proposals are approved or denied will inevitably be perceived by lower echelons as precedents for developing future goals or policies.

Managing coalitions

Power interactions among key players are important at this stage of solidifying progress. Each player has a different level of power determined by his or her information base, organizational position, and personal credibility.[25] Executives legitimately perceive problems or opportunities differently because of their particular values, experiences, and vantage points. They will promote the solutions they perceive as the best compromise for the total enterprise, for themselves, and for their particular units. In an organization with dispersed power, the key figure is the one who can manage coalitions.[26] Since no one player has all the power, regardless of that individual's skill or position, the action that occurs over time might differ greatly from the intentions of any of the players.[27] Top executives try to sense whether support exists among important parties for specific aspects of an issue and try to get partial decisions and momenta going for those aspects. As 'comfort levels' or political pressures within the top group rise in favour of specific decisions, the guiding executive might, within his or her concept of a more complete solution, seek – among the various features of different proposals – a balance that the most influential and credible parties can actively support. The result tends to be a stream of partial decisions on limited strategic issues made by constantly changing coalitions of the critical power centres.[28] These decisions steadily evolve toward a broader consensus, acceptable to both the top executive and some 'dominant coalition' among these centres.

As a partial consensus emerges, top executives might crystallize issues by stating some broad goals in more specific terms for internal consumption. Finally, when sufficient general acceptance exists and the timing is right, the goals may begin to appear in more public announcements. [...]

Formalizing commitment by empowering champions

As each major strategic thrust comes into focus, top executives try to ensure that some individual or group feels responsible for its goals. If the thrust will project the enterprise in entirely new directions, executives often want more than mere accountability for its success – they want real commitment.[29] A significantly new major thrust, concept, product, or problem solution frequently needs the nurturing hand of someone who genuinely identifies with it and whose future depends on its success. [...]

In some cases, top executives have to wait for champions to appear before committing resources to risky new strategies. They may immediately assign accountability for less dramatic plans by converting them into new missions for ongoing groups.

From this point on, the strategy process is familiar. The organization's formal structure has to be adjusted to support the strategy.[30] Commitment to the most important new thrusts has to be confirmed in formal plans. Detailed budgets, programs, controls, and reward systems have to reflect all planned strategic thrusts. Finally, the guiding executive has to see that recruiting and staffing plans are aligned with the new goals and that – when the situation permits – supporters and persistent opponents of intended new thrusts are assigned to appropriate positions.

Continuing the dynamics by eroding consensus

The major strategic changes studied tended to take many years to accomplish. The process was continuous, often without any clear beginning or end.[31] The decision process constantly moulded and modified management's concerns and concepts. Radical crusades became the new conventional wisdom, and over time totally new issues emerged. Participants or observers were often not aware of exactly when a particular decision had been made[32] or when a subsequent consensus was created to supersede or modify it; the process of strategic change was continuous and dynamic.

[. . .]

Once the organization arrives at its new consensus, the guiding executive has to move immediately to insure that this new position does not become inflexible. In trying to build commitment to a new concept, individual executives often surround themselves with people who see the world in the same way. Such people can rapidly become systematic screens against other views. Effective executives therefore purposely continue the change process, constantly introducing new faces and stimuli at the top. They consciously begin to erode the very strategic thrusts they may have just created – a very difficult, but essential, psychological task.

Integration of processes and of interests

In the large enterprises observed, strategy formulation was a continuously evolving analytical-political consensus process with neither a finite beginning nor a definite end. It generally followed the sequence described above. Yet the total process was anything but linear. It was a groping, cyclical process that often circled back on itself, with frequent interruptions and delays. Pfiffner aptly describes the process of strategy formation as being 'like fermentation in biochemistry, rather than an industrial assembly line.'[33]

Such incremental management processes are not abrogations of good management practice. Nor are they Machiavellian or consciously manipulative manoeuvres. Instead, they represent an adaptation to the practical psychological and informational problems of getting a constantly changing group of people with diverse talents and interests to move *together* effectively in a continually dynamic environment. Much of the impelling force behind logical incrementalism comes from a desire to tap the talents and psychological drives of the whole organization, to create cohesion, and to generate identity with the emerging strategy. The remainder of that force results from the interactive nature of the random factors and lead times affecting the independent subsystems that compose any total strategy.

An incremental – not piecemeal – process

The total pattern of action, though highly incremental, is not piecemeal in well-managed organizations. It requires constant, conscious reassessment of the total organization, its capacities, and its needs as related to surrounding environments. It requires continual attempts by top managers to integrate these actions into an understandable, cohesive whole.
[...]

Formal–Analytical Techniques

At each stage of strategy development, effective executives constantly try to visualize the new patterns that might exist among the emerging strategies of various subsystems. As each subsystem strategy becomes more apparent, both its executive team and top-level groups try to project its implications for the total enterprise and to stimulate queries, support, and feedback from those involved in related strategies. Perceptive top executives see that the various teams generating subsystem strategies have overlapping members. They require periodic updates and reviews before higher echelon groups that can bring a total corporate view to bear. They use formal planning processes to interrelate and evaluate the resources required, benefits sought, and risks undertaken *vis-à-vis* other elements of the enterprise's overall strategy. Some use scenario techniques to help visualize potential impacts and relationships. Others utilize complex forecasting models to better understand the basic interactions among subsystems, the total enterprise, and the environment. Still others use specialized staffs, 'devil's advocates', or 'contention teams' to make sure that all important aspects of their strategies receive a thorough evaluation.

Power–Behavioural Aspects: Coalition Management

All the formal methodologies help, but the real integration of all the components in an enterprise's total strategy eventually takes place only in the minds of high-level executives. Each executive may legitimately perceive the intended balance of goals and thrusts differently. Some of these differences may be openly expressed as issues to be resolved when new information becomes available. Some differences may remain unstated – hidden agendas to emerge at later dates. Others may be masked by accepting so broad a statement of intention that many different views are included in a seeming consensus, when a more specific statement might be divisive. Nevertheless, effective strategies do achieve a level of understanding and consensus sufficient to focus action.

Top executives deliberately manage the incremental processes within each subsystem to create the basis for consensus. They also manage the coalitions that lie at the heart of most controlled strategy developments.[34] They recognize that they are at the confluence of innumerable pressures — from stockholders, environmentalists, government bodies, customers, suppliers, distributors, producing units, marketing groups, technologists, unions, special issue activists, individual employees, ambitious executives, and so on — and that knowledgeable people of goodwill can easily disagree on proper actions. In response to changing pressures and coalitions among these groups, the top management team constantly forms and reforms its own coalitions on various decisions.[35]

Most major strategic moves tend to assist some interests — and executives' careers — at the expense of others. Consequently, each set of interests serves as a check on the others and thus helps maintain the breadth and balance of strategy.[36] To avoid significant errors some managers try to ensure that all important groups have representation at or access to the top.[37] The guiding executive group may continuously adjust the number, power, or proximity of such access points in order to maintain a desired balance and focus.[38] These delicate adjustments require constant negotiations and implied bargains within the leadership group. Balancing the forces that different interests exert on key decisions is perhaps the ultimate control top executives have in guiding and co-ordinating the formulation of their companies' strategies.[39]

Establishing, measuring, and rewarding key thrusts

Few executives or management teams can keep all the dimensions of a complex evolving strategy in mind as they deal with the continuous flux of urgent issues. Consequently, effective strategic managers seek to identify a few central themes that can help to draw diverse efforts together in a common cause.[40] Once identified, these themes help to maintain focus and consistency in the strategy. They make it easier to discuss and monitor proposed strategic thrusts. Ideally, these themes can be developed into a matrix of programs and goals, cutting across formal divisional lines and dominating the selection and ranking of projects within divisions. This matrix can, in turn, serve as the basis for performance measurement, control, and reward systems that ensure the intended strategy is properly implemented.

Unfortunately, few companies in the sample were able to implement such a complex planning and control system without creating undue rigidities. But all did utilize logical incrementalism to bring cohesion to the formal-analytical and power-behavioural processes needed to create effective strategies. Most used some approximation of the process sequence described above to form their strategies at both subsystem and overall corporate levels.

[...]

Conclusion

In recent years, there has been an increasingly loud chorus of discontent about corporate strategic planning. Many managers are concerned that despite elaborate strategic planning systems, costly staffs for planning, and major commitments of their own time, their most elaborately analysed strategies never get implemented. These executives and their companies generally have fallen into the trap of thinking about strategy formulation and implementation as separate, sequential processes. They rely on the awesome rationality of their formally derived strategies and the inherent power of their positions to cause their organizations to respond. When this does not occur, they become bewildered, if not frustrated and angry. Instead, successful managers in the companies observed acted logically and incrementally to improve the quality of information used in key decisions; to overcome the personal and political pressures resisting change; to deal with the varying lead times and sequencing problems in critical decisions; and to build the organizational awareness, understanding, and psychological commitment essential to effective strategies. By the time the strategies began to crystallize, pieces of them were already being implemented. Through the very processes they used to formulate their strategies, these executives had built sufficient organizational momentum and identity with the strategies to make them flow toward flexible and successful implementation.

Notes

1. This is the third in a series of articles based upon my study of ten major corporations' processes for achieving significant strategic change. The other two articles in the series are: J. B. Quinn, 'Strategic Goals: Process and Politics', *Sloan Management Review*, Fall 1977, pp. 21–37; J. B. Quinn, 'Strategic Change: "Logical Incrementalism" ', *Sloan Management Review*, Fall 1978, pp. 7–21. The whole study is published in a book entitled *Strategies for Change: Logical Incrementalism* (Homewood, IL: Dow Jones-Irwin, 1980). All findings purposely deal only with strategic changes in large organizations.
2. See R. M. Cyert and J. G. March, *A Behavioral Theory of the Firm* (Englewood Cliffs, NJ: Prentice-Hall, 1963) p. 123. Note this learning–feedback–adaptiveness of goals and feasible alternatives over time as organizational learning.

3. See J. B. Quinn, *Xerox Corporation (B)* (copyrighted case, Amos Tuck School of Business Administration, Dartmouth College, Hanover, NH, 1979).
4. See O. G. Brim, D. Glass *et al.*, *Personality and Decision Processes: Studies in the Social Psychology of Thinking* (Stanford, CA: Stanford University Press, 1962).
5. Crises did occur at some stage in almost all the strategies investigated. However, the study was concerned with the attempt to manage strategic change in an ordinary way. While executives had to deal with precipitating events in this process, crisis management was not – and should not be – the focus of effective strategic management.
6. For some formal approaches and philosophies for environmental scanning, see: W. D. Guth, 'Formulating Organizational Objectives and Strategy: A Systematic Approach', *Journal of Business Policy* (Autumn 1971) pp. 24–31; F. J. Aguilar, *Scanning the Business Environment* (New York: Macmillan Co., 1967). For confirmation of the early vagueness and ambiguity in problem form and identification, see H. Mintzberg, D. Raisinghani, and A. Théorêt, 'The Structure of "Unstructured" Decision Processes', *Administrative Science Quarterly* (June 1976) pp. 246–75.
7. For a discussion on various types of 'misfits' between the organization and its environment as a basis for problem identification, see R. Normann, *Management for Growth*, trans. N. Adler (New York: John Wiley & Sons, 1977) p. 19.
8. For suggestions on why organizations engage in 'problem search' patterns, see R. M. Cyert, H. A. Simon, and D. B. Trow, 'Observation of a Business Decision', *The Journal of Business* (October 1956) pp. 237–48. For the problems of timing in transitions, see L. R. Sayles, *Managerial Behavior: Administration in Complex Organizations* (New York: McGraw-Hill, 1964).
9. For a classic view of how these screens operate, see C. Argyris, 'Double Loop Learning in Organizations', *Harvard Business Review*, September–October 1977, pp. 115–25.
10. Cyert and March (1963) suggest that executives choose from a number of satisfactory solutions; later observers suggest they choose the first truly satisfactory solution discovered.
11. See F. F. Gilmore, 'Overcoming the Perils of Advocacy in Corporate Planning', *California Management Review*, Spring 1973, pp. 127–37.
12. See E. Rhenman, *Organization Theory for Long-Range Planning* (New York: John Wiley & Sons, 1973) p. 63. Here author notes a similar phenomenon.
13. See R. M. Cyert, W. R. Dill, and J. G. March, 'The Role of Expectations in Business Decision Making', *Administrative Science Quarterly* (December 1958) pp. 307–40. The authors point out the perils of top management advocacy because existing policies may unconsciously bias information to support views they value.
14. See H. Mintzberg, *The Nature of Managerial Work* (New York: Harper & Row, 1973). Note that this 'vision' is not necessarily the beginning point of the process. Instead it emerges as new data and viewpoints interact; Normann (1977).
15. See Mintzberg, Raisinghani, and Théorêt (June 1976). Here the authors liken

the process to a decision tree where decisions at each node become more narrow, with failure at any node allowing recycling back to the broader tree trunk.

16. H. E. Wrapp, 'Good Managers don't Make Policy Decisions', *Harvard Business Review* (September–October, 1967) notes that a conditioning process that may stretch over months or years is necessary in order to prepare the organization for radical departures from what it is already striving to attain.

17. See J. G. March, J. P. Olsen, S. Christensen *et al.*, *Ambiguity and Choice in Organizations* (Bergen, Norway: Universitetsforlaget, 1976).

18. For an excellent overview of the processes of co-optation and neutralization, see Sayles (1964). For perhaps the first reference to the concept of the 'zone of indifference', see C. I. Barnard, *The Functions of the Executive* (Cambridge, MA: Harvard University Press, 1938). The following two sources note the need of executives for coalition behaviour to reduce the organizational conflict resulting from differing interests and goal preferences in large organizations: Cyert and March (1963); J. G. March, 'Business Decision Making', in *Readings in Managerial Psychology*, H. J. Leavitt and L. R. Pondy, eds. (Chicago: University of Chicago, 1964).

19. Cyert and March (1963) also note that not only do organizations seek alternatives but that 'alternatives seek organizations' (as when finders, scientists, bankers, etc., bring in new solutions).

20. See March, Olsen, Christensen *et al.* (1976).

21. Much of the rationale for this approach is contained in B. Quinn, 'Technological Innovation, Entrepreneurship, and Strategy', *Sloan Management Review*, Spring 1979, pp. 19–30.

22. See C. Argyris, 'Interpersonal Barriers to Decision Making', *Harvard Business Review*, March–April 1965, pp. 84–97. The author notes that when the president introduced major decisions from the top, discussion was 'less than open' and commitment was 'less than complete', although executives might assure the president to the contrary.

23. See March (1964).

24. The process tends to be one of eliminating the less feasible rather than of determining a target or objectives. The process typically reduces the number of alternatives through successive limited comparisons to a point where understood analytical techniques can apply and the organization structure can function to make a choice. See Cyert and March (1963).

25. For more detailed relationships between authority and power, see: H. C. Metcalf and L. Urwick (eds) *Dynamic Administration: The Collected Papers of Mary Parker Follett* (New York: Harper & Brothers, 1941); A. Zaleznik, 'Power and Politics in Organizational Life', *Harvard Business Review*, May–June 1970, pp. 47–60.

26. See J. D. Thompson, 'The Control of Complex Organizations', in *Organizations in Action* (New York: McGraw-Hill, 1967).

27. See G. T. Allison, *Essence of Decision: Explaining the Cuban Missile Crisis* (Boston: Little, Brown & Company, 1971).

28. See C. E. Lindblom, 'The Science of "Muddling Through" ', *Public Admini-*

stration Review (Spring 1959) pp. 79–88. The author notes that the relative weights individuals give to values and the intensity of their feelings will vary sequentially from decision to decision, hence the dominant coalition itself varies with each decision somewhat.

29. Zaleznik (May–June 1970) notes that confusing compliance with commitment is one of the most common and difficult problems of strategic implementation. He notes that often organizational commitment may override personal interest if the former is developed carefully.
30. See A. D. Chandler, *Strategy and Structure: Chapters in the History of the Industrial Enterprise* (Cambridge, MA: MIT Press, 1962).
31. See K. J. Cohen and R. M. Cyert, 'Strategy: Formulation, Implementation, and Monitoring', *The Journal of Business* (July 1973) pp. 349–67.
32. March (1964) notes that major decisions are 'processes of gradual commitment'.
33. See J. M. Pfiffner, 'Administrative Rationality', *Public Administration Review* (Summer 1960) pp. 125–32.
34. See R. James, 'Corporate Strategy and Change – The Management of People' (monograph, The University of Chicago, 1978). The author does an excellent job of pulling together the threads of coalition management at top organizational levels.
35. See Cyert and March (1963) p. 115.
36. Lindblom (Spring 1959) notes that every interest has a 'watchdog' and that purposely allowing these watchdogs to participate in and influence decisions creates consensus decisions that all can live with. Similar conscious access to the top for different interests can now be found in corporate structures.
37. See Zaleznik (May–June 1970).
38. For an excellent view of the bargaining processes involved in coalition management, see Sayles (1964) pp. 207–17.
39. For suggestions on why the central power figure in decentralized organizations must be the person who manages its dominant coalition, the size of which will depend on the issues involved, and the number of areas in which the organizations must rely on judgemental decisions, see Thompson (1967).
40. Wrapp (September–October 1967) notes the futility of a top manager trying to push a full package of goals.

CHAPTER 3

Rethinking Incrementalism

GERRY JOHNSON

[...]

Introduction

The notion of incrementalism as a descriptor of strategic management processes has become current in the 1980s and has taken on normative implications (Quinn, 1980). Incrementalism has been seen as a management learning process (Mintzberg, 1977), indeed as 'logical', purposive (Quinn, 1980) and 'unfolding rationality' (Pondy, 1983). It has also been accounted for as the outcome of the political and social processes in the organizations (Pettigrew, 1977, 1985); certainly research studies have shown the extent to which strategic decisions are characterized by high degrees of bargaining, solicitation and political activity (Mintzberg, Raisinghani and Théorêt, 1976; Lyles, 1981; Fahey, 1981). Moreover it has been argued that there exists a 'logic' in incremental strategy development insofar as by 'learning through doing' it facilitates decision-making and implementation within a political organizational context (Lindblom, 1959; Quinn, 1980; Pondy and Huff, 1983). The phenomenon of incrementalism has also been accounted for in terms of the routing of strategic decisions through the programmes and routines of the organization (Nelson and Winter, 1980), thus building on its prehistory and current modes of operation; or more proactively, in which organizational routines provide opportunities which amount to 'solutions looking for issues to which they might be the answer' (Cohen, March and Olsen, 1972: 2). Incrementalism has also been seen as a cognitive process (Hedberg and Jonsson, 1977; Grinyer and Spender, 1979a,b; Miller and Friesen, 1980) in which collective managerial cognition results in enactment, selection and retention processes (Weick, 1979) that take form in incremental processes of strategic change.

There are, then, various explanatory accounts of the phenomenon of incrementalism, but the underlying theme is that the strategic development of an organization needs to be seen as building on current practice and managerial beliefs about organizational competences within a political and historical context. Clearly the explanations for incremental processes of strategic change are complex: yet there are still few studies which have examined these processes *in context* and *over time* so as to identify how they come about.

This paper uses as an illustration the strategic development of one firm, which we shall call 'Coopers'. It begins with an outline of the major strategic changes within that firm from 1970 onwards and demonstrates that incremental patterns of strategic change were manifest in that organization. There follows a brief explanation of the research methods used. In the remainder of the paper a number of the key strategic decisions are examined in their historical context, and these are examined so as to provide explanatory models accounting for incremental processes of change which integrate some previous explanations and challenge others.

The context of the study

The study on which this paper is based took place within three retail clothing companies operating mainly in the UK, and covered a time period of 1970 to 1985.
[. . .]
Fieldwork was undertaken within Coopers between the years 1980 and 1986 and, in particular, in the years 1980 and 1983. The company had experienced from 1970 to 1980 a decade of above-industry profitable growth, in which time it had concentrated on what the management saw as a defendable market niche – the working men's outerwear market – for which they provided relatively low-priced merchandise, a large percentage of which was imported from the Far East and sold through a national chain of specialist fairly small outlets. From 1970 onwards the company attempted to diversify into a number of other retail ventures, notably women's wear, children's wear and drugs and toiletries with varying degrees of success. The fieldwork of 1980 therefore provided an opportunity to reconstruct the strategic development of the business and some of the key strategic decisions during a period of undoubted success.

From 1981 to 1983 the company experienced a marked – and to the managers traumatic – decline in fortunes. Not only did the recession in the UK affect the spending on men's clothing, particularly the lower-income brackets, but other retailers, less successful in the 1970s, had significantly changed their strategies and were enjoying considerable success at Cooper's expense. During this time the management attempted first to rationalize and reduce costs and also shed some of the acquisitions of the late 1970s; and then substantially to reposition the business. The fieldwork of 1983 thus provided the opportunity to examine how managers coped with decline and attempts to turn the business around. In fact the attempts at turnaround were only partially successful from 1983 to 1985. In 1985 the company was taken over and a second round of strategic repositioning commenced.

This paper concentrates on the period from the early 1970s to 1983 and, in particular, on the incremental patterns of change evident during that time. An illustration of the strategies within Coopers during the period (see Figure 3.1) helps to show why the study provided a fertile basis of study. This 'map' of strategies not only summarizes their time scales and content but also provides a visual patterning of strategies as they developed between 1970 and 1983. In processual terms it supports the idea of an incremental pattern of strategy development, as for example observed by Mintzberg (1978). Whilst there are some relatively clear breaks in strategy, in the main strategic initiatives merge into each other, or grow out of one another.
[...]

1960s 1970 71 72 73 74 75 76 77 78 79 1980 81 82 83

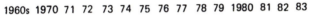

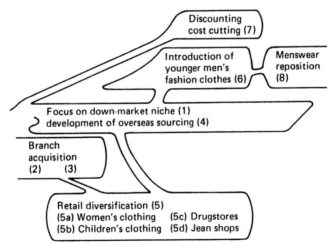

FIGURE 3.1   A pattern of strategy development

Research method

There have been few studies which have looked systematically at the processes of strategic change in context and over time. As Pettigrew has argued:

> There is still a dearth of studies which can make statements about the how and why of change, about the processual dynamics of change; in short which go beyond the *analysis of change* and begin to theorise about *changing* (Pettigrew, 1985, p. 15).

The research project sought to understand the complex processes of strategic change over time and within the cultural dimensions of organizations. With its focus on a limited number of companies (and on one in particular), the study is in the tradition of rich case research (Allison, 1971; Bower, 1972; Pettigrew, 1973, 1985; Biggart, 1977; Mintzberg and Waters, 1983; Pondy and Huff, 1983; Bartunek, 1984). In so doing it was possible to gain a depth of appreciation of the cultural, cognitive and political processes of management which form strategy, and thus achieve the 'application of conceptual knowledge about a phenomenon in a *specific and familiar* context' (Mintzberg, 1979, p. iv). [...]

Models of strategic management

There exist a number of models to account for the process of strategic management. We can build on these to provide a framework by which to examine some of the decision processes in Coopers. One such framework is provided by Chaffee (1985), who proposes three generic categories. Her first is the 'linear' model corresponding to what others have called the 'planning' (Mintzberg, 1973), 'rational' (Peters and Waterman, 1982), 'rational comprehensive' or 'synoptic' (Fredrickson, 1983) approach. It is a model of strategy-making which assumes a progressive series of steps of goal-setting, analysis, evaluation, selection and the planning of implementation to achieve an optimal long-term direction for the organization.

Chaffee's second category is the 'adaptive' model of strategic management, a term also used by Mintzberg (1973). This model corresponds to the idea of incremental strategic change discussed previously and, as we have seen, the explanations for this phenomenon vary considerably from those who see incrementalism as essentially 'logical' or 'rational' through to those who account for the phenomenon in terms of satisficing behaviour in a political, or programmed, context or within the cognitive limits of management.

It is this cognitive view of strategy formulation that leads us to Chaffee's third category – the 'interpretative' model. Weick argues that there is a 'presumption of logic' (Weick, 1983: 223) in meeting a complex situation; this logic is rooted in the beliefs and assumptions that managers hold, a cognitive map that provides a view of the world, helps interpret the changes the organization faces and provide appropriate responses. These organizational sets of beliefs and assumptions have been variously referred to in management literature as 'paradigms' (Sheldon, 1980; Pfeffer, 1981; Johnson, 1987), 'interpretative schemes' (Bartunek, 1984) and 'ideational culture' (Schein, 1985; Sathe, 1985). The result of the application of such cognitive maps is well documented: the danger is of 'groupthink' as the application of 'collective cognitive resources to develop rationalisations in line with shared illusions about the invulnerability of ... organizations' (Janis, 1985: 169). Other researchers have shown the extent to which symbolic aspects of the organization stories and myths (Schrank and Abelson, 1977; Wilkins, 1983), rituals and ceremonies (Meyer and Rowan, 1977; Trice and Beyer, 1984) and the language of the organization (Meyer, 1982) act to legitimize and preserve such core beliefs and assumptions held within the organization. Indeed Abravanel (1983) argues that symbolic devices provide a mediating role between fundamental organizational beliefs and potentially conflicting exigencies the organization faces.

Arguably these three models more generally embrace two broad thrusts about views on strategy formulation. The one is that strategy formulation can be accounted for by logical, rational processes either through the planning mode or through the adaptive, logical incremental mode. In either event the manager is a proactive strategy formulator consciously seeking to understand a complex environment, so as to establish causal patterns and formulate strategy by configuring organizational resources to meet environmental needs. The other view is an 'organizational action' view of strategy formulation where strategy is seen as the product of political, programmatic, cognitive or symbolic aspects of management. In what follows we will take a closer look at Coopers in order to assess the extent to which these differing views explain the strategic development of the company.

Explaining strategic management processes

A rational view of strategy formulation

Referring back to Figure 3.1 it might appear that the notion of strategy as a logical response to environmental change is supported at least in so far as, over the period, the company did apparently try to make strategic changes in response to a changing business environment.
[...]

However, the observation that strategies change given environmental change tells us little about the processes of strategic decision-making. If we were to account for such decisions in terms of 'linear, rational, planning' models, we would expect to find strong evidence and a significant impact of systematic environmental scanning, clear objective setting and evaluation of strategic options against such objectives, and probably a planning infrastructure through which this took place. In fact in Coopers throughout the period studied there was little evidence of any of this and, as will be seen, when such activity did take place, it had relatively little impact. We have to account for the observed strategic changes in other ways.

However, the managers themselves expressed views about the management of strategy which square well with rational but incremental models of strategic management – views which mirror closely Quinn's (1980) notion of logical incrementalism.

[...]

If the espousal of the logic of incrementalism is examined in the context of the company's performance to 1980, it would be tempting to concur with the managers' view that such a process was, indeed, beneficial. Coopers had enjoyed a decade of virtually continuous profit growth and a 4-year period in which it had achieved record profits, whilst most large competitors could only generate book profits through the sale of properties. There are, however, two dangers in this interpretation. The first is a danger of dubious causality: it is one thing to recognize the phenomenon of incrementalism, even to note the espousal of 'logical incrementalism'; it is quite another to support that a good record of profit performance can be explained by it. Indeed the dramatic decline in performance between 1980 and 1983 was to show that the processes of management in the firm were not adequate to prevent it. The second danger is that of assuming that the logic of the processes described by the managers is necessarily a reasonable description of the processes which account for strategy formulation. This research was concerned to study strategic change as a longitudinal, contextual process, rather than as the espoused theory of managers. It will be shown that a somewhat different picture of the process of strategic management emerges if patterns of development of strategy in the business are examined in terms of the events, dramas and routines of organization life and the belief systems of managers.

An 'organizational action' view of strategy formulation and implementation

An 'organizational action' view of strategy formulation argues that strategy can best be seen as the product of the political, cognitive and cultural fabric of the organization. The expectation would be that strategic decisions could be explained better in terms of political processes than analytical procedures; that cognitive maps of managers are better explanations of their perceptions of the environment and their strategic responses than are analysed position statements and evaluative techniques; and that the legitimacy of these cognitive maps is likely to be reinforced through the myths and rituals of the organization.

Discernible from the analysis of the interviews with managers was a common set of beliefs and assumptions taken for granted by those managers; it was tacit knowledge, primarily about the modes of operation in the organization, typically in terms of trading procedures, organization and control, seen as bestowing beneficial competences and capabilities on the organization.

[...]

This set of beliefs amounts to what other writers have referred to as a paradigm:

> those sets of assumptions, usually implicit, about what sort of things make up the world, how they act, how they hang together and how they may be known, ... such paradigms function as a means of imposing control ... (and) ... provide roles to be enacted in particular ways, particular settings, and in particular relation to other roles' (Brown, 1978: 373).

In the case of Coopers this paradigm was closely related to the dominance of routines and programmes in the organization: it is essentially an operational view of the world built up over time through the experience of operating and encapsulating what the managers saw as the distinctive competences of their business. In particular we will see the extent to which the buying routines played a substantial part in shaping strategy in the business.

It was also clear that political processes and the exercise of power were important. In Coopers over most of the years under study the buyers in particular exercised high degrees of power in the business. The link between the paradigm and the power bases in the company is an observation made by many researchers: 'power accrued to those sub-units which could best deal with organisational uncertainty' (Pfeffer and Salancik, 1974: 137; also Crozier, 1964; Hickson *et al.*, 1971; Hambrick, 1981). The merchandise strategy was perceived to have the effect of insulating the company from market threats; the price and margin advantages reduced the likelihood of competitive incursions and buffered them against downturns in demand. Changes in fashion were seen to be less important than for some other companies because they had elected to concentrate on 'commodity' merchandise policies. It was the merchandise strategy that became the mechanism through which company profits were to be guaranteed, and this became central within the set of assumptions about the basis upon which the business could compete in an uncertain world.

The dominance of buying and merchandise could be seen in the shop window displays of the 1970s, crowded with every item of merchandise the shop stocked with an emphasis given to that which the buyers had procured. The assumption of the dominant importance of merchandise and buying was also symbolized in the greater freedom and discretion enjoyed by buyers in an otherwise tightly controlled business. On the caring nature of management, managers told stories which emphasized the concern for staff and emphasized the difference between retailing and manufacturing because retailing was run on 'trust' and 'love'. Managers also emphasized the way in which they were given opportunity for career progression; promotion was always from within, and if someone was promoted beyond his competence, then he would still be 'looked after'. The emphasis on the importance of staff loyalty was also reflected in organizational stories; managers were proud to tell of how they and their staff would work extra hours or over the weekend to help with a store refit. The rituals of socialization ensured that everyone knew of the company way of retailing and acknowledged organizational features of loyalty, long service and deference to senior executives not only as proper but beneficial. The nature of top management in the firm, its perceived entrepreneurial flair, the speed of decision-making and the centrality of the chief executive, were enshrined in myths which showed how this had been so throughout the history of the company. In short the tenets of the paradigm were, indeed, legitimized symbolically.
[...]

Formalizing explanatory models

Examination of the processes of strategic change in Coopers bears out many of the phenomena which characterize incremental strategic change explained in terms of an organizational action perspective. The patterns of change are indeed evolutionary; strategic decisions build upon history, and what managers at least perceive to be the core strength of the business. Decisions came about following long periods of incubation following identification of problems or opportunities through highly qualitative assessment. High levels of solicitation and bargaining characterize both problem definition and the selection of solutions. The primacy of cognitive maps in the interpretation of environmental stimuli, the configuration of responses and strategy implementation, is also evident: and it becomes clear that these belief sets are relatively commonly held within the organization and persistent, forming an organizational paradigm. Moreover the mediatory and legitimizing role of symbolic aspects of the organization is also borne out. Building on all this we can move towards more integrated explanatory models of strategic management which arguably help to provide assistance in understanding the complexity of strategic management.

The nature of the paradigm

The paradigm is the set of beliefs and assumptions, held relatively common through the organization, taken for granted, and discernible in the stories and explanations of the managers, which plays a central role in the interpretation of environmental stimuli and configuration of organizationally relevant strategic responses. Although this is a phenomenon observed in other studies, a number of points of explanation emerge from the examination of the impact of the paradigm on strategic decisions in Coopers. We need to start by distinguishing between what is meant by the paradigm and what is meant by 'strategy'. Following Mintzberg (1978) we can distinguish between intended and realized strategy. Realized strategy is taken to mean the observable output of an organization's activity in terms of its positioning over time. By intended strategy is meant the strategy that managers espouse, perhaps in some sort of formal plan, public statement, or explanation. The paradigm, on the other hand, is a more generalized set of beliefs about the organization and the way it is or should be and, since it is taken for granted and not problematic, may be difficult to surface as a coherent statement. It is more likely to emerge in the explanations and stories of managers. The point is that both intended and realized strategy are likely to be configured within the parameters of the paradigm.

There were discernible reasons why the paradigm would be resistant to rapid change. First because the internal consistency of the paradigm as observed was self-preserving and self-legitimizing. For example the belief in Coopers in the efficacy of bulk buying was consistent with the accepted wisdom of centralized control of stocks and distribution; the belief that the company could be fast on its feet because of the entrepreneurial approach of top management and a loyal workforce helped account for how an apparently rigid and closed system could be regarded as capable of flexibility. It is not an easy matter to challenge or repudiate one construct of an internally supportive and consistent whole. Second, and particularly significant in terms of understanding management implications we need to understand the paradigm not just as a system of beliefs and assumptions; it is preserved and legitimized in a 'cultural web' of organizational action in terms of myths, rituals, symbols, control systems and formal and informal power structures which support and provide relevance to core beliefs (see Figure 3.2). In Coopers the

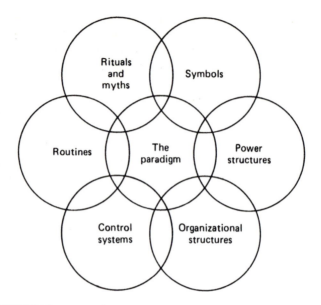

FIGURE 3.2   The cultural web of an organization

assumptions about the approach to buying and merchandising, and the
emphasis on centralized control of current costs and assets were not only
linked themselves, but institutionalized, indeed capitalized, in the stock
control and distribution systems. This is the inertia of technical organizational commitment, and is not likely ignored or overturned. The
significance of many of the operational aspects of managing the business
was, as has been seen, highlighted and arguably legitimized in the softer
rituals, myths and symbols of the organization (Wilkins, 1983; Daft,
1983; Dandrige, Mitroff and Joyce, 1980).

Further, the constructs of the paradigm are closely linked to the power
structures in the organization. In effect the paradigm represents the
internally constructed belief set about 'uncertainty reduction' so it is
likely that those most associated with operationalizing these beliefs will
be most powerful in the organization. This point is of some significance.
Strategic change processes traditionally advocated in the literature are
linked to rational analytical planning models. The notion that it is
through analysis of the business environment and the competitive
position of the firm that managers yield insights into strengths and
weaknesses which help identify the need for and opportunities for
change, overlooks the political implications of such analysis. Such
analysis was undertaken in Coopers – for example the market research
report of 1980. In the period following the analysis the evidence it
provided was either denied by management, discredited or led to

minimal change. The reason for this was not that the analysis lacked clarity or cogency; quite the reverse: it pointedly questioned tenets of beliefs fundamental to the strategies being followed by the organization; in other words it raised explicit challenges to the paradigm and, as such, constituted not an intellectual analytical questioning of strategy, but a political threat to those whose power was most associated with it. Clarity of analysis is not, in itself, a sufficient basis to break the powerful momentum of the fundamental assumptions embraced within the paradigm, and indeed can actually increase resistance to change.

Such were the characteristics discernible in relation to the paradigm in Coopers. It is not suggested that such characteristics will necessarily obtain in all organizations, of course. For example, such homogeneity of beliefs and assumptions will not always exist. However other empirical studies (e.g. Grinyer and Spender, 1979a,b; Miles and Snow, 1978; Davis, 1984; Janis, 1972; Smircich, 1983 and Wilkins and Ouchi, 1983) do suggest there are many organizations in which just such homogeneity around a core set of beliefs is common. Also noticeable about the paradigm in Coopers was its operational orientation, and Spender (1980) and to some extent Pettigrew (1985) note similar phenomena. However, this may not necessarily be the case in all organizations. Indeed if the arguments of Peters and Waterman (1982), Quinn (1980), and Kanter (1983) are to be accepted, it is those organizations with core belief sets of a relatively high order (mission statements) and yet at other levels rather heterogeneous sets of beliefs, which are the 'excellent' companies.

An integrated model of process

The proposition arising from the analysis of the events in Coopers is that environmental signals will be reordered in terms of the paradigm. We can discern a pattern in this which allows a clearer understanding of what is meant by 'relevant environmental change' (Rhenman, 1973). Specifically, some environmental signals will simply not be seen as relevant in terms of the paradigm, and will be ignored. For example, for managers the strategic repositioning in the late 1970s of tailoring companies not historically in direct competition with Coopers was interesting to observe, but seen as of limited consequence and requiring no specific action. Coopers was perceived to be in a distinct market sector with a distinct way of operating. Other signals might be seen as 'consonant' with the paradigm, in so far as they were capable of interpretation and action within the bounds of that paradigm. For example, the apparent decline in consumer expenditure within the target market, in 1980, was seen as a matter which could be handled by more aggressive sales effort from loyal staff, price competition and even tighter cost control. The paradigm here provided a ready-made menu of responses to a set of circumstances.

There might also be signals from the environment seen as 'dissonant' with the paradigm; that is they might be actual or potential perceived threats to its basis, or not capable of being dealt with strictly within its bounds. For example, managers saw that there was a growing expectation of more fashionable merchandise within the 'C2D market', and youngsters in particular were increasingly shopping elsewhere for clothes. This was clearly relevant to the merchandise formula of the company but, as we saw in the mid-1970s, not capable of being handled by the 'pile it high and sell it cheap' approach of that time. It would, of course, theoretically be possible to see the same signals in quite different ways; analytically it might be argued that their notion of a defensible market sector had become groundless; or that changing fashion expectations could not be dealt with simply by adjusting merchandise but also required changes in retail shop ambience. This, however, is to take an analytical perspective rather than a cognitive perspective. Market signals were not analysed in this sense but perceived in terms of organizationally and operationally relevant beliefs – what we have called the paradigm.

Given such perceived dissonance there appears to be a pattern of response. Dissonance with the paradigm is potentially threatening to its integrity. Given such a threat:

1. Dissonance will be mediated symbolically; that is the symbolic mechanisms within which the paradigm is embedded will perform the role of maintaining the legitimacy of the paradigm in the face of the apparent threat.
2. Since such a threat may take the form of a political challenge to those most associated with core constructs of the paradigm, such threats may well be strongly resisted.
3. The problem will be resolved by managers seeking for consonance within the paradigm. That is, managers will seek to resolve the extent to which elements of the environment and the paradigm are in a state of dissonance. It is here that the most significant acts of strategic adaptation take place. The evidence throughout the period under study here is that such consonance might be achieved by: (a) making sense of contra-stimuli in the terms of paradigm rather than questioning or reconstructing the paradigm – for example, defining changes in buying behaviour as relating to merchandise rather than indicating any fundamental change in the fundamental nature of the buyer; or (b) where necessary marginally adjusting the paradigm, but from within its own bounds, and whilst maintaining its essential form. For example, by shifting somewhat from a 'pile it high' conception of retailing to an admission of the relevance of 'fashionable' merchandise

– providing it can meet buying and margin requirements of course. Action is then taken in line with the (adjusted) paradigm.

Figure 3.3 outlines this process schematically.

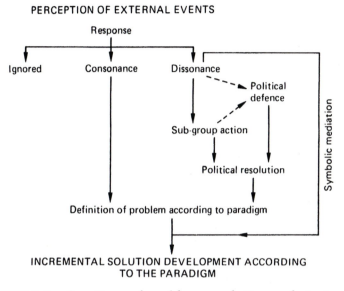

FIGURE 3.3   **A pattern of problem resolution and strategy formulation**

The notion of strategic drift

'Logical incrementalism' assumes a tension between identified environmental stimuli and 'the way we do things around here'. Indeed Quinn (1980) claims that such an approach explicitly recognizes the need for managing such ambiguity: in the terms of this chapter, the process allows for the admission of threats to the paradigm. The argument here is that the very nature of the cultural context of the paradigm means that it is likely to militate against and stifle such tensions and such threats. The paradigm effectively defines environmental 'reality' and responses to environmental change. Quinn's logical notion is that strategic change, through environmental sensing by managers within subsystems and the interplay between subsystems and continual testing out of new strategies, results in a learning and readjustment process in organization by which the organization keeps itself in line with environmental changes. It is a notion which is summarized in Figure 3.4. The argument here is different: it is that managers may well see themselves as managing

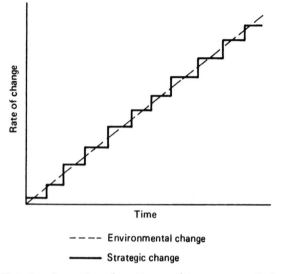

FIGURE 3.4   A notional pattern of incremental change

logically incrementally, but that such consciously managed incremental change does not necessarily succeed in keep .ng pace with environmental change. Indeed it is argued that there is a high risk that it will not. The situation in Coopers as it evolved throug the 1970s was not as shown in Figure 3.4, but rather as shown in Figure 3. ' Gradually the incrementally adjusted strategic changes, and the envi onmental, particularly market changes, moved apart.

This phenomenon of 'strategic drift' was found in all three companies studied and can be accounted for thus:

1. Sensing of external stimuli is muted because the stimuli are not meaningful in themselves; they take on a relevance, and responses are operationalized in terms of the paradigm.
2. Managers believe they are adapting to a changing environment when in fact they are adapting to signals which coincide with the paradigm.
3. There is likely to be resistance to 'deviant' interpretations of the environment if they threaten the paradigm. This results in political pressure for conformity or marginal adjustments to strategy.
4. Strategic drift is not easily discerned by managers. However, in the event of its detection remedial action is likely to take the form of solutions constructed within the bounds of the paradigm anyway.
5. Moreover these adjustments may well be enough to demonstrate the efficacy of the action to the satisfaction of stakeholders since, given the application of the familiar, there is a good chance that there will be some signs of performance improvement, at least in the short term.

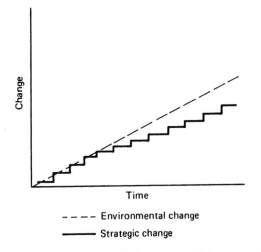

FIGURE 3.5 Incremental change and 'strategic drift'

This notion of strategic drift, whilst accounted for differently, is similar to phenomena observed by other researchers. Mintzberg (1978) shows how organizations go through periods of strategy adjustment characterized by continuity, flux or incremental change, but infrequently require more global changes. Greiner (1972) charts periods of evolution and revolution in corporate development, and Chandler (1962) also noted the resilience of current strategies and structures, as more recently did Grinyer and Spender (1979): indeed, Miller and Friesen summarize their own research thus:

> Managers demand a large potential benefit before they are willing to destroy the order and complementarity of elements inherent in the old gestalt and begin to construct a new one. The price paid for this sluggish responsiveness to the need for reversals in evolutionary trends is occasional revolutionary periods with all of their turmoil, expense and confusion (Miller and Friesen, 1980, pp. 612–13).

Conclusions and normative implications

The main purpose of this chapter has been to develop explanatory models relating to the phenomenon of incrementalism. It has not set out to be a normative management chapter. However, there are implications which arise from the study which should be highlighted. The first is that the integrated model of strategic decision-making rooted in the organizational action approach does lend itself to the prediction of likely responses given certain circumstances. The prediction would be that in the context of organizations exhibiting dominant paradigms of the sort we see in Coopers, likely responses in line with Figure 3.3 may be expected, and represent a very different explanation of the phenomenon of incrementalism than is found in the arguments of the logical incrementalists. Indeed it is argued that managers are likely to espouse such 'logical incrementalism' but that such espousals may disguise a system of management rooted in the currency of the paradigm. The question therefore remains as to how it might be possible to achieve more nearly effective adaptive incremental strategic management and avoid 'strategic drift'.

If strategy is to be managed effectively, adaptively there must exist a 'constructive tension' (Kanter, 1983) between that which is necessary to preserve and that which must be changed. A tension, for example, between the need for managers to question and challenge and the preservation of core values and organizational 'mission'; between the need for new ideas and directions and the need for continuity and preservation of the core business. This necessary tension is what Peters and Waterman (1982) call 'simultaneous loose–tight properties' or 'the coexistence of firm central direction and maximum individual autonomy' (p. 318). It is a view echoed elsewhere but, more specifically, at the cultural and cognitive levels. Meyer (1982) has argued that the reason an organization is more likely to adopt strategies more divergent from its previous strategies than other organizations is because it has a more heterogeneous organizational 'ideology', as manifested in terms of, for example, organizational images and symbols. It is a view supported by Friedlander (1983), who argues organizational learning in a 're-constructive' mode takes place more readily where there is such heterogeneity. A number of writers have argued that such ideological heterogeneity can be built into management systems in a variety of ways. For example through organic management styles with a removal or reduction of hierarchical lines of reporting and communication (Bartunek, 1984; Peters and Waterman, 1982; Pettigrew, 1985); through deliberate challenging and assumption surfacing devices, either formally promulgated (Mason and Mitroff, 1981) or as part of the organizational culture (Peters and Waterman, 1982; Kanter, 1983); through the active involvement of 'outsiders' with less adherence to organizational culture or the organizations paradigm (Mintzberg, 1978; Grinyer and Spender, 1979a; Schein, 1985) and through the avoidance of 'segmentalist' structures (Kanter, 1983).

Findings here also bear out those who argue the power of symbolic mechanisms for strategic management and change (Peters, 1978; Boje, Fedor and Rowland, 1982; Deal and Kennedy, 1982; Kotter, 1982; Martin and Powers, 1983; Sathe, 1985). The point that they argue is that strategic issues have, traditionally, been seen as linked to analytic, planning mechanisms of management, and as such run the risk of not being 'owned' by those within the organization. They point out that successful organizations are good at managing change, not by talking about it at an analytical level but by demonstrating it at a symbolic and therefore more meaningful level in terms of the interpretative models suggested here and as illustrated in Figure 3.2. Such organizations approach the management of change through the very artifacts (symbolic and political) that otherwise preserve the integrity of the paradigm and prevent change.

None of this is to say that the planning and analytical methods advocated in so much of the literature is of no relevance. It is rather to argue that planning and analysis are necessary but not sufficient, and need to be understood as mechanisms for problem and opportunity identification and strategy evaluation, rather than as a mechanism for strategic change. Indeed, the argument can be advanced that planning and analytical mechanisms are likely to give rise to resistance to change unless they take place within a context where the mechanisms for managing strategic change through the social, cultural, political, cognitive and symbolic devices of the organization are already in place.

Overall the results of the study emphasize the importance of understanding strategic management processes essentially in terms of organization action perspectives, and argue for the continued development of models which more precisely explain both strategy formulation and implementation in these terms.

References

Abravanel, H. (1983) 'Mediating Myth in the Service of Organization Ideology', in Pondy, L. R., Frost, P. G., Morgan, G., and Dandrige, T. C. (eds) *Organizational Symbolism* (Greenwich, CT: JAI Press).

Allison, G. T. (1971) *The Essence of Decision* (Boston: Little, Brown).

Bartunek, J. M. (1976) 'Changing Interpretive Schemes and Organizational Restructuring: The Examples of a Religious Order', *Administrative Science Quarterly*, **29**, pp. 355–72.

Biggart, N. W. (1977) 'The Creative–Destructive Process of Organizational Change: The Case of the Post Office', *Administrative Science Quarterly*, **22**, pp. 410–26.

Boje, D. M., Fedor, D. B., and Rowland, K. M. (1982) 'Myth Making: a Qualitative Step in O.D. Interventions', *Journal of Applied Behavioural Science*, **18**(1), pp. 17–28.

Bower, J. L. (1972) *Managing the Resource Allocation Process: a Study of Corporate Planning and Investment* (Homewood, IL: Irwin).

Brown, R. H. (1978) 'Bureaucracy as Praxis: Toward a Political Phenomenology of Formal Organizations', *Administrative Science Quarterly*, **23**, pp. 365–82.

Chaffee, E. E. (1985) 'Three Models of Strategy', *Academy of Management Review*, **10**(1), pp. 89–98.

Chandler, A. D. (1962) *Strategy and Structure* (Cambridge, MA: MIT Press).

Cohen, M. D., March, J. C., and Olsen, J. P. (1972) 'A Garbage Can Model of Organization Choice', *Administrative Science Quarterly*, **17**, pp. 1–25.

Crozier, H. (1964) *The Bureaucratic Phenomenon* (Chicago: University of Chicago Press).

Daft, R. L. (1983) 'Symbols in Organizations: A Dual-content Framework for Analysis', in Pondy, L. R., Frost, P. J., Morgan, G., and Dandrige, T. C. (eds) *Organizational Symbolism* (Greenwich, CT: JAI Press).

Dandrige, T. C., Mitroff, I., and Joyce, W. F. (1980) 'Organizational Symbolism: a Topic to Expand Organizational Analysis', *Academy of Management Review*, **5**, 1980, pp. 77–82.

Davis, S. M. (1984) *Managing Corporate Culture* (Cambridge, MA: Ballinger/ Harper & Row).

Deal, T. and Kennedy, A. (1982) *Corporate Cultures: The Rites and Rituals of Corporate Life* (Reading, MA: Addison Wesley).

Fahey, L. (1981) 'On Strategic Management Decision Processes', *Strategic Management Journal*, **2**, pp. 43–60.

Fredrickson, J. W. (1983) 'Strategic Process: Questions and Recommendations', *Academy of Management Review*, **8**, pp. 565–75.

Friedlander, F. (1983) 'Patterns of Individual and Organisational Learning', in Srivastva, S. (ed.) *The Executive Mind* (San Francisco: Jossey Bass).

Greiner, L. E. (1972) 'Evolution and Revolution as Organizations Grow', *Harvard Business Review*, July/August, pp. 37–46.

Grinyer, P. H. and Spender, J. C. (1979a) 'Recipes, Crises and Adaptation in Mature Businesses', *International Studies of Management and Organisations*, **9**, pp. 113–23.

Grinyer, P. H. and Spender, J. C. (1979b) *Turnaround: Managerial Recipes for Strategic Success: The Fall and Rise of the Newton Chambers Group* (London: Associated Business Press).

Hambrick, D. C. (1981) 'Environment, Strategy and Power within Top Management Teams', *Administrative Science Quarterly*, **26**, pp. 253–76.

Hedberg, B. and Jonsson, S. (1977) 'Strategy Making as a Discontinuous Process', *International Studies of Management and Organisation*, **7**, pp. 88–109.

Hickson, D. J., Hinings, G. R., Lee, C. A., Schneck, R. E., and Dennings, J. M. (1971) 'A Strategic Contingencies Theory of Intraorganizational Power', *Administrative Science Quarterly*, **16**(2), pp. 216–29.

Janis, I. L. (1972) *Victims of Groupthink* (Boston: Houghton Mifflin).

Janis, I. L. (1985) 'Sources of Error in Strategic Decision Making', in Pennings, J. M. (ed.) *Organizational Strategy and Change* (San Francisco: Jossey Bass) pp. 157–97.

Johnson, G. (1987) *Strategic Change and the Management Process* (Oxford: Blackwell).

Kanter, M. (1983) *The Change Masters: Innovation for Productivity in the American Corporation* (New York: Basic Books).

Kotter, J. P. (1982) *The General Managers* (New York: Free Press).

Lindblom, C. E. (1959) 'The Science of Muddling Through', *Public Administration Review*, **19**, Spring, pp. 79–88.
Lyles, M. A. (1981) 'Formulating Strategic Problems – Empirical Analysis and Model Development', *Strategic Management Journal*, **2**, pp. 61–75.
Martin, J. and Powers, M. E. (1983) 'Organizational Stories: More Vivid and Persuasive than Quantitative Data', in Staw, B. (ed.) *Psychological Foundations of Organizational Behavior* (Glenview, IL: Scott, Foresman) pp. 161–8.
Mason, R. O. and Mitroff, I. I. (1981) *Challenging Strategic Planning Assumptions* (New York: Wiley).
Meyer, A. D. (1982) 'How Ideologies Supplement Formal Structures and Shape Responses to Environments', *Journal of Management Studies*, **19**(1), pp. 45–61.
Meyer, J. W. and Rowan, B. (1977) 'Institutional Organizations: Formal Structures as Myth and Ceremony', *American Journal of Sociology*, **83**, pp. 340–63.
Miles, R. E. and Snow, C. C. (1978) *Organizational Strategy, Structure and Process* (New York: McGraw-Hill).
Miller, D. and Friesen, P. (1980) 'Momentum and Revolution in Organizational Adaptation', *Academy of Management Journal*, **23**(4), pp. 591–614.
Mintzberg, H. (1973) 'Strategy Making in Three Modes', *California Management Review*, Vol. **16**(2), Winter.
Mintzberg, H., Raisinghani, O., and Théorêt, A. (1976) 'The Structure of Unstructured Decision Processes', *Administrative Science Quarterly*, **21**, pp. 246–75.
Mintzberg, H. (1977) 'Strategy Formulation as a Historical Process', *International Studies of Management and Organization*, **7**(2) pp. 28–40.
Mintzberg, H. (1978) 'Patterns in Strategy Formation', *Management Science*, May, pp. 934–48.
Mintzberg, H. (1979) *The Structuring of Organizations* (Englewood Cliffs, NJ: Prentice-Hall).
Mintzberg, H. and Waters, J. A. (1979) 'The Mind of the Strategist(s)', in Srivastva, S. (ed.) *The Executive Mind* (San Francisco: Jossey Bass).
Nelson, R. R. and Winter, S. G. (1981) *An Evolutionary Theory of Economic Change* (Cambridge, MA: Harvard University Press).
Peters, T. (1978) 'Symbols, Patterns and Settings: An Optimistic Case for Getting Things Done', *Organizational Dynamics*, Autumn, pp. 2–23.
Peters, T. J. and Waterman, R. H. (Jr) (1982) *In Search of Excellence* (New York: Harper & Row).
Pettigrew, A. M. (1973) *The Politics of Organisational Decision Making* (London: Tavistock).
Pettigrew, A. M. (1977) 'Strategy Formulation as a Political Process', *International Studies of Management and Organization*, **7**(2), pp. 78–87.
Pettigrew, A. M. (1985) *The Awakening Giant* (Oxford: Blackwell).
Pfeffer, J. (1981) 'Management as Symbolic Action: The Creation and Maintenance of Organizational Paradigms', in Cummings, L. L. and Staw, B. M. (eds) *Research in Organizational Behavior*, vol. 3 (Greenwich, CT: JAI Press) pp. 1–15.
Pfeffer, J. and Salancik, G. R. (1974) 'Organizational Decision-making as a Political Process: The Case of a University Budget', *Administrative Science Quarterly*, **19**, 1974, pp. 135–51.

Pondy, L. R. (1983) 'Union of Rationality and Intuition in Management Action', in Srivastva, S. (ed.) *The Executive Mind* (San Francisco: Jossey Bass).

Pondy, L. R. and Huff, A. S. (1983) 'Budget-cutting in Riverside: Emergent Policy Re-framing as a Process of Analytic Discovery and Conflict Minimization', presented at a symposium on 'The Management of Hard Times', at the National Academy of Management, Dallas, August.

Quinn, J. B. (1980) *Strategies for Change* (Homewood, IL: Irwin).

Rhenman, E. (1973) *Organization Theory for Long Range Planning* (New York: Wiley).

Sathe, V. (1985) *Culture and Related Corporate Realities* (Homewood, IL: Irwin).

Schein, E. H. (1985) *Organizational Culture and Leadership* (San Francisco: Jossey Bass).

Schrank, R. and Abelson, R. (1977) *Scripts, Plans and Knowledge* (Hillsdale NJ: Erlbaum).

Sheldon, A. (1980) 'Organizational Paradigms: A Theory of Organizational Change', *Organizational Dynamics*, **8**(3) pp. 61–71.

Smircich, L. (1983) 'Organizations as Shared Meanings', in Pondy, L. *et al.* (eds) *Organizational Symbolism* (Greenwich, CT: JAI Press) pp. 55–68.

Spender, J. C. (1980) 'Strategy Making in Business', PhD thesis, School of Business, University of Manchester.

Trice, H. M. and Beyer, J. M. (1984) 'Studying Organizational Cultures through Rites and Ceremonials', *Academy of Management Review*, **9**(4) pp. 653–69.

Weick, K. E. (1979) *The Social Psychology of Organizing* (Reading MA: Addison Wesley).

Weick, K. E. (1983) 'Managerial Thought in the Context of Action', in Srivastva, S. (ed.) *The Executive Mind* (San Francisco: Jossey Bass).

Wilkins, A. L. (1983) 'Organizational Stories as Symbols which Control the Organization', in Pondy, L. R., Frost, P. J., Morgan, G., and Dandrige, T. C. (eds) *Organizational Symbolism* (Greenwich, CT: JAI Press).

Wilkins, A. L. and Ouchi, W. G. (1983) 'Effective Cultures: Exploring the Relation between Culture and Organisational Performance', *Administrative Science Quarterly*, **28**, pp. 468–81.

Paralysis by Analysis: is your planning system becoming too rational?

R. T. LENZ and MARJORIE A. LYLES

Is your planning becoming *too* rational?

[...]
During the past three years, we have been involved in a study of strategic planning processes in several financial and commercial organizations. Our findings, when combined with insight gathered from consulting relationships, reveal a disconcerting trend. With increasing frequency we have observed a variety of bureaucratic processes within organizations and technical developments from without that are causing many planning processes to become too rational. By this we mean a condition in which the strategic planning process has become inflexible, formalized and excessively quantitative. In this state, the planning system seems to develop an inertia all of its own that can stifle creative thought and frustrate the most able managers. It appears to be a major contributor to the disenchantment experienced by many line and staff members for whom planning has lost its glow.

Excessive rationality: its basic character and origins

Nothing would be more comforting than to suggest that the tendency toward excessive rationality in a planning system stems from a single source. If it were so, the problem would be easily recognizable and, probably, rather straightforward to resolve. Unfortunately, it appears that this tendency has multiple origins − none of which is abnormal in organizational life and all of which occur over rather lengthy periods of time. The collective effect of independent decisions and commitments made in the midst of daily administrative affairs can result in an overly rationalized planning process. Its early symptoms are usually felt by managers who sense that the demands placed on them to plan are burdensome in terms of time requirements, and that creativity, innovation and entrepreneurship are not rewarded. The resulting tension and frustration are mirrored in the remarks of one manager whose views are becoming increasingly widespread:

> Thank God it's over; now let's get back to work. This is my third strategy review. Same damn outcome. Nothing resolved. Every year we get together, fill in the forms — some of which don't even fit my business (and the planning instruction manual gets thicker by the year), make a two-and-one-half-hour presentation. We never get to the strategic issues. The discussion gets bogged down in nitpicking and number crunching; then we simply run out of time. Nobody really cares what's in the strategic plans. We must put on a good show, appear to be innovative, and go through the ritual. What really counts is the one-year operating budget.[1]

It would be misleading to suggest that either researchers, consultants or practitioners fully understand the constellation of forces that cause a planning process to become bureaucraticized and ritualistic. Precise answers to such questions will, undoubtedly, be forthcoming as more field studies of organizations are undertaken. As it now stands, however, it is clear that both basic administrative processes within most firms and technological developments from outside contribute to excessive rationality. Figure 4.1 includes some of the more salient processes whose overall effect, if not guarded against, is to generate inertia within the planning system toward an over-rationalized state.

Any classification of such diverse processes is at this point somewhat arbitrary. Nevertheless, the tendency toward too much rationality seems to be manifest in: (1) the growing professionalization of the planner's job; (2) excessive emphasis on quantification in strategic decision-making; (3) a drive to make planning routine and administratively efficient; and (4) the unqualified acceptance and improper use of techniques for strategic analysis. These processes influence each other in ways that can lead to a self-perpetuating cycle of organizational momentum. Gaining some appreciation for this requires more insight into each process.

Professionalizing the planner's job

One of the most important processes, particularly during the last decade, is the growth of planning as a profession. Both corporations and schools of business have done much to single out strategic planning as a high-potential career path. Fast-track programs in major business firms and university curricular developments have contributed to an aura and

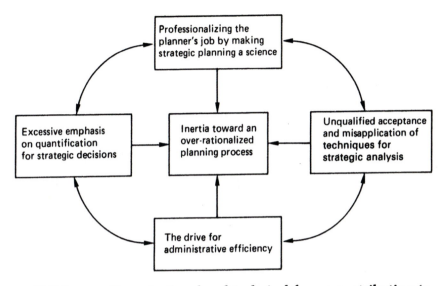

FIGURE 4.1 **Organizational and technical forces contributing to over-rationalized planning**

attractiveness that make careers in planning virtually irresistible. If popular business literature were to be taken at face value, one would come to believe that the corporate planner is a key influential who has the 'king's ear' on every strategic decision.

[...]

A requirement for maintaining the professional mystique of planning is to cast it into the mold of an exact science. With the help of academicians and consultants this is precisely what has occurred. First came the necessary jargon. Terms such as strategic business unit, growth-share matrix and GAP analysis became buzz words of the planning professional. These provided outward and visible signs required to gain and sustain respectability in organizational life. Accompanying this special vocabulary are a variety of research findings and analytical techniques reputed to reveal 'laws' of the market place. Armed with both an arcane language and a special knowledge of lawful (i.e. predictable) strategic relationships, corporate planning has come to be a 'scientific' profession.

The hazards of permitting the planning function to gain professional and scientific status in organizational life are manifold, and more will be said of it later. What is worth noting at this point is that planners are first and foremost staff. Therefore, they feel vulnerable with respect to their organizational status – particularly when going one-on-one with strong line managers. It should come as no surprise, then, that a safe harbor for the corporate planner is specialized knowledge and complex analytical procedures. These are more than tools of the trade: they are independent bases of power for offsetting the prerogatives and stature of line executives and serve as a means for surviving the vagaries of corporate life.

Excessive emphasis on quantification

A second process that can make a planning system overly rational is excessive emphasis on quantification. This emphasis is directed at both information used as inputs to the planning process and the level of detail embodied in the corporate plan itself. In each instance there operates an implicit belief that the level of quantification and certainty are directly correlated.
[...]
   A pervasive belief among many line and staff members is that only quantifiable data are sufficiently reliable bases for planning. Other data, though useful for explaining empirical relationships, lack the 'hardness' or certainty required for planning. Beliefs of this sort are seldom expressed – nor do they have to be. Nevertheless, they greatly bias the scope and character of information used to plan. Critically important qualitative information, especially that regarding emerging societal values, life-style changes, new directions in technology, etc., is frequently lost in the shuffle. Partly, this is because models for strategy analysis and most management information systems can only accommodate numbers.
   The desire of staff to establish solid planning assumptions is not the only factor contributing to the drive for quantification and certainty. Line managers also share part of the blame. One of the most often observed phenomena in organizational life is the direct correlation between the age of a planning system and the level of detail used for analysis and exhibited in the strategic plan. There are exceptions, of course, but the tendency is for line managers to demand and receive each year more detailed information for preparing plans. Corporate planners are then expected to incorporate such detail into the plan itself. In companies we have seen, the increasing emphasis on detail reflects a continuing quest for certainty. Unfortunately, in most firms this quest proves to be a mirage. What managers usually encounter with increasing levels of detail is not greater certainty, but more ambiguity. As strategic problems are 'sliced' into smaller and smaller pieces, they become fragmented and disjointed. What is lost is coherence.
[...]

The drive for administrative efficiency

A third force that can contribute to planning becoming too rational is a drive for administrative efficiency. This drive is not consciously co-ordinated and typically occurs simultaneously in many parts of an organization. It is usually undertaken to save time and make the planning process less of a chore to manage.

A central administrative problem in organizational life is that of sustaining commitment and enthusiasm to essential tasks. Planning is no exception. A distinct problem with planning processes, however, is that once they are implemented a raft of little decisions are made whose overall effect is to reduce the effectiveness of the process. In the early years of planning the process is usually 'loose'. That is, it is open to a wide spectrum of information and emphasis is placed on gaining fresh insight into emerging strategic issues. Typically there develops a dense, semi-structured pattern of executive interaction. As time passes this looseness begins to be regarded as inefficient. Steps are then taken to improve planning effectiveness by making the process more routine and predictable. Initial changes usually center on standardizing data inputs and the format of planning documents. Unfortunately, this even occurs when strategically significant differences in businesses and markets are blurred by a standard format. Subsequently, attention centers on establishing a timetable for data preparation, meetings, etc. to facilitate more systematic co-ordination of effort. These decisions are taken throughout an organization in the name of improving the efficiency of the planning process.

[...]

Our experience suggests that the dual forces of administrative efficiency and planning effectiveness pull in opposite directions. To obtain more of one you must be ready to give up some of the other. This duality is not merely an academic abstraction. Rather, it is an operational characteristic. As planning systems are made more efficient, the time devoted to creative thought is inevitably reduced. The driving force in the planning process becomes the agreed upon timetable. Demands for data in fixed formats and formalized executive interactions with a previously established agenda are not conducive to innovative thought and entrepreneurship.

In no sense are we suggesting that a planning process be left entirely unstructured. We are proposing that there is a delicate balance to be maintained between administrative efficiency and planning system effectiveness. And, unless executives are alert to this issue, the scale can easily be tipped in a way that undermines the prospect of an organization for achieving strategic success.

Unqualified acceptance and misapplication of analytical techniques

[...]

Findings stemming from the PIMS Program,[2] contributions from finance concerning capital budgeting, the Boston Consulting Group's concept of portfolio analysis[3] and recent outgrowths of industrial organization economics are milestones in strategic thought.[4] These and similar techniques are powerful tools for competitive analysis. However, their function and limits are often ignored in the quest for certainty in strategic decision-making. Planning becomes over-rationalized when one or more of these techniques become the dominant framework for defining and evaluating strategic choices. The following problems are typical of this condition.

(I) The particular analytical model used becomes a 'filter' that frames managerial thinking. In this mode the model's parameters and structure *define* strategic problems in such a way that the model can deal with them. Thus, emerging, ill-defined strategic issues that often prove decisive may not be detected because they either do not correspond to variables in the model or fall outside its analytical scope. In a sense, unqualified acceptance of a model for strategy analysis can seriously impair the capacity of an organization to spot problems sufficiently well in advance to formulate and implement a response.[5]

(II) Many strategy analysis techniques place undue emphasis on a single criterion as the basis for strategic decision-making. Both the present value method and the Boston Consulting Group's portfolio model are primarily concerned with cash flows. Their implication is that the strategic significance of investment decisions and managing a portfolio of diverse businesses is summarized by streams of cash. For the executive, strategic choices are a complex, multidimensional problem. They involve matters that cannot be incorporated by a single measure. Misapplication of these or similar techniques can lead to strategic errors biased by short-term financial considerations that undermine the infrastructure of an organization necessary to sustain it over the long run.[6,7]

(III) Proponents of particular analytical techniques usually make it a point to remind potential users of the scope, limits and assumptions of each technique. Unfortunately, these are often ignored at great risk. The PIMS findings, for example, are based on product life cycle. Whether lawful relationships revealed in this program hold under other circumstances is not known. Thus, generalizing can be perilous. The portfolio model and experience curve (which underpins the BCG portfolio matrix) also have limits.[8,9,10] Managers lulled into a false sense of security with these models can wake up to find that competitors placing greater emphasis on product innovation are expanding into new markets with higher rates of return.

(IV) Deterministic thinking often supplants entrepreneurial creativity in strategy-making. By this we mean when managers implicitly assume that relationships specified by an analytical model are inevitable and result from irresistible economic and technological trends. For example, some drawing on PIMS research argue that high profits are the outcome of a large market share. Therefore, one should pursue share. This is a case of over-generalizing a deterministic relationship. It ignores other factors such as profit margins, cost structure, barriers to industry competitors, etc. The potency of these factors is clear in the world of commerce which is replete with examples of firms with small market share that are extremely profitable.

[...]
The four processes presented in Figure 4.1 are primary contributors to excessive rationality in the planning process. Certainly, not all firms experience these in the same proportion. Some never experience them at all. The point is that such processes operate among evolutionary developments that facilitate the normal adaptation of planning systems as organizations grow. When planning becomes too rational it is onerous, dysfunctional and incapable of producing clear strategic thinking. Organizational consequences of this condition can be very serious.

Organizational consequences of an excessively rational planning process

When a planning process becomes too rational its effects are not localized. Instead, they affect persons in key roles throughout an organization. Of particular importance are the chief executive officer, the corporate planner, senior-level line managers and board members. Such persons experience the effects somewhat differently. For this reason each deserves individual consideration.

Chief Executive Officer

There are two discernible effects on a chief executive when a planning system becomes too rational. First, the shifting pattern of people, values, aspirations and commitments that comprise the milieu of executive action seems strangely irrelevant. The organization is discussed as if it were an abstraction to be referenced by carefully defined strategic variables and subject to immutable competitive laws. Intangible qualities of organization that constitute its social structure and sense of collective purpose seem unimportant in the wake of empirical data and statistically verified relationships. A second effect of excessive rationality concerns the role of the chief executive. If strategy formulation is developed within the parameters of a single model, the specification of strategy becomes merely a constrained choice problem. The executive's role is recast from that of institutional leader to one of clerk: in lieu of inventing a future for the organization is an annual endorsement of an inevitable course of action. Admittedly, these effects are exaggerated. But the central point remains that when planning becomes too rational it is devoid of meaning for many senior executives because of its incapacity to capture the complexity of strategic issues.

When confronted with this situation we have seen executives exhibit a variety of responses. Two of these are particularly detrimental to the success of the strategic planning process. One response is to withdraw support from and active participation in the process. It goes without saying that this seriously undermines the integrity of the planning effort by giving mixed signals to other executives. Without visible and enthusiastic support from the chief executive, strategic planning is doomed to failure.[11,12,13]

A second and equally destructive consequence of over-rationalized planning is for the CEO to form a coterie of senior managers for making strategic decisions. Such a group is usually comprised of certain key executives that share basic values with the chief executive and possess a similar 'view of the world'. Matters of real strategic significance are confronted and dealt with by this group outside of the formal process of strategic planning. Relatively mundane aspects of planning occur within prescribed channels. In this situation the formal planning process can take on the role of an annual exercise that affords little in the way of innovative thought. Few other executive actions have a greater negative impact on the overall effectiveness of the strategic planning than withdrawing visible support.

The corporate planner

Although to some it may seem ironic, corporate planners are often victims of excessive rationality in planning. In their effort to attain organizational respectability as vital contributors to strategic decision-making, the trappings of the 'science of planning' sometimes create a snare. The snare is slowly fashioned out of the increasingly intricate network of models, data, analytical techniques and formal procedures. If the process goes too far, these factors establish an intellectual cocoon of abstractions whose relationship to the administrative experiences of line managers is, at best, tenuous. Increasing sophistication can breed increasing irrelevance and the development of a ponderous planning apparatus.
[...]

An organizational consequence of such circumstances is to prevent the planner from acting as an otherwise creative agent in the planning process. In place of internal consultant, counsellor and confidant to managers struggling with tough strategic choices, the corporate planner becomes merely a 'gadfly' insuring that deadlines are met and procedures adhered to. The planning process ceases to be an instrument and becomes an end in itself. Administrative success is equated with completing the plan on schedule and in the correct format. For the planner there is little time for creative analysis of strategic opportunities sensed by line managers, since such projects are often precluded by the formal demands of the planning system. Innovation suffers as the planner's role changes from one of catalyst to one of weary coordinator.

Senior line managers

By now it must be clear that line managers too are victims of too much rationality in planning. They suffer at the hands of executive leadership when an over-rationality causes the CEO to withdraw from or by-pass the strategic planning process. Such executive actions communicate contradictory signals to mid-level managers. In one breath these managers are reminded of the importance of strategic planning. It is made clear that planning will require much of them and that they will be rewarded if well done. If, simultaneously, the CEO personally disengaged from the planning process, what are line managers to do?

Under such circumstances, managers expected to conduct the planning process experience role stress and feelings of ambiguity about planning.[14] These experiences often surface in the form of dysfunctional behaviors which reduce the effectiveness of the planning process. Mid-level managers often send the same mixed signals to subordinates that they have received from their chief executive. Thus, the facade of planning is maintained while the substance of planning is lost. There develops a mere chain of compliance. Managers at all levels come to view the strategic planning process as the nearly unbearable annual ritual that in the end means little.

When the quality of participation in the planning process gravitates from enthusiastic support to reluctant compliance, the capacity of the system to facilitate adaptation is severely impaired. Missing are the priceless inputs from line managers that help an organization sense out shifting environmental contingencies. Early signals of strategic significance are ignored. Without antennae of this sort, the corporation is, at least with respect to subtle changes in competitive conditions, 'flying blind'. If the planning process ceases to be a forum in which entrepreneurial thought and action are encouraged, ambitious, able managers are forced to find other outlets for their creativity. If these are not available, morale declines and a generation of future executives are compelled to conclude that strategic planning is simply another administrative burden they must bear while ascending the organizational hierarchy.

Board members

Board members are, perhaps, the most unwitting victims of excessive rationality in planning. This stems from the fact that they are usually trying to reach an accommodation between two conflicting pressures that make board membership difficult. One source of pressure is rising public expectations of a board member's responsibility for a corporation's strategic behavior.[15] Such expectations are reflected in a raft of litigation that is redefining the legal liability and role of directors. A second source of pressure is the difficulty even able board members have in comprehending the complexity and scope of corporate actions. Many directors, despite good intentions, have an inadequate understanding of both current strategy and broad issues affecting strategic success.

To the besieged board member the appearance of certainty conveyed by a highly rational planning process is alluring, indeed. Its pseudo-scientific trappings provide a sense of stability in a world that often appears turbulent. Armed with sophisticated planning procedures, executives can bring to board members in simple 'black and white' the immutable logic supporting their chosen course of action. If questions arise, staff can be summoned to deliver a litany of arcane terminology and statistical mumbo jumbo sufficient to blunt the most earnest inquiry. For the board member, an over-rationalized planning process can become an opiate for coping with the stress of rising expectations and the increasing complexity of strategic choices.
[...]

Guidelines for preventing an over-rationalized planning process

The occurrence of excessive rationality in strategic planning is a result of a myriad of complex administrative and technical processes. However, these processes are not inevitable in the sense that nothing can be done to arrest their momentum. At first blush, it may appear to be fruitful to engage the sources presented in Figure 4.1 directly. This approach, however, will probably yield only modest results. Instead, our suggestion is to take action on three broad fronts with the intent of blunting the overall inertia toward excessive rationality.

Developing a planning culture

Simply stated, a culture is a group of individuals who have shared values. For planning to succeed, it is essential that a culture be developed in which the purpose and limits of planning are widely recognized and fully understood.[16,17] This is a particularly important function of the president, but does not stop there. Organizations that we are familiar with that have experienced success in this area spend a great amount of energy to develop shared values. Typically, corporate planners work with line executives on a continuous basis and in a variety of roles. Stress is placed on consultation throughout the planning process. Efforts are made to counsel, coach when necessary and reflect organization-wide opinion to line executives preparing plans. For younger managers initially exposed to planning, a close relationship is fostered to build a shared sense of the nature and role of planning. In this way commitment is sustained and pitfalls are avoided. One firm went so far as to have each new corporate trainee participate in a competitive simulation exercise with seasoned executives from a variety of functional areas. The purpose is to introduce newcomers to competitive issues facing the business and to stress the importance of planning for corporate success.

Regardless of the specific approaches employed, persons must be made to understand that the strategic planning process is a means for the continual identification and response to strategic issues that may affect the long-term growth and development of an enterprise. In this capacity, it should facilitate problem formulation, sensing out of values and aspirations, consensus building and settling on a strategy consistent with a firm's unique capabilities. In no sense, however, is strategy-making an exact science. It is, instead, a combination of analytical techniques, administrative processes and human judgement that bears elements of both art and science. With this in mind, executives must effect a synthesis between analyses provided by limited, but powerful, techniques and equally important non-quantifiable properties of an organization.

Probing evaluation of plans

In most companies where planning has become too rational, plans are usually presented rather than scrutinized. This occurs, in part, because of the heavy emphasis on quantification. Managers tend to use planning meetings as a forum for providing information in the form of graphs, charts and tables. If evaluation does take place, it usually centers on the fine adjustments to particular numbers (e.g. sales, market share) rather than the strategy and tactics behind it.

In order to prevent this excessive concern with detail and producing the 'right numbers', two steps can be taken. First, during the strategy

formulation phase, stress should be placed on the assumptions underlying strategy alternatives. Every strategy alternative and final strategic plan are underpinned by a host of assumptions. Some assumptions may stem from data used during analysis (e.g. interest rates, GNP). Other assumptions are peculiar to specific analytical techniques (e.g. declining costs, cash flows, rates of technological innovation). If assumptions in either of these areas are unwarranted, conclusions that result are also likely to be unwarranted. In light of these circumstances, we suggest that staff and line executives be encouraged to examine in considerable detail assumptions supporting strategic alternatives facing a firm.
[...]

In addition to careful evaluation of assumptions, a second step is helpful in preventing excessive rationality in planning. During strategy review sessions, managers should be pressed to express in words the substance of their strategy and why they expect it to work. This compels managers to deal with qualitative factors likely to affect the proposed strategy (e.g. competitors' reactions, technological innovation). As one executive in our field study remarked: 'If my managers cannot explain their strategy in simple language, then they don't have a strategy – all they have are a bunch of numbers.' Lately, companies have been turning more and more toward a verbal synopsis of strategy in lieu of seemingly endless quantitative analyses. This changes the basic character and role of strategy review sessions. Instead of primarily serving as occasions for providing information, they become settings for careful thought and probing analysis. Thus, the prospect for creativity and innovation is enhanced.

Planning process audits

[...]
We recommend periodic audits of the strategic planning process. These may be conducted by a task force comprised of both participants in the planning process and those with no direct involvement. The latter could be a consultant, an outside board member or an executive from another firm or division. The team should develop audit criteria before initiating their evaluation. The following are some criteria for getting started. This list is by no means all inclusive.

1. Do those engaged in the planning process understand its basic purpose and structure?
2. Does the strategic planning process facilitate the identification and interpretation of strategic issues?
3. Is there a balance between quantitative and qualitative information that sets the stage for innovative thought and action?

4. Given the utility of information obtained, is the time required to gather and interpret it excessive?
5. Does the planning process provide a means for fully discussing dissenting viewpoints?
6. Are managers encouraged and rewarded for entrepreneurial initiatives?
7. Are intangibles such as managerial values, aspirations and acknowledged responsibilities to society explicitly incorporated into final strategic choices?
8. Does the process provide adequate time for strategy implementation and evaluation?

Conclusion

We have suggested that four basic processes found in and around most organizations can generate momentum that often causes a strategic planning process to become too rational. This condition exists when a planning system becomes excessively rigid, formalized, quantitative and deterministic. Excessive rationality does not arise suddenly, nor are all organizations necessarily susceptible to its debilitating effects. Managers in many firms recognize its early symptoms and take corrective action. Other managers do not. As a result, they suffer a decrease in the level of effectiveness of their planning process.

In order to lessen the inertia toward over-rationality, we suggest that action be taken on three fronts. First, it is necessary to instill and cultivate organizational values about planning that put into perspective its purpose, proper role and limits. Second, assumption-testing procedures should be incorporated into the planning process in conjunction with strategy review sessions stressing innovative thought. Finally, periodic audits of the planning process could be vitally important. If these steps are successful, they will contribute to the maintenance of a viable planning process sufficient to insure continuing adaptation to a changing competitive environment.

Notes

1. Charan, R. (1982) 'How to Strengthen Your Strategy Review Process', *Journal of Business Strategy*, **2** (3) pp. 50–60.
2. Schoeffler, S., Buzzell, R. and Heany, D. (1974) 'Impact of Strategic Planning on Profit Performance', *Harvard Business Review*, **52** (3) pp. 137–45.
3. The Boston Consulting Group (1971) 'Growth and Financial Strategies', *Perspectives* (Boston: Boston Consulting Group).

4. Porter, M. (1980) *Competitive Strategy* (New York: The Free Press).
5. Ansoff, H. (1977) 'Managing Surprise and Discontinuity: Strategic Response to Weak Signals', in H. Thorelli (ed.) *Strategy + Structure = Performance* (Bloomington, IN: Indiana University Press).
6. Abernathy, W. and Wayne, K. (1974) 'Limits of the Learning Curve', *Harvard Business Review*, **52** (5) pp. 109–19.
7. Hayes, R. and Garvin, D. (1982) 'Managing as if Tomorrow Mattered', *Harvard Business Review*, **60** (3) pp. 71–9.
8. Kiechel, W. (1981) 'The Decline of the Experience Curve', *Fortune*, pp. 139–46, 5 October.
9. Kiechel, W. (1981) 'Three (or four, or more) Ways to Win', *Fortune*, pp. 181–8, 19 October.
10. Kiechel, W. (1981) 'Oh Where, Oh Where Has My Little Dog Gone? Or My Cash Cow? Or My Star?', *Fortune*, pp. 140–54, 2 November.
11. Lorange, P. (1980) *Corporate Planning: An Executive Viewpoint* (Englewood Cliffs, NJ: Prentice-Hall).
12. Rothschild, W. (1980) 'How to Ensure the Continued Growth of Strategic Planning', *Journal of Business Strategy*, **1** (1) pp. 11–18.
13. Steiner, G. (1979) *Strategic Planning* (New York: The Free Press).
14. Lyles, M. and Lenz, R. (1982) 'Managing the Planning Process: A Field Study of the Human Side of Planning', *Strategic Management Journal*, **3** (2) pp. 105–18.
15. Donnell, J. (1976) 'Sixteen Commandments for Outside Directors', *Business Horizons*, **19** (1) pp. 45–58.
16. Cleland, D. and King, W. (1973) 'Developing a Planning Culture for More Effective Strategic Planning', Working Paper no. 31, University of Pittsburgh.
17. Emshoff, J. and Mitroff, I. (1978) 'Improving the Effectiveness of Corporate Planning', *Business Horizons*, **21** (5) pp. 49–60.

CHAPTER 5

Strategic Planning for the World Wildlife Fund

G. J. MEDLEY

[...]

Introduction

The National Organization of the World Wildlife Fund operating in the United Kingdom (WWF UK) is a not for profit organization registered as a charity. It was founded in 1961 with the object of promoting education and research on the conservation of world fauna and flora, water, soils and other natural resources. In its early years, it developed like the majority of 'not for profit' organizations using relatively low-paid staff who had a concern for the charity's objectives. By 1973 gross income had risen to around £750 000 per annum and it stayed in this region for the next 5 years.

In 1977 a new Chairman of Trustees, Sir Arthur Norman, was appointed who was, himself, chairman of a major British Corporation. He identified the necessity of bringing in sound business management to develop the charity and when the previous Chief Executive Officer (CEO) left in April 1977, he searched for a Senior Executive who had already demonstrated a sound and successful business career. The author took up appointment as CEO of WWF UK on 1 January 1978, arriving to a relatively demoralized staff who had been without direct leadership for 9 months.

Preparing for change

The first task was to identify, from the existing staff of 70, those who would fit in with a sound business approach compared to those who were working because of their interest and dedication to conservation. Whilst there was a need for good conservationists in the project departments, those in the fundraising areas needed to be capable of taking a wholly professional and sound business approach to their work. A structural reorganization took place in September 1978 and coincided with the introduction of strategic planning based on a 'management by objectives' (MBO) process developed by the author in his previous assignment as CEO of the subsidiary of a large multi-national. This was the first time that WWF UK had taken a hard look at its operations and it turned out to be a most revealing exercise.

The management team consisting of the Heads of each of the organization's departments of Promotions, Membership, Regional, Information, Education, Finance and Administration under the Chairmanship of the Director, met for the strategic planning exercises for two days at the end of September 1978.
[...]

Deciding on the purpose

The first essential was deciding the purpose of WWF UK. The purpose is the reference point which makes possible the formulation of clear and realistic objectives. Prior to the strategic planning exercise the general view was that WWF UK was a conservation organization. After some considerable discussion, however, it was recognized that in fact WWF UK was a fundraising business but that it also had as its purpose the proper spending of the funds raised. In 1978 the team decided that the purpose was 'to raise the maximum funds possible from UK sources and to ensure that the funds are used wisely for the benefit of conservation of the natural environment and renewable natural resources with emphasis on endangered species and habitats'.

Key areas

Having decided the purpose, attention was then turned to the result-influencing areas of the organization, specific areas in which success would contribute significantly to improve results or areas in which failure would have an adverse impact on results. The team were asked to give free range to their thinking and a list of some 60 possible areas emerged on the blackboard. Further analysis of these showed that many of them were in fact overlapping or similar and a final list of nine was chosen.

It is interesting to see that these nine can be matched to the more usual designations found when this process is followed in industry. 'Marketing' is the same word. 'Public Awareness' and 'Fund Status' relate to customer and shareholder perceptions of a business. 'Innovation' is the same concept as research and development and, most importantly, 'Net Funds' is the same as profitability. The full list is shown in Table 5.1.

TABLE 5.1   WWF UK key areas, 1978

1. Marketing
2. Public awareness
3. Fund status
4. Quality of application
5. Use of personal resources
6. Use of financial and physical resources
7. Administrative control
8. Innovation
9. Net funds

Each key area was then taken in turn and subjected to a strengths, weaknesses, opportunities and threats exercise. This systematic review identified the internal strengths and weaknesses of the organization and examined the external environment to identify the opportunities that might be available and the threats that might exist.

The marketing strengths of WWF UK in 1978 were seen largely to be its emotive and visually appealing message, its 'panda' logo and the uniqueness of its work. It was weak in its lack of a large donor base, its poor record on innovation and its lack of marketing penetration.

The rising awareness of the need to conserve the earth's natural resources, the size of the market-place and the general increase in disposable income, all presented opportunities to be tapped. On the other hand, competitive charities were also growing and some legislation proposals threatened certain freedoms to fundraising in specific areas, notably national lotteries.

In the key area of fund status, WWF UK's international connections and scientific authority were seen as strengths offset by the weakness that the organization was not itself active in conservation work nor was it campaigning.

A major effort to devise and publicize a strategy for world conservation was to be carried out in the near future by WWF's international scientific sister organization, the International Union for the Conservation of Nature and Natural Resources (IUCN) with the financial backing of WWF and the United Nations Environmental Programme (UNEP) and this was seen as a major opportunity to improve further the public perception of WWF UK. A concomitant threat was the Government's

disinterest in the environment and its reluctance to enhance existing legislation in this field.
[...]

Agreeing strategies

At this point in the exercise, comprehensive answers to questions such as (a) where are we now? (b) what do we think will happen in the future? and (c) where do we want to go? had been determined.

It was now necessary to devise guidelines – termed strategies – which would be developed for all future actions – a strategy is a guide for action. Clearly the marketing strategies concentrated on improving those areas of fund-raising that were perceived to be weaknesses. Thus the first strategy was to increase membership and the second to increase the number and yield effectiveness of WWF's volunteer supporter groups around the country. Business would be concentrated on through effective commercial promotions and licensing the 'panda' trade mark and increased efforts would be made to raise income from business and charitable trusts. As the donor list had been identified as a major weakness, significant efforts would be made to build these lists. At that time, the cleaned list yielded 12 000 members together with a further 25 000 trading customers.
[...]

This exercise covering all the nine key areas took two days, at the end of which WWF UK had a document setting out its clear objectives for the immediate and medium-term future.

The last key area – 'net funds' – equates to a corporation's profitability. The achievement of the net funds objectives would show the progress of the organization. Net fund objectives were therefore agreed by the management team for the coming 3 years.

Action plans

The next part of the process was to devise the actions needed to achieve the strategies. Each department was asked to take each of the strategies and write down the actions they proposed in the coming year to fulfil the strategy. Clearly a number of strategies were not applicable to all departments whereas others had impact across all departments. The final action plans from each department were amalgamated into a single document and this became the working forward plans for WWF UK.

Budgeting to meet objectives

At the end of this strategic planning exercise, written documentation existed to show what WWF UK was hoping to achieve in all the key areas and how each department was going to take action to fulfil these strategies. At this stage however, there were no financial figures determined. The second part of the planning process involved the compilation of departmental budgets designed to achieve the strategies. Each department produced both income and expenditure budgets for the coming year and forecasts for the next 2 years. The departmental budgets were then consolidated to produce the budget for WWF UK. It was a surprise to most members of the management team that when the departmental budgets were amalgamated the overall net fund projected for the budget year was extremely close to the objective net fund set in September as the final stage in the strategic planning exercise. This came as no surprise to the author because in his experience in the subsidiary of a major multi-national, the management team setting itself objectives with considerable 'stretch' produced budgets which met those objectives, and more importantly produced results which came within a very few percentage points of achieving the budgets.

The setting of objectives in a strategic planning process and the compiling of budgets to achieve those objectives, are of no use without adequate factual information to show progress and achievement. WWF UK's financial management was strengthened and systems set up to provide quarterly reporting by department against budget. At the end of each quarter departmental performance was assessed and where necessary corrective action was taken although the disciplines of budget and assessment of performance against budget led very rapidly to excellent control of expenditure.

The strategic planning exercises have been carried out each year in WWF UK and it is interesting to see how the process has evolved. The basic structure has remained unchanged but, over the years, a number of key areas have been identified and a number dropped. For example, regional activities became important but when the problems within the regional area were resolved, that area no longer merited the microscopic examination of the planning process. It is also interesting to look at three measures of success and to see how the planning process has helped in the achievement of these successes.

Measures of success

Net funds is the best measure of success. Net funds remained static between 1972 and 1977 at £400 000–£600 000. After the introduction of strategic planning in 1978, net funds grew steadily although there was a slight decline in 1983 due to an unexpected and unexplainable drop of significant proportions in income from legacies that year. The upward trend was resumed in 1984 and the past 2 years have been exceptional. Figure 5.1 shows the growth of net funds from 1972 to 1986.

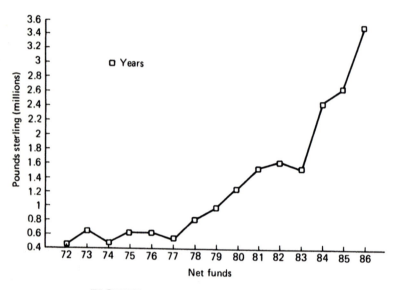

FIGURE 5.1   WWF UK net funds

FIGURE 5.2   WWF UK income per employee – productivity

Productivity in WWF UK is measured in terms of both gross and net income per employee. Staff numbers at 70 remained fairly constant from 1972 through to 1980 but since then marginal increases have occurred giving staff numbers at the end of 1986 of 85. With the growth in net funds by a factor of some eight times, it is clear that productivity will have increased substantially, as is shown in Figure 5.2.
[...]
One other measure of success is the growth in the size of the donor list. At the end of 1986, WWF UK had 110 000 members and a donor list of 450 000 names. This compares with the 12 000 and 25 000 in 1978.
[...]

Conclusion

When strategic planning was first suggested for WWF UK there was a considerable degree of scepticism coupled with a willingness to try a new business method which might bring good results for the organization. After the first year it became clear to the whole management team that the exercise was invaluable, giving an opportunity for the whole team to participate in the forward planning resulting in a feeling of commitment by the whole team to the objectives that had been agreed after full and open discussion. This commitment seemed to transfer itself to other staff members giving the whole organization a sense of purpose and of drive which, coupled with team work, produced the outstanding results that the organization has achieved. It is now inconceivable to think of WWF UK working without an annual strategic planning exercise, developing clear strategies in key areas with action plans to achieve those strategies. The success of this method of management by objectives must be seen in the light of WWF UK's performance in the last few years.

Reference

IUCN, *World Conservation Strategy* (1980) (Gland: Switzerland).

CHAPTER 6

Corporate Strategy and the Small Firm

SUE BIRLEY

Introduction

[...]
There is very little known about the interplay between the management development and strategic issues associated with the birth and growth of the firm.[1] Indeed, most of the advice, teaching, and other schemes tend to focus on relatively easy technical problems such as taxation, legislation or accounting procedures, and on solving problems rather than on the more difficult conceptual area of developing a total strategy.[2]

Moreover, implicit in any advisory or counselling work which is concerned with strategic development must lie assumptions about the process involved. Many assumptions have indeed been made and a great deal of valuable field experience has been gained, but with only a few notable exceptions, this experience has not been collated and analysed.[3] It is the contention of this paper that the strategic choices open to, and made by, the owner-manager differ in four fundamental ways from those facing his counterpart in the larger firm.

Corporate strategy

Corporate strategy is concerned with 'the determination of the basic long term goals and objectives of the enterprise, and the adoption of courses of action and the allocation of resources necessary for carrying out these goals'.[4] Thus it encompasses the totality of the firm and its interaction with the environment. However, this 'totality' is significantly different for the small firm than for the large firm; the choices which the small firm manager wishes, and indeed is able, to make often encompass a different set from those open to his counterpart in the larger firm. There are four

78

significant differences, all of which are concerned with the assumptions generally made when designing the framework for strategic analysis.

Goals

The first assumption concerns the goals or objectives to be chosen. In the small firm, ownership and management are usually held by the same person or persons,[5] and so the objectives of the firm and those of the owner become one and the same. The pressures which determine these objectives will encompass personal lifestyle and family considerations as well as commercial ones. Further, the entrepreneur often starts his own business with the declared intention of becoming independent and, once established, may have a clear intention of maintaining his independence by keeping day to day operational control.[6] To achieve this, his strategic goal becomes one of no growth or minimum growth consistent with survival. Moreover, the choices which he may wish to make will take into account personal lifestyles, personal interests and family considerations.[7] To the outside analyst, this can produce a company with a very strange profile, but one which is in fact pursuing a strategy which is internally consistent.

As considerations change in the market place and as the owner is forced to think both of his own possible retirement and of the future for his family, his personal objectives may change. Regardless of the needs of the business or, indeed, the skills and wishes of his children, he may wish to continue the family name in the firm and to continue to provide jobs for a loyal workforce. Alternatively he may wish to realise his lifetime investment and sell. In either case the firm's objectives and direction may need to change.

As time passes and the firm continues to survive, whether or not there is any real growth, ownership and management become more separate. Attempts to avoid personal taxation[8] by passing shares to family and employees, plus the natural growth of families, imply a widening of the ownership of the company. The shareholders become a different, although not necessarily a completely separate, set from the management. As this transition takes place, the pressures on the firm from the owners and from the market places are towards improving financial performance and growth. No longer is working in the firm part of the lifestyle of the owners, it is merely one of many possible ways of paying for a lifestyle. Thus dividends and capital growth become essential.
[...]

In medium and larger firms, this transition is complete and the conflict between the needs of the owners for a certain lifestyle and the needs of management for a continuing satisfying job are both realized in high profitability and dividends. Thus strategic objectives tend to focus almost exclusively on growth and/or profitability.

Product/market choices

The second difference between the small and large firm concerns the choices to be made in satisfying the goals already discussed. Not only will the large firm have developed a diverse ownership, but also probably a wide and even diverse range of products and markets. Therefore, in choosing a strategy the manager will aim to pick an optimum mix of products and markets. Indeed, the successful large firm is almost always market oriented. The successful small firm is, in the first place, the firm which manages to produce and sell one product or service. All the rest do not manage to get past first base. Thus success in the small sector initially means simply survival. Much of this 'success' is often a function of luck rather than strategic planning.

Once having survived long enough to prove his product in the market place, the owner manager has the opportunity to grow his business through new products or services or new geographic markets. Unlike the large firm, however, his ability to acquire knowledge and information upon which to base his decision is very limited. His own skills may be product or production based rather than market based and the resources upon which he can draw to test new ideas very limited. Moreover, the effect of the failure of a new venture on his business could be catastrophic. Thus he perceives a very narrow range of options open to him and indeed he is not rearranging a product/market portfolio as trading conditions change and products mature: he is trying to create one.

Resources

The third difference concerns management resources and skills. In simple terms, management exists as a function in the large firm. Indeed, there are likely to be functional managers for marketing, production, finance, often with specialist training. In some small firms the owner is attempting to create management, often without either training or help. In others, he may view management as bureaucracy, and have no wish to create systems or to delegate responsibility. Thus, the rate at which a small firm changes depends not only on factors like company size or market forces, but also on the abilities and inclination of the owner and the extent to which he is able or prepared to devolve management. In any event, the balance between skills which may be needed at particular points in the development of the firm has to be achieved within one or two 'jacks of all trade', not several functional specialists.

Organization structure

Most students of corporate strategy[9] suggest that once a strategy is decided upon, the company structure should be rearranged appropriately. Structure in this sense means an organizational arrangement which is consistent with both the product and market choices made, and the resources available. For the manager of the very small firm this is a very easy step, since all the resources – management, technical and financial – lie within himself. His concern is merely the division of his own time. Problems only arise as the firm begins to grow[10] and the manager is forced to make choices about what extra resources to provide. These choices may take into account his own lack of skill as well as his perception of the needs of the firm. For example, he may not understand the difference between bookkeeping and management accounting, or he may consider quality control an expensive function and one which he can do himself on an *ad hoc* basis. Further, he may view any devolving of responsibility as loss of his control of the firm and may resist setting up functions which the external observer would consider vital to the continued development of the firm. So the choice of structure for the small firm manager involves the creation of new functions which are consistent with his own skills and inclinations. The resultant structure is not easily put into the form of an organization chart and therefore not easily identifiable from the outside, as is usually the case in the larger firm.

The relationships previously described are complex, and while we can describe both the environment in which the small firm owner works and the particular problems which he is likely to face, we do not know how he copes. We do not know how a strategy and structure evolves. We simply know that it does. Until we have a clearer understanding of the corporate development process in the small firm, any teaching about the sector and any management development schemes for the sector will be pragmatic at best and at worst ineffective on any real scale.[11] For example, it may be that there are observable characteristics which separate the owner with the skills and inclination to grow from the rest of the small firm population. As a result he may require different help from that which the owner with inclination but no skills requires. Indeed, it has already been shown that, in the larger firm sector, those firms with tight planning systems and clear corporate strategies have a better success rate in their market place than those without. So for small firms it should be possible to better understand the strategic development process in order to devise more effective education and advisory schemes.

Notes

1. Dalgleish, R. (1972) 'Business Policy in the Small Firm with Reference to Company Development as a Policy Objective', *Management, Education and Development*, August, **3**(2).
2. Beesley, M. E. and Birley, S. J. (1976) 'Developing Education for Small Business: Toward a National Policy', *Management Education and Development*, December, **7**, part 3.
3. See, for example, Deeks, J. (1973) 'The Small Firm: Asset or Liability', *Journal of Management Studies*, February.
4. Chandler, A. D. (1962) *Strategy and Structure* (Cambridge, Mass: MIT Press).
5. See, for example, Stanworth, J. and Curran, J. (1977) *Management Motivation in the Smaller Business* (London: Gower Press).
6. See, for example, Golby, C. W. and Johns, G. (1971) *Attitude and Motivation*, Committee of Inquiry on Small Firms, Research Report 7 (London: HMSO).
7. This point is made very strongly in Barnes, L. B. and Hershon, S. A. (1976) 'Transferring Power in the Family Business', *Harvard Business Review*, July/ August.
8. The issue of taxation on death or sale is not only a British phenomenon. See, for example, Bannock, G. (1976) *The Smaller Firm in Great Britain and Germany* (Wilson House Publications, Anglo-German Foundation).
9. Scott, B. R. (1971) 'Stages of Corporate Growth', unpublished paper, Harvard Business School.
10. Stanworth, J. and Curran, J. (1976) 'Growth and the Small Firm: An Alternative View', *Journal of Management Studies*, May. In their conclusions, Stanworth and Curran suggest that in growth situations contradictions between the entrepreneur's self identity and his participation in the firm are likely to result.
11. Economists Advisory Group (1980) *The Promotion of Small Business: A Seven-country Study* (Shell UK Ltd). In this study Bannock suggests that the schemes for understanding, and thus encouraging, small firms in the UK are less well developed than in any other of the countries studied.

PART II

STRATEGY FORMULATION

Introduction

In this part we concentrate on strategic analysis and the formulation of strategy, building on Part I by introducing an analytic element to the strategic management process.

Strategic analysis is concerned with understanding the situation the organisation is in now, and then trying to appreciate how that may change in the future. This provides a basis for organizational choice as to its future direction. The process itself, and how it is managed, will also affect the strategies adopted, as will individual managers' perceptions of 'objective facts'. Consequently, the articles address a wide range of issues covering both task and process and this part of the book underpins the final part on managing strategic change. We conclude this part by stepping outside the usual boundaries of strategic management to introduce some ethical dimensions.

The chapters are, we think, a mixture of empirical and theoretical, prescriptive and descriptive approaches to strategic management. The fact that some of the papers appear to offer conflicting or contradictory messages reinforces our view that there is no 'one best way' to manage an organization.

We start with Greenley's article in which he examines the published empirical data on the relationship between strategic planning and performance in manufacturing companies. He found that the evidence was not conclusive in establishing such a relationship, but he did manage to identify some intrinsic values. McLellan and Kelly's research led them to hypothesise four different strategy formulation processes which we think may be useful in understanding how organizations go about determining their future strategy.

Engledow and Lenz examined the environmental analysis function in nine companies which were recognized for their expertise in this area. They noted the difficulty in performing such appraisals and concluded that it is a complex and difficult function to incorporate in the management process. In his 1979 paper Porter summarizes a model for assessing the external environment, in particular the competitive environment, which is developed much more comprehensively in his 1980 book *Competitive Strategy: Techniques for Analyzing Industries and Competitors*. This important work has, in our view, had a major influence on how we perceive the development of corporate strategy in organizations. Haspeslagh examined portfolio planning in large US corporations and found that such approaches help managers strengthen their planning process. He also found that the challenge lay in placing portfolio theory actually in the management process. Stevenson's paper makes an important contribution to our understanding of the analysis of strengths and weaknesses. He notes how an individual manager's position in the organization affects his selection and goes on to identify that different criteria appear to be used in judging either strengths or weaknesses.

Biggadike's article considers the issues involved in new ventures. As a result of his research Biggadike concludes that large scale entry is required for a new venture, and that building market share is crucial to long term success. Younger presents an analytical framework for assessing diversification through the development of an attractiveness/mesh matrix. This was developed as a result of his work with consultants Arthur D. Little Ltd. The extract from *Divestment and Strategic Change* by Coyne and Wright identifies a broad spectrum under the heading of divestment and considers a number of stages in the divestment process. Some empirical evidence on the impact of divestment is also included. Harrigan and Porter consider the alternatives open to organizations in declining industries by analysing first the determinants of competition (à la Porter, 1979) and second the structural factors which influence the attractiveness of a declining industrial environment. This is then used to choose an appropriate strategy. In his 1987 article Porter develops a theme from his 1985 book, *Competitive Advantage*. He examined the success or otherwise of diversification in the USA. In this hard-hitting paper Porter is very critical of portfolio management techniques and contends that the key lies in the transfer of skills or shared activities. Shim and McGlade report on the use of corporate planning models by looking at current practice, the state of the art, and recommended practices. They conclude that corporate modelling is likely to increase given the growth in microcomputers.

In Chapter 19 Sorell introduces business ethics by considering the ethical issues involved in what on the surface appear to be two straightforward questions concerning the late payment of creditors and creative accounting. In Chapter 20 he looks at some of the ethical issues involved in the 1986/7 takeover struggle between Pilkington Glass and BTR. A number of interesting issues are analysed including social responsibility, morality and self-interest. These concluding chapters raise interesting questions for managers in organizations.

Does Strategic Planning Improve Company Performance?

GORDON E. GREENLEY

Introduction

This article is concerned with the effectiveness of strategic planning in manufacturing companies. As a function of the overall management of an organization, the literature describes planning as being effective relative to its contribution to the performance, or end results, that the planning system was initially designed to achieve. [...] The first area of attention in this article is published reports of empirical data, which have examined such a relationship between strategic planning and company performance. However [...] it cannot be concluded that strategic planning is an effective, or indeed ineffective, tool for the overall management of organizations.

The problems associated with assessing effectiveness by measuring performance have been discussed by writers such as Dyson and Foster[1] and Greenley.[2] In an attempt to overcome these problems, writers such as Kotler,[3] Dyson and Foster and Heroux,[4] have proposed methods to assess the effectiveness of the planning system itself, as opposed to the end results that it produces. However, these methods are based upon a range of arbitrary attributes, the existence of which, in a particular planning system, is claimed to indicate that the system is likely to be effective. However, the major problem here is paradoxical when compared to a performance assessment, in that, even if the attributes are present, there is still no assurance that the required results will be achieved. However, there is still a range of potential advantages to be gained within a company due to the utilization of strategic planning, even if specific cause and effect relationships cannot, at this point in time, be established. In addition to such advantages, the article recognizes benefits which accrue from the utilization of strategic planning, which are inherent as a consequence of its utilization. These are labelled as being 'intrinsic values' of planning, which not only accrue to the organization, but also to external stakeholders. These potential advantages, plus intrinsic values, are the second area of attention in the article. [...]

Empirical data relative to strategic planning and company performance

The literature search revealed nine previous studies which are appropriate to the article. All utilized sample surveys, with all but one being carried out in the USA, the other had been in the UK. All the surveys investigated strategic planning within manufacturing companies, where sample sizes ranged from 10 to 386 companies. [...] Five conclude that companies which utilize strategic planning achieve higher levels of performance or end results than companies which do not utilize strategic planning. The five studies which claim such a relationship are: Ansoff et al.;[5] Gershefski;[6] Thune and House;[7] Herold[8] and Karger and Malik.[9,10]

The results of these surveys claimed that strategic planning is effective, in that higher levels of results have been achieved by the companies utilizing strategic planning. However, the remaining four studies do not claim such a relationship between strategic planning and end results. These four studies are: Fulmer and Rue;[11,12] Grinyer and Norburn;[13] Kudla,[14,15] and Leontiades and Tezel.[16]

Alternatively, from the results of these four surveys it was concluded that higher levels of end results did not necessarily relate to the utilization of strategic planning. Therefore, from this comparison of the overall results of each survey, the conflicting conclusions obviously indicate that a firm conclusion as to the relationship of strategic planning to performance cannot be arrived at. This means that further examinations of each study are necessary, relative to both the methodological rigour of the studies and their results.

Approaches to evaluate the methodological rigour of such studies have been given in the literature by writers such as Porras and Berg[17] and Terpstra.[18] The latter provides five criteria for the evaluation, as follows:

- sampling strategy; scores 1 if sample representative, 0 if it is not.
- sample size; scores 1 if $N > 30$, or 0 if $N < 30$.
- control group; scores 1 if a control was used, or 0 if one was not used.
- measurement strategy; scores 1 if a pre-test strategy was made; or 0 if one was not made.

- significance levels; scores 1 if significance levels are reported to at least the $P < 0.05$ level, or 0 if no reporting, or if $P > 0.05$.

Using these criteria, the resultant comparisons of the nine studies are given in Table 7.1.
[...]
Although Terpstra does not give any standards against which to compare such evaluating, the scores are perhaps self-evident and can be interpreted by visual inspection. Hence none of the studies can be considered to be particularly rigorous in their methodology, based on these criteria, except perhaps for the studies by Karger and Malik[9,10] and Kudla.[14,15] [...] Therefore, from this comparison of the studies, based upon these criteria of methodological rigour, an indication as to the relationship of strategic planning and performance is not evident.
[...]
The nature of the questions used and survey bias would be [...] valuable criteria, although both of these were not available. Other valuable criteria relate to the individual sample characteristics, geographical differences and timing. In the case of sample characteristics, most studies covered both industrial and consumer firms (although several did not disclose this information), information on the personnel responding was generally not reported, although sample size was readily available. Here the sample sizes within the studies which do claim an association between strategic planning and end results ranged from $N = 10$ to $N = 323$, with an average size of 110. However, the sample sizes within the studies which do not claim such an association ranged from $N = 21$ to $N = 386$, with an average size of 200. Although this is the only criterion which indicates any difference in methodological rigour, it can only be considered to be a slight indication of a possible difference. In the case of geographical location, this can perhaps be considered to be constant in that all but one of the surveys were based in the USA. However, in the case of timing there is a different situation. Within the studies which do claim an association between strategic planning and end results, four of the studies were before 1975, with the other study being reported at that time. However, within the studies which do not claim such an association, all but one are post-1975. Again this criterion can only be taken to be an indication of a possible difference in methodological rigour.

Therefore, from the overall comparison of the two groups of studies, based upon methodological rigour, an overall conclusion as to the relationship of strategic planning and performance cannot be arrived at. This, then, leads to an examination of the nature of the results of the studies.

TABLE 7.1 Comparison of surveys (i)

	Sampling strategy	Sample size	Control group	Measurement strategy	Significance level	Score for each study
Ansoff et al.[5]	1	1	0	0	1	3
Gershefski[6]	0	1	0	0	0	1
Thune and House[7]	1	1	0	1	0	3
Herold[8]	1	0	0	1	0	2
Karger and Malik[9,10]	1	1	0	1	1	4
Average score						2.6
Fulmer and Rue[11,12]	1	1	0	0	0	2
Grinyer and Norburn[13]	1	0	0	0	1	2
Kudla[14,15]	1	1	1	0	1	4
Leontiades and Tezel[16]	1	1	0	0	1	3
Average score						2.75

Nature of results: studies claiming a relationship

The results of these studies are summarized as follows.

Ansoff et al. (N = 93)

The study used 13 separate variables of financial performance using 21 different measures within these variables. These were measured in more than one way, in order to minimize the effects of bias from any one type of measure. The 13 variables used were: sales; earnings; earnings/share; total assets; earnings/equity; dividends/share; stock price; debt/equity; common equity; earnings/total equity; P/E ratio; payout (dividends/earnings) and price/equity ratio.

The values of these variables for companies which do extensive strategic planning were compared with the values of the companies which did little planning. With the exception of equity growth and growth of assets, the companies which do extensive strategic planning outperformed the other companies, with levels of statistical significance of these differences ranging from $P < 0.1$ to $P < 0.005$.

Gershefski (N = 323)

This survey compared the growth of sales in companies over a 5-year period before strategic planning was introduced, and over a period of 5 years after planning was introduced. The results of this comparison led the author to conclude that companies with formal strategic planning outperform companies with little planning and that this indicates that strategic planning is effective. However, the statistical significance of the differences between formal and informal planners were not reported and data were not made available to calculate levels of significance.

Thune and House (N = 36)

The approach taken in this study was to examine the performance of each company both before and after formal strategic planning was initiated. Although these periods of time were equal for each company, they did vary from firm to firm. Comparisons were then made of these changes, relative to both formal and informal planners. The variables which were used to measure changes in performance were: sales; stock prices; earnings per share; return on equity and return on capital employed.

The comparison of planners and informal planners showed that the planners outperformed the informal planners on all five measures. The authors report that these differences were statistically significant, but the actual levels of significance were not reported. In addition they found that formal planners outperformed their own performance after the introduction of formal planning.

Herold (N = 10)

This study was instigated in response to the Thune and House study, in an attempt to cross-validate and broaden the results of the latter. However, the study resulted in a survey of only 10 companies in the drugs and chemicals industry. The performance of formal and informal planners were compared over a 7-year period, using the variables of sales growth, profit growth and R & D expenditure as measures for comparison. The author concludes that formal planners outperform informal planners with respect to these measures, from the point in time when the formal strategic planning was initiated. Although it is claimed that these differences are significant they have not been statistically tested. Indeed Herold highlights that this was not done, due to the small sample size. However, he does conclude that the results support those of Thune and House.

Karger and Malik (N = 90)

The approach taken in this study was similar to that taken by Ansoff *et al.*, in that the values of a range of variables of planners were compared to the values of the same variables of non-planners. The range of variables used in this study are as follows: sales value; sales per share; cash flow per share; earnings per share; rate earned on net worth; operating margin; per cent of dividends to income; stock price; book value per share; net income; rate earned on capital; price/earning ratio and capital spending per share.

From these comparisons, the authors conclude that the planners outperformed the non-planners relative to all variables except capital spending, stock price and dividends to income. The comparison of each variable between planners and non-planners was tested for statistical significance. Here, six of the 13 comparisons were significant at the $P < 0.05$ level and a further two were significant at the $0.05 < P < 0.10$ level. The remaining five comparisons were insignificant at the 10 per cent level.

Nature of results: studies claiming no relationship

The results of these studies are summarized as follows:

Fulmer and Rue (N = 386)

The survey used in this study was firstly designed to classify the formality of the companies' strategic planning. The survey also measured the financial performance of the companies, using the following four variables to assess performance: sales growth; earnings/sales ratio; earnings growth and earnings/total capital.

In making the comparisons for each variable, the authors split the respondents into large and small firms, with the aim of making a more realistic comparison. The overall conclusion they came to is that there is no simple across the board relationship between the completeness of strategic planning and financial performance. However, they do not conclude that strategic planning does not affect end results, but that their study indicates that there is no clear relationship between strategic planning and these variables. In making these comparisons the authors did not report the use of statistical significance testing, nor do they volunteer why such testing was not applied.

Grinyer and Norburn (N = 21)

In this study a single measure of financial performance was adopted as follows:

$$\text{Return on net assets} = \frac{\text{Profit before interest and tax}}{\text{Fixed assets} + \text{current assets} - \text{current liabilities}}$$

The study involved correlation analysis of the relationship of financial performance with a common perception of objectives, role perception and formality of planning. In all cases they found that there was no association with financial performance, with none of the comparisons being statistically significant at the 0·05 level. As they could find no evidence, particularly none relating formality of planning to financial performance, the authors consider that their results call into question most of the basic assumptions on which strategic planning is established.

Kudla (N = 328)

The study did not use a range of financial performance measures, but restricted its assessment to comparing the payments made to shareholders. The hypothesis tested was that the shareholders of planning companies would receive higher returns than the shareholders of non-planning companies. The survey covered a period of 5 years before the planners introduced strategic planning to their companies and a 10-year period after its introduction. The study concluded that strategic planning had a negligible affect on the level of shareholders' earnings, with this result being statistically significant at the 0·05 level. Therefore, Kudla concludes that strategic planning and performance are not related and sees his results as being consistent with those of Grinyer and Norburn.

Leontiades and Tezel (N = 61)

In this study the authors firstly claim a weakness in previous studies, which they relate to subjectivity in defining the formality of strategic planning and consequently subjectivity in defining companies as being planners or non-planners. The approach they used was to get the Chief Executive and the Chief Planning Officer, of each company to assess the importance of strategic planning on a numerical bipolar, semantic differential scale, with the aim of providing a quantified variable which could then be compared with company performance. Five variables were used to measure this performance, as follows: return on equity; return on assets; price–earnings multiples; earnings per share growth and sales growth.

The variables were measured for each company over a 6-year period. The study tested several hypotheses that would have indicated that the ratings of strategic planning and performance were related, but none of these were statistically significant at the 10 per cent level. Therefore the authors conclude that there is no evidence, from their study, of an association between the perceived importance of strategic planning and company performance.

From the examination of these studies there are five major areas of criticism, relative to the investigation of the relationship. The first is that there are many other variables which can also affect performance/end results, so that the changes detected in company performance may not have been affected by strategic planning, or may have been only partially affected by strategic planning, or indeed affected only by strategic planning (although the latter is highly unlikely). [. . .] In addition, where an association between strategic planning and performance was claimed, a causal relationship would need to be established, which, due to the variation in results, cannot be asserted. In addition, the direction of the causality would need to be established. This could be that indeed strategic planning does improve company performance, but it could also be that improved performance gives the firm the capacity or ability to implement strategic planning, with improved profits yielding the re- sources for its utilization.
[. . .]
The second area of criticism relates to subjectivity within the studies. In all the studies subjectivity was evident in defining formality of planning and in differentiating between planners and non-planners. Not

only were these definitions subjective within each study, but the criteria of definition was not common across the studies. The studies can also be claimed to exhibit subjectivity in that only financial measures were included in determining company performance. Indeed there are other end results which are established in strategic planning objectives, which perhaps would need to be considered in such studies. These points lead on to the third area of criticism, which is concerned with bias. [...]

The fourth area of criticism relates to the lack of commonality in the studies, leading to difficulty in the cross validation of results. First there was the large variation in sample size, mix in type of company (between consumer and industrial products) and mix in companies by size. [...] Only one study compared large and small firms, but the definition of large and small was by comparison of sales turnover to an arbitrary level. The second area of lack of commonality was concerned with the variables used throughout the studies to measure financial performance. Here there was variation in the measures used with a tendency to measure financial performance orientated towards results required by shareholders. Although this can be claimed to be a valid measure, there are other stakeholder groups and associated financial measures which are also important, which relates back to the full range of established company objectives. The final area of lack of commonality is the time periods over which the studies were carried out. [...] Variations in external variables are likely to have differed over the various time periods of the studies, and such effects of these variables on the planning/performance relationship are likely to have been different. This is particularly pertinent as the studies did not give any evidence of having tackled such effects and indeed the intensity of such effects on performance is likely to vary from company to company.

The fifth and final area of criticism relates to the statistical significance of the results reported within each study. Of the studies which claim a relationship between strategic planning and performance, only two studies[5,9,10] report the statistical significance of their results. [...] Of the studies which did not claim a relationship between strategic planning and performance, only the study by Fulmer and Rue failed to report levels of significance.
[...]

Therefore from the assessments of both methodological rigour and the results of each study, it is concluded that the research published to date, relative to manufacturing companies, is far from conclusive in establishing a relationship between strategic planning and performance, or end results.

Potential advantages of strategic planning

Regardless of whether or not strategic planning can be claimed to affect company performance, several advantages are suggested within the literature, which are claimed to arise due to the utilization of strategic planning. Within the literature these are split between those prescribed by several writers as being potential advantages, and those which are given by managers as potential advantages, as revealed by previous research and reported in the literature. [...]

The overall advantage of strategic planning claimed within the literature is epitomized by Godiwalla, Meinhart and Warde.[19] This is that planning results in a viable match between the changing internal organizational conditions of the firm and its external environmental variables. The purpose of this match is to ensure that the plans continuously realign the firm's objectives and strategies to the changing conditions, to improve the long run performance of the company. In addition to this overall advantage, several specific advantages are given in the literature, being classified into those being concerned with the planning process and those concerned with the personnel involved with the planning. These have been extracted from the literature as follows, from works by writers such as Stern,[20] Loasby,[21] Hausler,[22] Walker,[23] and Wilson.[24]

Process advantages

- The identification and exploitation of future marketing opportunities.
- An objective view of management problems.
- The provision of a framework for the review of plan execution and control of activities.
- Minimization of effects of adverse conditions and changes.
- Major decisions can be more effectively related to established objectives.
- More effective allocation of time and resources to identified opportunities.
- Provides for co-ordination of the execution of the tactics of the plan.
- Allows for the combination of all marketing functions into a combined effort.
- Less resources and time need to be devoted to correcting erroneous *ad hoc* decisions.
- Creates a framework for internal communication between personnel.
- Allows for the identification of priorities within the timing of the plan.
- The utilization of planning provides an advantage over competitors.

Personnel advantages

- Helps to integrate the behaviour of individuals in the organization into a total effort.
- Provides a basis for the clarification of individual responsibilities, giving a contribution to motivation.
- Gives an encouragement to forward thinking on the part of personnel.
- Stimulates a co-operative, integrated and enthusiastic approach to tackling problems and opportunities.
- Encourages a favourable attitude to change.
- Gives a degree of discipline and formality to the management of a business function that would not exist without planning.

[...]

However, although these benefits are claimed, none of these writers substantiate these benefits. Therefore the next stage is to examine potential advantages given by managers in previous research. Higgins and Finn[25] found that companies with the most experience of corporate planning consider that it is more successful than companies with a lesser period of experience. However, they did find that only 40 per cent of firms found corporate planning to be of limited success, although all the companies using this form of planning considered it to be worth carrying on with. Taylor and Irving[26] found that all the respondents in their survey were enthusiastic about the benefits of strategic planning, although most found difficulty in being specific in defining what it had achieved. However, they do report a selection of the advantages reported by their respondents, although they do not cite the numbers who perceive these advantages. The examples they give are as follows.

- An indication of problems before they happen.
- A change of interests and attitudes of managers.
- A discipline that identifies change and allows for consequential action.
- The identification of a need to redefine the nature of the business.
- Improves co-ordination of effort towards predetermined objectives.
- Enables managers to have a clearer understanding of the business.

The benefits of strategic planning were also investigated in two separate surveys by Al-Bazzaz and Grinyer[27] and Ang and Chua.[28] These surveys found the following percentages of respondents claiming the following advantages (see Table 7.2).

As with the advantages of strategic planning prescribed by writers within the literature, those claimed by respondents within the above surveys are also not substantiated. [...] It is suggested that they do need to be substantiated, as opposed to being merely implied. [...]

TABLE 7.2 Comparison of surveys (ii)

Al-Bazzaz and Grinyer	%
Awareness of problems, strengths and weaknesses	85
Profits and growth	48
Information and communication	40
Systematic resource allocation	35
Co-ordination and control	29
Morale and industrial relations	17
Ang and Chua	
Able to explore more alternatives	66
Faster and better quality decision making	58
More timely information	49
Better understanding of the business process	45
More accurate forecasts	43
Cost savings	27

Intrinsic values of strategic planning

[...] The article [...] recognizes other values or qualities which accrue as a consequence of the utilization of strategic planning, which extend the intended advantages, encompassing not only the company but also its external environment. These are intrinsic in that they are inherent within the adoption of the process. However, like the claimed advantages of strategic planning, the literature does not provide evidence to substantiate such intrinsic values. Again all that can be offered is an *a priori* case that such intrinsic values are likely to accrue.

Indeed the concept of intrinsic values is not given direct treatment in the literature as a separate area of understanding. However, Camillus[29] uses the phrase 'intrinsic purposes' in explaining the benefits of planning, as the development of earlier work by Vancil.[30] [...] Another indication from the literature is from an article by Wilson.[31] Although the emphasis of this work is the integration of social responsibility and business needs, it emphasizes the broad, external social implications of company planning, based upon potential ramifications of planning within society as a whole and the consequential social responsibility that befalls the company.

The range of intrinsic values is considered to fall into three classifications. [...] Intrinsic values accruing from strategic planning in [...] these three areas are considered to be as follows.

General external environment

The strategic planning of the firm's business over a future time period is firstly seen to be of value to the owners/shareholders of the company. As a consequence of effective strategic planning, improved security of investment can be considered, as can future returns, as part of the role of the strategic planning process is the future assurance of such returns. These plans are also likely to give an indication of the timing of future additionally required investments, so that again the owners/shareholders can themselves plan their own future returns.

The second area of intrinsic values in this classification relates to the general public in contact with the company. One example here is that effective strategic planning allows for anticipated levels of future employment, with growth strategies likely to yield growth of employment opportunities. [...] In addition, as the strategic planning framework requires an improved understanding of the society as part of the macro environment, it is likely that intrinsic values relative to areas such as product liability, quality control and environmental pollution control, will improve. Finally, in its widest sense, the utilization of strategic planning can be considered to be a logical exercise in the allocation of resources, which, over a long period of time, can be considered to be a contribution to efficient allocation of the world's finite resources.

The final intrinsic value of strategic planning given in this classification relates to the economy of the country in which the company is located. Long-term stability within a company provides a contribution to the stability of the GNP and companies planning for growth provide a contribution to the planned economic growth of the country's economy.

The company's markets

This logical organization of the firm's business over a future time period, through strategic planning, can be expected to produce several intrinsic values to its customers. [...] The results of such planning could be expected to yield intrinsic values such as follows.

- Improvements to the benefits of offerings.
- Effective assessment of changes in customer requirements.
- The provision of improvements to the future product mix and the providing of future consumer benefits.
- Realistic unit prices relative to market price levels and company requirements.
- The avoidance of undue pressure from the communications output through the balancing of the elements of the marketing mix.
- The development and continuation of free competition within the market place, with the consequential benefits of such market conditions.

Effective strategic planning can also be considered to result in intrinsic values for suppliers of inputs to the firm's business. The demand for inputs and the required product development of such inputs will be more clearly identified at an earlier time, through the strategic planning of the company. This will have consequences for suppliers in that such requirements become part of the planning data for these companies and rationality in this data is likely to contribute to the effectiveness of the planning of suppliers.

The internal environment

The first area internally where strategic planning provides intrinsic values is in the co-ordination of the various business functions within the company. [...] The strategic planning process *per se* obviously has value in that, if it is effective then the total company is unified and integrated towards a common aim, giving an overall framework for the co-ordination of the individual business functions. [...] Effective strategic planning [...] provides a basis for the internal allocation of resources. Throughout the planning process the various decisions to participate in various product/market scopes, to aim at certain growth strategies, to participate in various market segments and to pursue certain marketing opportunities, are all decisions which result in the allocation of resources.

The final intrinsic value of strategic planning [...] relates to the company personnel. [...] The overall logical and rational framework given to the company by the strategic planning process is likely to contribute to a working environment in which not only is motivation, leadership and morale fostered, but in which security of operation gives a framework for overall personal development.

Conclusions and implications

This article has examined empirical data relative to strategic planning and company performance, examined the potential advantages of strategic planning, plus its intrinsic values. The conclusion of these examinations were:

- The research published to date, relative to manufacturing companies, is far from conclusive in establishing a relationship between strategic planning and company performance.
- Although there is a strong *a priori* case that strategic planning provides a range of both advantages and intrinsic values, empirical evidence is lacking to substantiate these.

Following on from these it cannot be concluded as to whether or not strategic planning is an effective tool for the overall management of organizations.

However, despite these conclusions, several implications are apparent. The first is that, over future periods of time, additional empirical data may be reported within the literature relative to the relationship of strategic planning and company performance, which may be indicative of the effectiveness of strategic planning. The second is that empirical data may be reported relative to the substantiation of the advantages and intrinsic values of strategic planning. Also, further works may strengthen the *a priori* case for strategic planning. The third implication is that further research may indicate that company performance is not a valid basis on which to assess effectiveness. As already mentioned in the introduction, research has already started in this area, notably from the works of Dyson and Foster,[1,32] and Greenley,[2] which has examined effectiveness relative to the nature of the planning process itself, as opposed to end results. The final implication is that, as a consequence of the above, the instigation of further research is obviously essential in order to consolidate the body of knowledge, with the aim of establishing the effectiveness of strategic planning as a tool for the overall management of organizations.

References

1. Dyson, R. G. and Foster, M. J. (1980) 'Effectiveness in strategic planning', *European Journal of Operational Research*, **5** (3), 163–70.
2. Greenley, G. E. (1983) 'Effectiveness in marketing planning', *Strategic Management Journal*, **4** (1), 1–10.
3. Kotler, P. (1977) 'From sales obsession to marketing effectiveness', *Harvard Business Review*, **55** (6), 67–75.
4. Heroux, R. L. (1981) 'How effective is your planning', *Managerial Planning*, **30** (2), 3–16.
5. Ansoff, H. I. *et al.* (1970) 'Does planning pay?' *Long Range Planning*, **3** (2), 2–7.
6. Gershefski, G. W. (1970) 'Corporate models – the state of the art', *Management Science*, **16** (6), 303–12.
7. Thune, S. S. and House, R. J. (1970) 'Where long range planning pays off', *Business Horizons*, **29**, August, 81–7.
8. Herold, D. M. (1972) 'Long range planning and organisational performance', *Academy of Management Journal*, **15**, March, 91–102.
9. Karger, D. W. and Malik, Z. A. (1975) 'Long range planning and organisational performance', *Long Range Planning*, **8** (6), 60–4.
10. Karger, D. W. and Malik, Z. A. (1975) 'Does long range planning improve company performance?' *Management Review*, September, 27–31.
11. Fulmer, R. M. and Rue, L. W. (1973) 'Is long range planning profitable?' *Proceedings of the Academy of Management*, 66–73.

12. Fulmer, R. M. and Rue, L. W. (1974) 'The practice and profitability of long range planning,' *Managerial Planning*, **22** (6), 1–7.

13. Grinyer, P. H. and Norburn, D. (1975) 'Planning for existing markets', *Journal of the Royal Statistical Society*, **138** (1), 70–97.

14. Kudla, R. J. (1980) 'The effects of strategic planning on common stock returns', *Academy of Management Journal*, **23** (1), 5–20.

15. Kudla, R. J. (1981) 'Strategic planning and risk', *Review of Business and Economic Research*, **17** (1), 2–14.

16. Leontiades, M. and Tezel, A. (1980) 'Planning perceptions and planning results', *Strategic Management Journal*, **1** (1), 65–75.

17. Porras, J. I. and Berg, P. O. (1978) 'Evaluation methodology in organisational development: an analysis and critique', *Journal of Applied Behavioural Science*, **14**, 151–73.

18. Terpstra, D. E. (1981) 'Relationship between methodological rigor and reported outcomes in organisation development evaluation research', *Journal of Applied Psychology*, **66** (5), 541–3.

19. Godiwalla, Y. M., Meinhart, W. A. and Warde, W. A. (1981) 'General management and corporate strategy', *Managerial Planning*, **30** (2), 17–29.

20. Stern, M. E. (1966) *Marketing Planning: A Systems Approach*, McGraw-Hill, New York.

21. Loasby, B. J. (1967) 'Long-range formal planning in perspective', *Journal of Management Studies*, **4** (3), 300–308.

22. Hausler, J. (1968) Planning: a way of shaping the future, *Management International Review*, **2** (3), 12-21.

23. Walker, K. R. (1976) 'How to draw up a marketing plan that will keep you on track', *Industrial Marketing*, September, 126–8.

24. Wilson, R. M. S. (1979) *Management Controls and Marketing Planning* London: Heinemann.

25. Higgins, J. C. and Finn, R. (1977) 'The organisation and practice of corporate planning in the UK', *Long Range Planning*, **10** (4), 88-92.

26. Taylor, B. and Irving, P. (1971) 'Organised planning in major UK companies', *Long Range Planning*, **4** (3), 10–26.

27. Al-Bazzaz, S. and Grinyer, P. H. (1980) 'How planning works in practice – a survey of 48 UK companies', *Long Range Planning*, **13** (4), 30–41.

28. Ang, J. S. and Chua, J. H. (1979) 'Long range planning in large US corporations', *Long Range Planning*, **12** (2), 99–102.

29. Camillus, J. C. (1975) 'Evaluating the benefits of formal planning systems', *Long Range Planning*, **8** (3), 33–40.

30. Vancil, R. F. (1970) 'The accuracy of long range planning', *Harvard Business Review*, **48** (5), 98–101.

31. Wilson, I. H. (1974) 'Reforming the strategic planning process: integration of social responsibility and business needs', *Long Range Planning*, **7** (5), 2–6.

32. Dyson, R. G. and Foster, M. J. (1982) 'The relationship of participation and effectiveness in strategic planning', *Strategic Management Journal*, **3** (1), 77–88.

CHAPTER 8

Business Policy Formulation: understanding the process

RON McLELLAN and GRAHAM KELLY

Introduction

This paper is based upon a study of the contrasting processes used to formulate business policy in a selection of European companies. The characteristics of these processes are discussed to provide insights for managers who need to formulate business policy to meet their own organization's needs.
[...]
    The current uncertain business environment of many European companies demands business policies that are more effective than those used in the past. The ability to cope with a fall in demand for goods and services, the increasing cost and scarcity of resources, the change in social trends towards greater participation by the organizations' stakeholders and the emergence of new competitors have combined to challenge even the most adroit strategist.
[...]
    As a result, many companies at the present time are dissatisfied with their effectiveness when designing a business policy that has to cope with the changing demands of their environment. This is despite the outpourings of a decade or more of advice and instruction designed to help managers formulate business policies to suit their organization's operations.[1] [...]
Often a best policy is prescribed for all companies regardless of their differences in size, history, operation and environment. In contrast, the

range of alternative processes available for formulating this policy is largely ignored, despite the fact that the process used may have a large effect upon the content of the policy and its successful implementation.[2]

It does seem that as the operating environments of organizations have become more volatile, managers are turning to formal processes for generating their business policies. As a result, formal systems are being introduced by organizations that previously relied upon more informal methods, although informality is sometimes assumed to allow organizations to respond quickly to the threats and opportunities of their environments. While it may be true that some individual managers believe they are more effective when unfettered by a formal system [...] it may be a romantic myth that their organizations can be equally as effective without some degree of formality. [...] Furthermore, companies that already use formal systems are expecting policies that can more effectively meet the challenge of a changing environment.[3] It is our contention that the selection of a suitable process for formulating business policy is the key to the generation by organizations of more effective business policies.

We have been able to identify four different patterns of the process used by companies to formulate their business policy. These patterns should not be regarded as pure and rigidly defined, or mutually exclusive, but as generalized representations of what are exceedingly complex processes of human interaction. We do not claim that the patterns that we have identified describe the only process used to formulate business policy, but that they are present in a number of organizations operating under different environmental conditions. We believe that they are distinguishable from each other and that these distinctions can provide an opportunity for managers to analyse the process currently in use in their own organization and, more importantly, to consider alternative processes that may help obtain a better fit between the organization's activities and the demands made upon it by the environment.

The four processes described below have been called Alpha, Beta, Gamma, and Delta.

Policy formulation processes

Alpha process

The Alpha pattern of policy formulation process is characterized by the formulation initiatives being taken by the operational units of the organization. Their policy decisions are then passed upward in the structure for approval and for aggregation with similar decisions made by

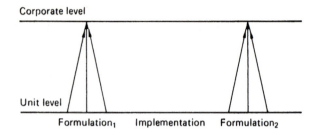

FIGURE 8.1   Alpha process

other units to form a corporate policy for the organization. It is essentially a convergent process, as illustrated in Figure 8.1.
[...]

At a unit level, within an organization using an Alpha process, each policy is designed to match the particular circumstances of each unit. Each policy tends to emphasize the unit's existing areas of activity and consolidate its position; any new business initiatives tend to be extensions of existing activities. Formulation of the policies is mainly carried out by the unit's managers. A relatively large number of managers are involved throughout the organization who can be expected to be conversant with the detailed operation of their unit's business. Corporate management may be informally involved during the formulation phase. When the unit policies have been formulated, they are passed upwards through the organization for approval, and for the corporate level executives to aggregate them with the policies of the other units to form a corporate policy. Since each unit's policies are specific to its own situation, the summation of the unit policies may result in a rather irregular, ill-fitting corporate policy – one that may not match the environmental demands being made on the organization as a whole. Approval may tend to be a relatively passive affair because informal, downward influence during the formulation phase ensures that unit policies are in an approvable state when presented. The company may expect all their units to use the same standardized documentation for the formulation and presentation of their policies. The convergent formulation process tends to occur periodically, usually annually. Between these periodic formulation phases, the unit managers are mainly concerned with the implementation of the policies they have helped to devise. They may also be reflecting upon the appropriateness of these policies for their unit's business in readiness for the next formulation phase.

Beta process

In the Beta pattern, the creation of an organization's business policy is the province of corporate management. Unlike the Alpha process, only a relatively small proportion of the company's managers are involved in the formulation process.

[...]

In general, the Beta process results in a well-rounded business policy undistorted by the irregularities that the Alpha process may produce. The policy reflects the corporate management's expectations for their company rather than a summation of the policies of the business units.

The policies formulated in companies using the Beta process are not approved by managers higher in the organizations' structure as in the Alpha process but are generally approved by the corporate managers themselves. The policy is then subdivided and distributed to the business units for implementation as shown in Figure 8.2.

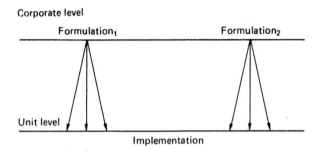

FIGURE 8.2   Beta process

Implementation by the business unit of corporate business policy is continuous and is only interrupted when the periodic output of the corporate formulation process requires a change in the business unit's operations. The managers of the business units implement their component of the corporate policy which may involve initiatives and changes in whose devising they have not been involved. The targets derived from the corporate business policy may provide the base for business unit performance appraisal.

Gamma process

In the Gamma pattern of policy formulation process, corporate and business unit managers jointly formulate a unit's business policy. It is [...] the result of the influences and approval of both groups of managers.

The process is participative and the resulting negotiated business policies reflect the linkage between corporate managers' expectations and the unit managers' knowledge of their operations. It may be seen to combine aspects of both the Alpha and Beta processes. Negotiation during the formulation process may be relatively lengthy but this may be compensated for by the speed of the approval and implementation phases. The process is illustrated in Figure 8.3.

The formulation process involves short bursts of activity in each business unit in turn as the corporate management successively negotiate each business unit's business policy. Corporate management may define the form of documentation and procedure to be used; this may be the same for each business unit. Each unit's business policy is collated and normalized by corporate management to provide an integrated corporate business policy. Implementation of these policies does not involve any changes in direction by the business unit that have not previously been agreed by the unit's manager.
[...]

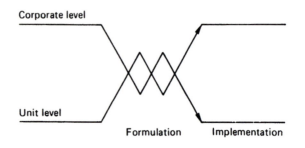

Corporate level

Unit level

Formulation   Implementation

FIGURE 8.3   Gamma process

Delta process

The Delta pattern of policy formulation process is distinguished by formulation occurring at two relatively isolated levels in the organization. At the business unit level, policy formulation is carried out periodically by individual units, with corporate management only involved in the approval of these policies. At corporate level, there is a continuous process of investigation and decision-making concerned with the organization's objectives for the future, with only occasional outputs being fed into the activities of the units. The Delta process is illustrated in Figure 8.4.
[...]

At the business unit level, in organizations with a Delta process, policy is formulated to suit each unit's own particular set of circumstances and objectives, much like the Alpha process. Once formulated, each unit submits its policies for approval at corporate level. This formulation

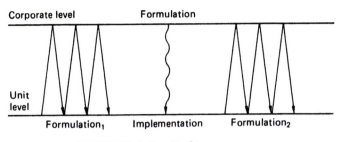

FIGURE 8.4 Delta process

activity tends to take place at regular intervals, usually every twelve months.

At the corporate level, policy formulation is a continuous activity, with the emphasis being placed on identifying new directions for the organization. In a process of this kind, the output of corporate policies is spasmodic. sometimes occurring several times in one year or sometimes not for several years. Outputs of the corporate process may occur during a unit's regular formulation phase or while it is implementing a recently formulated policy. When an output occurs, it may be fed into the activities of the existing units or may require the establishment of a new unit. The absorption of these corporate decisions by the units may be disruptive or result in the unit's own 'made-to-measure' policies becoming inappropriate. Unit managers may have to implement corporate policies in whose creation they have not been involved. In terms of the impact that unit policy formulation may have upon the corporate process, it would seem likely that the approval of unit policies will provide corporate executives with access to some of the ideas of their business unit managers and may help in their search for new directions for their company.

Discussion

Information

The upsurge of interest in formal systems for formulating business policy may have resulted from the increasing uncertainty of the environment in which companies are operating. [. . .] The uncertainty experienced by an organization may be related to the difference between the information it requires to perform its tasks and the amount of information it already possesses.[4] Organizations without an effective mechanism for gathering the information they require may miss information that could enhance their performance.

The construction of an effective information system requires some knowledge of the location of suitable information. [...] The Alpha process of formulating business policy actively involves the operating managers, and companies using this process can be expected to be knowledgeable of their short-term environment. Conversely, the bias of the Beta process towards the input of the corporate managers may result in companies that use this process feeling well informed about their organization's long-term future. The Gamma formulation process combines these two approaches to provide a blend of short and long-term information and may reveal a more realistic picture of the organization's future. This contrasts with the effect of the isolation of the inputs from the operating and corporate managers in the Delta process where the information possessed by the organization may not be combined and used to its full advantage.

The sources of information outside an organization are usually more numerous than is generally recognized. Managers may be slightly naive and assume they are aware of all the sources of information that are relevant to their business. In a changing environment, an organization's external sources of information can be expected to wax and wane in usefulness and they may need to develop new sources, possibly by involving outsiders in their formulation processes.

Rewards

[...] A common intervening factor that may govern the functioning of the [formulation] process is the organization's reward system.[5] This may help or hinder the process and influence the policies that are generated. [...]

An operating unit manager can be expected to be rewarded for effectively utilizing the resources of his unit. This may tend towards the maintenance of the present business and provide little incentive to innovate in areas outside his main line of business. [...] It may not be surprising if organizations using the Alpha process, with its dependence upon the input from unit managers, do not receive many new business ideas. This situation may be corrected if the reward system specifically recognizes an expected innovative function of unit managers. On the other hand, the reward system may provide such a strong motivation for a corporate manager to create new business initiatives, that he pays scant attention to their effect upon the organization's existing businesses. [...] This could occur when the Beta formulation process is used because of its reliance upon the inputs from corporate managers.

It may be necessary for the organization's reward system to stimulate managers to meet the goals of the business policy formulation process as well as to meet their day-to-day responsibilities. This may require a managerial reward system with two sets of critical – effective maintenance of today's business and the successful development of tomorrow's.

Leverage

From our investigations, we have found that organizations tend to focus their policy formulation activity at a particular point or level in their structure – in organizations with an Alpha process, it is centred on the managers at the operational unit level, whereas with a Beta process, formulation resides at a corporate level. The ability of the managers involved to influence their company's business policy will depend upon the leverage they possess.[6] [. . .]

An organizational role that may carry more leverage than most is that of Chief Executive or President. His personal style of management may well determine the nature and operation of the organization's policy formulation process; he may specify which particular formulation process is used by the organization. His influence may also pervade the actual operation of the formulation process once established. [. . .]

Another role that may carry a high degree of leverage in the policy formulation process is that of Corporate Planner. We have found that in organizations with a Beta or Delta process, for example, the Corporate Planner may well play a more central, expert role advising corporate management on future company policy and likely environmental trends. In Alpha process organizations, he tends to play a relatively peripheral role acting, if anything, as a facilitator rather than as an expert. In a Gamma process organization, he may tend to be in a central, facilitative role, helping to ensure constructive interaction and negotiation between corporate and unit level managers. [. . .]

Standardization

We have found that companies often use a standardized policy formulation process characterized by an annual formulation period during which all policy formulation for the year is carried out and often presented for approval using a standard format. [. . .] Whilst the potential benefits of control and co-ordination of a standard process are recognized, it may not suit the nature of all the business unit's activities and policy formulation needs.
[. . .]

Time-horizons

When formulating policy, there is a need to specify how far ahead one is going to look; what time-horizon is going to be applied to the formulation process? We have found some evidence that organizations feel that having too great a time-horizon may lead to unit managers who are formulators of business policy becoming less concerned with the current operational performance of their unit, in the belief that tomorrow must be better than today. [...] Again, it would seem important to match this aspect of the formulation process to the particular nature of the company's business and its environment. There may also be difficulties if the same time-horizon is used by unit formulators who are operating in situations with different time-scales.

Approval

A phase of any formulation process which should not be underestimated in terms of its effect on the behaviour and effectiveness of an organization's executives is that of approval. We have found two general patterns of approval, reflecting the amount of informal communication that occurs in a particular organization. In some organizations using an Alpha process, we have found that during the formulation process at unit level there is a continuous checking out of ideas with more senior executives, thus making the eventual formal presentation of unit policies a virtual rubber-stamping operation. In other organizations with a similar Alpha process, this informal feedback may not exist and therefore the eventual presentation session may be perceived as a high-risk situation, with the possibility of policies being totally rejected. In an organization using a Beta process, approval is integrated with formulation because both processsses are performed by corporate level executives. In a Gamma process organization, approval still resides at the corporate level, but because of their close involvement with the formulation of the policy, there should be a mutual feedback system operating between corporate and unit level managers.

Approval in organizations using the Delta process may be similar to that of the Alpha process for policies devised by the unit managers, and similar to the Beta process for the policies decided at corporate level. Whatever approval system is used, there is the possibility that it may be perceived as a hurdle that faces the formulators rather than an opportunity for them to gain organizational commitment for their ideas. There is a danger of policy being formulated to maximize the chances of approval, rather than optimizing the business operation.
[...]

Overall impact

When considering the impact of a formulation process upon an organization, we can identify two main dimensions along which we can usefully structure our thoughts. Firstly, its influence on the tasks the organization undertakes, and secondly its effect upon its managers who have to perform these tasks.

The formulation process used by organizations will influence the business policy formulated by governing who contributes to its generation. [. . .] A policy formulation process that does not involve managers at all levels in the organization and utilize their talents may be deprived of valuable creative ideas. Business initiatives that might result from the interaction between managers may also be lost and organizations may find it difficult to break out of their existing business profiles. [. . .] Where successful task performance requires the effective utilization of certain types of expertise, a formulation process that excludes individuals who possess this expertise may well suffer at the implementation stage.

Apart from affecting task performance, the formulation process can have an effect upon the attitudes, feelings and behaviour of an organization's managers. Whatever the process used, it will be in the nature of things to include some people and exclude others. [. . .] One of the strengths of the Gamma process, as we see it, is that executives from both corporate and unit level are involved in policy formulation. Even here, however, some of the organization's executives may be excluded from the process.

In addition to the feelings associated with being included or excluded in the policy formulation process, the process used can influence the type of behavioural response likely from those managers who are included in the formulation activity. We have found, for example, that unit level managers formulating policy in an Alpha process situation may be likely to adopt a maintenance orientation to their thinking. Their main concern will be to maintain or consolidate their unit's existing business activities and only develop them in closely related areas. This is intimately tied up with the organizational reward system, since, if rewards come from effective maintenance of the existing organizational activities, the manager's behaviour will tend to be oriented that way. Alternatively, in an organization with a Beta process where policy formulation is performed at corporate level, there may be a greater likelihood of innovative behaviour, such as the generation of ideas for new and radically different activities since, at a corporate level, rewards may be more closely linked with innovation.

The policy formulation process can therefore be seen as having an effect on two closely interrelated aspects of an organization, the performance of its task, and the attitudes, feelings and behaviour of those people responsible for task performance. How managers face up to the challenge of devising a suitable business policy formulation process may determine, to a large extent, the effectiveness of their organization's business policy and the future performance of their company.

Notes and references

1. Ansoff, H. I. (1979) *Strategic Management* (London: Macmillan); Taylor, B. and Sparkes, J. R. (eds.) (1977) *Corporate Strategy and Planning* (London: Heinemann).
2. For some consideration of the formulation process see Ackoff, R. L. (1970) *A Concept of Corporate Planning*, chapter 7 (New York: Wiley); Dror, Y. (1971) *Ventures in Policy Sciences*, chapter 10 (American Elsevier); Nurmi, R. (1976) 'Developing a Climate for Planning', *Long Range Planning*, June, pp. 48–53; Saunders, C. B. (1973) 'What Should We Know about Strategy Formulation?', *Academy of Management Proceedings*, USA, August, pp. 29–35; Wheelwright, S. C. and Banks, R. L. (1979) 'Involving Operating Managers in Planning Process Evolution', *Sloan Management Review*, Summer, pp. 43–59.
3. For a summary of the situation see Ansoff, H. I. (1979) 'The Changing Shape of the Strategic Problem', *Journal of General Management*, 4(4); Hussey, D. E. (1979) *Introducing Corporate Planning*, chapter 1 (London: Pergamon); Warren, K. E. (1966) *Long Range Planning: The Executive Viewpoint*, ch. 3 (London: Prentice-Hall).
4. Galbraith, Jay (1977) *Organisational Design* (London: Addison Wesley) p. 36.
5. Galbraith, Jay (1977) *Organisational Design*, ch. 16 (London: Addison Westley).
6. Bauer, R. A. and Gergen, K. J. (eds.) (1968) *The Study of Policy Formulation*, ch. 5 (New York: Free Press).

CHAPTER 9

Whatever Happened to Environmental Analysis?

JACK L. ENGLEDOW and R. T. LENZ

[...]

Introduction

For the past several years, environmental analysis has been a popular topic in the management literature. Under titles such as environmental analysis, environmental scanning, issues analysis, issues management, and others, a variety of published materials has discussed the desirability of the activity, and how it could or should be accomplished.[1] Two assumptions are explicit or implicit in many of these works: that the function will increase in importance over time,[2] and that there is merit in organizing the activity as a free-standing, real time staff function within the firm (either in concert with strategic planning,[3] or in a unit *outside* the normal planning process, cutting across organizational hierarchies).[4]

There is ample evidence to support the two propositions. Rapid growth in the activity has been reported,[5] the newly-formed Issues Management Association has over 500 members; 'how-to' manuals have been written;[6] and consulting firms have been formed to offer a variety of related services. Yet there is also evidence that only a small proportion of firms are undertaking continuous scanning;[7] there is frustration in knowing how and what to analyse and how to get the information utilized by line managers;[8] there is some general disenchantment by active firms;[9] and once-active firms have curtailed their involvement.[10] In summarizing his study, one researcher was reluctant to recommend establishment of corporate level scanning units, commenting: 'Environmental scanning is one of those many ideas which look good on paper, but prove intractable in implementation'.[11] Given this contradictory commentary, there would seem to be merit in tapping the cumulative experience of firms which have demonstrated a commitment to this activity and have a substantive history, rather than depending upon cross-sectional observations of randomly chosen firms, as in most of the above studies.

Nature of the study

Rationale

This article is a discussion of part of a study of the environmental analysis function in ten corporations specifically identified as 'leading-edge' firms in the field. The purpose of the overall study was to gain an understanding of how this function was organized, how it linked to planning, and what problems, strengths and weaknesses have been uncovered by the firms as they put the process to use. The focus here is on that portion of the study dealing with the evolution of these ten units over time: the nature of change which has taken place, and its implications – the *dynamics* of building systems for environmental analysis. The purpose is to compare and contrast the evolving structures and cumulative experience among the ten firms, both to test the propositions listed and to identify principles which would be helpful to other managers facing the task of organizing environmental analysis in their own firms.

The total study also generated a considerable body of cross-sectional observations and conclusions about more specific aspects of the analysis process and how the results are injected into planning. Readers interested in more specifics on organization and linkages to planning will find greater detail on those areas in Lenz and Engledow (1984).[12]

Sampling

Since the purpose was an in-depth understanding of advanced practice, an attempt was made to identify firms and individuals with a commitment to environmental analysis, a reputation for expertise, and several years of experience in the field. A panel of academics, management consultants and practitioners was asked to identify individuals who were recognized as leading practitioners of and contributors to environmental analysis. Individuals were ranked according to numbers of mentions by the panel. The firms were thus selected by identification of the heads of their units as being among the best in their field. It was felt that any performance criteria were too indirectly and tenuously related to environmental analysis to be said to select 'successful' firms at this early stage of the function's development.

The final sample was comprised of nine firms in the US and one in Canada. Though the firms studied were selected with environmental

analysis expertise as the only criterion, they are all large (sales volumes from $2 billion to $35 billion) and they are highly diverse as to industry and type (manufacturing and service; industrial and consumer, etc.). The function has been in existence from three to fifteen years in the firms studied; all but two units began within the last eight years.
[. . .]

Information gathering

In-depth interviews lasting from two to five hours were conducted with the heads of environmental analysis units of the ten firms, and, in several cases, with other analysts or specialists in the same firm. The interviews were based on a structured questionnaire containing sections on: structure of analysis process; links to planning; models of the environment; problems in process and implementation; history of the unit; and number and nature of personnel involved. Relevant written documents were also collected, and follow-up calls were made to clarify and supplement the initial interviews. The longitudinal data relating to the firms and their analysis units came from these regular field interviews as well as written materials collected during the interviews, some multiple visits with the same firms, follow-up calls to interviewees and other knowledgeable individuals, and miscellaneous secondary materials.

Analytic procedures

To analyse the nature and causes of evolution in the firms more systematically and to address the propositions to be tested in the study, the units were classified on two dimensions.[13]

1. The status of the analysis unit as either a *freestanding* function, or one which was *combined* with other responsibilities. The unit was considered to be *free standing* if the director and/or at least one professional analyst under his or her immediate supervision were assigned specific responsibility for some version of environmental analysis, and spent essentially full time at that task. If environmental analysis was only part of their duties, the unit was classified as *combined*.
2. The type of *role* which environmental analysis seems to play in the given firm. In another part of this same study, the authors found that the units might be classified based upon the roles and purposes which they played in their firms' planning activities.[14] The three roles used for classification were: *policy-oriented; strategic planning integrated*; and *function-oriented*. The rationale for these distinctions is contained in the section immediately following.

The roles and purposes of environmental analysis: an important side issue

Though each of the firms in this study was deeply involved in something which could be described generally as 'environmental analysis', it became obvious as the study progressed that there were significant differences among them in the purposes served by the analysis and in the role which the analysis unit played in the organization.

[. . .]

A careful evaluation of the structures and procedures of the various units led to the conclusion that three separate *roles* could be described.

- *Policy-oriented* – Unit generally at corporate level with direct access to top management. Focus is on early detection of broad strategic issues in the macro environment (shifts in attitudes, norms, laws, social roles) which are likely to result in public policy impact on the corporation as a whole. Search is relatively unstructured, and the connection to planning is usually indirect and informal (through reports and interlocking committee structures). Basic purpose is to help define the relevant environment, sensitize top management and avoid 'blind siding' by major emerging issues.
- *Strategic planning integrated* – Unit may be at either corporate or divisional level, reporting to or operating as part of planning staff. Has specific role in the strategic planning process, usually including both: (i) preparing an environmental forecast to generate basic assumptions at beginning of planning cycle, and (ii) providing more detailed information about parts of the environment at later stages of the planning process. Analysis is at both macro and task environment levels. Basic purpose is both to sensitize managers from top through business levels, and to inject specific issues directly into the planning process, helping link corporate to business level plans.
- *Function-oriented* – Unit attached to a particular function at either corporate or business level, with activities tightly tied to that function's specific environment. Search and analysis confined to factors related to the future of current activities or concerns (products, laws, public opinion, etc.). Linked to planning process via its function's usual reporting paths. May use technically sophisticated monitors and outside consultants. Basic purpose is to improve future functional performance (better products; effective lobbying; timely compliance) by providing forward-looking information.

Table 9.1 summarizes in greater detail the characteristics of these roles including the quite different *purposes* served by analysis in the three different categories. The three categories seem to represent loci on a continuum, with the policy-oriented role the broadest, most highly placed, and most loosely connected with planning; the function oriented role the most specific, most tightly tied to current activities and most readily implemented; and the strategic planning integrated role somewhere in the middle – attempting to bridge the substantive gap between the two and provide specific links to the planning process at multiple levels.

This categorization proved helpful in the overall study for systematizing comparisons among the units and for summarizing the advantages and disadvantages of various organizational arrangements for analysis.[15] But the results presented below suggest that it also offers valuable insights regarding the *evolution* of units over time.

Results

Table 9.2 shows the result of categorizing the ten firms as to role and freestanding/combined status both at their time of origin and at the present, along with time spans covered and brief comments as to the nature of changes which have occurred. Figure 9.1 more concisely summarizes the information on change.

One fact is apparent: there has been little standing pat. In eight of the ten units there have been significant changes in some combination of the size and nature of the unit, number of individuals involved, and relation to the firm's planning system.

Jain,[16] in a study prior to 1979, suggested that development of environmental scanning in an organization was likely to involve progression over time through a series of steps of increasing sophistication. He labelled the steps: primitive, *ad hoc*, reactive and proactive; characterized each, and theorized on what factors were prerequisites for a smooth progression through these steps. Our study revealed no such pat hierarchy of effectiveness and no such predictable progress through stages. What our study does seem to have tracked is a series of interesting organizational experiments reflecting individual managements' attempts to cope with a new and complex analytical problem. In these experiments stages have been skipped, boundaries between stages are blurred and evolution has not been consistently 'forward' by Jain's definition.

Each of the ten firms within the last 15 years launched into some form of environmental analysis. The specific reasons were as varied as the firms themselves. [...] Whatever the specific impetus for forming the unit, the generalized purpose was to make the organization better prepared to cope with 'its environment', which was generally perceived

TABLE 9.1 Organizational roles of environmental analysis units

	Organizational roles		
Characteristics	*Policy-oriented*	*Strategic planning integrated*	*Function-oriented*
Scope of environmental analysis	● General environment	● General environment ● Task environment	● Task environment ● Specific functional area concerns: Product development Public affairs Public relations, etc.
Focus of analysis	● Broad societal trends	● Economic and legislative conditions ● Business-level strategic issues	● Per functional area, as: Product use and technology Legal structure Public opinion
Locus of analysis and interpretation	● Board subcommittee ● Corporate management	● Corporate management ● Group management ● Business management	● Per functional area, as: Product line managers Functional department managers Legal, public policy staff

Use of environmental analyses	• Condition thinking of CEO and Board • Help CEO, Board to define relevant environment • Public policy formulation	• Statements on public policy issues • Multi-level strategy formulation	• Per functional area, as: Product design and materials selection Public policy lobbying/compliance Public relations programs
Link with strategic decision processes	• No linkage (or) • Memberships on interdepartmental committees	• Integral part of the strategic planning process	• Per functional area, as: Product development system Reports to function managers and planning staff Legal guidelines, policies
Primary users of environmental information	• Board • Chief executive and operating officers	• Corporate and group line executives • Strategic planning staff	• Per functional area, as: Functional and business line executives Product dev. staff, teams Legal staff

TABLE 9.2 Changes in role and form in ten environmental analysis units

Company	Original role/form	No. years activity in existence	Current role/form	Rationale/comment
Appco	Function orient/comb.	15	Same	Environmental analysis developed gradually from technological forecasting, as part of product development process.
Chemco	Policy orient/free	7	Strategic plan/comb.	Reporting line changed, after 6 years, from public affairs to strategic planning. Director now part of regular planning staff. Has responsibility for integrating environmental analysis into planning process, but has other planning duties as well.
Consco	Strategic plan/comb.	—	Disbanded in 8th year	Corporation acquired by major consumer goods firm, less staff-oriented. CEO and planning head left within a year, and environmental analysis unit disbanded.
Diverco	Strategic plan/free	15	Strategic plan/comb.	After 10 years, activity dispersed into four different planning units; consistent with original idea of freestanding unit as catalyst to introduce, stimulate environmental analysis. Also consistent with lean-staff approach of new management which took charge soon after this change.

Enerco	Strategic plan/free	3	Same	Though linked directly into strategic planning process, manager and analysts have specific, full time function in environmental analysis.
Foodco	Policy orient/free	—	Disbanded after 1 year	Director had other duties, but spent major portion of time developing environmental analysis system. Never fully in operation, the unit disbanded in 1 year, following a management change.
Pipeco	Policy orient/free	6	Strategic plan/comb.	After 4 years, activity integrated into corporate and division strategic planning activities. Original task of freestanding unit in establishing awareness, developing methods seen as accomplished.
Retco	Policy orient/free	8	Policy orient/comb.	Unit reduced in size after 5 years, shifted from division to corporate. Director now spends only part time at environmental analysis.
Servco	Policy orient/free	6	Same	Basic public policy orientation unchanged, but evolving toward more interaction with strategic planning process.
Teleco	Strategic plan/free	—	Disbanded in 6th year	Change in corporate structure eliminated specific planning activity which was most important function of unit.

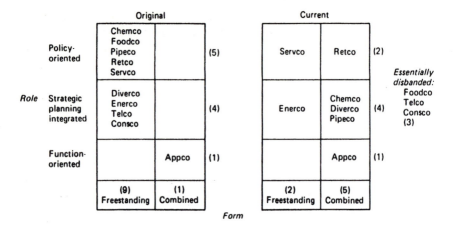

FIGURE 9.1   Summary of role and form changes

as rapidly-changing and largely untractable by existing planning and forecasting methods.

Though specific practice and guidance were lacking, most followed the developing consensus to form a full-time department with responsibility for continuous scanning of the environment and reporting of results. Nine of the units began as some type of free standing, full time analysis unit, with one or more analysts fully dedicated to environmental studies of some description. Some grew in size (Telco − 4 analysts; Diverco − 4 analysts; Enerco − 6 analysts; Retco − 9 analysts and clerks; Chemco − 2 part-time analysts plus director), while others remained as essentially one-person shops with secretarial backup. Even the latter usually had a mandate to leverage their resources by tapping other organization personnel to serve on committees and task forces, or as monitors.

From these similar beginnings as freestanding units, there has been considerable evolution of the various units as management has sought effective means of fitting this new function to their own organizations. Several general observations are possible:

1. Mortality has been relatively high. Among these ten firms, all large and recognized as leading edge, three have now drastically de-emphasized or abandoned the formal attention to environmental analysis.
2. The freestanding form has not proven robust. Of the nine units which began as freestanding, with full-time directors and/or staff, only two remain. One of those two is the newest of the ten units in the study. No unit has moved from combined to free standing.
3. There has been a proportionate shift toward the Strategic Planning

Role. Four of the remaining seven units fit that description; four of ten were originally of that form. Two firms have switched from policy-oriented to strategic planning oriented, and no firms have moved away from strategic planning to some other role (though two disbanded).
4. The proposition that environmental analysis would become 'more important' over time is not supported, at least in terms of numbers of firms and numbers of individuals within firms in this study. In these firms, at the peak of the activity ten units of some description were operating and approximately 26 full-time equivalent directors and analysts were employed. At the end of the observation period, only seven units were operating (including five combined into other planning activities, as noted above) and approximately eleven and one-half full-time equivalent directors and analysts were doing environmental analysis of some type (six in one firm).[17]

Discussion

The cases studied here fail to support the conventional wisdom that there would be steady and unambiguous growth in environmental analysis activities and that much of the action would take place in freestanding units with full-time responsibilities. Instead, a literal reading of the results above would lead to the conclusion that 'on the average' in these ten firms environmental analysis began as an autonomous function located where it was visible and available to top management and had, after much experimentation, settled in among other planning procedures as a much more routine and lower level activity.

It does not follow *per se* that environmental analysis is unimportant or that it cannot or should not be sustained as a viable element in planning. What the experiences do illustrate is that the function is even more complex and harder to do than originally envisioned. The evolutions traced in these ten case histories seem not so much to illustrate disenchantment with the concept of environmental analysis itself or strengths and weaknesses of any given analytical structure, but rather to reflect the emergence of four basic principles regarding effective implementation of the environmental analysis function:

1. Environmental analysis must be linked, conceptually and practically, to current planning and operations.
2. Environmental analysis serves a number of separate purposes, and different analytic structures and systems may be required to achieve those different purposes.

3. Systems for environmental analysis must fit the culture and decision-making styles of the organization and areas they serve.
4. Continuing support from internal champions is required to sustain environmental analysis in an organization over time.

The following sections will discuss these four criteria in more detail.

Links to current activities

By almost everyone's definition, environmental analysis has the explicit purpose of leading executive thinking beyond current activities and short time horizons. Yet it was an almost universal observation among the experts interviewed that frequent and sensible *linkages* to current activities must be established to attain credibility and keep the analysis function viable. As one director noted: 'It doesn't help to have a 16 cylinder engine, if it isn't connected to the wheels'.

The most frequently employed means for accomplishing this linkage were by directly involving line managers in the analysis process, and/or by translating broad issues to specific product/market/operations concerns.

[. . .]

Much of the fragility of the freestanding arrangement seems to stem from inherent difficulty in getting that structure 'attached to the wheels'. It has been argued convincingly by policy experts that environmental analysis should be a separate function from 'regular' strategic planning because of the danger that the broad-range, long run perspective will be overwhelmed by bias toward current activities and squeezed out by the time pressure and specificity of current operations.[18] That fear is not unfounded. One director of a unit newly-combined with Strategic Planning said that 'the number still wins 90 per cent of the time' in their firm, which is filled with engineers used to dealing with the 'facts'. Another said that it would be the 'kiss of death' for his activity if he were assigned to strategic planning, since his output was considered very 'soft science' in comparison to their 'hard science' economic forecasts and modeling. Following an early switch in reporting of the unit from public policy to strategic planning at Diverco, the director expressed frustration at being 'overwhelmed by the better structured economic stuff'.

Yet the weakness of the freestanding unit is the same as its strength: its personnel are 'estranged' from the organization, and it is difficult to tie back to planning and operations. When a crisis or organizational change occurs, the separate unit is visible, relatively costly, and has a tenuous tie to implementation and bottom line.

[. . .]

The straight reporting of environmental 'facts' by staff, without

connection to plans and policies, was often seen as worthless. [...] Excessive detail and formality are also seen as creating barriers to usage. [...] Several directors commented upon the necessity of gradually building credibility by small successes and creating a climate of frankness and honesty.
[...]

Varied purposes for environmental analysis

The role types identified (Table 9.1) suggest that firms use environmental analysis for a number of distinct purposes. In the Policy-Oriented Role, environmental analysis is, in effect, an extension of and complement to top management. Analysts in this role must have a broad, flexible perspective, and be readily available to CEOs and other top managers. A Function-Oriented Role requires a close working knowledge of the specific function to which environmental analysis is attached (e.g. product development; public affairs) and an ability to help translate environmental data into effective action (new products; effective lobbying). The Strategic-Planning Integrated Role is an attempt to bridge the gap between the other two roles by creating specific inputs into the planning process at multiple levels. Ideally, it encompasses the basic qualities of each, coupled with the systems and/or political skill to integrate all into a workable whole. In practice, this ideal is difficult to achieve.

To some degree, each of these purposes exists in any firm at any given time, though the weighting given a particular purpose and the importance of the total function may vary for many reasons, including differing management styles, and differing perceptions of environmental turbulence. It seems unlikely, given the differences in environmental scope, specifity, organizational level and audience, that any 'one best way' will serve all purposes.

The units which have survived and stayed close to their original forms seem to be those which had clear-cut definitions of their purpose from the beginning and have remained true to their last.
[...]

Both Servco's and Appco's units have retained the same basic structure since their beginning, and both seem well integrated with their firm's planning activities, though in quite different ways. The Servco unit's job is to sensitize top management and it impacts product development only in a very indirect way, while the Appco unit's input is technical and is injected well below the top management level. [...] Different objectives require different structures and philosophies.

Stability of the unit is not in and of itself a virtue; changed objectives may require changed structures. Both Diverco and Pipeco stated that one reason for their move from a policy/freestanding to a strategic planning/ combined form was that the initial period of sensitizing executives, identifying key issues, and gaining acceptance for the function was complete, and it was time to put it to work where it would be more effective.

Fit to corporate culture and decision-making style

Like any other management activity, to be effective, environmental analysis must fit well with the basic culture and style of the organization or area where it operates. In interviews during this study, one consistent admonition by successful practitioners was that both personnel and analytic systems exist for the sole purpose of serving existing management, and that they must fit not only the corporate culture, but also the personal information needs of the managers to whom they report. This view was well summarized by one director who suggested: 'You must understand the vocabulary and environment of the organization – the culture, the psychology, the political environment' and by another who said: 'the *client* is the CEO and key senior level executives. Their needs must be served.'

A large proportion of the instability in the units studied seems to stem either from mismatches with their organizations from the beginning, or from substantive organizational or environmental change which resulted in mismatches.

[...]

Directors and analysts who came from outside the organizations they served all alluded to some scepticism and 'turf' problems, and spent a large proportion of their early time on the job learning their organizations and working for acceptance and credibility. One cited the necessity for 'high sensitivity to the politics of the organization', and noted that she had worked hard at enlisting the support of key executives and getting their participation in the analysis process. Directors who had come from inside their organizations often felt that outsiders would lack credibility and a feel for the fitness of things, and simply could not succeed. 'Outsiders, MBA Specialists, and others do not have much of a chance,' said one insider. There is some evidence to the contrary, but there is also evidence that the basic concerns are well-founded.

All this suggests that, particularly in the policy-oriented role, the unit should be custom-built to serve the particular group of managers who will put the information to use, not constructed by a prescriptive formula. If one accepts the notion of Weick[19] that it is not the physical environment, but rather the *enacted* environment – the one which exists in the collective 'cause maps' (perceptions) of top management – which is critical, then the environment may very literally change importantly with each major management change – calling for a rethinking of structures for environmental analysis.

Paradoxically, this would suggest that even well-designed environmental analysis systems may be systematically less stable at the policy level than at the functional level. Though executives at the top level deal with broader concerns and longer time horizons, they generally do so with prerogatives (or even imperatives) for adopting more unique and creative perspectives than those of lower level executives. So, at the policy level, there is rationale that analysis should change form and style frequently to fit to the needs of the current ruling *individuals*, while at the functional level it may be argued that it should be standardized to the more routinized *systems* which are required for efficiency and continuity there. A failure of planning systems to deliver this 'personalized' information may account for Quinn's[20] finding that most top managers rely upon informal and external sources for important environmental information, rather than depending upon their firm's forward planning activities.

The role of champions in environmental analysis

Another finding of the study, evidenced both by outcomes and by comments in interviews, is the importance of sustained support for environmental analysis by top management or some individual in top management. It is axiomatic that any major activity within an organization ultimately requires high level support to survive. It seems particularly critical to this function, which is so expressly long range and so fuzzily tied to near term results. 'Top management support is critical' was a nearly universal comment. One director said: 'CEO support is helpful, but not decisive.' The unit was disbanded a year later.

In most of the ten organizations studied, particular top management individuals could be associated with initiating and/or sustaining environmental analysis. [...] These executive champions serve two main functions: to provide the power and resources required to sustain the activity within the organization, and to provide personal leadership to encourage injecting results into executive thinking and the planning process [...] They make the process possible and the use of output more likely.

Besides these *executive champions*, who furnish power and legitimacy to the function, it is also apparent from the study that there is an important role for a *working champion* who can provide expertise and credibility. Environmental analysis is a relatively new, poorly defined activity which does not have a historical role in the planning process, and which is always in danger of being smothered by more conventional and more easily justified concerns. So not only must there be generalized top level support for the activity to survive, there must also be an individual who makes it work. His or her job is to organize the activity, gain the confidence of planners and line executives, and aggressively press for including environmental concerns in planning decisions. At this stage of development and acceptance of environmental analysis, this individual's task seems more closely akin to that of the new product champion[21] than that of a conventional planning director or staff specialist. In most organizations, these working champions seemed to combine a strong belief in the inherent worth of the activity with missionary zeal. Like product champions, they tend to be a bit fanatic. As noted above, to be successful they must not only be broad-thinking individuals with knowledge of relevant analytical methods, they must also have a keen sense of the philosophy and politics of the organization and the decision-making styles of key executives.

In several organizations which have moved from freestanding to combined analysis, the original working champions have moved into new positions, but maintained some responsibilities for environmental analysis. It will be interesting to note whether these will eventually be succeeded by new 'champions', and, if not, whether environmental analysis has become firmly enough entrenched in the systems to survive without this type of support.

Implications and conclusions

This study has confirmed the general findings of earlier ones[22] that firms have difficulty in doing environmental analysis, fitting it to the planning process and evaluating its contributions. A superficial and literal interpretation of these results might suggest that environmental analysis has been tried and found wanting, and is fading from popularity as an element in planning. The above discussion has suggested that this is oversimplistic. A more tenable conclusion is that it is a more complex and difficult function to accomplish than first imagined, and that these firms have been engaged in ongoing organization experiments on how best to fit the activity to the particular needs of their firms over time. Though changed in form, the function remains as an important adjunct to planning in most of the firms. Even in the three firms which have 'abandoned' the activity in its original form, rudiments of the function still exist in some part of the organization. What seems to have happened to environmental analysis is that it is growing up ... painfully.

All of the conclusions discussed above weigh against stable, pat solutions and one best way. These ten firms – all serious about the activity and all large enough to bring extensive resources to bear on it – had arrived at much different structures and philosophies at the end of the measurement period, after fairly homogeneous beginnings. There was more evolution toward the strategic planning/combined mode than any other, but even here there was much variation in the specific form taken and reasons for being there.

Overall, the study suggests that firms hoping to establish a successful environmental analysis program should address themselves to these principles:

1. *Make a long-term commitment*
   Given the non-conventional nature and long run orientation of the function, plus its tenuous connection to the bottom line, it will have little chance of achieving its purposes without sustained top level support and excellent implementation. This would imply that a firm undertaking environmental analysis should have modest short-run expectations, enthusiastic executive and working champions, and an accompanying, reasonable, resource commitment.

2. *Continually evaluate objectives*
   There is a profound difference between evaluating a series of interacting social trends which may subvert an organization's mission, and tracking a new technology which may make a production machine more efficient. It is unlikely that either the parties interested or the analytical techniques used will be the same. Yet much of the literature and experience available fails to discriminate well (if at all) among alternative purposes and methods. More careful preliminary analysis of problems to be solved and decision-makers to be served will help avoid some of the mismatches and failures which have characterized earlier attempts at the function.[23] The above experiences suggest that objectives change; so the evaluation process must be continuous.

3. *Demand linkages to present strategies and operations*
   Environmental analysis is by definition at the fringes of present operations or beyond. Yet to be effective, it must engage the attention of current decision-makers and enter into current decisions. This requires careful blending of: line and staff participation; outside-in and inside-out perspectives; and present *vs* prospective future strategies. This blending, in turn, requires an expert, politically savvy staff with strong top-level backing.

4. *Fit the style and culture of your own organization*
   It is one of the strongest findings of this study that environmental analysis must be 'custom designed' to fit both the culture of the organization and the decision-making style of its key executives. Emulating techniques developed elsewhere give no assurance of effectiveness. Understanding the organization and its people is at least as important as understanding the environment and its strategic issues.

5. *Design flexible, versatile systems*
Different purposes suggest different methods, and purposes and their
relative importance change over time. The experience of the above
firms suggests that stable, highly structured systems may be an
unattainable, and perhaps even an undesirable goal. A large, freestanding system is unlikely to survive, and a routinely combined system
may be smothered. Multiple purposes and flexibility over time might
be accomplished by designing a simple core structure of expertise,
championship, and resources which could spin off a variety of
temporary and semi-permanent activities on demand, aiding in linking
them into a cohesive whole within the planning framework. In this
case, the working champion or champions would become more the
instigators, co-ordinators, and resource persons monitoring a changing bundle of activities, than the directors of a specific system. Such an
arrangement potentially retains some of the 'away from the system'
perspective valued by Ansoff,[24] avoids some of the bureaucratization
of highly formal planning systems, and provides a minimum, continuous core of commitment and expertise which might bend, but not
break in a major management change or cost crisis. The success of
such an arrangement would depend heavily upon not only the
attention to purpose and commitment noted above, but also on a
generally supportive organizational culture.

There is ample room for further research and organizational experimentation, based upon these five principles.
[...]

References

1. For instance: F. Aquilar (1967) *Scanning the Business Environment* (New York: Macmillan Company); H. Ansoff (1979) *Strategic Management* (New York: John Wiley and Sons); I. Wilson (1974) 'Socio-political Forecasting: A New Dimension to Strategic Planning', *Michigan Business Review*, pp. 15–25, July; E. Segev (1979) 'Analysis of the Business Environment', *Management Review*, **63**, 58–61, August; M. J. Kami (1976) 'Planning in Times of Unpredictability', *Columbia Journal of World Business*, Summer.
2. Ansoff, H. (1980) 'Strategic Issue Management', *Strategic Management Journal*, **1** (2), 131–48; Kami, op. cit.; S. Jain (1984) 'Environmental scanning in US Corporations', *Long Range Planning*, **17** (2), 117–128.
3. Wilson, I. (1983) 'Evaluating the Environment: Social and Political Factors', Working Paper, SRI International; R. Ewing, 'Modeling the Process', in J. Magelschmidt (ed.) *The Public Affairs Handbook* (New York: AMACON, 1982).
4. Ansoff (1980), op. cit.

5. *Wall Street Journal*, 8 August (1981); P. Thomas (1980) 'Environmental Scanning – the State of the Art', *Long Range Planning*, **13**, February.
6. *This Business of Issues: Coping with the Company's Environments*, Conference Board (1979).
7. L. Fahey and W. King (1977) 'Environmental Scanning in Corporate Planning', *Business Horizons*, pp. 61–71, August.
8. J. Diffenbach (1983) 'Corporate Environment Analysis in Large US Corporations', *Long Range Planning*, **16** (3), 107–16.
9. C. Stubbart (1982) 'Are Environmental Scanning Units Effective?', *Long Range Planning*, **15**, 139–45.
10. Stubbart, op. cit.
11. Stubbart, op. cit., p. 144.
12. T. Lenz and J. Engledow (1984) 'Environmental Analysis and Strategic Decision Making: A Field Study of Selected "Leading-Edge" Corporations', Working Paper, Strategy Research Center, Columbia University.
13. The categorization (irregular, regular and continuous) proposed by Fahey and King (op. cit.) is not helpful in discriminating among firms here, since, because of the manner of selection, all would be classified as continuous. The same basically applies to the 'phases of evolution' suggested by Jain (op. cit.). Further discussion of the latter is included below.
14. Lenz and Engeldow, op. cit.
15. See the discussion in Lenz and Engeldow, op. cit.
16. Jain, op. cit.
17. It is unlikely that either of the figures covering numbers of personnel is totally accurate, given the difficulty of measuring shared duties, ambiguity in delimiting environmental analysis from other planning activities, and likelihood of other types of environmental analysis taking place in parts of the organization not uncovered by the interview process. Any bias introduced by these measurement difficulties is unlikely to be systematic, or to change the basic conclusion.
18. Ansoff (1980), op. cit.; M. Porter (1980) *Competitive Strategy* (New York: Free Press).
19. K. Weick (1979) *The Social Psychology of Organizing* (2nd edn) (Reading, Massachusetts: Addison-Wesley).
20. J. Quinn (1980) *Strategies for Change: Logical Incrementalism* (Homewood, Illinois: Irwin).
21. T. Peters and R. Waterman (1982) *In Search of Excellence* (New York: Harper & Row).
22. Fahey and King, Stubbart, Diffenbach, all op. cit.
23. One interesting finding in the study was the ambiguity in, or, in some cases, the complete lack of attention to defining 'the environment', though analysing the environment was the task at hand. There was no consensus between organizations and little consensus within organizations as to how to approach the problem of describing the organization's environment and delimiting the units' domain for search. This ambiguity almost certainly causes misunderstandings in expectations for the activity, confusion in the use of terminology, and lack of efficiency and effectiveness in analysis.

There is a need for direct attention to the question of how to conceptualize the firm's environment. (See the discussion in T. Lenz and J. Engledow (1983) 'Alternative "Models" for Analyzing Organizational Environments: Theoretical Issues and Administrative Implications', Working Paper, Strategy Research Center, Columbia University.)

24. Ansoff (1980) op. cit.

[...]

CHAPTER 10

How Competitive Forces Shape Strategy

MICHAEL E. PORTER

Introduction

The essence of strategy formulation is coping with competition. Yet it is easy to view competition too narrowly and too pessimistically. While one sometimes hears executives complaining to the contrary, intense competition in an industry is neither coincidence nor bad luck.

Moreover, in the fight for market share, competition is not manifested only in the other players. Rather, competition in an industry is rooted in its underlying economics, and competitive forces exist that go well beyond the established combatants in a particular industry. Customers, suppliers, potential entrants, and substitute products are all competitors that may be more or less prominent or active depending on the industry.

The state of competition in an industry depends on five basic forces, which are diagrammed in Figure 10.1. The collective strength of these forces determines the ultimate profit potential of an industry. It ranges from *intense* in industries like tires, metal cans, and steel, where no company earns spectacular returns on investment, to *mild* in industries like oil field services and equipment, soft drinks, and toiletries, where there is room for quite high returns.

In the economists' 'perfectly competitive' industry, jockeying for position is unbridled and entry to the industry very easy. This kind of industry structure, of course, offers the worst prospect for long-run profitability. The weaker the forces collectively, however, the greater the opportunity for superior performance.

Whatever their collective strength, the corporate strategist's goal is to find a position in the industry where his or her company can best defend itself against these forces or can influence them in its favour. The collective strength of the forces may be painfully apparent to all the antagonists; but to cope with them, the strategist must delve below the surface and

133

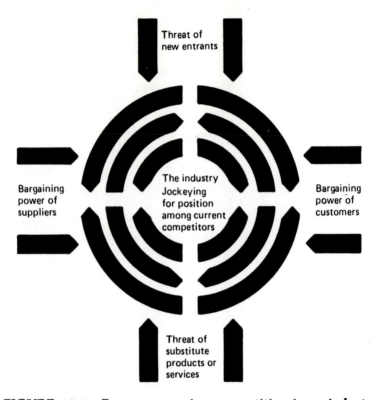

FIGURE 10.1   Forces governing competition in an industry

analyse the sources of each. For example, what makes the industry vulnerable to entry? What determines the bargaining power of suppliers?

Knowledge of these underlying sources of competitive pressure provides the groundwork for a strategic agenda of action. They highlight the critical strengths and weaknesses of the company, animate the positioning of the company in its industry, clarify the areas where strategic changes may yield the greatest payoff, and highlight the places where industry trends promise to hold the greatest significance as either opportunities or threats. Understanding these sources also proves to be of help in considering areas for diversification.

Contending forces

The strongest competitive force or forces determine the profitability of an industry and so are of greatest importance in strategy formulation. For example, even a company with a strong position in an industry unthreatened by potential entrants will earn low returns if it faces a superior or a lower-cost substitute product – as the leading manufacturers of vacuum tubes and coffee percolators have learned to their sorrow. In such a situation, coping with the substitute product becomes the number one strategic priority.

Different forces take on prominence, of course, in shaping competition in each industry. In the ocean-going tanker industry the key force is probably the buyers (the major oil companies), while in tires it is powerful OEM buyers coupled with tough competitors. In the steel industry the key forces are foreign competitors and substitute materials.

Every industry has an underlying structure, or a set of fundamental economic and technical characteristics, that gives rise to these competitive forces. The strategist, wanting to position his company to cope best with its industry environment or to influence that environment in the company's favor, must learn what makes the environment tick.

This view of competition pertains equally to industries dealing in services and to those selling products. To avoid monotony in this article, I refer to both products and services as 'products'. The same general principles apply to all types of business.

A few characteristics are critical to the strength of each competitive force. I shall discuss them in this section.

Threat of entry

New entrants to an industry bring new capacity, the desire to gain market share, and often substantial resources. Companies diversifying through acquisition into the industry from other markets often leverage their resources to cause a shake-up [. . .].

The seriousness of the threat of entry depends on the barriers present and on the reaction from existing competitors that the entrant can expect. If barriers to entry are high and a newcomer can expect sharp retaliation from the entrenched competitors, obviously he will not pose a serious threat of entering.

There are six major sources of barriers to entry:

1. *Economies of scale* – These economies deter entry by forcing the aspirant either to come in on a large scale or to accept a cost disadvantage. Scale economies in production, research, marketing, and service are probably the key barriers to entry in the mainframe computer industry. [. . .] Economies of scale can also act as hurdles in distribution, utilization of the sales force, financing, and nearly any other part of a business.

2. *Product differentiation* – Brand identification creates a barrier by forcing entrants to spend heavily to overcome customer loyalty. Advertising, customer service, being first in the industry, and product differences

are among the factors fostering brand identification. It is perhaps the most important entry barrier in soft drinks, over-the-counter drugs, cosmetics, investment banking, and public accounting. [...]

3. *Capital requirements* – The need to invest large financial resources in order to compete creates a barrier to entry, particularly if the capital is required for unrecoverable expenditures in up-front advertising or R&D. Capital is necessary not only for fixed facilities but also for customer credit, inventories, and absorbing start-up losses. While major corporations have the financial resources to invade almost any industry, the huge capital requirements in certain fields, such as computer manufacturing and mineral extraction, limit the pool of likely entrants.

4. *Cost disadvantages independent of size* – Entrenched companies may have cost advantages not available to potential rivals, no matter what their size and attainable economies of scale. These advantages can stem from the effects of the learning curve (and of its first cousin, the experience curve), proprietary technology, access to the best raw materials sources, assets purchased at preinflation prices, government subsidies, or favorable locations. Sometimes cost advantages are legally enforceable, as they are through patents. [...]

5. *Access to distribution channels* – The new boy on the block must, of course, secure distribution of his product or service. A new food product, for example, must displace others from the supermarket shelf via price breaks, promotions, intense selling efforts, or some other means. The more limited the wholesale or retail channels are and the more that existing competitors have these tied up, obviously the tougher that entry into the industry will be. Sometimes this barrier is so high that, to surmount it, a new contestant must create its own distribution channels, as Timex did in the watch industry in the 1950s.

6. *Government policy* – The government can limit or even foreclose entry to industries with such controls as license requirements and limits on access to raw materials. Regulated industries like trucking, liquor retailing, and freight forwarding are noticeable examples; more subtle government restrictions operate in fields like ski-area development and coal mining. The government also can play a major indirect role by affecting entry barriers through controls such as air and water pollution standards and safety regulations.

The potential rival's expectations about the reaction of existing competitors also will influence its decision on whether to enter. The company is likely to have second thoughts if incumbents have previously lashed out at new entrants or if:

• The incumbents possess substantial resources to fight back, including

excess cash and unused borrowing power, productive capacity, or clout with distribution channels and customers.
- The incumbents seem likely to cut prices because of a desire to keep market shares or because of industrywide excess capacity.
- Industry growth is slow, affecting its ability to absorb the new arrival and probably causing the financial performance of all the parties involved to decline.

Changing conditions

From a strategic standpoint there are two important additional points to note about the threat of entry.

First, it changes, of course, as these conditions change.

[...]

Second, strategic decisions involving a large segment of an industry can have a major impact on the conditions determining the threat of entry. [...]

Powerful suppliers and buyers

Suppliers can exert bargaining power on participants in an industry by raising prices or reducing the quality of purchased goods and services. Powerful suppliers can thereby squeeze profitability out of an industry unable to recover cost increases in its own prices. [...] Customers likewise can force down prices, demand higher quality or more service, and play competitors off against each other – all at the expense of industry profits.

The power of each important supplier or buyer group depends on a number of characteristics of its market situation and on the relative importance of its sales or purchases to the industry compared with its overall business.

A *supplier* group is powerful if:

- It is dominated by a few companies and is more concentrated than the industry it sells to.
- Its product is unique or at least differentiated, or if it has built up switching costs. Switching costs are fixed costs buyers face in changing suppliers. These arise because, among other things, a buyer's product specifications tie it to particular suppliers, it has invested heavily in specialized ancillary equipment or in learning how to operate a supplier's equipment [...] or its production lines are connected to the supplier's manufacturing facilities [...].
- It is not obliged to contend with other products for sale to the industry. For instance, the competition between the steel companies

and the aluminum companies to sell to the can industry checks the power of each supplier.

● It poses a credible threat of integrating forward into the industry's business. This provides a check against the industry's ability to improve the terms on which it purchases.

● The industry is not an important customer of the supplier group. If the industry *is* an important customer, suppliers' fortunes will be closely tied to the industry, and they will want to protect the industry through reasonable pricing and assistance in activities like R&D and lobbying.

A *buyer* group is powerful if:

● It is concentrated or purchases in large volumes. Large-volume buyers are particularly potent forces if heavy fixed costs characterize the industry [. . .] which raise the stakes to keep capacity filled.

● The products it purchases from the industry are standard or undifferentiated. The buyers, sure that they can always find alternative suppliers, may play one company against another, as they do in aluminum extrusion.

● The products it purchases from the industry form a component of its product and represent a significant fraction of its cost. The buyers, are likely to shop for a favorable price and purchase selectively. Where the product sold by the industry in question is a small fraction of buyers' costs, buyers are usually much less price sensitive.

● It earns low profits, which create great incentive to lower its purchasing costs. Highly profitable buyers, however, are generally less price sensitive (that is, of course, if the item does not represent a large fraction of their costs).

● The industry's product is unimportant to the quality of the buyers' products or services. Where the quality of the buyers' products is very much affected by the industry's product, buyers are generally less price-sensitive.
[. . .]

● The industry's product does not save the buyer money. Where the industry's product or service can pay for itself many times over, the buyer is rarely price sensitive; rather, he is interested in quality.
[. . .]

● The buyers pose a credible threat of integrating backward to make the industry's product. The Big Three auto producers and major buyers of cars have often used the threat of self-manufacture as a bargaining lever. But sometimes an industry engenders a threat to buyers that its members may integrate forward.

Most of these sources of buyer power can be attributed to consumers as a group as well as to industrial and commercial buyers; only a modification of the frame of reference is necessary. Consumers tend to be more price sensitive if they are purchasing products that are undifferentiated, expensive relative to their incomes, and of a sort where quality is not particularly important.

The buying power of retailers is determined by the same rules, with one important addition. Retailers can gain significant bargaining power over manufacturers when they can influence consumers' purchasing decisions [...].

Strategic action

A company's choice of suppliers to buy from or buyer groups to sell to should be viewed as a crucial strategic decision. A company can improve its strategic posture by finding suppliers or buyers who possess the least power to influence it adversely.

Most common is the situation of a company being able to choose whom it will sell to – in other words, buyer selection. Rarely do all the buyer groups a company sells to enjoy equal power. Even if a company sells to a single industry, segments usually exist within that industry that exercise less power (and that are therefore less price sensitive) than others. For example, the replacement market for most products is less price-sensitive than the overall market.

As a rule, a company can sell to powerful buyers and still come away with above-average profitability only if it is a low-cost producer in its industry or if its product enjoys some unusual, if not unique, features. [...]

If the company lacks a low-cost position or a unique product, selling to everyone is self-defeating because the more sales it achieves, the more vulnerable it becomes. The company may have to muster the courage to turn away business and sell only to less potent customers. [...]

As the factors creating supplier and buyer power change with time or as a result of a company's strategic decisions, naturally the power of these groups rises or declines. [...]

Substitute products

By placing a ceiling on prices it can charge, substitute products or services limit the potential of an industry. Unless it can upgrade the quality of the product or differentiate it somehow (as via marketing), the industry will suffer in earnings and possibly in growth.

Manifestly, the more attractive the price-performance trade-off offered by substitute products, the firmer the lid placed on the industry's profit potential.
[...]
Substitutes not only limit profits in normal times; they also reduce the bonanza an industry can reap in boom times.
[...]
Substitute products that deserve the most attention strategically are those that (a) are subject to trends improving their price-performance trade-off with the industry's product, or (b) are produced by industries earning high profits. Substitutes often come rapidly into play if some development increases competition in their industries and causes price reduction or performance improvement.

Jockeying for position

Rivalry among existing competitors takes the familiar form of jockeying for position – using tactics like price competition, product introduction, and advertising slugfests. Intense rivalry is related to the presence of a number of factors:

● Competitors are numerous or are roughly equal in size and power. In many US industries in recent years foreign contenders, of course, have become part of the competitive picture.
● Industry growth is slow, precipitating fights for market share that involve expansion-minded members.
● The product or service lacks differentiation or switching costs, which lock in buyers and protect one combatant from raids on its customers by another.
● Fixed costs are high or the product is perishable, creating strong temptation to cut prices. Many basic materials businesses, like paper and aluminum, suffer from this problem when demand slackens.
● Capacity is normally augmented in large increments. Such additions, as in the chlorine and vinyl chloride businesses, disrupt the industry's supply-demand balance and often lead to periods of overcapacity and price cutting.
● Exit barriers are high. Exit barriers, like very specialized assets or management's loyalty to a particular business, keep companies competing even though they may be earning low or even negative returns on investment. Excess capacity remains functioning, and the profitability of the healthy competitors suffers as the sick ones hang on.[1] If the entire industry suffers from overcapacity, it may seek government help – particularly if foreign competition is present.
● The rivals are diverse in strategies, origins, and 'personalities'. They

have different ideas about how to compete and continually run head-on into each other in the process.

As an industry matures, its growth rate changes, resulting in declining profits and (often) a shakeout.
[...]

An acquisition can introduce a very different personality to an industry [...]. Technological innovation can boost the level of fixed costs in the production process, as it did in the shift from batch to continuous-line photo finishing in the 1960s.

While a company must live with many of these factors – because they are built into industry economics – it may have some latitude for improving matters through strategic shifts. For example, it may try to raise buyers' switching costs or increase product differentiation. A focus on selling efforts in the fastest-growing segments of the industry or on market areas with the lowest fixed costs can reduce the impact of industry rivalry. If it is feasible, a company can try to avoid confrontation with competitors having high exit barriers and can thus side-step involvement in bitter price cutting.

Formulation of strategy

Once the corporate strategist has assessed the forces affecting competition in his industry and their underlying causes, he can identify his company's strengths and weaknesses. The crucial strengths and weaknesses from a strategic standpoint are the company's posture *vis-à-vis* the underlying causes of each force. Where does it stand against substitutes? Against the sources of entry barriers?

Then the strategist can devise a plan of action that may include (i) positioning the company so that its capabilities provide the best defense against the competitive force; and/or (ii) influencing the balance of the forces through strategic moves, thereby improving the company's position; and/or (iii) anticipating shifts in the factors underlying the forces and responding to them, with the hope of exploiting change by choosing a strategy appropriate for the new competitive balance before opponents recognize it. I shall consider each strategic approach in turn.

Positioning the company

The first approach takes the structure of the industry as given and matches the company's strengths and weaknesses to it. Strategy can be viewed as building defenses against the competitive forces or as finding positions in the industry where the forces are weakest.

Knowledge of the company's capabilities and of the causes of the competitive forces will highlight the areas where the company should confront competition and where avoid it. If the company is a low-cost producer, it may choose to confront powerful buyers while it takes care to sell them only products not vulnerable to competition from substitutes.

[...]

Influencing the balance

When dealing with the forces that drive industry competition, a company can devise a strategy that takes the offensive. This posture is designed to do more than merely cope with the forces themselves; it is meant to alter their causes.

Innovations in marketing can raise brand identification or otherwise differentiate the product. Capital investments in large-scale facilities or vertical integration affect entry barriers. The balance of forces is partly a result of external factors and partly in the company's control.

Exploiting industry change

Industry evolution is important strategically because evolution, of course, brings with it changes in the sources of competition I have identified. In the familiar product life-cycle pattern, for example, growth rates change, product differentiation is said to decline as the business becomes more mature, and the companies tend to integrate vertically.

These trends are not so important in themselves; what is critical is whether they affect the sources of competition. Consider vertical integration. In the maturing minicomputer industry, extensive vertical integration, both in manufacturing and in software development, is taking place. This very significant trend is greatly raising economies of scale as well as the amount of capital necessary to compete in the industry. This in turn is raising barriers to entry and may drive some smaller competitors out of the industry once growth levels off.

Obviously, the trends carrying the highest priority from a strategic standpoint are those that affect the most important sources of competition in the industry and those that elevate new causes to the forefront.

[...]

The framework for analysing competition that I have described can also be used to predict the eventual profitability of an industry. In long-range planning the task is to examine each competitive force, forecast the magnitude of each underlying cause, and then construct a composite picture of the likely profit potential of the industry.

[...]

The framework for analysing industry competition has direct benefits in setting diversification strategy. It provides a road map for answering the extremely difficult question inherent in diversification decisions: 'What is the potential of this business?' Combining the framework with judgement in its application, a company may be able to spot an industry with a good future before this good future is reflected in the prices of acquisition candidates.

Multifaceted rivalry

Corporate managers have directed a great deal of attention to defining their businesses as a crucial step in strategy formulation. Theodore Levitt, in his classic 1960 article in HBR, argued strongly for avoiding the myopia of narrow, product-oriented industry definition.[2] Numerous other authorities have also stressed the need to look beyond product to function in defining a business, beyond national boundaries to potential international competition, and beyond the ranks of one's competitors today to those that may become competitors tomorrow. As a result of these urgings, the proper definition of a company's industry or industries has become an endlessly debated subject.

One motive behind this debate is the desire to exploit new markets. Another, perhaps more important motive is the fear of overlooking latent sources of competition that someday may threaten the industry. Many managers concentrate so single-mindedly on their direct antagonists in the fight for market share that they fail to realize that they are also competing with their customers and their suppliers for bargaining power. Meanwhile, they also neglect to keep a wary eye out for new entrants to the contest or fail to recognize the subtle threat of substitute products.

The key to growth — even survival — is to stake out a position that is less vulnerable to attack from head-to-head opponents, whether established or new, and less vulnerable to erosion from the direction of buyers, suppliers, and substitute goods. Establishing such a position can take many forms — solidifying relationships with favorable customers, differentiating the product either substantively or psychologically through marketing, integrating forward or backward, establishing technological leadership.

Notes

1. For a more complete discussion of exit barriers, see my article, 'Please note Location of Nearest Exit', *California Management Review*, Winter 1976, p. 21.
2. Theodore Levitt, 'Marketing Myopia', reprinted as an HBR Classic, September–October 1975, p. 26.

CHAPTER 11

Portfolio Planning: uses and limits

PHILIPPE HASPESLAGH

Reprinted by permission of *Harvard Business Review*. Extracts from 'Portfolio Planning: Uses and Limits' by Philippe Haspeslagh, Jan/Feb 1982. Copyright © 1982 by the President and Fellows of Harvard College; all rights reserved.

Introduction

The diversity of large industrial – and mostly multinational – corporations can be at once their greatest source of competitive advantage and the wellspring of their most fundamental difficulties. Diversity provides an opportunity for these companies to use cash flow generated by their mature basic businesses to gain new leadership positions. Internally, however, this same diversity also creates a managerial gap between the corporate level, which has the power to commit resources but often only a superficial knowledge of each business, and the business level, where managers have the substantive knowledge required to make resource allocation decisions but lack the 'big corporate picture'.
[. . .]
    In the late 1970s, a new generation of strategic planning approaches called 'portfolio planning' spread across a wide range of companies in response to the problems and prospects of managing diversity. On the basis of my survey, I estimate that, as of 1979, 36% of the *Fortune* '1000' and 45% of the *Fortune* '500' industrial companies had introduced the approach to some extent. Each year during the last five years, another 25 to 30 organizations have joined the ranks.
    Advocated by consulting firms like the Boston Consulting Group, McKinsey, and Arthur D. Little and touted by organizations like General Electric, Mead, and Olin, portfolio planning has struck the minds of many corporate executives. [. . .] Portfolio planning seems to have profoundly affected the way executives think about the management of their companies.
    But what is all the fuss about? What is portfolio planning – as preached – and as practiced? How widespread is its application? What are the problems with its implementation? Does it really work? Or is it just

144

another set of words that consultants have sold to top management — words that must be learned but that are then easily forgotten?

In 1979, I set out to investigate the impact of portfolio planning and its implications for corporate administration in a survey of *Fortune* '1000' companies sponsored by the *Harvard Business Review* [...]. From subsequent conversations and interviews with planners, financial officers, and CEOs, I found that portfolio planning approaches are widespread among large diversified industrial companies and being increasingly introduced.

There seem to be some limits to the practice of portfolio planning as well as tremendous — and sometimes latent — opportunities. Among the more serious limits are that:

1. The road to portfolio planning is a long one; therefore, companies often get stuck trying to implement it and cannot realize the full potential of the approach.
2. If a company looks on portfolio planning as merely an analytic planning tool, it will not realize its benefits.
3. In implementing portfolio planning, companies often write in biases that block its usefulness, including the tendency to focus on capital investment rather than resource allocation — or cost-efficiency at the expense of organizational responsiveness.
4. Portfolio planning seems unable to successfully address the issue of new business generation.

Despite these difficulties, the corporate managers surveyed want to press ahead with portfolio planning, largely because the approach:

1. Promotes substantial improvement in the quality of strategies developed at both the business and the corporate level.
2. Produces selective resource allocation.
3. Provides a framework for adapting their overall management process to the needs of each business.
4. Furnishes companies with a greatly improved capacity for strategic control when portfolio planning is applied intelligently and with attention to its pitfalls.

[...]

Before I explain the findings in detail, I will briefly review the challenge facing diversified companies, the reason behind the widespread application of the portfolio planning approaches, and the characteristics they have in common. Then I will delve closely into the findings before I offer some advice on the introduction of the technique and speculate on its future.

The challenge: how best to manage diversity

The basic challenge for the modern corporation lies in the sheer number of businesses over which it holds sway. Managers of large companies in the 1980s cannot possibly be familiar with all the relevant strategic aspects of each unit of their organizational structure.

Faced with this challenge, companies react in two ways. They may seek a substantive solution and simplify the problem by limiting their activities to businesses that are easy to comprehend or that share a common strategic logic. Or, to avoid the complexity of managing interrelatedness, they may treat their businesses as stand-alone units.

Usually, however, companies tackle the problem by developing a supra-administrative capability. The typical organization creates intermediate organizational levels (groups or sectors) and uses intermediate managers and administrative systems to measure, evaluate, and reward performance. Yet for all their sophistication, modern companies still experience difficulty in managing diversity.

Often top management is aware only of the short-term financial performance of its business (and even that is buried in the fragmentation of profit centers and the aggregation of reporting structures). Senior executives often end up delegating major decisions, which then become based on individual track records and managerial influence and heavily weighted by short-term career risks. Corporate top management becomes actively involved when dramatic across-the-board moves are called for. The uniformity of administrative systems indeed makes it very difficult to escape uniform pressures across all businesses.

As a result, a range of conflicts buffets almost any company. Even supposedly well-run organizations oscillate between periods of uniform emphasis on profits and emphasis on growth – often coinciding with the tenure of a particular CEO. What is needed to counter these problems is a management system that provides (i) corporate-level visibility of performance on both strategic and financial terms, (ii) selectivity in resource allocation, and (iii) differentiation in administrative attention among businesses.

The essence of portfolio planning: how it helps

Portfolio planning recognizes that diversified companies are a collection of businesses, each of which makes a distinct contribution to the overall corporate performance and which should be managed accordingly. Putting the portfolio planning philosophy into place takes three steps as the typical company:

1. Redefines businesses for strategic planning purposes as strategic business units (SBUs), which may or may not differ from operating units.
2. Classifies these SBUs on a portfolio grid according to the competitive position and attractiveness of the particular product market.
3. Uses this framework to assign each a 'strategic mission' with respect to its growth and financial objectives and allocates resources accordingly.

The approach, then, allows management to see business performance as largely determined by the company's position within the industry. Companies can theoretically assess the strategic position of each of their enterprises and compare these positions using cash flow as the common variable. A verbal and graphic language facilitates communication across organizational levels. Finally, the approach helps build a framework for allocating resources directly and selectively and for differentiating strategic influence.

Focusing debate on the real issues

Given the attractiveness of portfolio planning theory and its rapid acceptance by major companies, it is not surprising that the approach has stirred up much debate. Most of it has been ill focused, however, for proponents and critics alike are more interested in a dialogue about analytic techniques than in solving the practical problems inherent in implementation.

So they argue about which 'portfolio grid' technology a company should choose between – the Boston Consulting Group growth/share matrix or the General Electric-McKinsey industry attractiveness/business position grid, the Arthur D. Little industry maturity/competitive position grid or the Shell Directional Policy matrix.

That discussion is sterile; the question of which grid to use and where to place a business on it is least important. The real issue is how a company can best define an SBU and assign a strategic mission to it. In short, what is a company to do with each of its businesses?

The decision on a strategic mission always requires a broad analysis of industry characteristics, competitive positions, expected competitive responses, financial resources, and the opportunities of other businesses in the portfolio. Whatever grid it chooses, a corporation's assessment comes down to a judgement heavily influenced by administrative considerations.

In selling a company on the 'what', the consultants sometimes forget the 'how'. They make it appear that portfolio planning will emerge like a *deus ex machina* out on the corporate landscape – that its administration will pose no difficulties as long as top management has the will to implement it. [...]

The first steps

If the experience with previous generations of planning approaches furnishes any lesson, the usefulness of portfolio planning is determined, of course, by the success a company has with its implementation. In formulating the basis for my survey, I made a number of assumptions. The first is most basic – that administrative rather than technical problems create the greatest difficulties for companies implementing any portfolio system.

My assumption was subsequently borne out as respondents reported that administrative problems loomed the largest. In fact, managers found the labels commonly used with the grid technologies to be largely irrelevant and often the source of psychological problems during the introduction of the technique. A lot of the 'better' portfolio planning companies avoid their use and focus on what to do with the business.

Another important judgement involves the kinds of categories companies work with. Any theory will mean different things to different practitioners, so I devised categories to help distinguish among the various forms portfolio planning has taken.

My interpretations of the data allowed me to make distinctions among companies [...]

No portfolio planning – No intention to introduce the technique.
Analytic portfolio planning – Use confined to a planning tool at the corporate level, no intention to negotiate explicit strategic missions with managers, and business strategies influenced by traditional administrative tools and profit pressures.
Process portfolio planning – Portfolio planning as a central part of the ongoing management process, as evidenced by the explicit negotiation of strategic missions with SBU managers.

As could be expected, getting to process portfolio planning is a long road, so I had to develop subcategories to take into account the various stages of introduction, like companies with:

New portfolio planning – Having just introduced the approach, the companies are still in the process of constructing the portfolio.
Undecided portfolio planning – The initial grid analysis completed, the companies have not yet decided at the corporate level what to do with the businesses or which strategic missions to assign to the SBUs.

Unassigned portfolio planning – Corporate-level decisions are reached on the strategic mission for each business unit, but companies hold no explicit negotiations yet with the unit managers.

The use of portfolio planning

Diversified companies, particularly the large ones, widely practise the art of portfolio planning; for most of them, it is indeed much more than an analytic tool. At the corporate level, 75% practice or are implementing process portfolio planning.

Despite the enthusiasm with which companies are jumping onto the bandwagon, I estimate that only 14% of the *Fortune '1000'* have reached the most advanced (the process) stage. The average travel time seems to be at least five years. [...] Capital-intensive process industries such as chemicals, petroleum, and paper – and technology-intensive (but industrially mature) industries such as appliances, abrasives, and industrial equipment – are most likely to use some form of this planning process. [...]

Since they face the greatest challenges, the bigger and more diverse among *Fortune '1000'* companies have introduced the technique. But, among diversified industries, conglomerates rarely use portfolio planning, while diversified industrials often do.

Two-thirds of portfolio planning companies oversee businesses that are related in some way. The majority not only overlap along one dimension (such as technology or market) but also along multiple dimensions (for example, technology, market, and raw materials). Moreover, companies usually attempt to integrate the management of these related businesses through the use of shared resources and staff at the corporate and group levels. [...]

It is because of the difficulty they have in assessing the strategic performance of each of their businesses and allocating resources selectively that diversified industrials need a formal tool like portfolio planning. Conglomerates, on the other hand, speak portfolio planning prose like Monsieur Jourdain in Molière's *Le Bourgeois Gentilhomme – sans savoir*. How well companies can incorporate these interdependencies in applying portfolio planning will be crucial to the success of the approach.

Portfolio planning companies tend to be international and likely to manage through complex organizational structures. Again, the ease with which the planning approach incorporates both a product and a market dimension will prove crucial to the company's success.

Structuring the strategic business units

Before the introduction of portfolio planning, most companies divide up the corporate whole into organizational units (like divisions) on the basis of operating control considerations. Often these units lack the necessary autonomy appropriate for strategic planning and resource allocation.

Defining what constitutes a business unit is the first step in all strategic – not just portfolio – planning. In the case of portfolio planning, two theoretical principles underline the definition:

1. An organization must identify its various business units so that they can be regarded as independent for strategic purposes.
2. Companies then should allocate resources directly to these SBUs to support whatever strategies are chosen.

The first principle is an attempt to solve the problem of inappropriate planning units by arriving at a good business definition on the basis of industry economics. Based on the experience curve, this definition sees a business as strategically independent if its value-added structure is such that market leadership in that business alone permits successful performance. To put it another way, a company looks at each market segment to see whether it can survive if it competes only in that segment.

The second principle, tying resource allocation directly to each SBU's strategic mission, attempts to solve the problems companies face with typical administrative systems. It hypothesizes that the practice of allocating resources on a project-by-project basis and the step-by-step aggregation of corporate operating results tend to shorten the focus of corporate management and create uniform rather than selective policies. To forge a dynamic strategy throughout the company, the theory states, a company must allocate its resources selectively and directly to strategically independent businesses.

SBUs without the theoretical mask

But that is the theory. It is the application of the theory of portfolio planning to the realities of corporate activities that is most difficult. Anyone simply reading the description of companies employing portfolio planning could list a multitude of obstacles and administrative hurdles; the ordinary manager is dumbfounded by all the possibilities for failure.

In practice, of course, SBUs are not – and cannot be – strategically autonomous units rooted in an industry's structure. A company can only determine the size, shape, and number of SBUs in the light of prior organizational constraints and history, the limits of its managers' intelligence and imagination, and the multiple interdependencies among businesses.

According to my survey results, companies try to apply the theory;

70% of all organizations started off their introduction of portfolio planning by comprehensively re-examining the definition of each of their businesses. In 75% of these organizations, the reevaluation led to the classification of SBUs as sometimes or usually different from operating units. The larger the company, the more likely it is to have SBUs that do not coincide with operating units.

However, let us not assume that the companies started an administrative revolution. Despite the fact that they do not coincide with operating units *per se*, the resulting SBUs are generally aggregations of existing operating units or segments of single units; they clearly cut across organizational lines in only 7% of the cases. A close examination reveals that careful strategic analysis is rarely followed by an alignment of organizational units; rather, there is strong pressure to define SBUs quickly and good reason, in practice, to put the units clearly within the boundaries of existing organizational structure.

The administrative reality

Lest the theoreticians judge too harshly, the degree of diversification of most large companies obviates the possibility of simultaneous consideration of each relevant product/market segment at the corporate level. If the theory were strictly applied, a resulting grid would in most portfolio planning companies have over 100 bubbles and in some over 500. It is no mere coincidence that portfolio planning companies – small and large alike – have ended up with, on the average, only 30 SBUs.

The end result is that, instead of single, homogeneous units, most companies (58% of those in my survey, 72% of those among the *Fortune* '1000') consider each SBU as a portfolio itself – not of different businesses but rather of product/market segments that often may have quite diverse grid positions and strategic missions. In fact, the more experienced companies are with portfolio planning, the more likely they are to treat the exercise as a multilevel operation.

The impact of this redefinition comes alive when you realize the degree to which related businesses of each company share resources along different dimensions. Companies create SBUs at the organizational level, where shared resources can be managed. Top management should therefore see nothing inherently wrong with business units that cut across different market segments and that have widely different positions on the grid or a variety of strategic missions. To the contrary, forcing uniform strategic missions onto the managers of business units leads to either rejection of the mission or buildup of inappropriate strategies.

Those companies most advanced in the art of portfolio planning structure it on two levels. When analysing the whole corporate portfolio and making trade-offs among businesses, they look at the company in the aggregate. In this larger picture, the companies look at SBUs that are in most cases organizational units and assign them strategic missions that reflect the expected cash flow contribution to the whole company.

During the corporate plan review process, however, companies take a disaggregate view and look within those SBUs at the relevant strategic segments. These strategic segments are more likely to result from an analysis of the industry than from an accommodation to existing organizational structure. Their missions reflect the particular strategy the company wants a business unit manager to follow in each of his competitive arenas.

The definition of SBUs and strategic segments evolves throughout the introduction of the process. As the companies go through more planning cycles, the SBUs become more an organizational reality and the segment definition becomes finer. Often the segments are revised but the original SBU definition stays the same.

The definition of SBUs in each company raises two critical issues: how the company should define SBUs so as to accommodate the interdependencies and how a company can achieve the strategic aggregation and disaggregation that portfolio planning requires.

The question of interdependence for example, creates nasty problems of the chicken–egg variety. One product/market segment may share manufacturing facilities with a few others, basic technology with an even broader group, and a sales organization with a different set of product/market segments. With all these differing dimensions, trade-offs must always be made. The guiding principle is that a company must define the SBU to incorporate control over those resources that will be the key strategic variables in the future.

[...]

Looking closer at the way in which the surveyed companies make these trade-offs in practice, you detect a bias toward cost efficiency in relation to responsiveness. Indeed, the business economics orientation of portfolio planning pushes cost structure as the only basis for business definition. In most industrial products and consumer durables companies, the market-based part of costs is small. Moreover, things like an SBU's responsiveness to local market conditions or governments are not quantifiable. As a result, these companies define SBUs along technological and manufacturing rather than market lines. Particularly in the international arena, many companies find that their worldwide SBUs are less responsive to local issues and cooler toward international activities than they were under the former international division structure and country plans.

A hypothetical case

As seen from the corporate level of a large diversified company, business strategy is the outcome of a process of administrative influence. While no one could expect a solar cell producer and an independent electrical wire manufacturer to perform under a similar set of administrative systems, as divisions of a hypothetical — and of course typical — US diversified industrial company they are subject to fairly uniform sets of pressures and patterns of influence.

A theorist reasonably expects organizations to alter administrative systems to make way for portfolio planning, so planners would encourage this company to change its administrative systems — to be selective, not uniform, in its strategic decision-making. In that way, new patterns of influence arise that correspond to the nature of the business, its competitive position, and strategic mission.

[...]

In constructing the survey questionnaire, I tried to see if companies altered administrative processes to fit strategic missions. I asked whether they adjusted the financial planning system, the capital investment approval process, the incentive compensation system, or the strategic planning system itself.

Few formal administrative changes

I found that in practice (except for considerations of capital investment and, of course, the strategic planning system itself) companies do not alter formal administrative systems in accordance with the strategic missions of SBUs. (If they did, theorists would see a high level of formal differentiation across businesses.) On one level, this attitude simply reflects the time needed to implement the planning system. For example, one company (acknowledged as a leader in portfolio planning) finally brought its management compensation system into line seven years after it had introduced the portfolio planning process.

In addition, the reluctance to modify administrative systems across businesses is a good indication of the perceived benefits of administrative simplicity. Controllers have excellent arguments for keeping administrative procedures uniform.

More profoundly, however, the basis for this reluctance may lie within the nature of the SBUs themselves. As I've said, diversified industrials look at SBUs as portfolios of various segments; tying the formal systems to portfolio planning would mean going beyond the business units and would require the company to gear itself to the specific strategic mission of each segment.

The importance of informal systems

Though successful companies did not change administrative systems to

accommodate portfolio planning, their managers did informally adapt systems to fit the various businesses. Time and time again in the survey, this informal differentiation seemed to make the difference between portfolio planning as an isolated exercise and as an integral part of the management process. In fact, implementation depends on how well the CEO and other top managers can tailor their attention to each SBU, especially how they monitor strategic plans, how they weight the financial numbers *in light of the planning process*, and how and where they promote managers.
[...].

The impact of portfolio planning is most profound on the corporate review process and the capital investment appraisal process. Corporate review of business plans becomes more intense and focuses on different variables than in other companies. Generally, portfolio planning companies separate their strategic plan review from their financial review, so the planning process remains as meaningful as possible. As companies gain experience, the review goes into more and more of the detail of each segment within an SBU. My evidence indicates that the review process does shift from emphasis on short-term profits and sales objectives to long-term profits and sales targets and competitive analysis. [...]

Tying resource allocation to strategy

In a diversified company, strategy is essentially about resource allocation across businesses. In most companies, however, formal strategic planning is one thing and the capital investment appraisal process quite another.

My investigations show that companies engaging in process portfolio planning try to correct this inherent contradication by tying the capital investment process closely to strategic planning. [...] Not that many allocate resources primarily on the basis of strategies (only 14% do), but at least the business plan becomes an explicit element in the evaluation process for investment projects. Unfortunately, very few organizations tackle the allocation of strategic expenses (that is, investments that are expensed rather than capitalized, such as R&D, marketing, applications engineering) in the same way.

How managers perceive the benefits

Despite the difficulties associated with the implementation of portfolio planning, almost all the managers surveyed indicated that the process had a positive impact on management. The clearest evidence may be that only one of the 176 respondents that were introducing portfolio planning said it would hold less importance for the organization in the years to come. In fact, managers credit the approach with an array of benefits, with respect to not only the quality of strategy generation but also the commitment of resources and implementation [...]

In the first place, companies gain a better understanding of each of their businesses. In turn, this allows them to make appropriate strategic decisions. One reason is the approach's emphasis on a company's ability to decipher industry logic and assess its competitive position. Another is the introduction of verbal and graphic languages that facilitate improved communication in strategic, not just financial, terms.

According to the comments of managers, all of these benefits lead to improving resource commitments, for they improve resource allocation and facilitate strategic reorientation as well as entry and divestment decisions. Managers even credit the approach with improved operations since it encourages focus, objectivity, and commitment.

A question of direct impact

If resource allocation is what strategy is all about, then a fundamental question is whether portfolio planning actually affects the allocation of resources in the companies that adopt it. Since my survey format did not allow me to study the shifts in allotments readily, I measured the impact as perceived by managers. I asked them how serious the following list of common allocation problems were for their companies on a scale from one (no problem) to five (severe problem):

1. We waste resources by continually subsidizing marginal businesses.
2. Our high-return businesses tend to underinvest.
3. Our low-return businesses tend to overinvest.
4. We do not fund our existing growth opportunities adequately.
5. We have a hard time generating new growth opportunities internally.

To reduce subjectivity, I did not ask for an assessment of improvement but rather for separate descriptions of the current situation as well as that before the introduction of portfolio planning. [...] In general, the introduction of portfolio planning coincides with a perceived improvement in the allocation process. Both process and analytic portfolio planning help the company face the problem of marginal businesses. Changing the investment behavior of basic businesses or their attitudes toward risk that lead to inadequate funding of existing growth opportunities, however, requires a process approach to portfolio planning.

The one problem the approach does not address is the difficulty of generating new internal growth opportunities. I would add that on the basis of interviews I have conducted, the impact – if there is one at all – is rather negative. In theory, portfolio planning is about the allocation of all resources. In practice, however, companies focus on capital investment. The generation of new business requires explicit emphasis on human resource decisions and strategic expenses such as R&D and market research, only later to be followed by capital allocations.

On the most fundamental level, however, it appears that the impact of portfolio planning on resource allocation is a function of the degree and quality of its introduction. We can draw a road map of the potential benefits according to the stages of introduction. First, companies face up to those businesses with untenably weak market positions, make divestments, and inaugurate programs to increase market share. Next, businesses with growth opportunities feel liberated from short-term performance pressure and propose major growth programs from which the corporate level may not yet be ready to select.

In most cases, the investment inclination of base businesses changes slowly and requires the full commitment of top management behind certain power shifts. If a company has been overinvesting, all these resource demands may result in a resource crunch. The way that crunch is handled, in fact, gives a good indication of the degree to which portfolio planning has taken hold. If the company takes into account the various strategic missions of SBUs and counters the resource crunch selectively, then it has firmly established portfolio priorities. If, however, it institutes an across-the-board cut, you have a good sign that nothing has changed from the old days.

Success – or failure

Some companies in my sample reached the process portfolio planning stage very quickly, while others had not quite gotten there even though they had gone through five planning cycles. The difference between such fast and slow introductions coincided well with how successful or unsuccessful portfolio planning was.

In a set of telephone interviews, I compared the experience of 27 companies that had reached the process portfolio planning stage in three years with the experience of 24 organizations that, after five years or more, were still not negotiating strategic missions explicitly. I found that in these cases five factors determined the ease with which portfolio planning could be implemented. Most are endemic to the corporate situation; planners can do little about them. Yet they allow the corporate planner to gauge the magnitude of challenges that lie ahead.

The performance problem: shock

Portfolio planning reallocates resources and thus implies a redistribution

of power. As with all such shifts, a performance crisis – often, according to our data, arising from a profit crunch when fast growth goes out of control – triggers the initial decision to introduce the approach and greatly reduces the resistance.
[...]

CEO role: commitment

In all cases, a strong and continuous commitment from the CEO is the key to a fast introduction, even though in many companies the initial force comes from someone else – often the corporate planner. [...] Lack of real commitment was the source of major problems that companies in my sample ultimately faced.

Resource imbalance level: low resistance

Shifts in resource allocation can range anywhere from the improvement of segment strategies in divisions that can 'stand on their own two feet' to major shifts across group, and even sector, levels. The degree of inertia and political resistance encountered within the corporate structure is a function of how important (or how high up in the structure) the shifts need to be.

Previous planning experience: capability

Though the approach usually provides a dramatic jump in the quality of strategic analysis, its introduction as an ongoing process is based on the previous planning experience. Outside consultants cannot offer a good substitute for the strategic thinking of line managers and the experience acquired in earlier planning exercises. Skillful corporate planners often elicit support for portfolio planning by avoiding what line managers disliked about previous planning formats (for example, by reducing the amount of paperwork and financial information required).

Previous MBO experience: focus

As I've pointed out, good portfolio planning often requires the ability to treat SBUs as portfolios of segments. Companies with a tradition of management by objectives easily introduce the appropriate set of objectives specific to each segment and thereby mold the review process so that it incorporates both an aggregate and a detailed view.

Some important advice

Unfortunately, these five factors are largely out of the planner's control. My research turned up some valuable information about other variables which the planner can control and which will help him set the right priorities in introducing portfolio planning.

The following advice deals with the broad issues involved and applies to most companies independent of their specific situations:

1. *Move quickly*   Companies introduce portfolio planning initially on a 'wave', the strength of which depends on the extent of CEO support or the existence of a dramatic performance problem. It is important to establish the legitimacy of portfolio planning by pushing through some resource allocation decisions before their immediacy in the corporate atmosphere disappears. Many planners get bogged down because corporate attention shifts elsewhere.

   If that happens, advocates may have to carry their selling job 'upstairs' as well as 'downstairs'. The best advice is to demonstrate the strength of the approach through successfully implementing it in one part of the company rather than pushing for across-the-board improvements.

2. *Educate line managers*   Portfolio planning is not a planner's exercise. It depends on improved strategic thinking at all levels of line management. From that perspective, many organizations – even though they invite consultants to analyse myriad divisions – have not taken advantage of the opportunity presented by the approach to improve the quality of management.

   Successful companies usually conceive their planning process as a learning exercise for line management. They also invest heavily in education to allow managers to become familiar with both the basic thinking behind the approach and how best to use its tools.

3. *Redefine strategic business units explicitly*   Defining SBUs is the genesis – and nemesis – of portfolio planning. The units reflect and constrain corporate strategy in the most fundamental way. The period during which the company initially defines their scope gives astute managers the most leverage they will ever have to change strategic focus. This time should not be cut short and will prove to be time well spent if the right questions are asked and the practical problems and organizational biases taken into account.

4. *Avoid labels; focus on missions*   The successful portfolio planning company shuns labels and does not haggle over grids. It focuses on a fundamental discussion of practical strategies for each SBU. Unhappily, many companies still leave fundamental decisions unmade and

allocate resources continually by default. If portfolio planning is focused well, it can help by forcing the issue.

5. *Acknowledge SBUs as portfolios to be managed* In practice, companies often determine what is a manageable number of SBUs around technological or market-based resources. These SBUs consist of many product/market segments. Successful companies, then, tend to accept portfolio planning as a multilevel approach. On the one hand, they develop the capability to take a detailed view of each segment when a strategic issue arises and, on the other, an aggregate view of the SBU when they discuss overall portfolio balance and resource commitments.

6. *Invest corporate management time in the review process* Portfolio planning is a facilitating framework that allows substantive discussion between the corporate and the business levels. As such, the quality and extent of corporate review are crucial. Successful companies set aside time for reviewing strategic as well as financial plans, but they emphasize strategic planning. When analysed at the same time, the financial numbers tend to drive out fundamental discussion of the strategic issues.

Good companies also maximize the time their top managers spend on strategic plan reviews. Though the theory of portfolio planning would call for reviewing all SBUs simultaneously, many companies spread out their review during the year in order to allow senior executives the most exposure possible.

7. *Avoid across-the-board treatment* Portfolio planning companies do keep formal administrative systems uniform. However, they rely on a flexible, informal management process to differentiate influence patterns at the SBU level. Every corporate manager should remember an important caveat: have no across-the-board treatment. At a certain point the introduction of portfolio planning is likely to place demands on corporate resources. Those demands should be met squarely without equalizing the pain through uniform reductions. Any other method will dilute the real impact portfolio planning has.

8. *Tie resource allocation to the business plan* The approach has no teeth without formal links to the resource allocation system. Forcing congruence between resource allocation, on the one hand, and the nature of the business and its strategic mission, on the other, is vital. In successful companies this link takes the form of setting an asset growth rate objective as well as approving a 'quota' for various types of spending. Subsequent requests are evaluated first for their fit within this agreed-on spending pattern.

Such an approach actually alleviates the review burden because it allows decentralization of nonstrategic investments and facilitates approval of those projects that fall within agreed-on strategic priorities.

9. *Consider strategic expenses and human resources as explicitly as capital investment*   Portfolio planning is about the reallocation of all resources. Many companies subvert the process by focusing solely on the allocation of capital to investment. That can work in industries that are highly capacity-oriented, such as paper or steel, especially when the main problem is a deficient selection process between competing investments.

   In most industries, however, strategic expenses in R&D, marketing, applications engineering, and recruiting hold the key to portfolio planning, especially if the company's main problem is the creation of growth. Companies that formally attempt to monitor the allocation of these resources tend to be the most successful.

10. *Plan explicitly for new business development*   Though it addresses the resource allocation imbalance in existing businesses, portfolio planning does not address the issue of new business generation. As a matter of fact, the way companies implement the system tends to inhibit innovative behavior at the business level. Companies with excellent track records of internal business development generally introduce some way to focus attention on the issue in their planning formats.

11. *Make a clear strategic commitment to a few selected technologies and/or markets early*   Corporate management can make specific portfolio choices only on the basis of strategy inputs from SBUs. Business unit managers, on the other hand, need guidance from the top to develop specific strategic proposals. When many companies in the survey could not initially decide on strategic missions, for example, business managers felt as if they were in limbo.

   The best companies will announce firm commitments to a certain set of technologies and markets as early as possible. Setting up workable frames of reference to guide business level planning allows them to make better product/market decisions later on. Such commitments not only facilitate the introduction of portfolio planning, but in a planning approach that regards essentially interdependent businesses as stand-alone units, they also inject a dimension of commonality in a way that provides leverage for individual business strategies.

Current fad or basic breakthrough?

Does portfolio planning constitute a step forward in the management of diversity, or is it simply a passing phenomenon? Often an administrative change, such as the introduction of a new planning system, is the way a CEO can address an organizational imbalance that might be at the root of a performance problem. Successful introduction may be self-defeating. The new system removes the problem and its own *raison d'être*.

It is true that in most companies the introduction of portfolio planning is triggered by a performance crisis and the need to allocate resources selectively in a capital-constrained environment. Also, portfolio planning is not the discovery of the wheel. As I have defined it – the explicit recognition that a diversified company is a portfolio of businesses, each of which should make a distinct contribution to the overall corporate performance and should be managed accordingly – portfolio planning was practised *de facto* by many companies before the development of formal 'technology'.

Yet along with most managers, I feel that, in contrast to previous generations of planning approaches, portfolio planning is here to stay and represents an important improvement in management practice. After the initial portfolio imbalance is redressed, the approach can give companies a permanent added capacity for strategic control because it provides a framework within which the management process can be adapted to the evolving needs of the business. It also helps companies out of the dilemma between stifling centralization and dangerous decentralization. It allows them to reassert the primacy of the center in creating profit potential yet leave their strategic business units maximum operational autonomy in realizing that potential.

Portfolio planning can deliver on three fronts. The first is in the generation of good strategies, by promoting competitive analysis at the business level, more substantive discussion across levels, and strategy that capitalizes on the benefits of diversity at the corporate level. The second contribution is the promotion of more selective resource allocation trade-offs, not by solving the problems or eradicating the power game but by providing a focus for the issues and a vehicle for negotiation.

The most important contribution that portfolio planning can add is to the management process. The essence of managing diversity is the creation in each business of a pattern of influence that corresponds to the nature of the business, its competitive position, and its strategic mission. The benefit a company gets out of portfolio planning depends on its ability to create such a differentiated management process. Putting the approach into practice presents the company with some of its greatest challenges.

Success is based more on coping with administrative issues than on developing sophisticated analytic techniques. It requires a real commitment to good management and demands that an elegant theory be stretched to fit a complex reality.

CHAPTER 12

Defining Corporate Strengths and Weaknesses

HOWARD H. STEVENSON

[...]

Introduction

Business organizations have certain characteristics – strengths – which make them uniquely adapted to carry out their tasks. Conversely they have other features – weaknesses – which inhibit their ability to fulfil their purposes. Managers who hope to accomplish their tasks are forced to evaluate the strengths and weaknesses of the organization over which they preside. Many managers may not think in terms of 'defining strengths and weaknesses'. However, the evaluations which they make in determining areas for action reflect judgments of their organizations' capabilities related to either a competitive threat or a belief about what 'ought to be'.

Many corporate activities are aimed at helping a manager to understand what his own unit and the other units with which he comes into contact are doing well or poorly. Internally gathered information provides data for evaluating the performance of parts of the organization. Externally supplied information provides an understanding of the company's place in its competitive spectrum. It has become common for business organizations to formalize such information into a 'resource evaluation program', a 'capability profile', or other formally communicated assessments.

Although many organizations have undertaken such studies, the results have often been difficult to integrate into an effective planning cycle. Many of the statements which emerged were either of the 'motherhood' type or else did not readily lead to operational decisions. The research for this article examined some of the characteristics which create these operational difficulties.

Research methodology

Defining strengths and weaknesses is viewed by management theorists as an important prelude to the development of an organizational commitment to strategic purpose.[1] In the book *Business Policy: Text and Cases*, the authors identify the following four components of strategy:[2]

- Market opportunity,
- Corporate competences and resources,
- Personal values and aspirations,
- Acknowledged obligations to segments of society other than stockholders.

These components are integrated into an overall program of strategy formulation. [...]

Other writers clearly put the objective appraisal of strengths and weaknesses high on the list of necessary activities for a company which desires to grow.[3] Almost all work available has emphasized the normative aspects of the resource evaluation process. Even those authors examining practice have to a large extent focused on the formal methods by which the evaluation process is carried out.

The study which this article presents examined the process from the viewpoint of output. Fifty managers from six companies were asked for their evaluation of the corporate strengths and weaknesses and the reasons underlying those evaluations. The sample was structured so that it provided a relatively broad representation of managers within an organization. The dimensions shown in Table 12.1 were studied. From analysis of the 191 responses examined, typologies were constructed and an evaluation was made of the consistencies of responses.

The companies selected were:

- Paperco – a diversified paper converter,
- American Ink – a specialty chemical producer,
- Hitech – an integrated electronic manufacturer,
- Pumpco – a heavy machinery manufacturer,
- National Gas – a manufacturer of gas products and transmission equipment,
- Electrico – an electrical equipment manufacturer.

164

TABLE 12.1 Steps in the process of assessing strengths and weaknesses

Which attributes can be examined?	What organizational entity is the manager concerned with?	What types of measurements can the manager make?	What criteria are applicable to judge a strength or a weakness?	How can the manager get the information to make these assessments?
Organizational structure	The corporation	Measure the existence of an attribute	Historical experience of the company	Personal observation
Major policies	Groups			Customer contacts
Top manager's skills	Divisions	Measure an attribute's efficiency	Intracompany competition	Experience
Top manager's experience	Departments			Control system documents
Information system	Individual employees	Measure an attribute's effectiveness	Direct competitors	Meetings
Operation procedures				Planning system documents
Planning system			Other companies	Employees
Employee attitudes				Subordinate managers
Manager's attitudes			Consultants' opinions	Superordinate managers
Union agreements				Peers
Technical skills			Normative judgments based on management's understanding of literature	Published documents
Research skills				Competitive intelligence
New product ideas				Board members
Production facilities				Consultants
Demographic characteristics of personnel			Personal opinions	Journals
Distribution network				Books
Sales force's skill			Specific targets of accomplishment such as budgets, etc.	Magazines
Breadth of product line				Professional meetings
Quality control procedures				Government economic indicators
Stock market reputation				
Knowledge of customer's needs				
Market domination				

Despite other differences these companies had a strong commonality in their product lines. Annual sales of the selected companies ranged from $200 million to over $2 billion.

The results of the study brought into serious question the value of formal assessment approaches. It was found that an individual's cognitive perceptions of the strengths and weaknesses of his organization were strongly influenced by factors associated with the individual and not only by the organization's attributes. Position in the organization, perceived role, and type of responsibility so strongly influenced the assessment that the objective reality of the situation tended to be overwhelmed. In addition, there were wide variations among standards of measurement and criteria for judgment employed.

Few members of management agreed precisely on the strengths and weaknesses exhibited by their companies. To facilitate further analysis the responses were classified within twenty-two categories. These categories were further reduced into the five major groups shown in Table 12.2.

The individual attributes listed are neither mutually exclusive nor

TABLE 12.2 Categories for assessing strengths and weaknesses

General category	Includes these attributes
Organization	Organizational form and structure Top management interest and skill Standard operating procedures The control system The planning system
Personnel	Employee attitude Technical skills Experience Number of employees
Marketing	Sales force Knowledge of the customer's needs Breadth of the product line Product quality Reputation Customer service
Technical	Production facilities Production techniques Product development Basic research
Finance	Financial size Price-earnings ratio Growth pattern

collectively exhaustive in partitioning each of the general categories. They do, however, represent the focal point of the responses from among the managers interviewed.

Analysis of strengths and weaknesses reported

The list of attributes identified by the managers interviewed is notable both for the factors which have been included and for those which were not mentioned. Also important is the overall distribution of responses among each of the general categories and the individual attributes. Absent from the list were such items as: quality control procedures, channels of distribution, relationships with unions, share of market data, characteristics of the customers, growth rate of the industries in which the company is participating, purchasing and contract administration techniques, and competitive relationships.

The most obvious feature of the overall distribution of responses is the relatively equal importance attached to each of the general categories of attributes. Marketing related attributes were the subject of 26.7 per cent of the responses, and technical, organizational, and personnel related attributes each accounted for over 20 per cent. Since one might have predicted that the relationship to markets and customers would have been most important to the companies studied, its lack of dominance comes as a surprise. This is especially true given that over 48 per cent of the responses came from managers with a marketing background. The overall distribution of the responses is shown in Table 12.3.

TABLE 12.3   The relative importance of attributes identified as strengths and weaknesses (all managers)

General category	Percent of response
Organizational	22.0
Personnel	21.5
Marketing	26.7
Technical	22.0
Financial	7.9

The study indicates that there is a variety of influences impinging upon the manager as he analyses the strengths and weaknesses of his corporation. These influences are shown diagrammatically in Figure 12.1. As would be expected the distribution of responses differed from

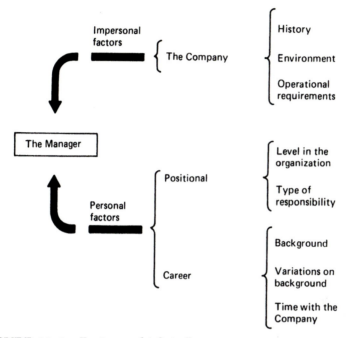

FIGURE 12.1   **Factors which influence a manager in defining strengths and weaknesses**

TABLE 12.4   **The attributes examined in relation to the companies studied**

	Paperco	American Ink	Hitech	Pumpco	Overall
Organizational	30.4%	16.5%	18.2%	20.0%	22.0%
Personnel	36.2	7.7	27.3	30.0	21.5
Marketing	15.9	36.3	45.5	10.0	26.7
Technical	14.5	29.7	—	25.0	22.0
Financial	2.9	9.9	9.1	15.0	7.9
	100%	100%	100%	100%	100%
Number of responses	69	91	11	20	191

company to company. The pattern of responses among the companies is shown in Table 12.4.

Some generalizations of particular interest can be drawn from this small sample. It would appear that the following statements are true:

● There are some aspects of a company that are of concern in all companies.
● Managers within any company examine a broad range of attributes. There is no consensus on 'the corporation's strengths and weaknesses'.

Attributes of common concern

One of the interesting phenomena observed was that there were many attributes which received roughly equal consideration from all companies. There was not a statistically significant difference among the attributes examined by the companies. Evidence of the interest of the company in a particular type of problem was shown by a tendency to examine additional attributes of the same category.

The clearest examples of this phenomenon were the 'organization' and 'marketing' categories. Within these categories, there were similar responses for some individual attributes, for example, organizational form.
[...]

Managers in all companies were concerned with the attributes listed in Table 12.5. Variations arose as the managers examined other attributes which affected their companies' strengths and weaknesses in the organizational, personnel, marketing, technical and financial categories.

The range of concern

The broad range of attributes examined in each company should at once

TABLE 12.5 Attributes of common concern to the companies studied (percentage of all responses from the managers citing attributes)

	Paperco	American Ink	Hitech	Pumpco
Organizational Form	7.2%	5.5%	5.6%	5.0%
Attitudes	18.8	4.4	9.1	15.0
Technical Skills	13.0	1.1	18.2	10.0
Breadth of Line	10.1	7.7	15.5	5.0
Growth Pattern	1.4	3.3	5.0	10.0
Percentage of Total Response for Company	37.7%	22.2%	36.9%	45.0%

be a comfort and a warning signal to those interested in the process of defining strengths and weaknesses. Paperco managers evaluated seventeen of the twenty-two categories. American Ink managers had at least one response in each category. Even in the companies where only three or four executives were questioned, more than half of the list of twenty-two attributes were cited as being either a strength or a weakness.

This broad dispersal of responses indicated [...] [that] there was apparently an effective, if informal, division of the effort of 'scanning the internal environment'. The managers assumed certain territories upon which they felt qualified and responsible for judgment. These territories did not overlap; therefore, a majority of the important aspects of the company's existence was surveyed for relative strengths or weaknesses.

Most attributes were found to be both strengths and weaknesses. The results of the definition process were therefore ambiguous. [...] The resolution of the process of defining strengths and weaknesses into a list often did not produce the expected results. Further management judgment needed to be applied in order to develop a meaningful guide to action.

Although the strengths which a manager identifies depend in part upon his company affiliation, it is also apparent that certain characteristics of the manager's position influence his evaluations. Level in the organization, type of responsibility, functional background, time with the company and variations in background were all studied as possible explanatory variables. The results indicated that only level in the organization and type of responsibility were significantly related to the attributes which a manager cited as being strengths or weaknesses.

Importance of the manager's level in the organization

The traditional theory of organization rests on the differentiation of responsibility within a hierarchical structure. With this as a framework, the hypothesis is that the attributes which are cited as strengths and weaknesses will vary by organizational level within a company. The results of the study show variations which are consistent from company to company. Table 12.6 shows variations among the overall sample in the attributes examined as they were related to the organizational level of the respondent. The organizational levels are defined as follows: level one is presidents and board chairmen; level two reports to either the company president or board chairman; level three is two steps removed; and level four is three or more steps removed from the company's executive officers.

Table 12.6 suggests several tentative conclusions. The level of responsibility is connected with the type of attribute cited. Personnel attributes, for example, are of increasing concern as the level of

TABLE 12.6   The relationship between the category of attribute
examined and the manager's organizational level

	One	Two	Three	Four	Overall
Organizational (as %)	25.0	17.3	24.2	26.9	22.0
Personnel	32.1	22.7	17.7	15.4	21.5
Marketing	10.7	28.0	33.9	23.1	26.7
Technical	7.1	24.0	21.0	34.6	22.0
Financial	25.0	8.0	3.2		7.9
Percentage of total response by level	14.7	39.3	32.5	13.6	100.0

responsibility goes up. This finding is consistent with the frequently
made statement that the problems of managers at higher levels of
responsibility increasingly become questions of the management of
people. Comments have often been heard that judgments have to be
made on the basis of whether the person is right for the job rather than
on other more measurable dimensions. An interesting aspect of the
citation of personnel attributes is that an individual's technical skills and
experience tended to be examined equally at all levels. The consideration
of attitudes of the individual, on the other hand, was definitely an
increasing function of the organizational level of the examiner.
[. . .]
    Technical attributes exhibited the opposite pattern from that observed
in the personnel attributes. Managers at higher levels were less concerned with the technical aspects of running the business. This finding is
consistent with the traditional theory. Among the four attributes which
comprise the technical category, only facilities and basic research were
cited at all by the top management personnel (level one). Techniques and
product development were of roughly equal concern to each of the other
three levels. Facilities were of increasing concern to the lower levels of
management.
[. . .]
    The financial attributes were of more interest to higher organizational
levels. The concern for the price – earnings ratio and growth pattern was
confined to the executive officers and their immediate subordinates. The
only element of the financial category which was of concern to lower
levels was the ability and willingness of the corporation to serve as a
source of funds.
    The organizational category showed no clear-cut pattern. There was
approximately equal concern for the organizational aspects at all levels of
the company. The control system, the planning system, and the interest
and skills of top management were not cited with any clearly identifiable

pattern according to organizational level. These attributes were of importance to particular individuals for a variety of reasons identified with their job responsibility, such as planning vice-president or assistant controller. It is of interest to note, however, that some of the particular attributes cited among the organizational categories varied distinctly and predictably by level. The attributes of organizational form and standard operating procedures fit nicely with conventional wisdom [. . .] organizational form was a concern of higher management while standard operating procedures were a concern to primarily the lowest level of management.

The marketing category showed no clear pattern, other than a slight tendency for the attributes to be of more concern to the lower levels, three and four, than to the upper levels of management. The specific attributes exhibited no recognizable pattern.

Another result of strengths and weaknesses by level is the apparent difference in perceptions of where a company is strong and where it may be weak according to the level of the evaluator within the company. Overall a pattern of greater optimism exists at higher organizational levels. One explanation for the trend is that the further down in an organization a manager is, the more levels there are above him to point to his mistakes and the weaknesses surrounding him. His comments reflect these evaluations.

The overall pattern of recognizing more strengths than weaknesses at higher levels was not consistent among all categories of attributes. Some categories were perceived differently at the different levels of management. The organizational elements were increasingly perceived as strengths the higher the level of the respondent. Marketing and financial attributes were perceived more positively by lower levels of management. Personnel and technical attributes also had slight tendencies toward more positive ratings by lower levels of management. Table 12.7 shows these results.

TABLE 12.7 Percentage of responses identifying category as a strength at each organizational level

	Organizational level				
Attributes	*One*	*Two*	*Three*	*Four*	*Overall*
Organizational	85.7%	38.4%	83.3%	28.6%	42.9%
Personnel	66.7	58.8	27.3	50.0	51.2
Marketing	66.7	57.1	86.7	66.7	70.6
Technical	50.0	55.5	38.4	44.4	47.6
Financial	14.3	66.7	100.0	—	46.7

It appears that the manager's organizational level influences both his choice of which attributes to examine and his perception of them as either strengths or weaknesses. This effect is quite consistent across company boundaries, confirming the influence of the changing organizational perspective upon what is at least theoretically an objective exercise.

Strengths and weaknesses were judged differently

Managers utilize differing criteria in defining corporate strengths and weaknesses. The following three types of criteria seem to be in use:

- Historical
  - Historical experience of the company
  - Intracompany comparisons
  - Budgets
- Competitive
  - Direct competition
  - Indirect competition
  - Other companies
- Normative
  - Consultants' opinions
  - Management's understanding of management literature
  - Rules of thumb
  - Opinion

The impact of the use of differing criteria is striking. Strengths are judged by different criteria than weaknesses. As shown in Table 12.8, 90 per cent of historical criteria are used to identify a strength while only 21 per cent of normative criteria are used to identify a strength.

The nature of the criteria determines whether they will be used for judging strengths or weaknesses. The utilization of the historical criteria for judging strengths occurs because managers are constantly searching for improvements in problem areas which they have previously identified. The base from which these improvements are made then becomes the standard by which the current attributes of the organization are judged. The converse is true with respect to weaknesses. The organiza-

TABLE 12.8 The association of specific criteria with identification of strengths and weaknesses

	Strengths	Weaknesses
Historical	90%	10%
Competitive	67	33
Normative	21	79

tion's current position is only a step on the way to where the managers wish it were. The gap is then measured between the current position and the goal which reflects a normative judgment of what ought to be. This relationship is depicted in Figure 12.2.

The same differentiation carries over to the relationship between the criteria employed and the attribute examined. It is evident that managers have developed models against which they test the strengths or weaknesses of their organization. These models reflect both the historical position and a normative sense of the possible.

This differentiation was especially critical for organizational questions. Every individual attribute within the organizational category was judged at least 50 per cent of the time according to normative standards. The almost total absence of competitive judgment is noticeable. It seems apparent that the managers were not comfortable in comparing their companies' organizational attributes with other companies' characteristics. They contented themselves with comparisons to 'what was in the past' or 'what should be'.

[...]

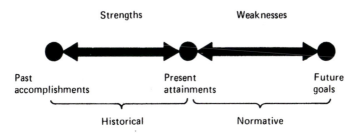

FIGURE 12.2   Criteria used to judge an attribute

Conclusions of the study

The research study which this article presents was exploratory in the broadest sense of the word. The aim of the study was to provide insights and to develop understanding of a complex measurement process. No effort was made to test scientifically formulated propositions. Several generalizations emerge from the study:

● Managers tend to treat strengths differently from weaknesses.
● The underlying steps in the process of defining strengths and weaknesses are similar in all the companies studied. The particular factors which are examined and, the criteria for judgment vary according to the operational requirements of the business and its history.

- The manager's position and responsibility in the organization are crucial influences on the way in which he carries out the process of defining strengths and weaknesses.
- There is no single type of measurement or criterion relevant to the measurement of all attributes as strengths and weaknesses.

The results show that traditional notions about strengths and weaknesses are in need of further examination. The factors studied reflect upon the difficulty of establishing meaningful procedures for the transmission and evaluation of lower-level managers' analysis of strengths and weaknesses. The 'adding of apples to oranges' syndrome is all too prevalent.

In addition to the procedural difficulties which emerged in the study of the process, several situational factors contributed to difficulties encountered by managers in implementing a program for defining corporate strengths and weaknesses. The factors resulted from general causes: the need for situational analysis, the need for self-protection, the desire to preserve the *status quo*, and the problems of definition and computational capacity. Each of these problems was observed not from statistical data but from analysis of anecdotal evidence.

The most common single complaint of managers who did not feel that the definition of strengths and weaknesses was meaningful was that they had to be defined in the context of a problem. [. . .] [They] did not believe in the efficacy of *a priori* definitions which were not related to a specific situation.

Suggestions for managers

The process of defining strengths and weaknesses should ideally require the manager to test his assumptions and to analyse the *status quo* in relationship to the requirements for future success given the competition and the changing environment. The analysis performed by managers is rarely so dispassionate. There is a great tendency toward inertia.

On other occasions, managers are faced with the necessity of recommending changes which include abolition of organizational subunits. There is tremendous pressure to identify the problem with personalities or environmental conditions rather than in a fashion which would prejudice the existence of a whole organizational subunit. Often the definition of the problem prescribes the solution. Managers are aware of this connection and shy away from making definitions which contribute to inevitable change.

Managers cannot and do not explore every existing or potential attribute in order to arrive at new evaluations of the corporation's strengths and weaknesses. They must make choices and decide when they are sufficiently certain. They can then examine areas about which there is less certainty or for which the payoff of an accurate assessment is larger.

The results of the study lead to suggestions for improvement of the process of defining strengths and weaknesses. The manager should:

- Recognize that the process of defining strengths and weaknesses is primarily an aid to the individual manager in the accomplishment of his task.
- Develop lists of critical areas for examination which are tailored to the responsibility and authority of each individual manager.
- Make the measures and the criteria to be used in evaluation of strengths and weaknesses explicit so that managers can make their evaluations against a common framework.
- Recognize the important strategic role of defining attributes as opposed to efficiency or effectiveness.
- Understand the difference in the use of identified strengths and identified weaknesses.

Overall, the assessment of strengths and weaknesses is an important element of strategic planning. The actual items being evaluated are not specific occurrences: rather they are directions, strategies, overall policy commitments, and past practices. The conscious process of defining the strengths and weaknesses of a firm provides a key link in a feedback loop. It allows managers to learn from the success or failure of the policies which they initiate. According to Wiener:

> feedback is a method of controlling a system by reinserting into it the results of its past performance ... If ... the information which proceeds backward from the performance is able to change the general method and pattern of performance, we have a process which may well be called learning.[4]

[...]

A strategic planning system which emphasizes the feedback learning aspects of defining strengths and weaknesses [would include] the comparison of attainments with goals using normative, competitive, or historical judgment criteria.[5] [...] In [the traditional] system the definition of strengths and weaknesses was not part of a closed loop. It was an input, a hurdle goal which each new opportunity had to clear. Once past this initial barrier, the planning process left the definition of corporate strengths and weaknesses alone until a new opportunity was presented.

The research for this article shows that organizational acceptance of the necessity of a process of defining strengths and weaknesses depends on whether the information gathered can be integrated meaningfully into the manager's individual strategic planning efforts. Definitions of strengths and weaknesses generally applicable for whole organizations were not found. However, there appear to be definitions which can aid the individual manager in doing his own job. The use of a formal assessment program developed from the budgeting process seems unlikely to succeed because the information gathered at one organizational level is not directly additive with information from other levels. A program which carefully defines the relevant attributes to be examined and which imposes rigorous and consistent criteria may provide important assistance in the strategic planning process.

Notes

1. See Selznick.
2. See Learned *et al.*
3. See Ansoff; Cordiner; Drucker; Golde; Leavitt, and Simon, Smithburg and Thompson.
4. See Wiener.
5. For further discussion about the requirements of a learning system see Leavitt.

References

Ansoff, H. I. (1956) *Corporate Strategy* (New York: McGraw-Hill) p. 92.
Cordiner, R. J. (1956) *New Frontiers for Professional Managers* (New York: McGraw-Hill) pp. 95–8.
Drucker, P. (1964) *Managing for Results* (New York: Harper & Row) p. 313 *et. seq.*
Golde, R. A. (1964) 'Practical Planning for Small Businesses', *Harvard Business Review*, September–October, p. 147.
Learned, E. P., Christensen, C. R.,Andrews, K. R. and Guth, W. D. (1965) *Business Policy: Text and Cases.* (Homewood, Ill.: Richard D. Irwin) p. 21.
Leavitt, H. (1964) *Managerial Psychology* (Chicago: University of Chicago Press) p. 77 *et. seq.*
Leavitt, T. (1965) *Innovations in Marketing* (New York: McGraw-Hill) p. 176.
Selznick, P. (1957) *Leadership in Administration* (New York: Harper & Row), p. 143.
Simon, H. A., Smithburg, D. W. and Thompson, V. A. (1950) *Public Administration* (New York: Knopf) p. 24.
Wiener, N. (1954) *The Human Use of Human Beings: Cybernetics and Society* (Garden City, N.Y.: Doubleday & Company) p. 58.

CHAPTER 13

The Risky Business of Diversification

RALPH BIGGADIKE

Reprinted by permission of *Harvard Business Review*. Extracts from 'The Risky Business of Diversification' by Ralph Biggadike, May/June 1979. Copyright © 1979 by the President and Fellows of Harvard College; all rights reserved.

Introduction

One way companies grow is to launch new businesses into product markets where they have not previously competed.
[...]
Corporate growth through the addition of new businesses has received further impetus from the 'product portfolio' concept, which argues that if a company is both to grow and to allocate resources wisely it must mix established with new businesses.
[...]
Launching new businesses is risky. Achieving a balanced product portfolio appears to be more difficult in practice than in theory. Articles on the product portfolio concept reinforce this perception of risk by referring to new businesses as 'wildcats', 'sweepstakes', or 'question marks' — hardly the most reassuring of terms. From this viewpoint, corporate diversification resembles Russian roulette.

Conversely, some executives and economists argue that big losses are rare events. Venturing by established companies, they suggest, is much less risky than venturing by individuals. Some of the problems of individual ventures, such as acquiring capital, a brand reputation, and economies of scale, are less severe for established companies.

Another question concerning negative results is, 'How long do we have to put up with losses?' While most managers do not expect immediate profits, few accept several years of losses. Indeed, any corporate venture that promises losses for a period longer than the job horizon of most managers seems unlikely to survive. One company has a firm rule: 'Kill new businesses if they are not profitable at the end of year 3.'

The problem is that, with current knowledge of corporate ventures, one just does not know whether large losses for several years are the common experience or the exception. There is no known rationale for saying that new ventures should be profitable at the end of three years. In addition, it is not clear how much cash, on the average, a wildcat business will demand and over what time period.

This article deals with these issues. First, I present data on the performance of a sample of corporate new ventures. I seek to evaluate their initial performances and to determine the average length of time needed to achieve profitability. Second, I will address the question, 'How might performance be improved?' and suggest some guidelines for future management of corporate ventures.

The sample

The data in this article are from a sample of corporate ventures launched in the United States by the top 200 companies in the *Fortune* '500' and a sample of established businesses in the PIMS project.[1] A corporate venture is defined as a business marketing a product or service that the parent company has not previously marketed and that requires the parent company to obtain new equipment or new people or new knowledge. A business is defined as a division, product line, or other profit center within its parent company selling a distinct set of products or services to an identifiable group or groups of customers in competition with a well-defined set of competitors. Corporate acquisitions were included in the venture sample only if the acquiring company had committed significant resources to the business and altered its strategy after purchase.

The sample included 68 ventures launched by 35 companies that supplied data on their first two years of operations. Of these ventures, 47 had been operating for four years, allowing analysis of the second two-year period of operation as well. The sample consisted mainly of industrial goods businesses. Data were provided by managers of the parent company and of the venture and were disguised by the managers, thus limiting analysis to ratios only, not absolute dollar values.

All these ventures entered existing markets. Markets were defined at a segment level, a more narrowly defined market than those identified by, say, the Bureau of the Census. Thus the data used to measure market size and growth rates cover only the specific products or services, customer types, and geographic areas in which each corporate venture actually operates.

The population from which this sample was derived can be summarized as surviving corporate ventures, launched in the late 1960s and early 1970s by a subset of the *Fortune* top 200 companies mentioned earlier and characterized by a high degree of diversification. These results probably do not apply to ventures that individuals launched or that had to create entirely new markets (e.g., the first business to introduce penicillin).

The data base does, however, embrace entrants that entered existing markets with incremental innovations (e.g., the first business to introduce electronic calculators) and that had a 'me too' technology. It also includes entrants to concentrated and fragmented markets and entrants to rapid growth and mature markets. Participating executives describe the ventures as typical examples of the new businesses that their parent companies have launched.

Financial performance

The sample indicates that corporate ventures, on average, suffer severe losses through their first four years of operations. Table 13.1 shows that the ROI for the median business was − 40% in the first two years and − 14% in the second two years.

TABLE 13.1   Financial performance in the first four years of operations

| | Median value* | |
Performance ratio	Years 1 and 2	Years 3 and 4
Return on investment†	− 40%	− 14%
Cash flow − investment‡	− 80	− 29
Pretax profit − sales	− 39	− 10
Gross margin − sales§	+ 15	+ 28
Number of businesses	68	47

*I show performance of the median business because the sample performance was spread over a wide range. The median is not affected by extreme cases and therefore is less likely to mislead.
†The ratio of net pretax income to average investment. Income is calculated after deduction of corporate expenses but prior to interest charges. Investment is calculated as working capital plus fixed capital (valued at net book value).
‡Cash generated by aftertax earnings *minus* cash absorbed by increased working capital and increased *net* investment in plant and equipment.
§Sales revenues *minus* purchases, manufacturing, and depreciation as a ratio to sales revenues.

A few businesses achieved profits in the first two years − specifically, 12 out of 68, or 18% of the sample. The most profitable venture recorded an ROI of + 80%; the lowest ROI was − − 42%. By the end of year 4, of the 47 ventures with four years of data, 18, or 38%, had made a profit. These 18 do not include 7 of the 12 businesses profitable in year 2. Early profitability in a venture, therefore, does not necessarily guarantee continued profitability.

One can now more precisely assess new businesses' appetite for cash.

The ratio of cash flow to investment was − 80% in the first two years and − 29% in the second two years. No business had a positive cash flow in the first two years; 6 businesses had a positive cash flow in the second two years.

The ratio of gross margin to sales revenue showed the most favorable picture. Of the 68 ventures, 48, or 70%, reported a positive gross margin in their first two years, which points to marketing and R&D expense as contributors to the negative income statements. Table 13.2 shows that the median marketing expense to sales revenue ratio, at 38%, was the second highest operating ratio in the first two years; R&D expense to sales revenue ratio was a hefty 19%.

Most operating and capital ratios showed some improvement in the second two years. For example, Table 13.2 shows that marketing − sales revenue ratio improved to 22% and investment − sales revenue ratio improved from 98% to 73%. However, these ratios did not improve because of any declining outlays on operating and capital items. In fact, outlays continued to rise in the second two years. Rather, growth in sales revenues − at 45% per year for the median venture − rose faster than outlays.

TABLE 13.2   Operating and capital ratios in the first four years of operations

	Median value	
	Years 1 and 2	Years 3 and 4
Operating ratios		
Purchase − sales	46%	44%
Manufacturing − sales	28	25
Marketing − sales	38	22
R&D − sales	19	8
Capital ratios		
Inventory − sales	24	22
Receivables − sales	16	12
Investment − sales	98	73
Number of businesses	68	47

The key to improving financial statements, then, is to obtain rapid sales growth with a less than proportionate increase in outlays. While not surprising, this perspective is in contrast to the common approach of forecasting improvement because of declines in initial launch outlays. According to this sample, both expenses and capital items go only one way − up.

Another common view, that the problem with new businesses is that initial returns are low because of high capital requirements, is also wide of the mark. Rather, in this sample the problem is that there is no return at all – net income is negative. The appellations wildcats or sweepstakes thus appear uncomfortably accurate descriptions of corporate new ventures.

Losses for how long?

Severe losses over the first four years of operations raise the question 'How long, on the average, do corporate new ventures take to improve performance?' I estimated an answer to this question by extracting from the PIMS data base two groups of businesses in more advanced stages of development. One group of businesses, termed 'adolescents', had data on their fifth through their eighth year of operations. The other group of businesses are, on average, 18 years old and describe their product or service as mature; these businesses can be regarded as established and were called 'mature'. These groups allow us to compare performance over three stages of business development: start-up, adolescence, and maturity.

It appears that new ventures need, on the average, eight years before they reach profitability. Note in Table 13.3 that ROI did not become positive until the seventh and eighth years, with the median business earning 7%. However, the adolescents still have some way to go before attaining the 17% reported by mature businesses. In fact, a simple time projection of the results in the first eight years suggests that ten to twelve years elapse before the ROI of ventures equals that of mature businesses.

Figures drawn from this comparison must be regarded as estimates because we cannot be sure that the businesses in the adolescent and mature samples were, in *their* first four years, structurally similar to the businesses in the venture sample. However, even if we limit accuracy to plus or minus two to three years, this length of time to reach profitability is not encouraging.

Cash flow does not become positive for the median business in the first eight years. A similar time projection suggests that twelve years are needed before ventures generate cash flow ratios similar to those of mature businesses.

Some executives previewing these results were initially astonished. This reaction led them, and me, to review personal experiences with corporate ventures. The overriding question was, 'Could the financial results be that bad for that long?' Managers found that the sample data were so provocative that they had to test them against their own venture experiences.

TABLE 13.3 Median performance in start-up, adolescent, and mature stages

Performance ratio	Start-up		Adolescence		Maturity
	Years 1 and 2	Years 3 and 4	Years 5 and 6	Years 7 and 8*	Average age about 18 years
Return on investment	− 40%	− 14%	− 8%	+ 7%	+ 17%
Cash flow − sales	− 90	− 29	− 13	− 4	+ 3
Pretax profit − sales	− 39	− 10	− 5	− 4	+ 9
Gross margin − sales	+ 15	+ 28	+ 19	+ 22	+ 26
Number of businesses	68	47	61	61	454

*Profit to sales is negative while ROI is positive because these averages are medians, not means (mean ROI is + 5% and mean profit to sales is + 1%).

Although these personal recollections cannot be used analytically, the executives eventually concluded that the sample results squared with many of their companies' venture experiences.
[. . .]

Market performance

Although the median corporate venture in the first four years increased sales revenues at 45% per year, this sales growth did not lead to a strong market position. The median venture achieved 7% share in the first two years and 10% in the second two years. Relative share (defined as the venture share divided by the combined share of the three largest competitors) is a more relevant measure of competitive position. The medium corporate venture held 11% and 13% in the first and second two-year periods, respectively.

Although the low initial share level might be expected for a new business, the apparent difficulty in improving share is disturbing. Although 39 of the 47 businesses with four years of share data gained share in the second two years, one-third gained less than a single point and only one-quarter gained more than four points. The impressive sales revenue growth for many ventures was negligible in the context of a market growing slightly faster and a starting position of zero share.

Market share and financial performance

Persuasive theoretical arguments and a good deal of concrete evidence suggest that high market share improves financial performance.[2] Although this previous research was done on established businesses, it seems likely that share will similarly benefit new businesses. However, few researchers have discussed the financial impact of building share. One can argue from common sense that building share should damage financial performance in the same time period.

Building share can require higher quality, broader marketing, lower prices, and extended capacity – all expensive items that damage both income statements and balance sheets. Furthermore, some rapid share builders are starting from both a low share position and an inferior cost position. Their financial results will thus experience a 'double whammy'.

Earlier research leads one to expect a positive relationship between financial performance and share for new ventures. Conversely, in the same time period, a negative relationship between financial performance and share building should be expected. While the small sample size and the wide variability in the data prevent rigorous testing of these relationships, one can say that the evidence of this sample supports them.

Effect of market share

To get the data on these relationships, I divided the venture sample into three approximately equal-sized groups – low, medium, and high relative market share ventures in their first and second two years. Table 13.4 shows data on the first relationship: businesses with low relative share reported − 93% ROI, and businesses with high relative share reported − 21% ROI in the first two years – a difference of 72 points. The impact of relative share on profit margin and cash flow/investment was similar. The advantages of high relative share continued in the second two years of operations. The benefits of share are similar to those cited for established businesses: profit margin increases sharply, and the purchases-to-sales and marketing-to-sales ratios decline.[3]

Effect of building share

Having share and building it produce quite different effects on financial performance. Table 13.5 shows that the greater the rate of gain in relative share, the poorer the financial performance. Rapid share builders reported a median ROI of − 20% for the first four years of operations compared to − 4% ROI for those who were not building share. That is to say, a strategy of rapid relative share building carried a short-term penalty of 16 percentage points in ROI over the alternative of holding relative share.

As might be expected, the penalty on the cash-flow-to-investment ratio was even more severe. Rapid relative share builders reported a median cash-flow–investment ratio of − 58% while share holders reported − 19%, a difference of 30 points.

On the average, the market share of rapid share builders was lower than that of the share holders throughout the first four years of operations. Gaining share from a low share base was doubly handicapping. Rapid share builders, on the average, had price-cost margins worse than those of the share holders. That is, they charged lower prices and carried higher direct costs than did their competitors. To gain share from a low share position, several ventures had to offer customers a better bargain, at the same time bearing the financial disadvantages of low share. This combination is surely the quintessence of the double whammy.

Share before profits

The foregoing findings demonstrate that ventures cannot report both good financial and good market performance in the same time period:

TABLE 13.4 Relationship between financial and market performance

Performance ratio	First two years median value relative share*			Second two years median value relative share*		
	Low (below 4%)	Medium (4% to 42%)	High (over 42%)	Low (below 7%)	Medium (8% to 33%)	High (over 50%)
Return on investment	− 93%	− 40%	− 21%	− 20%	− 5%	− 6%
Cash flow − investment	− 110	− 67	− 74	− 39	− 22	− 23
Pretax profit − sales	− 95	− 35	− 21	− 29	− 2	− 5

*Relative share is the venture share divided by the combined share of the three largest competitors.

TABLE 13.5   Financial performance and change in relative share, first four years

	Median value		
Performance ratio	Rapid share builders	Moderate share builders	Holders or losers of share
Return on investment	− 20%	− 10%	− 4%
Cash flow − investment	− 58	− 20	− 19
Pretax profit − sales	− 24	− 6	− 2

these two aspects of performance conflict. But we know from other studies that the highest ROI for established businesses goes to the highest market share holder. If a business can have both good financial and good market performance only when share is established, the management implication is clear: a venture's objective for its early years should be to build share, regardless of short-run financial performance.

If we accept this objective, it follows that corporate ventures should enter on a large scale for the best results. Obviously, only a business with a large capacity relative to the size of the market has the potential to gain a large market share. This approach is often referred to as building capacity ahead of demand. But it is a controversial strategy and, some executives have argued, counterintuitive, because it raises the required investment and therefore the risk. Yet my findings here suggest the opposite: perhaps the biggest risk is entering too small. It may be true, in corporate venturing as in love, that faint heart never won fair lady.

Entry scale

To obtain further evidence for the idea that to enter on a large scale is the best strategy, I analysed these ventures according to the size of their entry. I used two measures of scale: production and market scales. Production scale is defined as the initial production capacity of the business, expressed as a percentage of the market size. Market scale is defined as the number of customers served and the breadth of product line offered by the venture, relative to its competitors. Production and market scale together represent the maximum potential share a business can obtain. We need both measures of scale because economies of a large plant can be realized only if the output is continuously sold.

Table 13.6 shows the distribution of this sample on these measures. Just over half the sample, 37 businesses, entered with a capacity less than 20% of the size of the market. Similarly, about half the sample offered

TABLE 13.6   Distribution of sample on entry scale, first two years

Production scale: capacity as percentage of market size		
Less than 10%	21	31%
10%–19%	16	24
20%–29%	5	7
30%–39%	4	6
40%–49%	4	6
50%–59%	2	3
60% +	15	22
	67	99%
Median = 19%		
Marketing scale product line breadth		
Less broad*	44	65%
Same breadth	13	19
Broader	11	16
	68	100%
Segment size		
Fewer customers*	25	37%
About the same	36	54
More customers	6	9
	67	100%

*Relative to competitors

product lines less broad than their competitors'; more than one-third served fewer customers than did their competitors. Thus, on the average, our sample consists of small-scale entrants.

When we look at performance by different sizes of entry scale, we see that the small-scale strategy failed to reduce losses. And neither did it build share. Table 13.7 shows performance in the first two years by an index of entry scale, which is simply production and market scales combined. The big losers were those ventures with the smallest entry scale: these had a median ROI of − 41%, compared with − 24% for those with the largest entry scale. The second two years showed similar performances.

Table 13.7 also returns us to relative share: the large-scale entrants achieved the highest relative share as well as the least negative financial performance. For a few businesses, therefore, the conflict between financial and market performance was less severe. Although these ventures still sustained losses, they were at least building market position.

TABLE 13.7   Performance by index of entry scale, first two years

	Median value		
	Small scale	Medium scale	Large scale
Return on investment	− 41	− 47	− 24
Relative share	1	12	64

These findings provide persuasive support for the argument that entering on a large scale is likely to lead to better financial results earlier than does the intuitively obvious approach, entering on a small scale. In fact, small-scale entries are doubly handicapped. Their immediate financial performance is terrible, and satisfactory market position remains undeveloped.

Managers' intentions

I asked managers whether they had deliberately chosen the small-scale entry strategy. Most venture managers had indeed targeted a low initial market share. [...] 34 entrants, half the sample, set for the first two years a market share objective below 10%. Therefore, I judge that the poor performance of this sample was largely self-inflicted. In effect, these entrants obtained the market share they deserved, and this share in turn contributed to their financial losses. They could not generate enough revenue to cover their entry costs and to overcome their relative direct cost disadvantage.

An important management question here is, 'Why would executives seek a low share?' At least four explanations come to mind:

1. Perhaps there is still a widespread lack of awareness of the relationship between profitability and share. I suggest this explanation because, if executives were aware of this relationship, they would realize that they must build share in the start-up phase of a venture – ideally, reaching the number one position.
2. Perhaps middle managers (presumably the proposers of new businesses) fear that, if they ask for too much capital and launching expenses, their idea will not be approved by top management. Thus they plan a small-scale entry to minimize their financial demands. Maybe capital budgeting criteria emphasize financial results prematurely, thus fostering the practice of taking several small dips at the corporate well rather than one large scoop.
3. Venture managers probably expect to be evaluated more on their own

goals than on the long-run success of the particular venture. Therefore, they project a small share because they are more likely to attain it.

[. . .]

4. Another explanation could be that executives believe that starting small is prudent. After all, seeking high share requires larger investment for capacity and more marketing expenses to generate the sales to fill that capacity – all for a new business in an unknown, often still evolving market. As one executive put it, 'Far better to enter small, learn as you go, and expand with experience'.

[. . .]

Management implications

The clearest recommendation from this study is the need for large-scale entry. Such a recommendation might appear foolhardy in view of the financial results of this sample. Recall from Table 13.7, however, that large-scale entrants reported the least negative results. I suggest that the eight years, on average, taken to reach positive net income would be reduced if higher relative share were achieved in the early years. Larger scale entries might require less managerial patience.

One might argue that market segmentation would allow profitable small-scale entries. However, as I explained while describing the sample, markets for the PIMS program are defined narrowly, at least compared with census definitions. Segmentation, therefore, has already occurred. We have been examining the performance of corporate ventures into parts of industries, rather than into entire industries. To illustrate this point, a venture marketing hospital pharmacy equipment confined the definition of its market to pharmacy equipment only, not to all types of hospital equipment. Therefore, its market share was its share of pharmacy equipment sales, not of hospital equipment sales.

I do not, however, recommend large spending on every opportunity in sight. Corporate diversification should not be played like Russian roulette. I do recommend that fewer ventures be launched, so that each can have the advantage of adequate resources to achieve a good market position, right from year 1. Starting too many ventures at the same time diffuses the company's effort.

The recommendation for fewer ventures leads to another: one should back a new business and its managers as long as they continue to build share. Similarly, one should withdraw resources from a profitable venture if profits have been gained at the cost of share. It may be hard to realize in the heat of today's decisions, but a profitable corporate venture sitting on a low share is in fact tomorrow's dog. Conversely, the unprofitable venture gaining share and demanding ever more cash is tomorrow's winner.

The recommendation to enter on a large scale means that middle-level managers should 'call it as they see it'. I have seen too many corporate venture plans with, for example, marketing-sales ratios only slightly higher than those for established businesses and profits forecast for the second year. According to this sample, such a corporate venture rarely exists.

Middle-level executives must estimate what it will take to build a successful business and see that top executives know what they are getting into. This sample tells us that share points are gained only slowly and after the commitment of substantial resources. Middle managers should study the most recent venture pro forma they have been working on. If its operating and capital ratios are better than those shown in Table 13.2, they should ask themselves, 'Why will *this* venture outperform the median venture in a sample of corporate ventures?'

Similarly, if profits are forecast early in the life of the venture, they should ask, 'What is relative market share in the first year of profitability?' It is quite probable that early profitability has been forecast at the expense of a long-term market position.

Summing up

The data in this article tell us, more precisely than we knew before, about the risks in corporate ventures. The odds are unattractive. Indeed, many managers will find them daunting. But, at the same time, managers know that they have to build a balanced corporate product portfolio. I believe that the way to improve the odds and build the portfolio is to commit substantial resources to each venture and to defer immediate financial performance in favor of market position. Launching new businesses takes large entry scale and continual commitment; it is not an activity for the · impatient or for the faint-hearted.

Notes

1. See Sidney Schoeffler, Robert D. Buzzell, and Donald F. Heany, 'Impact of Strategic Planning on Profit Performance', *Harvard Business Review*, March–April 1974, p. 137; and Robert D. Buzzell, Bradley T. Gale and Ralph G. M. Sultan, 'Market Share – A Key to Profitability', *Harvard Business Review*, January–February 1975, p. 97.
2. See Buzzell, Gale and Sultan, 'Market Share – A Key to Profitability'.
3. Ibid.

CHAPTER 14

Assessing Opportunities for Diversification: an analytical approach

MICHAEL YOUNGER

Introduction

A company on a diversification exercise is like a man searching for a mate. He can rely on chance meetings and the immediate attractions of visual appeal and hope for love at first sight. But will he enjoy living with her 10 years later? Or he can rely on a computer dating service and search for the perfect match with similar interests and preselected characteristics. But when he meets her, will he be able to stand an evening with her?

A company has similar problems. It can rely on brokers, runners, its merchant bank, and chance meetings at the annual association dinner or on the plane to New York and end up with juicy opportunities that are wholly unsuitable. Or it can systematically and analytically work through a screening process and end up with an unexciting perfect match. Neither approach is entirely satisfactory and while the individual will probably prefer to enjoy the excitement of random selection, the company should look to a combination of the two strategies.

This article is concerned with an analytical system for the selection of industry sectors for diversification which can not only cope with the chance opportunity but provides a framework for assessing it alongside other possibilities. In this article, we describe how we have recently used the system to select and assess diversification opportunities for a large British consumers goods company.

The system provides the facility for assessing and measuring each business sector against a number of different criteria so that a judgment can be reached on two separate factors: the attractiveness of the sector as an investment in its own right and the extent to which the qualities required for success in the sector match the company's own strengths.

Each sector is assessed qualitatively against each criterion and these judgments are then translated into numerical scores to provide a consistent basis on which sectors can be compared. This involves the risk of turning unquantifiable judgments into numerical results; the subjective judgments are, however, firmly based on an understanding of the structure of each sector, including a number of statistical measures.

Step-by-step, the approach for this particular project [. . .] was as follows:

- From the total base of British industry, eliminate sectors not meeting broad initial criteria – e.g. executive industries, engineering, electronics.
- Assess the 'attractiveness' of each of the remaining sectors on the basis of industry maturity and profitability, by allocating scores to each.
- Assess each sector's 'mesh' with the company's strengths.
- Plot the position of each sector on an attractiveness/mesh matrix and select sectors according to the strategy the company has decided to follow.
- Define the criteria for selecting companies and identify candidates for analysis and negotiation.

Figure 14.1 summarizes the building up of the various factors and scores to result in the attractiveness/mesh matrix.

Assessment of the attractiveness of a sector

The assessment of the attractiveness of a sector as an area of potential investment is based on its profitability and 'maturity'.

The profitability of a sector was measured in terms of the return on capital employed (ROCE) of the principal companies within the sector. Although there was usually a wide range, the average profitability of each sector was assessed. Points were then allocated according to a schedule:

TABLE 14.1   Profitability

Profitability (ROCE)	Score
< 10%	2
Close to 10%	3
10–15%	4
Close to 15%	5
15–25%	6
Close to 25%	7
> 28%	8

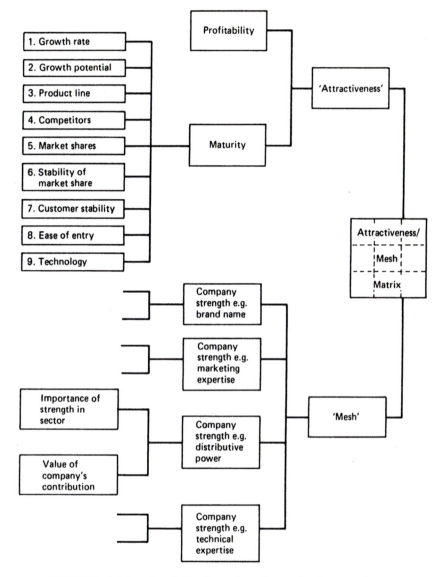

FIGURE 14.1 Analytical system for selecting sectors

TABLE 14.2 System for classifying sectors according to degree of maturity

Factor \ Stage of maturity	Embryonic	Growth	Mature	Ageing
Growth rate	?	> GNP	≤ GNP	< 0
Predictability of growth	?	Uncertain	Well known	Well known
Product line	Basic	Proliferating	Being renewed	Shrinking
Competitors	Increasing	Large number and increasing, then decreasing	Few and stable	Declining
Market shares	Fragmented	Fragmented; some leaders	Concentration	More concentration
Stability of market share	Volatile	Leaders switching positions	Leaders entrenched	High stability
Customer stability	Little or none	Some; buyers aggressive	High loyalty – buying pattern established	Stable
Ease of entry	Very easy	Usually easy	Difficult	Difficult unattractive
Technology	Concept development, product engineering	Product line refinement and extension	Product line renewal; processes and materials	Minimal

Industry maturity is a concept developed as part of Arthur D. Little's strategic planning system. Industries or sectors are classified as 'embryonic', 'growth', 'mature' or 'ageing', on the basis of nine different factors:

Growth rate:	real past growth of the sector and projected growth.
Predictability of growth:	the certainty with which growth can be forecast.
Product line:	the extent to which the product line is expanding or contracting.
Competitors:	the number of competitors and whether they are increasing or decreasing.
Market shares:	the concentration or fragmentation of market shares.
Stability of market share:	the stability of the shares held by each company.
Customer stability:	the loyalty of customers to a company's brands.
Ease of entry:	the ease with which a new company can enter the sector.
Technology:	the importance of technology and whether it is directed at developing the product or improving the product process.

Table 14.2 shows how sectors were classified on this basis. For example, a sector which is growing at a rate faster than the gross national product (GNP) was classified as 'growth' on the growth rate factor; if the market leaders are few and well-entrenched, with high market shares, the sector was classified as 'mature' on the stability-of-market-share factor. Each sector was allocated a score for each factor, as shown in Table 14.2; these nine scores were totalled to give one maturity score for each sector.

From the structure and maturity of a sector, certain general conclusions

TABLE 14.3   Scoring system for sector maturity

Maturity	Score
Ageing	0
Mature/late mature	2
Early mature	4
Late growth	6
Growth	8
(Early growth	10)

can be drawn on the factors critical for success, its investment characteristics and possibly entry routes. For example:

- In an embryonic sector, market shares and consumer brand loyalty are unimportant; direct entry is very acceptable but the acquisition of a small group of companies may not be possible in either instance; further investment is essential but can be risky.
- In a growth sector, high market share at the time of entry is not crucial; opportunities exist for rationalization/consolidation; further investment is normally needed; direct entry or acquisition of a group of small companies are acceptable.
- In a mature sector, high market share at the time of entry is critical; cost-cutting and control is important; further major investment is generally inappropriate and direct entry is virtually impossible, except into a 'niche' or segment which continues to grow.
- In an ageing sector, a high market share at the time of entry is critical; little or no further investment is desirable and no direct entry is possible.

The scoring for the overall attractiveness of each sector is then arrived at by adding the score for profitability to the score for maturity.

Measure of extent of synergy – mesh

Although the prime purpose of a diversification exercise is normally to obtain increased earnings, we believe that there must be some industrial logic to any acquisitions and that the risk involved in the investment is reduced if it bears some kind of relationship to the company's existing business. Companies will be acquired not only because they are good investments. They must be related to the acquiring company in some way, either positively, so that one company can add something to the other, or defensively, so that if the acquisition goes sour, management has the ability to step in and sort matters out. We therefore went to some lengths to ensure that the sector selection process included an assessment of the extent to which the company's management could understand and contribute to the potential acquisition.

Our assessment of the company's strengths was made on the basis of interviews with the company's central and technical staff, an appraisal of the company's corporate and strategic planning decisions, business plans and special studies, interviews with retailers, wholesalers and other buyers and a general evaluation of the company's operations. We classified the company's strengths into four areas:

• Brand: all strengths associated with the company's brand names, including reputation with the consumer.
• Marketing/promotion: all marketing strengths such as skills in advertising, promotion, product development and packaging design.
• Distribution power: all strengths relating to the company's existing distribution links with retail and wholesale customers, such as its reputation with the trade, its sales force, its retail skills and its physical distribution network.
• Technical: all technical strengths in product technology, production, processing and purchasing of raw materials.

An acquisition in a sector that has a high mesh with the company's strengths will increase the upside potential of the investment (because the company can add something to the operations) and will decrease the downside risk (because management will have experience of the sort of problems that are likely to occur). A sector that has a low mesh with the company's strengths should not be ruled out, but an acquisition within it should be treated as a higher risk proposition, requiring a greater degree of self-sufficiency in the candidate's management.

The extent to which a sector will mesh with – i.e. use and benefit from – the company's special strengths was rated by plotting the importance of the strength within the sector against the contribution that the particular company strength could make in that sector (see Figure 14.2).

Value of the company's contribution	Critical (4)	High (3)	Medium (2)	Low (1)	None (0)
Excellent (4)	16	12	8	4	0
High (3)	12	9	6	3	0
Medium (2)	8	6	4	2	0
Low (1)	4	3	2	1	0
None (0)	0	0	0	0	0

Importance of strength in sector

FIGURE 14.2   System for appropriateness of a sector to a company's strengths-mesh

For example, a good brand name may be of critical importance in a sector, but the value of the company's own brand name may be low. Conversely, distributive power may be of medium importance in a sector and the value of the company's selling and distribution techniques in that sector excellent. The placing of each sector within the matrix (one for each of the areas of particular company strengths) was determined by a combination of factors and statistics, experience and judgment. Each square in the matrix contains a number; this number is scored by the sector that falls into that square. (The numbers in the squares are obtained by multiplying the values assigned to each category along the two axes.)

Totalling the scores of each sector within the four matrices, we obtained an overall score for our assessment of the mesh of each sector with the company's strengths.

Attractiveness/mesh matrix

Having rated each sector's attractiveness and mesh, we could relate one to the other. Because the two measures are independent of each other, one would expect some sectors to score high on mesh and low on attractiveness whereas other sectors will score higher on attractiveness and low on mesh with the company's strengths. Because of this independence, it makes no sense to add the scores together nor to look at the characteristics independently. We therefore developed a further and final matrix, plotting attractiveness on one axis against mesh on the other (see Figure 14.3).

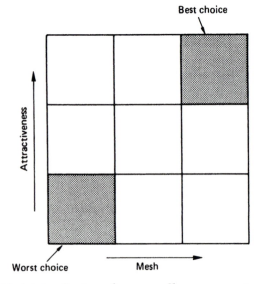

FIGURE 14.3   System for overall assessment of sectors

The best opportunities are obviously those that score high on both characteristics. The selection of sectors from elsewhere within the matrix then depends on the strategy the company selects. If it wishes to go for growth and earnings and pay low regard to the relationship which a sector has with the company's strengths, it would select the sectors falling into the categories in the order of preference shown for Strategy A in Figure 14.4. If it wishes to minimize risk and pursue business in those sectors which mesh best with its own strengths, it would select sectors in the order shown for Strategy B. If the company wishes to select areas for business development on the basis of both measures – attractiveness and mesh – it would select sectors in the order shown for Strategy C.

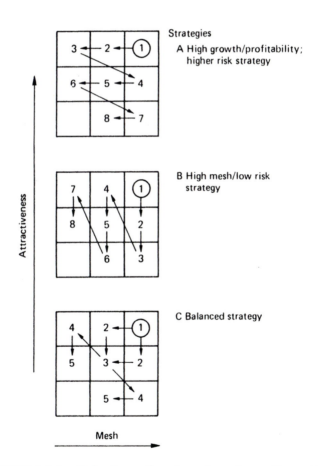

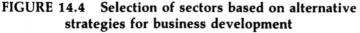

FIGURE 14.4 Selection of sectors based on alternative strategies for business development

Summing up

We hope to have demonstrated that the system provides an analytical method for assessing both the attractiveness of an opportunity area as an investment and the extent to which it will match a company's current operations and their strengths and weaknesses. The attractiveness/mesh matrix system provides a systematic procedure for finding the best date. But it also provides a framework against which to assess and compare the girl you meet in the pub.

CHAPTER 15

An Introduction to Divestment: the conceptual issues

JOHN COYNE and MIKE WRIGHT

Introduction

Until the 1980s a disproportionate amount of attention was given to the growth and development of companies by merger and acquisition. Whilst many acquisitions were part of other groups, little attention was given to the decision to sell and almost exclusive focus was brought to bear on the decision to buy. The performance of companies post-acquisition has been the subject of enquiry and there has been some dissatisfaction that the doctrine of 'big is best' has not been proven and the anticipated economies of scale not realized (Meeks 1977; O'Brien 1978; Utton 1974).

Nevertheless the focus on the divorce between ownership and control is understandable within the framework of theories of the firm which place emphasis on the discretionary power of management. Acquisitive behaviour fits well with the emphasis on empire building and the extension of authority (Mueller 1972; Marris and Mueller 1980). The decision to sell, however, is an equally important decision in the realization of company or managerial corporate objectives, and it may well be the case that something has to be sold before something else can be bought. It seems only logical, therefore, that attention should be focused on the decisions to sell and the attainment of corporate objectives through a realignment of subsidiaries within large groups.

The future of divestment, and the way companies adapt to their changing commercial environment, is the subject of this chapter [...] As divestment is so little examined, the chapter spells out quite carefully the adjustment process and the way in which divestments can occur, and the different forms they can take from partial to complete severance, and by various routes.

The stages through which a company progresses which precede the divestment are outlined, and the limited literature on post-divestment performance of both the former parent and the divestee is reviewed. In particular the effects on both efficiency and share price performance are examined.
[...]

The divestment spectrum

Divestment may be described in simple terms as the sale by an organization of one part of itself to another party. The impression given by such a definition is that the severance of ownership is always complete and final. Whilst this is very often the case, it is clear from Table 15.1 that such an approach does not provide a complete description of the process. It is useful to classify the various types of divestment by the nature of the ownership severance involved, the relative frequency with which it takes place and the post-divestment ownership form for the part disposed of.
[...]

For some types of product or service, franchising is the means by which trade can take place. The precise form varies, but normally involves some kind of competition for the exclusive right to produce a firm's product or service in a particular area for a given period. Contracting-out has similarities with franchising, in that firms engage in tenders for the production of a service. However, the distinction may be made that contracting-out involves the provision of a specific good or service to the parent company. To all intents and purposes, the contractor obtains a monopoly position for the period of the contract, and the service or good will normally be provided by a contractor who is a specialist in that area. Thus the benefits of economies of scale may be obtained (not least by the contractee through the payment for lower cost services) which the contractee, who is a non-specialist in that area, could not enjoy. In this way a company may 'dispose' of part of the operation which it does not wish to exploit internally but maintain an ownership interest.

A sell-off is likely to be a permanent arrangement involving an identifiable business unit rather than the provision of a good or service. For the reasons elaborated below, a sell-off may involve units that are small in relation to the parent either in a series of divestments, a one-off divestment or a large sell-off, but in all cases the subsidiary either becomes independent or part of another organization. In the case of management or leverage buy-outs, for example, where a part of a large

TABLE 15.1 Spectrum of divestment

Type	Ownership severance	Relative frequency	New ownership form
(1) Franchising	Complete; limited period	Frequent	Subsidiary or independent
(2) Contracting-out	Complete, but trading relationship remains	Frequent	Subsidiary
(3) Sell-off	Complete; usually permanent	Small sell-offs frequent; part of a series Large sell-offs – function of crisis	Subsidiary
(4) Management/ leverage buy-out	Usually complete and permanent; parent may retain equity interest	Small – frequent Large – becoming more frequent in UK; frequent in US	Independent
(5) Spin-off/demerger	Split rather than severance; may involve dilution of ownership; usually permanent	Small – frequent, especially in high technology, where management takes equity stake	Quasi-independent
(6) Asset-swap/ strategic trade	Complete, but exchange involved so size of parent maintained	Unusual; small asset-swaps may arise in anti-trust divestitures; large asset-swaps voluntary	Subsidiary

company is sold to its management or a consortium of institutions, it becomes an independent entity. In some cases, especially in the US, the parent may retain a short- or medium-term equity interest which effectively amounts to a deferral of payment.

Where spin-offs occur, the question of immediate and complete ownership severance does not arise. Rather, part of the parent company becomes a separate legal entity but remains substantially owned by the same shareholders as the parent (Burgelman 1984). Some dilution of ownership may occur in the short-term if managers are given a significant equity stake, as in spin-offs of new high-technology developments (Garvin 1983) or where the shares of both parts are traded on separate stock exchanges [. . .] The part which is spun off may be regarded as quasi-independent since it can decide its own management structure and raise finance in its own right.

The case of asset-swaps or strategic trades are treated separately because, strictly speaking, little if any funds change hands. Transfer of ownership is effected by exchanging some of the assets of one firm for some of those of another. A match is required, but this is not between what one company has to sell and what another is prepared to pay; it is, rather, between what one company has which it wishes to dispose of and what part of another company is prepared to accept, and vice versa. It might thus be expected that the available market is considerably narrowed.

In all the cases of divestment just described, the part of the organization disposed of may be small (say 10 per cent) or large (greater than 10 per cent) in relation to the parent. Having outlined the types of divestment, attention is now turned to a consideration of how the need for divestment might arise and the circumstances under which each of the above might be appropriate.

The growth of firms and adaptation of the organization

Firms may seek to grow in order to satisfy a number of objectives, the major ones of which are likely to be the maximization of shareholder wealth or managerial welfare. In both cases the avoidance of takeover and the maintenance of the firm as an independent entity are likely to weigh heavily in determining managements' behaviour.

In order to obtain growth, a company has seven broad policy options available to it: the expansion of existing activities and markets; vertical integration; diversification; innovation; international operations; defence of an existing market; or divestment and restructuring (Chiplin 1982). The individual options are not mutually exclusive and the last two named may require some degree of marking-time or contraction before longer-term growth is possible. International operations may involve elements of the other options as a company may integrate backwards by securing essential raw material supplies overseas or seek to exploit some technical superiority in widening its sales into an international context (Franco 1976; Dunning in Casson 1983; Caves 1982). Growth may be achieved through any of these options by internal (organic) or by external (acquisition) means.

Before embarking upon any action designed to achieve growth, a company determines its corporate strategy, which compares where the firm is at present with where it wants to be, to indicate what needs to be done to meet its objectives.

[...]

The benefits to the company as a whole from the successful implementation of the above growth strategy may accrue from technical economies of scale or by the synergy released as two or more separate entities are forced together. It has increasingly come to be argued in recent years that benefits may also accrue to the company from the reduction in transactions costs which are derived from the internalization of transactions previously carried out through market contracts (see Williamson 1981). Such internalization of transactions is considered to reduce opportunistic behaviour on the part of customers or suppliers. However, in order to be successful it may be necessary for the management hierarchy in the company to become divisionalized so that opportunistic behaviour by managers within the company may be minimized (Teece 1984). The divisionalized management organization may be accompanied by a centralization of the finance function, and in particular an internal capital market may be set up so as to allocate investment funds between competing divisions according to the firm's own investment criteria. It has been argued that as greater information is likely to be available internally, such allocations of investment funds should be more efficiently carried out than if recourse was made to the external capital market (Williamson 1975).

[...]

The emergence of a need to change

The corporate strategy adopted by a firm and the consequent direction of action is a response to the company's perceived current weaknesses and the current environment and how that is expected to change. Such change may take three main forms [...] arising from the spread of markets occupied by the company, threatening actions from various sources, and the speed and variability of such change. The interdependence of the environmental factors seems to intensify the pressures on the organization.

Management structures may well be required to change in line with a strategy designed to cope with change. However, in a dynamic environment it is likely that the organization will be attempting to hit a moving target. More precisely, if a particular firm operates in several areas (both in terms of products and geography), it may be viewed as attempting to hit several targets which are moving at different rates.

For firms faced with the problem of adaptation to a changing environment, recent research has proposed a number of solutions (e.g. Aaker 1984). Whilst divestment has figured amongst these solutions, there has been no systematic attempt to discuss when divestment might be appropriate, the various forms it might take and when each form might itself be appropriate. The interrelated issues influencing the need for change may be considered under the headings of product-market changes; managerial and control inadequacies, which include the issue of incomplete labour contracts; financial problems; the type of management structure to be adopted; and the need to reassess corporate strategy in the light of the other issues. Change itself may, for simplicity, be divided into 'ordered' and 'crisis' change, although in practice the degree of change may lie along a spectrum from static to dynamic (Waterhouse and Tiessen 1978). As regards ordered change, the company may be able to adapt gradually to changed circumstances, whereas in crisis conditions, rapid and major structural adjustment is called for. In both cases, change may be for better or worse!

Now consider the 'key' interrelated areas in ordered and crisis conditions of change (see Table 15.2). First, the case of ordered change is examined. Where finance becomes either more or less freely available within the company, perhaps in terms of rising or falling profits or changes in the cost of borrowing new funds, the appropriate hurdle rate for new investment projects may be changed accordingly. As jobs develop with growth of the company or change in the nature of its products, an extension of payments and incentive structures may be required to monitor and control opportunism on the part of management. In terms of gradual changes in the product market, the company may most obviously adapt by riding out cyclical falls in demand or by developing product differentiation. Alternatively, the established dominant firm may engage in expenditure to maintain excess capacity and so deter the entry of new firms into the market. The existing management structure itself does not require major change at this stage but is able to deal with change either through supervision of the existing managers, recruitment of further managers or the non-replacement of those who leave. Overall corporate strategy may well have been set in terms of

TABLE 15.2 Divestment change and breakdown in key areas

	Finance	Labour contracts	Product markets	Management structure	Corporate strategy
Normal/ ordered change	Adjust hurdle rates for new investment	Change payment and incentive structures	Rideout cyclical falls; encourage product differentiation; excess capacity, greater expenditure to deter entry	Extend existing structure	Absorb incremental changes
'Crisis' conditions	Severe funding constraint; internal capital market fails	Insufficient incentives; inability to monitor; divisional employees require parity with co-workers; inability to change pay and incentive structure	Long-term decline in market; affinities with other product areas breakdown; entry deterrence requires ownership change	Change structure (monitoring system U → M)	Structural shift

aiming for an annual substantial increase in profits within which incremental changes may be comfortably accommodated.

As far as divestment is concerned at this stage, though it may take place it would probably be limited. The most likely form that this might take is for small subsidiaries to be sold off to new parents or to the managers. The conditions under which these types of divestment might occur may be when the parent has made an acquisition of a group which includes parts that are of no interest to it or in which it has no expertise. Considerations of the failure of the subsidiary leading to divestment may arise where it does not achieve its target return on investment but nevertheless earns some profits. Divestments might also occur through the spinning-off of companies to exploit new developments which are insignificant for the parent to deal with itself.

In crisis conditions the possibilities for divestment are greatly enhanced. Consider the key areas shown in Table 15.2. Crisis conditions may be manifested in poor performance of an organization, though this may be relative to what could be achieved and not necessarily an absolute position. However, structural changes may be necessary to deal with these conditions as change cannot be accommodated by incremental adjustment in the organization (Miller 1982).

Initially, as we have seen, a move from a unitary style of management to a divisionalized form may be appropriate. But a divisionalized form or organization may also reach its own limits for a number of reasons. Firstly, as Dugger (1983) has pointed out, the divisionalized form of organization, with its central office acting as a monitor, may prevent opportunism in the subsidiaries but the gains may be appropriated to the head office managers in the form of increased salaries rather than being passed on to shareholders. Opportunism is generally understood to refer to behaviour by the managers of the subsidiary which is not compatible with the objectives of the organization as a whole and hence is detrimental to its performance.

Secondly, the organization may become too diverse and large so that the central office is unable to prevent opportunism occurring in the divisions, as it cannot enforce incomplete contracts of the management (Klein 1983). This position may occur regardless of whether or not a trading relationship exists between the subsidiaries (Wright 1986).

The third reason concerns the whole question of the meaning of 'opportunism'. Where the possibility for opportunism exists, monitoring is required to ensure that subsidiary managers follow the organization's goals. Such a view is acceptable if the organization's goals are optimal, but this may not necessarily be true in a dynamic or turbulent environment. A rapidly changing environment may hinder the subsidiary management's ability to adapt to changed circumstances, and hence poor performance results through control loss (Wright *et al.* 1983).

Alternatively, subsidiary entrepreneurship ('intrapreneurship') may be stifled such that new opportunities which would benefit the organization are missed. Burgelman (1984) has suggested a framework by which senior management should encourage corporate 'intrapreneurship' and find ways of integrating it into the organization for the benefit of the company as a whole. Senior management should assess both the strategic importance and operational relatedness of each new entrepreneurial initiative. Actions can then be determined as to how best to deal with such opportunities. Depending upon the importance of the new opportunity, actions may range from direct integration, through setting up new business departments/units/divisions, to contracting out or even complete spinning off of the activity.

[...]

Alternatively, and of more relevance for divestment, there may be the incentive for some managers to leave the organization and set up in direct competition to the parent company (Frank 1984). However, the pushing may come from the other side. That is, if managers engage in opportunistic behaviour which cannot be resolved internally by improved incentives so that monitoring is imperfect, the parent itself may encourage managers to buy out the company [...] The divestment of the company in this way may have an effect on performance, which the parent can benefit from, in its trading relationships with the former subsidiary. The threat, however, must exist for other competitors in the market place to take over the trading relationship with the former parent, and the former subsidiary must to some extent remain dependent on the parent for some time. Effective competition may have been prevented previously as the subsidiary was protected by being part of the parent's organization.

The problem of employees being aware of what employees in other divisions are earning may make it difficult to alter remuneration packages in an ailing subsidiary so as to make it viable. Spinning off the subsidiary and retaining an equity stake may make it easier to effect the required changes and obtain rewards from continued ownership.

Where reliance has to be placed on the workings of a capital market internal to the firm, problems may arise for newer opportunities either because the project may only exceed the organization's required rate of return in the longer term, and is hence subject to risk and uncertainty, or because it may lose out to the political bargaining processes which exist between divisions. Such a position may be difficult but not fatal where sufficient funds are available in the firm as a whole. As the majority of investment funds of UK firms are generated internally (e.g. in 1983 the figure was 56.3 per cent), severe problems may arise where performance of the firm is weak. Alternatively, a part of the business may demand large injections of funds to finance major investment which is required if

it is to remain competitive. The parent may be quite profitable but unable to generate internally the level of funds required, so that the internal capital market breaks down. Recourse may then be made to the external capital market in order to raise the additional funds.
[...]
The ability to raise extra finance externally may [...] be highly restricted for the firm as a whole. It can be even more restricted for a division which usually would have no independent means of raising funds. Possibilities may exist for foreign subsidiaries to raise some debt-funding on overseas capital markets, which could be more sympathetic than the parent's home capital market, but in general the options available are likely to be severely limited.

Where the lack of finance is absolute, parents may sell off subsidiaries which are the greatest drain on resources or, in some severe cases, those which provide the easiest means of raising funds quickly. In a deep recession the size of the divestments may be expected to rise steeply, as was certainly the case in the UK during the early 1980s (Coyne and Wright 1982).

Long-term decline or serious poor performance in a market area in which the organization operates may lead it to consider divestment as a means of adjustment (Harrigan 1980). The extent to which this route is possible is a function of the barriers to exit faced by the organization (Porter 1976). The price that may be obtained by the vendor is closely related to the extent to which asymmetry of information exists between the parties to the transaction (Chiplin and Wright 1980). Where buyers are available, barriers to exit for the parent may be reduced even though the assets being transferred are specific to a particular industry. Buyers may arise from either inside or outside the firm, both believing that the subsidiary to be disposed of may be made to perform better under new ownership. The question of sale to the current managers may be a vexed one where they are in a bargaining position which enables them to obtain the subsidiary at a discount by the threat of vetoing external purchasers. This problem may be particularly acute where the parent is desperate to sell, where the incumbent management constitute a substantial part of the worth of the subsidiary and where few alternative purchasers exist. In the UK, where such management buy-outs have occurred, discounts on the book value of assets was a common feature of transactions in the early 1980s (Coyne and Wright 1982). However, more recently the *offensive* strategy of parents to remove subsidiaries has been counter-balanced in a number of cases by a *defensive* strategy to prevent management seeking to buy out (since they are now more aware of the possibilities), especially where this is not in accord with corporate policy. One result of this shift has been for the discounts on management buy-outs to disappear (Wright and Coyne 1985).

A long-term decline in a product market may accompany breakdowns in the traditional affinities with other product areas that the organization has been associated with (Rumelt 1982). The economic rationale for affinities with other areas may be related to vertical integration, horizontal integration or risk-spreading conglomerate behaviour. Where rapid change makes integration a less attractive option (e.g. it may be difficult to control across integrated processes, or integration in different markets may now be required) or where a change of markets to achieve effective conglomerate risk spreading is required, affinities may break down and accelerate the need for divestment.

For a firm faced with a threat to its dominant market position, entry-deterring pre-emptive action may usually take the form of investment in excess capacity (Spence 1977). However, in some circumstances capacity reduction through divestment may be warranted (Lewis 1983). By following this route a firm may reduce the cost to itself of future entry-deterring behaviour since by selling capacity it will depress prices. This route to divestment may be dangerous, though, if capacity is sold to a competitor or a parent who is able to engage in cross-subsidization. As a result, firms may prefer to close down capacity rather than divest in order to gain strength from the profitable use of remaining capacity.
[...]

Stages of divestment

The types and course of divestment discussed in the preceding sections need to be placed in the context of the development of an organization's corporate strategy. A firm may at a period of time, engage in all the types of divestment shown in Table 15.2, but their appropriateness will depend on the circumstances facing it.

An approach to fitting divestment into the development of corporate strategy is shown in Figure 15.1. The organization is assumed in Stage 1 to be in a state of fuzziness (Amey 1979). In other words, it is unclear about its objectives and as a consequence is engaged in a set of activities which display little underlying strategic logic. Arrival at this position may be the result of previous activities which have not been directed towards a coherent strategy or where the strategy has been inappropriate to the changing environment. At some point the need to reassess the position arises. This point may emerge because of a change in management, the new management reading early warning signs and deciding that change is required. In this type of case the degree of change undertaken may be quite minor. Alternatively, management's hand may eventually be forced as performance deteriorates sharply. Management may also have its hand forced in two other ways. Firstly, it could be

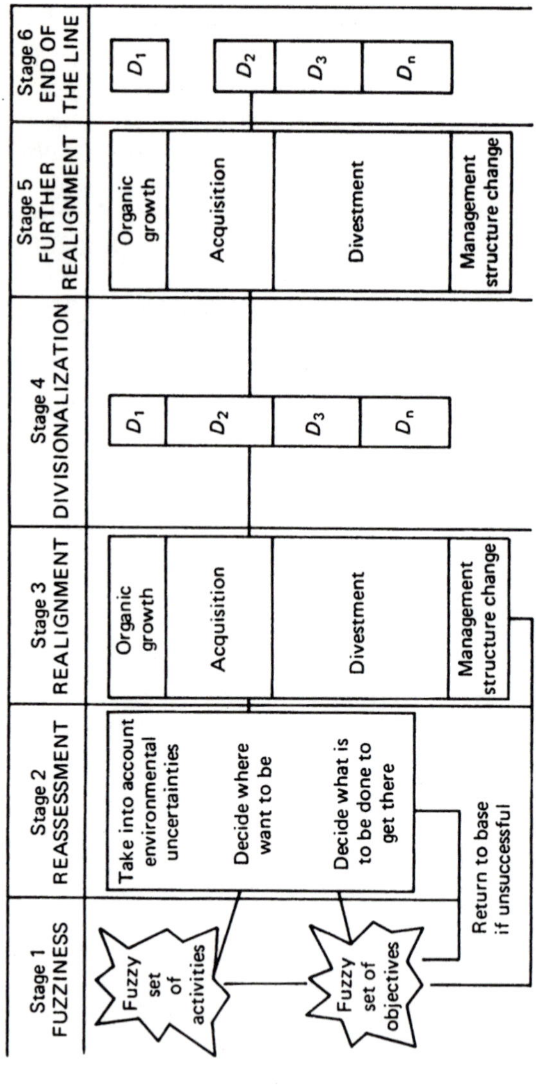

212

FIGURE 15.1 Route to adaptation through ownership change

compelled to sell off a part of the business as a requirement of competition policy. [...] Secondly, as has been the case recently in the UK, governmental privatization policy may seek to break up large state-owned monopolies.

Initially consider that the company's environment is changing slowly so that the pressures faced, as outlined in Table 15.2, are less severe. Management in Stage 2 of Figure 15.1 is able to reassess the organization's corporate strategy by taking into account environmental uncertainties, deciding the direction to go and what is to be done to get there. The required action to achieve the reassessed strategy may involve a combination of organic growth, acquisition, divestment and a change in the management structure to ensure effective monitoring. At this point, Stage 3, changes in the management structure are likely to concern additions and extensions to the existing position. [...]

Realignment in Stage 3 may not succeed, particularly if the speed of change in the environment is under-estimated, with consequential implications for internal aspects of the firm and the effectiveness of monitoring. The organization may thus find itself back in Stage 1 and be required to start again. If Stage 3 is successful, growth may require divisionalization of the organizational structure to secure effective monitoring. However, assume now that rapid change in the environment begins to occur with consequential effects on the key areas identified in Table 15.2. Further realignment is called for in Stage 5, but on a larger scale than in Stage 3. The divestment element may involve large sell-offs and/or a series of smaller ones as the parent company attempts to extricate itself from areas which are an excessive drain on resources, are difficult to monitor, are suffering a large decline in demand or require changes to correct problems which are difficult to digest within the current organization. Asset-swaps may also be called for at this stage, though, as explained earlier, the circumstances under which they are likely to occur are rather specialized.

At Stage 5 the structural changes made by the parent may effectively deal with the problem. However, in some circumstances the underlying pressure may be that whilst the constituent parts of the company have been reorganized on a sound basis, they are incompatible when put together. As a result, they grow further apart as time passes. The solution is no longer to return to earlier stages and attempt reassessment or realignment, but rather to recognize that the end of the line has been reached. By spinning off or demerging, the owners of the parent company are able to maintain ownership of the same assets which are now repackaged as two (or more) separate entities. The owners may gain both from being able to adjust their investment decisions as to the amount of stock they wish to hold in each part, and from any efficiency gains which arise from improved monitoring and control that separation may bring.

It is worth pointing out at this juncture the different performance implications of divestments (sell-offs) and demergers (spin-offs). Divestment may normally be regarded as involving some element of failure through either a misfit with the parent or unsatisfactory performance. To some extent in demergers the problem is one of success – there are difficulties from strategic and managerial points of view if the two parts remain within the same parental organization, but there may well be shareholder gains to separation, i.e. demerger may release negative synergy in that the two parts on their own are greater than the whole. Maintaining ownership through the form afforded by demerger may produce a greater return to shareholders than would be available if one part was sold off completely and the resulting funds reinvested in new or existing ventures. As is shown in the next section, such benefits may, in practice, be quite substantial.

Studies of the effects of divestment on performance

The effects of three main types of divestment have hitherto been examined in the literature, all of them relating to the USA. These types of divestment have been voluntary sell-offs, voluntary spin-offs/demergers and involuntary actions which are the result of competition policy.

The studies have focused on the effects on shareholder wealth, as an indicator of the change in performance of the firm, following divestment. As the reasons for divestment differ, the effects on shareholder wealth may also be expected to vary. In the case of enforced divestitures as part of competition policy, it is argued that if a monopoly has been enjoying its market power, the shareholders will lose by the removal of that power. Sell-offs may be undertaken as an investment decision by management. If management is interested in wealth creation, such a decision should have a positive NPV and accordingly this should provide a signal to investors which results in an upward movement in the share price. Upward movements in the share price of companies involved in spin-offs should be observed for four main reasons which may be viewed as changes in existing contracts.

First, demerger may improve the efficiency of the firm. Second, demerger may alter the contractual relations between shareholders and regulators. As a result, the manner in which rates are regulated may be relaxed to the overall benefit of shareholders. The third and fourth reasons result from transfers to the initial shareholders without the total value of the firm increasing. Either, following Hakansson (1982) and Hite and Owers (1983), shareholders benefit from an increase in the opportunity set of securities available to them or, according to Galai and Masulis (1976), shareholders may benefit from an overall transfer from debtholders. The opportunity set of securities is increased as the initial shareholders can, following demerger, adjust the proportion of shares held in the two separate entities to suit their own risk–return preferences. A transfer from debtholders to shareholders may be said to occur when, upon demerger, shares are distributed solely to the shareholders of the parent corporation, resulting in them 'stealing away' a portion of debtholders' collateral as they no longer have any claim on the assets of the newly independent entity.

Empirical studies of the effects on shareholder wealth have essentially focused upon the measurement of abnormal returns which arise on the announcement of each particular form of divestment and relate to the USA. Studies of the effects of enforced divestitures have produced conflicting results which may be partly attributable to methodological weaknesses, particularly in the earlier studies (Brown and Warner 1980). Burns (1977, 1983), examining divestiture in the early part of the century, found positive increases in shareholder wealth, whilst studies of more recent cases by Kudla and McInish (1981) and Boudreaux (1975) have observed negative effects. Even where negative effects are recorded, it may well be that these are insufficient to outweigh the large positive abnormal returns that have been accumulated over a number of years leading up to the divestiture (Ellert 1976).

Tests on both spin-offs and sell-offs have indicated positive announcement effects on share prices. The early study by Boudreaux (1975) of 138 firms that made voluntary divestitures between 1965 and 1970 found positive effects, but he did not perform significance tests nor did he distinguish between sell-offs and spin-offs. Miles and Rosenfield (1983) analysed 55 voluntary spin-offs for the period 1963–80, Schipper and Smith (1983) examined 91 such cases for the period 1962–81 and Hite and Owers (1983) tested the effect on shareholder returns of 123 spin-offs for 1963–81. All three studies found significantly positive abnormal returns to shareholders. In examining the sources of these gains, it is interesting that both the Miles and Rosenfield and the Hite and Owers studies found that large spin-offs had a statistically significant greater positive impact on share prices. From the viewpoint of the improvement in efficiency of operation that demerger may bring, it is important to note the findings by both Schipper and Smith and Hite and Owers that there is little or no evidence to support the view that gains to shareholders arise because of transfer from bondholders. On the contrary, gains in shareholder wealth are found to be mainly attributable to the improvements in efficiency which derive from a reduction in the diversity of interests controlled by the parent company and from the increased ability provided by the new financial and operating structures for the two separate entities created on demerger to pursue their own investment opportunities.

The only recent study to date to focus solely on sell-offs is that by Alexander *et al.* (1984) which found slight positive announcement effects on shareholder returns. However, examination of the returns obtained in the period before divestment takes place reveals important differences between sell-offs and spin-offs. Sell-offs appear to be announced after a period of generally negative abnormal returns, whilst spin-offs are likely to be preceded by a period of generally positive abnormal returns. This finding seems to indicate that sell-offs are more likely to be associated with problems of failure whilst spin-offs are associated with problems of success. Overall, then, there seems to be a strong consensus in the empirical studies that demerging improves shareholder wealth. This increase in shareholder wealth appears to be derived from real efficiency gains resulting from the removal of control loss, rather than from changes in the opportunity set with which shareholders are presented.
[. . .]

References

Aaker, D. A. (1984) 'How to select a business strategy', *California Management Review*, **26**, Spring.
Alexander, G. J., Benson, P. G. and Kampmeyer, J. M. (1984) 'Investigating the valuation effects of announcement of voluntary corporate sell-offs', *Journal of Finance*, **39**(2), June.
Amey, L. R. (1979) *Budget Planning and Control Systems* (Boston: Pitman).
Boudreaux, K. J. (1975) 'Divestiture and share price', *Journal of Financial and Quantitative Analysis*, November.
Brown, S. J. and Warner, J. B. (1980) 'Measuring security price performance', *Journal of Financial Economics*, **8**.
Buckley, P. and Casson, M. (1976) *The Future of the Multinational Enterprise* (London: Macmillan).
Burgelman, R. A. (1984) 'Designs for corporate entrepreneurship in established firms', *California Management Review*, **26**(3), Spring.
Burns, M. R. (1977) 'The competitive effects of trust-busting: portfolio analysis', *Journal of Political Economy*, **85**.
Burns, M. R. (1983) 'An empirical analysis of stockholder injury under S.2 of The Sherman Act', *Journal of Industrial Economies*, **31**.
Casson, M. (1983) *The Growth of International Business* (London: George Allen & Unwin).
Caves, R. E. (1982) *Multinational Enterprise and Economic Analysis* (New York: McGraw-Hill).
Chiplin, B. (1982) 'Corporate strategy', Ch. 11 in J. Bates and J. Parkinson (eds) *Business Economics* (Oxford: Basil Blackwell) 3rd edn.
Chiplin, B. and Wright, M. (1980) 'Divestment and structural change in UK industry', *National Westminster Bank Review*, February.

Coyne, J. and Wright, M. (1982) 'Buy-outs in British industry', *Lloyds Bank Review*, October.

Dugger, W. M. (1983) 'The transactions cost analysis of Oliver E. Williamson: a new synthesis?', *Journal of Economic Issues*, **17**(1), no. 1, March.

Ellert, J. C. (1976) 'Mergers, antitrust law enforcement and shareholder returns', *Journal of Finance*, **31**.

Franco, L. G. (1976) *The European Multinationals* (London: Harper & Row).

Frank, R. H. (1984) 'Are workers paid their marginal products?', *American Economic Review*, **74**(4), September.

Galai, D. and Masulis, R. W. (1976) 'The option pricing model and the risk factor of stock', *Journal of Financial Economics*, **3**(1).

Garvin, D. A. (1983) 'Spin-offs and the new firm formation process', *California Management Review*, **25**, January.

Hakansson, N. H. (1982) 'Changes in the financial market: welfare and price effects', *Journal of Finance*, **28**(3), September.

Harrigan, K. R. (1980) *Strategies for Declining Business* (Lexington, Mass.: Lexington Books).

Hite, G. L. and Owers, J. E. (1983) 'Security price reactions, around corporate spin-offs announcement', *Journal of Financial Economics*, **12**, December.

Klein, B. (1983) 'Contracting costs and residual claims', *Journal of Law and Economics*, **26**(2).

Kudla, R. J. and McInish, R. S. (1981) 'The microeconomic consequences of an involuntary corporate spin-off', *Sloan Management Review*, **22**(2), Summer.

Lewis, T. R. (1983) 'Pre-emption, divestiture and forward contracting in a market dominated by a single firm', *American Economic Review*, **73**(5), December.

Marris, R. and Mueller, D. C. (1980) 'The corporation, competition and the invisible hand', *Journal of Economic Literature*, **18**.

Meeks, G. (1977) *Disappointing Marriage; A Study of the Gains from Merger* (University of Cambridge, Dept. of Applied Economics, Occasional paper, CUP).

Miles, J. A. and Rosenfield, J. D. (1983) 'The effect of voluntary spin-off announcements on shareholder wealth', *Journal of Finance*, **38**(5), December.

Miller, D. (1982) 'Evolution and revolution: a quantum view of structural change in organisation', *Journal of Management Studies*, **19**(2).

Mueller, D. C. (1972) 'A life-cycle theory of the firm', *Journal of Industrial Economics*, **20**.

O'Brien, D. P. (1978) 'Mergers – time to turn the tide', *Lloyds Bank Review*, October.

Panzar, J. C. and Willig, R. D. (1981) 'Economics of scope', *American Economic Review (Papers and Proceedings)*, May.

Porter, M. (1976) 'Please note location of nearest exit', *California Management Review*, **19**(2), Winter.

Rumelt, R. P. (1982) 'Diversification strategy and profitability', *Strategic Management Journal*, **3**.

Schipper, K. and Smith, A. (1983) 'Effects of recontracting on shareholder wealth: the case of voluntary spin-offs', *Journal of Financial Economics*, December.

Spence, M. A. (1977) 'Entry, capacity, investment and oligopolistic pricing', *Bell Journal of Economics*, **8**, Autumn.

Teece, D. J. (1984) 'Economic analysis and strategic management', *California Management Review*, **26**(3), Spring.

Utton, M. A. (1974) 'On measuring the effects of industrial mergers', *Scottish Journal of Political Economy*, February.

Utton, M. A. (1977) 'Large firm diversification in British manufacturing industry', *Economic Journal*, **87**.

Waterhouse, J. H. and Tiessen, P. (1978) 'A contingency framework for management accounting systems research', *Accounting, Organisations and Society*.

Williamson, O. E. (1975) *Markets and Hierarchies* (New York: Free Press).

Williamson, O. E. (1981) 'The modern corporation: origins, evolution and attributes', *Journal of Economic Literature*, **19**, December.

Wright, M. (1986) 'The make-buy decision and managing markets: the case of management buy-outs', *Journal of Management Studies*, **23**, July.

Wright, M. and Coyne, J. (1985) *Management Buy-Outs* (Beckenham: Croom Helm).

Wright, M., Rhodes, D. and Jarrett, M. (1983) 'Growth, survival and control in small manufacturing systems', *European Journal of Operational Research*, **9**.

CHAPTER 16

End-game Strategies for Declining Industries

KATHRYN RUDIE HARRIGAN and MICHAEL E. PORTER

Reprinted by permission of *Harvard Business Review*. Extracts from 'End-game Strategies for Declining Industries' by Kathryn Rudie Harrigan and Michael E. Porter, July/August 1983. Copyright © 1983 by the President and Fellows of Harvard College; all rights reserved.

Introduction

End game *n* **1:** the last stage (as the last three tricks) in playing a bridge hand **2:** the final phase of a board game; specifically the stage of a chess game following serious reduction of forces.[1]

As early as 1948, when researchers discovered the 'transistor effect', it was evident that vacuum tubes in television sets had become technologically obsolete. Within a few years, transistor manufacturers were predicting that by 1961 half the television sets then in use would employ transistors instead of vacuum tubes.

Since the 1950s, manufacturers of vacuum tubes have been engaged in the industry's end game. Like other end games, this one is played in an environment of declining product demand where conditions make it very unlikely that all the plant capacity and competitors put in place during the industry's heyday will ever be needed. In today's world of little or no economic growth and rapid technological change, more and more companies are being faced with the need to cope with an end game.

Because of its musical chair character, the end game can be brutal. Consider the bloodbath in US gasoline marketing today. Between 1973 and 1983, in response to high crude oil prices and conservation efforts by consumers, the output from petroleum refineries declined precipitately. Uncertainty concerning supply and demand for refined products has made predicting the speed and extent of decline difficult, and an industry consensus has never evolved. Moreover, the competitors in this end game are very diverse in their outlooks and in the tactics they use to cope with the erratic nature of decline.

As in the baby food industry's end game, where a ten-year price war raged until demand plateaued, gasoline marketers and refiners are fighting to hold market shares of a shrinking pie. As industry capacity is painfully rationalized and companies dig in for the lean years ahead in their end game, a long period of low profits is inevitable.

In the vacuum tube industry, however, the end game was starkly different. Commercialization of solid-state devices progressed more slowly than the transistor manufacturers forecast. The last television set containing vacuum tubes was produced in 1974, and a vast population of electronic products requiring replacement tubes guaranteed a sizable market of relatively price-insensitive demand for some years. In 1983, several plants still produce tubes. Where obsolescence was a certainty and the decline rate slow, the six leading vacuum tube manufacturers were able to shut down excess plant capacity while keeping supply in line with demand. Price wars never ruined the profitability of their end game, and the companies that managed well during the decline earned satisfactorily high returns, particularly for declining businesses.

To recoup the maximum return on their investments, managers of some declining businesses are turning with considerable success to strategies that they had used only when demand was growing. In the past, the accepted prescription for a business on the wane has been a 'harvest' strategy – eliminate investment, generate maximum cash flow, and eventually divest. The strategic portfolio models managers commonly use for planning yield this advice on declining industries: do not invest in low- or negative-growth markets; pull cash out instead.

Our study of declining industries suggests, however, that the nature of competition during a decline and the strategic alternatives available for coping with it are complex [. . .] The experiences of industries that have suffered an absolute decline in unit sales over a sustained period differ markedly. Some industries, like vacuum receiving tubes, age gracefully, and profitability for remaining competitors has been extremely high. Others, like rayon, decline amid bitter warfare, prolonged excess capacity, and heavy operating losses.

The stories of companies that have successfully coped with decline vary just as widely. Some companies, like GTE Sylvania, reaped high returns by making heavy investments in a declining industry that made their businesses better sources of cash later. By selling out before their competitors generally recognized the decline, and not harvesting, other companies, like Raytheon and Du Pont, avoided losses that competitors subsequently bore.

In this article we discuss the strategic problems that declining demand poses, where decline is a painful reality and not a function of the business cycle or other short-term discontinuities. Sometimes, of course, innovations, cost reductions, and shifts in other circumstances may reverse a decline.[2] Our focus here, however, is on industries in which available remedies have been exhausted and the strategic problem is coping with decline. When decline is beyond the control of incumbent companies, managers need to develop end-game strategies.

First, we sketch the structural conditions that determine if the environment of a declining industry is hospitable, particularly as these affect competition. Second, we discuss the generic end-game strategy alternatives available to companies in decline. We conclude with some principles for choosing an end-game strategy.

What determines the competition?

Shrinking industry sales make the decline phase volatile. The extent to which escalating competitive pressures erode profitability during decline, however, depends on how readily industry participants pull out and how fiercely the companies that remain try to contain their shrinking sales.

Conditions of demand

Demand in an industry declines for a number of reasons. Technological advances foster substitute products (electronic calculators for slide rules) often at lower cost or higher quality (synthetics for leather). Sometimes the customer group shrinks (baby foods) or buyers slide into trouble (railroads). Changes in life-style, buyers' needs, or tastes can also cause demand to decline (cigars and hatmaking equipment). Finally, the cost of inputs or complementary products may rise and shrink demand (recreational vehicles). The cause of decline helps determine how companies will perceive both future demand and the profitability of serving the diminished market.

Companies' expectations concerning demand will substantially affect the type of competitive environment that develops in an end game. The process by which demand in an industry declines and the characteristics of those market segments that remain also have a great influence on competition during the decline phase.

Uncertainty

Correct or not, competitors' perceptions of demand in a declining industry potently affect how they play out their end-game strategies. If managers in the industry believe that demand will revitalize or level off, they will probably try to hold onto their positions. [...] efforts to maintain position despite shrinking sales will probably lead to warfare. On the other hand, if [...] managers in different companies are all certain that industry demand will continue to decline, reduction of capacity is more likely to be orderly.

Companies may well differ in their perceptions of future demand, with those that foresee revitalization persevering. A company's perception of the likelihood of decline is influenced by its position in the industry and its difficulty in getting out. The stronger its stake or the higher its exit barriers, the more optimistic a company's forecast of demand is likely to be.

Rate and pattern of decline

Rapid and erratic decline greatly exacerbate the volatility of competition. How fast the industry collapses depends partly on the way in which companies withdraw capacity. In industrial businesses [...] where the product is very important to customers but where a substitute is available, demand can fall drastically if one or two major producers decide to retire and customers doubt the continued availability of the original product. Announcements of early departure can give great impetus to the decline. Because shrinking volume raises costs and often prices, the decline rate tends to accelerate as time passes.

Structure of remaining demand pockets

In a shrinking market, the nature of the demand pockets that remain plays a major role in determining the remaining competitors' profitability. [...]

If the remaining pocket has favorable structure, decline can be profitable for well-positioned competitors.
[...]

In general, if the buyers in the remaining demand pockets are price insensitive [...] or have little bargaining power, survivors can profit. Price insensitivity is important because shrinking sales imply that companies must raise prices to maintain profitability in the face of fixed overhead.

The profit potential of remaining demand pockets will also depend on whether companies that serve them have mobility barriers that protect them from attack by companies seeking to replace lost sales.

Exit barriers

Just as companies have to overcome barriers in entering a market, they meet exit barriers in leaving it. These barriers can be insurmountable even when a company is earning subnormal returns on its investment. The higher the exit barriers, the less hospitable the industry is during the industry's decline. A number of basic aspects of a business can become exit barriers.

Durable and specialized assets

If the assets, either fixed or working capital or both, are specialized to the

business, company, or location in which they are being used, their diminished liquidation value creates exit barriers. A company with specialized assets such as sole-leather tanneries must either sell them to someone who intends to use them in the same business, usually in the same location, or scrap them. Naturally, few buyers wish to use the assets of a declining business.
[...]
Particularly if it represents a large part of assets and normally turns over very slowly, specialized inventory may also be worth very little in these circumstances. The problem of specialized assets is more acute where a company must make an all-or-nothing exit decision (e.g., continuous process plants) versus a decision to reduce the number of sites or close down lines.

If the liquidation value of the assets is low, it is possible for a company to show a loss on the books but earn discounted cash flows that exceed the value that could be realized if management sold the business. When several companies perform this same analysis and choose to remain in a declining industry, excess capacity grows and profit margins are usually depressed.

By expanding their search for buyers, managers can lower exit barriers arising from specialized assets. Sometimes assets find a market overseas even though they have little value in the home country. But as the industry decline becomes increasingly clear, the value of specialized assets will usually diminish.
[...]

High costs of exit

Large fixed costs – labor settlements, contingent liabilities for land use, or costs of dismantling facilities – associated with leaving a business elevate exit barriers. Sometimes even after a company leaves, it will have to supply spare parts to past customers or resettle employees. A company may also have to break long-term contracts, which, if they can be abrogated at all, may involve severe cancellation penalties. In many cases, the company will have to pay the cost of having another company fulfil such contracts.

On the other hand, companies can sometimes avoid making fixed investments such as for pollution control equipment, alternative fuel systems, or maintenance expenditures by abandoning a business. These requirements promote getting out because they increase investment without raising profits, and improve prospects for decline.

Strategic considerations

A diversified company may decide to remain in a declining industry for c reasons even if the barriers just described are low. These reasons

Interrelatedness A business may be part of a strategy that involves a group of businesses, such as whiskey and other distilled liquors, and dropping it would diminish overall corporate strategy. Or a business may be central to a company's identity or image [...] and leaving could hurt the company's relationships with key distribution channels and customers or lower the company's purchasing clout. Moreover, depending on the company's ability to transfer assets to new markets, quitting the industry may make shared plants or other assets idle.

Access to financial markets Leaving an industry may reduce a company's financial credibility and lessen its attractiveness to acquisition candidates or buyers. If the divested business is large relative to the total, divestment may hurt earnings growth or in some way raise the cost of capital, even if the write-off is economically justified. The financial market is likely to ignore small operating losses over a period of years buried among other profitable businesses while it will react strongly to a single large loss. While a diversified company may be able to use the tax loss from a write-off to mitigate the negative cash flow impact of exit decisions, the write-off will typically still have an effect on financial markets. Recently the markets have looked favorably on companies who take their losses on businesses with little future, an encouraging sign.

Vertical integration When companies are vertically integrated, barriers to exit will depend on whether the cause of decline touches the entire chain or just one link. [...] In our study of end-game strategies, we found that most vertically integrated companies 'deintegrated' before facing the final go/no go decision.

Information gaps The more a business is related to others in the company, and especially when it shares assets or has a buyer-seller relationship, the more difficult it can be for management to get reliable information about its performance. For example, a failing coffee perco-lator unit may be part of a profit center with other small electrical housewares that sell well, and the company might not see the percolator unit's performance accurately and thus fail to consider abandoning the business.

Managerial resistance Although the exit barriers we've described are based on rational calculations, or the inability to make them because of failures in information, the difficulties of leaving a business extend well beyond the purely economic. Managers' emotional attachments and commitments to a business — coupled with pride in their accomplishments and fears about their own futures — create emotional exit barriers. In a single-business company, quitting the business costs managers their jobs and creates personal problems for them such as a blow to their pride, the stigma of having 'given up', severance of an identification that may have been longstanding, and a signal of failure that reduces job mobility.

It is difficult for managers of a sick division in a diversified company to propose divestment, so the burden of deciding when to quit usually falls on top management. But loyalty can be strong even at that level, particularly if the sick division is part of the historical core of the company or was started or acquired by the current CEO.
[...]

In some cases, even though unsatisfactory performance is chronic, managerial exit barriers can be so strong that divestments are not made until top management changes.[3] Divestments are probably the most unpalatable decisions managers have to make.[4]

Personal experience with abandoning businesses, however, can reduce managers' reluctance to get out of an industry. In an industry such as chemicals where technological failure and product substitution are common, in industries where product lives are historically short, or in high-technology companies where new businesses continually replace old ones, executives can become used to distancing themselves from emotional considerations and making sound divestment decisions.

Social barriers Because government concern for jobs is high and the price of divestiture may be concessions from other businesses in the company or other prohibitive terms, closing down a business can often be next to impossible, especially in foreign countries. Divestiture often means putting people out of work, and managers understandably feel concern for their employees. Workers who have produced vacuum tubes for 30 years may have little understanding of solid-state manufacturing techniques. Divestiture can also mean crippling a local economy. In the depressed Canadian pulp industry, closing down mills means closing down whole towns.[5]

Asset disposition The manner in which companies dispose of assets can strongly influence the profitability of a declining industry and create or

TABLE 16.1   Structural factors that influence the attractiveness of declining industry environments

Structural factors	Environmental attractiveness	
	Hospitable	Inhospitable
Conditions of demand		
Speed of decline	Very slow	Rapid or erratic
Certainty of decline	100% certain predictable patterns	Great uncertainty, erratic patterns
Pockets of enduring demand	Several or major ones	No niches
Product differentiation	Brand loyalty	Commodity-like products
Price stability	Stable, price premiums attainable	Very unstable, pricing below costs
Exit barriers		
Reinvestment requirements	None	High, often mandatory and involving capital assets
Excess capacity	Little	Substantial
Asset age	Mostly old assets	Sizable new assets and old ones not retired
Resale markets for assets	Easy to convert or sell	No markets available, substantial costs to retire
Shared facilities	Few free-standing plants	Substantial and inter-connected with important businesses
Vertical integration	Little	Substantial
'Single product' competitors	None	Several large companies
Rivalry determinants		
Customer industries	Fragmented, weak	Strong bargaining power
Customer switching costs	High	Minimal
Diseconomies of scale	None	Substantial penalty
Dissimilar strategic groups	Few	Several in same target markets

destroy exit barriers for competitors. If a company doesn't retir
plant but sells it to a group of entrepreneurs at a low price, the
capacity does not change but the competition does. The new er
make pricing decisions and take other actions that are rational for it but
cripple the competition. Thus if the owners of a plant don't retire assets
but sell out instead, the remaining competitors can suffer more than if the
original owners had stayed on.

Volatility of end game

Because of falling sales and excess capacity, competitors fighting in an
end game are likely to resort to fierce price warfare. Aggression is
especially likely if the industry has maverick competitors with diverse
goals and outlooks and high exit barriers, or if the market is very
inhospitable (see Table 16.1).

As an industry declines, it can become less important to suppliers
(which raises costs or diminishes service) while the power of distributors
increases. [...] On the other hand, if the industry is a key customer,
suppliers may attempt to help fight off decline.
[...]
Perhaps the worst kind of waning-industry environment occurs when
one or more weakened companies with significant corporate resources
are committed to stay in the business. Their weakness forces them to use
desperate actions, such as cutting prices, and their staying power forces
other companies to respond likewise.

Strategic alternatives for declining businesses

Discussions of strategy for shrinking industries usually focus on divestment or harvest strategies, but managers should consider two other
alternatives as well – leadership and niche. These four strategies for
decline vary greatly, not only in their goals but also in their implications
for investment, and managers can pursue them individually or, in some
cases, sequentially:

Leadership A company following the market-share leadership strategy
tries to reap above-average profitability by becoming one of the few
companies remaining in a declining industry. Once a company attains
this position, depending on the subsequent pattern of industry sales, it
usually switches to a holding position or controlled harvest strategy. The
underlying premise is that by achieving leadership the company can be
more profitable (taking the investment into account) because it can exert
more control over the process of decline and avoid destabilizing price

competition. Investing in a slow or diminishing market is risky because capital may be frozen and resistant to retrieval through profits or liquidation. Under this strategy, however, the company's dominant position in the industry should give it cost leadership or differentiation that allows recovery of assets even if it reinvests during the decline period.

Managers can achieve a leadership position via several tactical maneuvers:

- Ensure that other companies rapidly retire from the industry. [...]
- Reduce competitors' exit barriers. GTE Sylvania built market share by acquiring competitors' product lines at prices above the going rate. American Viscose purchased — and retired — competitors' capacity. (Taking this step ensures that others within the industry do not buy the capacity.) General Electric manufactured spare parts for competitors' products. Rohm & Haas took over competitors' long-term contracts in the acetylene industry. Proctor-Silex produced private-label goods for competitors so that they could stop their manufacturing operations.
- Develop and disclose credible market information. Reinforcing other managers' certainty about the inevitability of decline makes it less likely that competitors will overestimate the prospects for the industry and remain in it.
- Raise the stakes. Precipitating the need of other competitors to reinvest in new products or process improvements makes it more costly for them to stay in the business.

Niche   The objective of this focus strategy is to identify a segment of the declining industry that will either maintain stable demand or decay slowly, and that has structural characteristics allowing high returns. A company then moves pre-emptively to gain a strong position in this segment while disinvesting from other segments. [...] To reduce either competitors' exit barriers from the chosen segment or their uncertainty about the segment's profitability, management might decide to take some of the actions listed under the leadership strategy.

Harvest   In the harvest strategy, undergoing a controlled disinvestment, management seeks to get the most cash flow it can from the business. [...] To increase cash flow, management eliminates or severely curtails new investment, cuts maintenance of facilities, and reduces advertising and research while reaping the benefits of past goodwill. Other common harvest tactics include reducing the number of models produced; cutting the number of distribution channels; eliminating small customers; and eroding service in terms of delivery time (and thus reducing inventory), speed of repair, or sales assistance.

Companies following a harvest strategy often have difficulty maintaining suppliers' and customers' confidence, however, and thus some businesses cannot be fully harvested. Moreover, harvesting tests managers' skills as administrators because it creates problems in retaining and motivating employees. These considerations make harvest a risky option and far from the universal cure-all that it is sometimes purported to be.

Ultimately, managers following a harvest strategy will sell or liquidate the business.

Quick divestment   Executives employing this strategy assume that the company can recover more of its investment from the business by selling it in the early stages of the decline, as Raytheon did, than by harvesting and selling it later or by following one of the other courses of action. The earlier the business is sold, the greater is potential buyers' uncertainty about a future slide in demand and thus the more likely that management will find buyers either at home or in foreign countries for the assets.

In some situations it may be desirable to divest the business before decline or, as Du Pont did with its acetylene business, in the maturity phase. Once it is clear that the industry is waning, buyers for the assets will be in a strong bargaining position. On the other hand, a company that sells early runs the risk that its forecast will prove incorrect, as did RCA's judgement of the future of vacuum tubes.

Divesting quickly will force the company to confront its own exit barriers, such as its customer relationships and corporate interdependencies. Planning for an early departure can help managers mitigate the effect of these factors to some extent, however. For example, a company can arrange for remaining competitors to sell its products if it is necessary to continue to supply replacements, as Westinghouse Electric did for vacuum tubes.

Choosing a strategy for decline

With an understanding of the characteristics that shape competition in a declining industry and the different strategies they might use, managers can now ask themselves what their position should be:

1. Can the structure of the industry support a hospitable, potentially profitable, decline phase (see Table 16.1)?
2. What are the exit barriers that each significant competitor faces? Who will exit quickly and who will remain?

3. Do your company's strengths fit the remaining pockets of demand?
4. What are your competitors' strengths in these pockets? How can their exit barriers be overcome?

In selecting a strategy, managers need to match the remaining opportunities in the industry with their companies' positions. The strengths and weaknesses that helped and hindered a company during the industry's development are not necessarily those that will count during the end game, where success will depend on the requirements to serve the pockets of demand that persist and the competition for this demand.

Figure 16.1 displays, albeit crudely, the strategic options open to a company in decline. When, because of low uncertainty, low exit barriers, and so forth, the industry structure is likely to go through an orderly decline phase, strong companies can either seek leadership or defend a niche, depending on the value to them of remaining market segments. When a company has no outstanding strengths for the remaining segments, it should either harvest or divest early. The choice depends, of course, on the feasibility of harvesting and the opportunities for selling the business.

When high uncertainty, high exit barriers, or conditions leading to volatile end-game rivalry make the industry environment hostile, investing to achieve leadership is not likely to yield rewards. If the company

	Has competitive strengths for remaining demand pockets	Lacks competitive strengths for remaining demand pockets
Favorable industry structure for decline	Leadership or niche	Harvest or divest quickly
Unfavorable industry structure for decline	Niche or harvest	Divest quickly

FIGURE 16.1   Strategies for declining businesses

has strengths in the market segments that will persist, it can try either shrinking into a protected niche, or harvesting, or both. Otherwise, it is well advised to get out as quickly as its exit barriers permit. If it tries to hang on, other companies with high exit barriers and greater strengths will probably attack its position.

This simple framework must be supplemented by a third dimension of this problem – that is to say, a company's strategic need to remain in the business. For example, cash flow requirements may skew a decision toward harvest or early sale even though other factors point to leadership, as interrelationships with other units may suggest a more aggressive stance than otherwise. To determine the correct strategy a company should assess its strategic needs vis-à-vis the business and modify its end-game strategy accordingly.

Usually it is advantageous to make an early commitment to one end-game strategy or another. For instance, if a company lets competitors know from the outset that it is bent on a leadership position, it may not only encourage other companies to quit the business but also gain more time to establish its leadership. However, sometimes companies may want to bide their time by harvesting until indecisive competitors make up their minds. Until the situation is clear, a company may want to make preparations to invest should the leader go, and have plans to harvest or divest immediately should the leader stay. In any case, however, successful companies should *choose* an end-game strategy rather than let one be chosen for them.

The best course, naturally, is anticipation of the decline. If a company can forecast industry conditions, it may be able to improve its end-game position by taking steps during the maturity phase (sometimes such moves cost little in strategic position at the time):

● Minimize investments or other actions that will raise exit barriers unless clearly beneficial to overall corporate strategy.
● Increase the flexibility of assets so that they can accept different raw materials or produce related products.
● Place strategic emphasis on market segments that can be expected to endure when the industry is in a state of decline.
● Create customer-switching costs in these segments.

Avoiding checkmate

Finding your company's position in Figure 16.1 requires a great deal of subtle analysis that is often shortchanged in the face of severe operating problems during decline. Many managers overlook the need to make strategy in decline consistent with industry structure because decline is viewed as somehow different. Our study of declining industries revealed other factors common to profitable players:

They recognize decline   With hindsight, it is all too easy to admonish companies for being over-optimistic about the prospects for their declining industries' revitalization. Nevertheless, some executives, such as those of US oil refineries, fail to look objectively at the prospects of decline. Either their identification with an industry is too great or their perception of substitute products is too narrow. The presence of high exit barriers may also subtly affect how managers perceive their environment; because bad omens are so painful to recognize, people understandably look for good signs.

Our examination of many declining industries indicates that the companies that are most objective about managing the decline process are also participants in the substitute industry. They have a clearer perception concerning the prospects of the substitute product and the reality of decline.

They avoid wars of attrition   Warfare among competitors that have high exit barriers, such as the leather tanning companies, usually leads to disaster. Competitors are forced to respond vigorously to others' moves and cannot yield position without a big investment loss.

They do not harvest without definite strengths   Unless the industry's structure is very favorable during the decline phase, companies that try to harvest without definite strengths usually collapse. Once marketing or service deteriorates or a company raises its prices, customers quickly take their business elsewhere. In the process of harvesting, the resale value of the business may also dissipate. Because of the competitive and administrative risks of harvesting, managers need a clear justification to choose this strategy.

They view decline as a potential opportunity   Declining industries can sometimes be extraordinarily profitable for the well-positioned players, as GE and Raytheon have discovered in vacuum tubes. Companies that can view an industry's decline as an opportunity rather than just a problem, and make objective decisions, can reap handsome rewards.

Notes

1. *Webster's Third New International Dictionary* (Springfield, Mass.: Merriam, 1976). This term has also been used for an existentialist play by Samuel Beckett.
2. See Michael E. Porter, *Competitive Strategy* (New York: Free Press, 1980)

ch. 8. The book also contains a treatment of exit barriers and other industry and competitor characteristics discussed in this chapter.
3. See, for example, Stuart C. Gilmour, 'The Divestment Decision Process', DBA dissertation, Harvard Graduate School of Business Administration, 1973; and Kathryn Rudie Harrigan, *Strategies for Declining Businesses* (Lexington, Mass.: D. C. Heath, 1980).
4. See Michael E. Porter, *Interbrand Choice, Strategy and Bilateral Market Power* (Cambridge, Mass.: Harvard University Press).
5. See Nitin T. Mehta, 'Policy Formulation in a Declining Industry: The Case of the Canadian Dissolving Pulp Industry', DBA dissertation, Harvard Graduate School of Business Administration, 1978.

CHAPTER 17

From Competitive Advantage to Corporate Strategy

MICHAEL E. PORTER

Reprinted by permission of *Harvard Business Review*. Extracts from 'From Competitive Advantage to Corporate Strategy' by Michael E. Porter, May/June 1987. Copyright © 1987 by the President and Fellows of Harvard College; all rights reserved.

Introduction

Corporate strategy, the overall plan for a diversified company, is both the darling and the stepchild of contemporary management practice — the darling because CEOs have been obsessed with diversification since the early 1960s, the stepchild because almost no consensus exists about what corporate strategy is, much less about how a company should formulate it.

A diversified company has two levels of strategy: business unit (or competitive) strategy and corporate (or companywide) strategy. Competitive strategy concerns how to create competitive advantage in each of the businesses in which a company competes. Corporate strategy concerns two different questions: what businesses the corporation should be in and how the corporate office should manage the array of business units.

Corporate strategy is what makes the corporate whole add up to more than the sum of its business unit parts.

The track record of corporate strategies has been dismal. I studied the diversification records of 33 large, prestigious US companies over the 1950–1986 period and found that most of them had divested many more acquisitions than they had kept. The corporate strategies of most companies have dissipated instead of created shareholder value.

The need to rethink corporate strategy could hardly be more urgent. By taking over companies and breaking them up, corporate raiders thrive on failed corporate strategy. Fueled by junk bond financing and growing acceptability, raiders can expose any company to takeover, no matter how large or blue chip.

Recognizing past diversification mistakes, some companies have initiated large-scale restructuring programs. Others have done nothing at all. Whatever the response, the strategic questions persist. Those who have restructured must decide what to do next to avoid repeating the past; those who have done nothing must awake to their vulnerability. To survive, companies must understand what good corporate strategy is.

A sober picture

While there is disquiet about the success of corporate strategies, none of the available evidence satisfactorily indicates the success or failure of corporate strategy. Most studies have approached the question by measuring the stock market valuation of mergers, captured in the movement of the stock prices of acquiring companies immediately before and after mergers are announced.

These studies show that the market values mergers as neutral or slightly negative, hardly cause for serious concern.[1] Yet the short-term market reaction is a highly imperfect measure of the long-term success of diversification, and no self-respecting executive would judge a corporate strategy this way.

Studying the diversification programs of a company over a long period of time is a much more telling way to determine whether a corporate strategy has succeeded or failed. My study of 33 companies, many of which have reputations for good management, is a unique look at the track record of major corporations. [. . .] Each company entered an average of 80 new industries and 27 new fields. Just over 70% of the new entries were acquisitions, 22% were start-ups, and 8% were joint ventures. IBM, Exxon, Du Pont, and 3M, for example, focused on start-ups, while ALCO Standard, Beatrice, and Sara Lee diversified almost solely through acquisitions.

My data paint a sobering picture of the success ratio of these moves. I found that on average corporations divested more than half their acquisitions in new industries and more than 60% of their acquisitions in entirely new fields. Fourteen companies left more than 70% of all the acquisitions they had made in new fields. The track record in unrelated acquisitions is even worse – the average divestment rate is a startling 74%. Even a highly respected company like General Electric divested a very high percentage of its acquisitions, particularly those in new fields. [Some] companies achieved a remarkably low rate of divestment. Some bear witness to the success of well-thought-out corporate strategies. Others, however, enjoy a lower rate simply because they have not faced up to their problem units and divested them.

I calculated total shareholder returns (stock price appreciation plus dividends) over the period of the study for each company so that I could compare them with its divestment rate. While companies near the top of the list have above-average shareholder returns, returns are not a reliable measure of diversification success. Shareholder return often depends heavily on the inherent attractiveness of companies' base industries. Companies like CBS and General Mills had extremely profitable base businesses that subsidized poor diversification track records.

I would like to make one comment on the use of shareholder value to judge performance. Linking shareholder value quantitatively to diversification performance only works if you compare the shareholder value that is with the shareholder value that might have been without diversification. Because such a comparison is virtually impossible to make, my own measure of diversification success — the number of units retained by the company — seems to be as good an indicator as any of the contribution of diversification to corporate performance.

My data give a stark indication of the failure of corporate strategies.[2] Of the 33 companies, 6 had been taken over as my study was being completed. Only the lawyers, investment bankers, and original sellers have prospered in most of these acquisitions, not the shareholders.

Premises of corporate strategy

Any successful corporate strategy builds on a number of premises. These are facts of life about diversification. They cannot be altered, and when ignored, they explain in part why so many corporate strategies fail.

Competition occurs at the business unit level   Diversified companies do not compete; only their business units do. Unless a corporate strategy places primary attention on nurturing the success of each unit, the strategy will fail, no matter how elegantly constructed. Successful corporate strategy must grow out of and reinforce competitive strategy.

Diversification inevitably adds costs and constraints to business units   Obvious costs such as the corporate overhead allocated to a unit may not be as important or subtle as the hidden costs and constraints. A business unit must explain its decisions to top management, spend time complying with planning and other corporate systems, live with parent company guidelines and personnel policies, and forgo the opportunity to motivate employees with direct equity ownership. These costs and constraints can be reduced but not entirely eliminated.

Shareholders can readily diversify themselves   Shareholders can diversify their own portfolios of stocks by selecting those that best match their preferences and risk profiles.³ Shareholders can often diversify more cheaply than a corporation because they can buy shares at the market price and avoid hefty acquisition premiums.

These premises mean that corporate strategy cannot succeed unless it truly adds value – to business units by providing tangible benefits that offset the inherent costs of lost independence and to shareholders by diversifying in a way they could not replicate.

Passing the essential tests

To understand how to formulate corporate strategy, it is necessary to specify the conditions under which diversification will truly create shareholder value. These conditions can be summarized in three essential tests:

1. *The attractiveness test*   The industries chosen for diversification must be structurally attractive or capable of being made attractive.
2. *The cost-of-entry test*   The cost of entry must not capitalize all the future profits.
3. *The better-off test*   Either the new unit must gain competitive advantage from its link with the corporation or vice versa.

Of course, most companies will make certain that their proposed strategies pass some of these tests. But my study clearly shows that when companies ignored one or two of them, the strategic results were disastrous.

How attractive is the industry?

In the long run, the rate of return available from competing in an industry is a function of its underlying structure, which I have described in another HBR article.⁴ An attractive industry with a high average return on investment will be difficult to enter because entry barriers are high, suppliers and buyers have only modest bargaining power, substitute products or services are few, and the rivalry among competitors is stable. An unattractive industry like steel will have structural flaws, including a plethora of substitute materials, powerful and price-sensitive buyers, and excessive rivalry caused by high fixed costs and a large group of competitors, many of whom are state supported.

Diversification cannot create shareholder value unless new industries have favorable structures that support returns exceeding the cost of capital. If the industry doesn't have such returns, the company must be able to restructure the industry or gain a sustainable competitive advantage that leads to returns well above the industry average. An industry need not be attractive before diversification. In fact, a company might benefit from entering before the industry shows its full potential. The diversification can then transform the industry's structure.

In my research, I often found companies had suspended the attractiveness test because they had a vague belief that the industry 'fit' very closely with their own businesses. In the hope that the corporate 'comfort' they felt would lead to a happy outcome, the companies ignored fundamentally poor industry structures. Unless the close fit allows substantial competitive advantage, however, such comfort will turn into pain when diversification results in poor returns. Royal Dutch Shell and other leading oil companies have had this unhappy experience in a number of chemicals businesses, where poor industry structures overcame the benefits of vertical integration and skills in process technology.

Another common reason for ignoring the attractiveness test is a low entry cost. Sometimes the buyer has an inside track or the owner is anxious to sell. Even if the price is actually low, however, a one-shot gain will not offset a perpetually poor business. Almost always, the company finds it must reinvest in the newly acquired unit, if only to replace fixed assets and fund working capital.

Diversifying companies are also prone to use rapid growth or other simple indicators as a proxy for a target industry's attractiveness. Many that rushed into fast-growing industries (personal computers, video games, and robotics, for example) were burned because they mistook early growth for long-term profit potential. Industries are profitable not because they are sexy or high tech; they are profitable only if their structures are attractive.

What is the cost of entry?

Diversification cannot build shareholder value if the cost of entry into a new business eats up its expected returns. Strong market forces, however, are working to do just that. A company can enter new industries by acquisition or start-up. Acquisitions expose it to an increasingly efficient merger market. An acquirer beats the market if it pays a price not fully reflecting the prospects of the new unit. Yet multiple bidders are commonplace, information flows rapidly, and investment bankers and other intermediaries work aggressively to make the market as efficient as possible. In recent years, new financial instruments such as junk bonds have brought new buyers into the market and made even large companies vulnerable to takeover. Acquisition premiums are high and reflect the acquired company's future prospects – sometimes too well.

Philip Morris paid more than four times book value for Seven-Up Company, for example. Simple arithmetic meant that profits had to more than quadruple to sustain the preacquisition ROI. Since there proved to be little Philip Morris could add in marketing prowess to the sophisticated marketing wars in the soft-drink industry, the result was the unsatisfactory financial performance of Seven-Up and ultimately the decision to divest.

In a start-up, the company must overcome entry barriers. It is a real catch-22 situation, however, since attractive industries are attractive because their entry barriers are high. Bearing the full cost of the entry barriers might well dissipate any potential profits. Otherwise, other entrants to the industry would have already eroded its profitability.

In the excitement of finding an appealing new business, companies sometimes forget to apply the cost-of-entry test. The more attractive a new industry, the more expensive it is to get into.

Will the business be better off?

A corporation must bring some significant competitive advantage to the new unit, or the new unit must offer potential for significant advantage to the corporation. Sometimes, the benefits to the new unit accrue only once, near the time of entry, when the parent instigates a major overhaul of its strategy or installs a first-rate management team. Other diversification yields ongoing competitive advantage if the new unit can market its product, through the well-developed distribution system of its sister units, for instance. This is one of the important underpinnings of the merger of Baxter Travenol and American Hospital Supply.

When the benefit to the new unit comes only once, the parent company has no rationale for holding the new unit in its portfolio over the long term. Once the results of the one-time improvement are clear, the diversified company no longer adds value to offset the inevitable costs imposed on the unit. It is best to sell the unit and free up corporate resources.

The better-off test does not imply that diversifying corporate risk creates shareholder value in and of itself. Doing something for shareholders that they can do themselves is not a basis for corporate strategy. (Only in the case of a privately held company, in which the company's and the shareholder's risk are the same, is diversification to reduce risk valuable for its own sake.) Diversification of risk should only be a by-product of corporate strategy, not a prime motivator.

Executives ignore the better-off test most of all or deal with it through arm waving or trumped-up logic rather than hard strategic analysis. One reason is that they confuse company size with shareholder value. In the drive to run a bigger company, they lose sight of their real job. They may justify the suspension of the better-off test by pointing to the way they manage diversity. By cutting corporate staff to the bone and giving business units nearly complete autonomy, they believe they avoid the pitfalls. Such thinking misses the whole point of diversification, which is to create shareholder value rather than to avoid destroying it.

Concepts of corporate strategy

The three tests for successful diversification set the standards that any corporate strategy must meet; meeting them is so difficult that most diversification fails. Many companies lack a clear concept of corporate strategy to guide their diversification or pursue a concept that does not address the tests. Others fail because they implement a strategy poorly.

My study has helped me identify four concepts of corporate strategy that have been put into practice—portfolio management, restructuring, transferring skills, and sharing activities. While the concepts are not always mutually exclusive, each rests on a different mechanism by which the corporation creates shareholder value and each requires the diversified company to manage and organize itself in a different way. The first two require no connections among business units; the second two depend on them (see Table 17.1). While all four concepts of strategy have succeeded under the right circumstances, today some make more sense than others. Ignoring any of the concepts is perhaps the quickest road to failure.

Portfolio management

The concept of corporate strategy most in use is portfolio management, which is based primarily on diversification through acquisition. The corporation acquires sound, attractive companies with competent managers who agree to stay on. While acquired units do not have to be in the same industries as existing units, the best portfolio managers generally limit their range of businesses in some way, in part to limit the specific expertise needed by top management.

The acquired units are autonomous, and the teams that run them are compensated according to unit results. The corporation supplies capital and works with each to infuse it with professional management techniques. At the same time, top management provides objective and dispassionate review of business unit results. Portfolio managers categorize units by potential and regularly transfer resources from units that generate cash to those with high potential and cash needs.

In a portfolio strategy, the corporation seeks to create shareholder value in a number of ways. It uses its expertise and analytical resources to spot attractive acquisition candidates that the individual shareholder could not. The company provides capital on favorable terms that reflect corporatewide fund-raising ability. It introduces professional management skills and discipline. Finally, it provides high-quality review and coaching, unencumbered by conventional wisdom or emotional attachments to the business.

The logic of the portfolio management concept rests on a number of vital assumptions. If a company's diversification plan is to meet the attractiveness and cost-of-entry tests, it must find good but undervalued companies. Acquired companies must be truly undervalued because the parent does little for the new unit once it is acquired. To meet the better-off test, the benefits the corporation provides must yield a significant competitive advantage to acquired units. The style of operating through highly autonomous business units must both develop sound business strategies and motivate managers.

In most countries, the days when portfolio management was a valid concept of corporate strategy are past. In the face of increasingly well-developed capital markets, attractive companies with good managements show up on everyone's computer screen and attract top dollar in terms of acquisition premium. Simply contributing capital isn't contributing much. A sound strategy can easily be funded; small- to medium-size companies don't need a munificent parent.

Other benefits have also eroded. Large companies no longer corner the market for professional management skills; in fact, more and more observers believe managers cannot necessarily run anything in the absence of industry-specific knowledge and experience. Another supposed advantage of the portfolio management concept – dispassionate review – rests on similarly shaky ground since the added value of review alone is questionable in a portfolio of sound companies.

The benefit of giving business units complete autonomy is also questionable. Increasingly, a company's business units are interrelated, drawn together by new technology, broadening distribution channels, and changing regulations. Setting strategies of units independently may well undermine unit performance. The companies in my sample that have succeeded in diversification have recognized the value of interrelationships and understood that a strong sense of corporate identity is as important as slavish adherence to parochial business unit financial results.

But it is the sheer complexity of the management task that has ultimately defeated even the best portfolio managers. As the size of the company grows, portfolio managers need to find more and more deals just to maintain growth. Supervising dozens or even hundreds of disparate units and under chain-letter pressures to add more, management begins to make mistakes. At the same time, the inevitable costs of being part of a diversified company take their toll and unit performance

TABLE 17.1 Concepts of corporate strategy

	Portfolio management	Restructuring	Transferring skills	Sharing activities
Strategic prerequisites	Superior insight into identifying and acquiring undervalued companies	Superior insight into identifying restructuring opportunities	Proprietary skills in activities important to competitive advantage in target industries	Activities in existing units that can be shared with new business units to gain competitive advantage
	Willingness to sell off losers quickly or to opportunistically divest good performers when buyers are willing to pay large premiums	Willingness and capability to intervene to transform acquired units	Ability to accomplish the transfer of skills among units on an ongoing basis	Benefits of sharing that outweigh the costs
	Broad guidelines for and constraints on the types of units in the portfolio so that senior management can play the review role effectively	Broad similarities among the units in the portfolio	Acquisitions of beachhead positions in new industries as a base	Both start-ups and acquisitions as entry vehicles
	A private company or undeveloped capital markets	Willingness to cut losses by selling off units where restructuring proves unfeasible		Ability to overcome organizational resistance to business unit collaboration
	Ability to shift away from portfolio management as the capital markets get more efficient or the company gets unwieldy	Willingness to sell units when restructuring is complete, the results are clear, and market conditions are favorable		

Organizational prerequisites	Autonomous business units	Autonomous business units	Largely autonomous but collaborative business units	Strategic business units that are encouraged to share activities
	A very small, low-cost, corporate staff	A corporate organization with the talent and resources to oversee the turnarounds and strategic repositionings of acquired units	High-level corporate staff members who see their role as integrators	An active strategic planning role at group, sector, and corporate levels
	Incentives based largely on business unit results	Incentives based largely on acquired units' results	Cross-business-unit committees, task forces, and other forums for capturing and transferring skills	High-level corporate staff members who see their roles primarily as integrators
			Objectives of line managers that include skills transfer	Incentives based heavily on group and corporate results
			Incentives based in part on corporate results	
Common pitfalls	Pursuing portfolio management in countries with efficient capital marketing and a developed pool of professional management talent	Mistaking rapid growth or a 'hot' industry as sufficient evidence of a restructuring opportunity	Mistaking similarity or comfort with new businesses as sufficient basis for diversification	Sharing for its own sake rather than because it leads to competitive advantage
	Ignoring the fact that industry structure is not attractive	Lacking the resolve or resources to take on troubled situations and to intervene in management	Providing no practical ways for skills transfer to occur	Assuming sharing will occur naturally without senior management playing an active role
		Ignoring the fact that industry structure is not attractive	Ignoring the fact that industry structure is not attractive	Ignoring the fact that industry structure is not attractive
		Paying lip service to restructuring but actually practicing passive portfolio management		

slides while the whole company's ROI turns downward. Eventually, a new management team is installed that initiates wholesale divestments and pares down the company to its core businesses. The experiences of Gulf & Western, Consolidated Foods (now Sara Lee), and ITT are just a few comparatively recent examples. Reflecting these realities, the US capital markets today reward companies that follow the portfolio management model with a 'conglomerate discount'; they value the whole less than the sum of the parts.

In developing countries, where large companies are few, capital markets are undeveloped, and professional management is scarce, portfolio management still works. But it is no longer a valid model for corporate strategy in advanced economies. Nevertheless, the technique is in the limelight today in the UK, where it is supported so far by a newly energized stock market eager for excitement. But this enthusiasm will wane – as well it should. Portfolio management is no way to conduct corporate strategy.

Restructuring

Unlike its passive role as a portfolio manager, when it serves as banker and reviewer, a company that bases its strategy on restructuring becomes an active restructurer of business units. The new businesses are not necessarily related to existing units. All that is necessary is unrealized potential.

The restructuring strategy seeks out undeveloped, sick, or threatened organizations or industries on the threshold of significant change. The parent intervenes, frequently changing the unit management team, shifting strategy, or infusing the company with new technology. Then it may make follow-up acquisitions to build a critical mass and sell off unneeded or unconnected parts and thereby reduce the effective acquisition cost. The result is a strengthened company or a transformed industry. As a coda, the parent sells off the stronger unit once results are clear because the parent is no longer adding value and top management decides that its attention should be directed elsewhere.
[...]
When well implemented, the restructuring concept is sound, for it passes the three tests of successful diversification. The restructurer meets the cost-of-entry test through the types of company it acquires. It limits acquisition premiums by buying companies with problems and lackluster images or by buying into industries with as yet unforeseen potential. Intervention by the corporation clearly meets the better-off test. Provided that the target industries are structurally attractive, the restructuring model can create enormous shareholder value. Some restructuring

companies are Loew's, BTR, and General Cinema. Ironically, many of today's restructurers are profiting from yesterday's portfolio management strategies.

To work, the restructuring strategy requires a corporate management team with the insight to spot undervalued companies or positions in industries ripe for transformation. The same insight is necessary to actually turn the units around even though they are in new and unfamiliar businesses.

These requirements expose the restructurer to considerable risk and usually limit the time in which the company can succeed at the strategy. The most skillful proponents understand this problem, recognize their mistakes, and move decisively to dispose of them. The best companies realize they are not just acquiring companies but restructuring an industry. Unless they can integrate the acquisitions to create a whole new strategic position, they are just portfolio managers in disguise. Another important difficulty surfaces if so many other companies join the action that they deplete the pool of suitable candidates and bid their prices up.

Perhaps the greatest pitfall, however, is that companies find it very hard to dispose of business units once they are restructured and performing well. Human nature fights economic rationale. Size supplants shareholder value as the corporate goal. The company does not sell a unit even though the company no longer adds value to the unit. While the transformed units would be better off in another company that had related businesses, the restructuring company instead retains them. Gradually, it becomes a portfolio manager. The parent company's ROI declines as the need for reinvestment in the units and normal business risks eventually offset restructuring's one-shot gain. The perceived need to keep growing intensifies the pace of acquisition; errors result and standards fall. The restructuring company turns into a conglomerate with returns that only equal the average of all industries at best.

Transferring skills

The purpose of the first two concepts of corporate strategy is to create value through a company's relationship with each autonomous unit. The corporation's role is to be a selector, a banker, and an intervenor.

The last two concepts exploit the interrelationships between businesses. In articulating them, however, one comes face-to-face with the often ill-defined concept of synergy. If you believe the text of the countless corporate annual reports, just about anything is related to just about anything else! But imagined synergy is much more common than real synergy. GM's purchase of Hughes Aircraft simply because cars were going electronic and Hughes was an electronics concern demonstrates the folly of paper synergy. Such corporate relatedness is an ex post facto rationalization of a diversification undertaken for other reasons.

Even synergy that is clearly defined often fails to materialize. Instead of co-operating, business units often compete. A company that can define the synergies it is pursuing still faces significant organizational impediments in achieving them.

But the need to capture the benefits of relationships between businesses has never been more important. Technological and competitive developments already link many businesses and are creating new possibilities for competitive advantage. In such sectors as financial services, computing, office equipment, entertainment, and health care, interrelationships among previously distinct businesses are perhaps the central concern of strategy.

To understand the role of relatedness in corporate strategy, we must give new meaning to this often ill-defined idea. I have identified a good way to start — the value chain.[5] Every business unit is a collection of discrete activities ranging from sales to accounting that allow it to compete. I call them value activities. It is at this level, not in the company as a whole, that the unit achieves competitive advantage.

I group these activities in nine categories. *Primary* activities create the product or service, deliver and market it, and provide after-sale support. The categories of primary activities are inbound logistics, operations, outbound logistics, marketing and sales, and service. *Support* activities provide the input and infrastructure that allow the primary activities to take place. The categories are company infrastructure, human resource management, technology development, and procurement.

The value chain defines the two types of interrelationships that may create synergy. The first is a company's ability to transfer skills or expertise among similar value chains. The second is the ability to share activities. Two business units, for example, can share the same sales force or logistics network.

The value chain helps expose the last two (and most important) concepts of corporate strategy. The transfer of skills among business units in the diversified company is the basis for one concept. While each business unit has a separate value chain, knowledge about how to perform activities is transferred among the units. For example, a toiletries business unit, expert in the marketing of convenience products, transmits ideas on new positioning concepts, promotional techniques, and packaging possibilities to a newly acquired unit that sells cough syrup. Newly entered industries can benefit from the expertise of existing units and vice versa.

These opportunities arise when business units have similar buyers or channels, similar value activities like government relations or procurement, similarities in the broad configuration of the value chain (for example, managing a multisite service organization), or the same strategic concept (for example, low cost). Even though the units operate separately, such similarities allow the sharing of knowledge.

Of course, some similarities are common; one can imagine them at some level between almost any pair of businesses. Countless companies have fallen into the trap of diversifying too readily because of similarities; mere similarity is not enough.

Transferring skills leads to competitive advantage only if the similarities among businesses meet three conditions:

1. The activities involved in the businesses are similar enough that sharing expertise is meaningful. Broad similarities (marketing intensiveness, for example, or a common core process technology such as bending metal) are not a sufficient basis for diversification. The resulting ability to transfer skills is likely to have little impact on competitive advantage.
2. The transfer of skills involves activities important to competitive advantage. Transferring skills in peripheral activities such as government relations or real estate in consumer goods units may be beneficial but is not a basis for diversification.
3. The skills transferred represent a significant source of competitive advantage for the receiving unit. The expertise or skills to be transferred are both advanced and proprietary enough to be beyond the capabilities of competitors.

The transfer of skills is an active process that significantly changes the strategy or operations of the receiving unit. The prospect for change must be specific and identifiable. Almost guaranteeing that no shareholder value will be created, too many companies are satisfied with vague prospects or faint hopes that skills will transfer. The transfer of skills does not happen by accident or by osmosis. The company will have to reassign critical personnel, even on a permanent basis, and the participation and support of high-level management in skills transfer is essential. Many companies have been defeated at skills transfer because they have not provided their business units with any incentives to participate.

Transferring skills meets the tests of diversification if the company truly mobilizes proprietary expertise across units. This makes certain the company can offset the acquisition premium or lower the cost of overcoming entry barriers.

The industries the company chooses for diversification must pass the attractiveness test. Even a close fit that reflects opportunities to transfer skills may not overcome poor industry structure. Opportunities to transfer skills, however, may help the company transform the structures of newly entered industries and send them in favorable directions.

The transfer of skills can be one-time or ongoing. If the company exhausts opportunities to infuse new expertise into a unit after the initial post-acquisition period, the unit should ultimately be sold. The corporation is no longer creating shareholder value. Few companies have grasped this point, however, and many gradually suffer mediocre returns. Yet a company diversified into well-chosen businesses can transfer skills eventually in many directions. If corporate management conceives of its role in this way and creates appropriate organizational mechanisms to facilitate cross-unit interchange, the opportunities to share expertise will be meaningful.

By using both acquisitions and internal development, companies can build a transfer-of-skills strategy. The presence of a strong base of skills sometimes creates the possibility for internal entry instead of the acquisition of a going concern. Successful diversifiers that employ the concept of skills transfer may, however, often acquire a company in the target industry as a beachhead and then build on it with their internal expertise. By doing so, they can reduce some of the risks of internal entry and speed up the process. Two companies that have diversified using the transfer-of-skills concept are 3M and Pepsico.

Sharing activities

The fourth concept of corporate strategy is based on sharing activities in the value chains among business units. Procter & Gamble, for example, employs a common physical distribution system and sales force in both paper towels and disposable diapers. McKesson, a leading distribution company, will handle such diverse lines as pharmaceuticals and liquor through superwarehouses.

The ability to share activities is a potent basis for corporate strategy because sharing often enhances competitive advantage by lowering cost or raising differentiation. But not all sharing leads to competitive advantage, and companies can encounter deep organizational resistance to even beneficial sharing possibilities. These hard truths have led many companies to reject synergy prematurely and retreat to the false simplicity of portfolio management.

A cost–benefit analysis of prospective sharing opportunities can determine whether synergy is possible. Sharing can lower costs if it achieves economies of scale, boosts the efficiency of utilization, or helps a company move more rapidly down the learning curve. The costs of General Electric's advertising, sales, and after-sales service activities in major appliances are low because they are spread over a wide range of appliance products. Sharing can also enhance the potential for differentiation. A shared order-processing system, for instance, may allow new features and services that a buyer will value. Sharing can also reduce the cost of differentiation. A shared service network, for example, may make more advanced, remote servicing technology economically feasible. Often, sharing will allow an activity to be wholly reconfigured in ways that can dramatically raise competitive advantage.

Sharing must involve activities that are significant to competitive advantage, not just any activity. P&G's distribution system is such an instance in the diaper and paper towel business, where products are bulky and costly to ship. Conversely, diversification based on the opportunities to share only corporate overheads is rarely, if ever, appropriate.

Sharing activities inevitably involves costs that the benefits must outweigh. One cost is the greater co-ordination required to manage a shared activity. More important is the need to compromise the design or performance of an activity so that it can be shared. A salesperson handling the products of two business units, for example, must operate in a way that is usually not what either unit would choose were it independent. And if compromise greatly erodes the unit's effectiveness, then sharing may reduce rather than enhance competitive advantage.

Many companies have only superficially identified their potential for sharing. Companies also merge activities without consideration of whether they are sensitive to economies of scale. When they are not, the co-ordination costs kill the benefits. Companies compound such errors by not identifying costs of sharing in advance, when steps can be taken to minimize them. Costs of compromise can frequently be mitigated by redesigning the activity for sharing. The shared salesperson, for example, can be provided with a remote computer terminal to boost productivity and provide more customer information. Jamming business units together without such thinking exacerbates the costs of sharing.

Despite such pitfalls, opportunities to gain advantage from sharing activities have proliferated because of momentous developments in technology, deregulation, and competition. The infusion of electronics and information systems into many industries creates new opportunities to link businesses. The corporate strategy of sharing can involve both acquisition and internal development. Internal development is often possible because the corporation can bring to bear clear resources in launching a new unit. Start-ups are less difficult to integrate than acquisitions. Companies using the shared-activities concept can also make acquisitions as beachhead landings into a new industry and then integrate the units through sharing with other units. Prime examples of companies that have diversified via using shared activities include P&G,

Du Pont, and IBM. The fields into which each has diversified are a cluster of rightly related units.

[...]

Following the shared-activities model requires an organizational context in which business unit collaboration is encouraged and reinforced. Highly autonomous business units are inimical to such collaboration. The company must put into place a variety of what I call horizontal mechanisms — a strong sense of corporate identity, a clear corporate mission statement that emphasizes the importance of integrating business unit strategies, an incentive system that rewards more than just business unit results, cross-business-unit task forces, and other methods of integrating.

A corporate strategy based on shared activities clearly meets the better-off test because business units gain ongoing tangible advantages from others within the corporation. It also meets the cost-of-entry test by reducing the expense of surmounting the barriers to internal entry. Other bids for acquisitions that do not share opportunities will have lower reservation prices. Even widespread opportunities for sharing activities do not allow a company to suspend the attractiveness test, however. Many diversifiers have made the critical mistake of equating the close fit of a target industry with attractive diversification. Target industries must pass the strict requirement test of having an attractive structure as well as a close fit in opportunities if diversification is to ultimately succeed.

Choosing a corporate strategy

Each concept of corporate strategy allows the diversified company to create shareholder value in a different way. Companies can succeed with any of the concepts if they clearly define the corporation's role and objectives, have the skills necessary for meeting the concept's prerequisites, organize themselves to manage diversity in a way that fits the strategy, and find themselves in an appropriate capital market environment. The caveat is that portfolio management is only sensible in limited circumstances.

A company's choice of corporate strategy is partly a legacy of its past. If its business units are in unattractive industries, the company must start from scratch. If the company has few truly proprietary skills or activities it can share in related diversification, then its initial diversification must rely on other concepts. Yet corporate strategy should not be a once-and-for-all choice but a vision that can evolve. A company should choose its long-term preferred concept and then proceed pragmatically toward it from its initial starting point.

Both the strategic logic and the experience of the companies I studied over the last decade suggest that a company will create shareholder value through diversification to a greater and greater extent as its strategy moves from portfolio management toward sharing activities. Because they do not rely on superior insight or other questionable assumptions about the company's capabilities, sharing activities and transferring skills offer the best avenues for value creation.

Each concept of corporate strategy is not mutually exclusive of those that come before, a potent advantage of the third and fourth concepts. A company can employ a restructuring strategy at the same time it transfers skills or shares activities. A strategy based on shared activities becomes more powerful if business units can also exchange skills. [. . .] A company can often pursue the two strategies together and even incorporate some of the principles of restructuring with them. When it chooses industries in which to transfer skills or share activities, the company can also investigate the possibility of transforming the industry structure. When a company bases its strategy on interrelationships, it has a broader basis on which to create shareholder value than if it rests its entire strategy on transforming companies in unfamiliar industries.

My study supports the soundness of basing a corporate strategy on the transfer of skills or shared activities. The data on the sample companies' diversification programs illustrate some important characteristics of successful diversifiers. They have made a disproportionately low percentage of unrelated acquisitions, *unrelated* being defined as having no clear opportunity to transfer skills or share important activities. Even successful diversifiers such as 3M, IBM, and TRW have terrible records when they have strayed into unrelated acquisitions. Successful acquirers diversify into fields, each of which is related to many others. Procter & Gamble and IBM, for example, operate in 18 and 19 interrelated fields respectively and so enjoy numerous opportunities to transfer skills and share activities.

Companies with the best acquisition records tend to make heavier-than-average use of start-ups and joint ventures. Most companies shy away from modes of entry besides acquisition. My results cast doubt on the conventional wisdom regarding start-ups. While joint ventures are about as risky as acquisitions, start-ups are not. Moreover, successful companies often have very good records with start-up units, as 3M, P&G, Johnson & Johnson, IBM, and United Technologies illustrate. When a company has the internal strength to start up a unit, it can be safer and less costly to launch a company than to rely solely on an acquisition and then have to deal with the problem of integration. Japanese diversification histories support the soundness of start-up as an entry alternative.

My data also illustrate that none of the concepts of corporate strategy works when industry structure is poor or implementation is bad, no matter how related the industries are. Xerox acquired companies in related industries, but the businesses had poor structures and its skills were insufficient to provide enough competitive advantage to offset implementation problems.

An action program

To translate the principles of corporate strategy into successful diversification, a company must first take an objective look at its existing businesses and the value added by the corporation. Only through such an assessment can an understanding of good corporate strategy grow. That understanding should guide future diversification as well as the development of skills and activities with which to select further new businesses. The following action program provides a concrete approach to conducting such a review. A company can choose a corporate strategy by:

1. *Identifying the interrelationships among already existing business units*   A company should begin to develop a corporate strategy by identifying all the opportunities it has to share activities or transfer skills in its existing portfolio of business units. The company will not only find ways to enhance the competitive advantage of existing units but also come upon several possible diversification avenues. The lack of meaningful interrelationships in the portfolio is an equally important finding, suggesting the need to justify the value added by the corporation or, alternately, a fundamental restructuring.

2. *Selecting the core businesses that will be the foundation of the corporate strategy*   Successful diversification starts with an understanding of the core businesses that will serve as the basis for corporate strategy. Core businesses are those that are in an attractive industry, have the potential to achieve sustainable competitive advantage, have important interrelationships with other business units, and provide skills or activities that represent a base from which to diversify.

   The company must first make certain its core businesses are on sound footing by upgrading management, internationalizing strategy, or improving technology. My study shows that geographic extensions of existing units, whether by acquisition, joint venture, or start-up, had a substantially lower divestment rate than diversification.

   The company must then patiently dispose of the units that are not core businesses. Selling them will free resources that could be better deployed elsewhere. In some cases disposal implies immediate liquidation, while in others the company should dress up the units and wait for a propitious market or a particularly eager buyer.

3. *Creating horizontal organizational mechanisms to facilitate interrelation-ships among the core businesses and lay the groundwork for future related diversification*   Top management can facilitate interrelationships by emphasizing cross-unit collaboration, grouping units organizationally and modifying incentives, and taking steps to build a strong sense of corporate identity.

4. *Pursuing diversification opportunities that allow shared activities*   This concept of corporate strategy is the most compelling, provided a company's strategy passes all three tests. A company should inventory activities in existing business units that represent the strongest foundation for sharing, such as strong distribution channels or world-class technical facilities. These will in turn lead to potential new business areas. A company can use acquisitions as a beachhead or employ start-ups to exploit internal capabilities and minimize integrating problems.

5. *Pursuing diversification through the transfer of skills if opportunities for sharing activities are limited or exhausted*   Companies can pursue this strategy through acquisition, although they may be able to use start-ups if their existing units have important skills they can readily transfer.

    Such diversification is often riskier because of the tough conditions necessary for it to work. Given the uncertainties, a company should avoid diversifying on the basis of skills transfer alone. Rather it should also be viewed as a stepping-stone to subsequent diversification using shared activities. New industries should be chosen that will lead naturally to other businesses. The goal is to build a cluster of related and mutually reinforcing business units. The strategy's logic implies that the company should not set the rate of return standards for the initial foray into a new sector too high.

6. *Pursuing a strategy of restructuring if this fits the skills of management or no good opportunities exist for forging corporate interrelationships*   When a company uncovers undermanaged companies and can deploy adequate management talent and resources to the acquired units, then it can use a restructuring strategy. The more developed the capital markets and the more active the market for companies, the more restructuring will require a patient search for that special opportunity rather than a headlong race to acquire as many bad apples as possible. Restructuring can be a permanent strategy, as it is with Loew's, or a way to build a group of businesses that supports a shift to another corporate strategy.

7. *Paying dividends so that the shareholders can be the portfolio managers*
Paying dividends is better than destroying shareholder value through diversification based on shaky underpinnings. Tax considerations, which some companies cite to avoid dividends, are hardly legitimate reason to diversify if a company cannot demonstrate the capacity to do it profitably.

Creating a corporate theme

Defining a corporate theme is a good way to ensure that the corporation will create shareholder value. Having the right theme helps unite the efforts of business units and reinforces the ways they interrelate as well as guides the choice of new businesses to enter. NEC Corporation, with its 'C&C' theme, provides a good example. NEC integrates its computer, semiconductor, telecommunications, and consumer electronics businesses by merging computers and communication.

It is all too easy to create a shallow corporate theme. CBS wanted to be an 'entertainment company', for example, and built a group of businesses related to leisure time. It entered such industries as toys, crafts, musical instruments, sports teams, and hi-fi retailing. While this corporate theme sounded good, close listening revealed its hollow ring. None of these businesses had any significant opportunity to share activities or transfer skills among themselves or with CBS's traditional broadcasting and record businesses. They were all sold, often at significant losses, except for a few of CBS's publishing-related units. Saddled with the worst acquisition record in my study, CBS has eroded the shareholder value created through its strong performance in broadcasting and records.

Moving from competitive strategy to corporate strategy is the business equivalent of passing through the Bermuda Triangle. The failure of corporate strategy reflects the fact that most diversified companies have failed to think in terms of how they really add value. A corporate strategy that truly enhances the competitive advantage of each business unit is the best defense against the corporate raider. With a sharper focus on the tests of diversification and the explicit choice of a clear concept of corporate strategy, companies' diversification track records from now on can look a lot different.

Notes

1. The studies also show that sellers of companies capture a large fraction of the gains from merger. See Michael C. Jensen and Richard S. Ruback, 'The Market for Corporate Control: The Scientific Evidence', *Journal of Financial Economics*, April 1983, p. 5; and Michael C. Jensen, 'Takeovers: Folklore and Science', *HBR*, November–December 1984, p. 109.

2. Some recent evidence also supports the conclusion that acquired companies often suffer eroding performance after acquisition. See Frederick M. Scherer, 'Mergers, Sell-Offs and Managerial Behavior', in Lacy Glenn Thomas (ed.) *The Economics of Strategic Planning* (Lexington, Mass.: Lexington Books, 1986) p. 143; and David A. Ravenscraft and Frederick M. Scherer, 'Mergers and Managerial Performance', paper presented at the Conference on Takeovers and Contests for Corporate Control, Columbia Law School, 1985.

3. This observation has been made by a number of authors. See, for example, Malcolm S. Salter and Wolf A. Weinhold, *Diversification Through Acquisition* (New York: Free Press, 1979).

4. See Michael E. Porter, 'How Competitive Forces Shape Strategy', *HBR* March–April 1979, p. 86.

5. Michael E. Porter, *Competitive Advantage* (New York: Free Press, 1985).

CHAPTER 18

The Use of Corporate Planning Models: past, present and future

JAE K. SHIM and RANDY McGLADE

Introduction

Corporate planning models are of recent origin in comparison with the more standard tools of business managers and analysts. Since the 1960s, planning models have advanced from an obscure concept for large corporations to a credible tool for planning in a broad size-range of companies. The proliferation of planning models has been due largely to the increasing availability of computers over the last 20 years, which quickly enhanced the applications and practicality of modelling for all types of business. This report provides an overview of the concept, developments and future of corporate planning models.

Definition and history of modelling

Definition

The definition of a planning model varies somewhat with the scope of its application. For instance, financial planning models may have a very short planning-horizon and entail no more than a collection of accounting formulae for producing *pro forma* statements (Kingston, 1977). Corporate planning models are often considered a separate kind of model in which the quantitative and logical inter-relationships among a corporation's financial, marketing and production activities are simulated (Naylor, 1976). In this sense, the model has greater utility because any of the co-ordinated subroutines composing the comprehensive model may be isolated for narrower applications. Therefore, the definition of a corporate planning model in the present discussion includes any type of planning model (e.g. financial, accounting, production, etc.), since financial and physical modules can be combined to form larger routines (Power, 1975). Planning models can be categorized according to two approaches: simulation and optimization (Hammond, 1974; Power, 1975). Simulation models are attempts to represent mathematically the operations of the company or of the conditions in the external economic environment. By adjusting the values of controllable variables and assumed external conditions, the future implications of present decision-making can be estimated. Probabilistic simulation models incorporate probability estimates into the forecast sequence, while deterministic simulation models do not. Optimization models are intended to identify the best decision, given specific constraints. The typical framework for financial planning models is discussed in a later section.

History of models

Naylor (1983) places the rudiments of corporate modelling in the early 1960s with the large, cumbersome simulation models developed by major corporations, e.g. AT&T, Wells Fargo Bank, Dow Chemical, IBM and Sun Oil. Most of the models were written in one of the general programming languages (GPLs, e.g. FORTRAN) and were used for generating *pro forma* financial statements. The models typically required several man-years to develop and, in some cases, never provided benefits sufficient to outweigh the costs of development. Financial models were considered an untested concept, suitable only for those corporations large enough to absorb the costs and risks of development.

Important advancements in computer technology in the early 1970s provided the means for greater diversity and affordability in corporate modelling. Interactive computing facilities allowed for faster and more meaningful input/output sequences for modellers; trial-and-error adjustments of inputs and analyses were possible while on-line to the central computer or to an outside timesharing service. The advent of corporate simulation languages enabled analysts with little experience with GPLs to write modelling programs in an English-like programming language (e.g. EXPRESS, SIMPLAN and XSIM). By 1979, nearly every Fortune 1000 company was using a corporate simulation model.

As companies gained experience in developing basic, deterministic simulations, renewed effort was directed toward consolidating and integrating smaller models into the larger corporate models first attempted in the 1960s. Furthermore, certain companies were attempting the more difficult optimization models and were increasing predictive power by using econometric models to link their simulations with product markets and the external economy. Early successes with the simpler models led to a boom in modelling, but an increasing number of failures in more ambitious projects soon moderated the general enthusiasm. As the economy entered a recession and became more unstable (less predictable), the weaknesses in the rationale underlying many corporate models were revealed. Managers realized that the purpose of a model must be well-defined and that the end-users should be involved in its development. Although the bad experiences of the mid 1970s have jaded some executives against models to the present day, most veterans of the period have developed a realistic attitude toward the capabilities of models and are employing recent advancements in techniques to construct more serviceable models.

Current practices of modelling

Surveys of corporations

Several surveys of financial model-making in US and UK firms have been conducted over the last 15 years. The firms represented a broad cross-section of industries and services, with sales ranging from one million to over one billion dollars annually. The specific purposes of the surveys varied somewhat between researchers, but each was designed to estimate the general acceptance and development of corporate financial modelling. While different sample sizes and populations prevent pooling the results, it is instructive to discuss important issues and common findings.

The earliest survey results, reported by Gershefski (1969), revealed that 63 (20%) of 323 firms sampled in 1968 were working with corporate planning models. Naylor and Schauland (1976) found that 253 (73%) of 346 firms were using or developing corporate planning models in 1975. Recent surveys by McLean and Neale (1980) and by Klein (1982) indicated that 85% of companies surveyed (410 and 204, respectively) were using some type of financial model. The results indicate that corporate financial modelling has become a common tool in US business firms (Table 18.1).

Among the reasons cited by corporations for using planning models were (1) economic uncertainty, (2) shortages of resources, (3) diminishing increase in productivity, (4) international competition, (5) tight money and inflation, (6) political upheavals (affecting foreign operations), (7) environmental problems, and (8) new business opportunities (Naylor, 1976). There was general agreement that models enabled managers to run alternative analyses and to adjust decision variables, while reducing the time needed for report writing. The many possible applications of corporate planning models are listed in Table 18.2. Financial forecasting/planning and *pro forma* balance-sheet statements were the most common

TABLE 18.1   Results of surveys for the use of corporate planning models

Author	Sample size (response)	Companies using or developing models
Gershefski (1969)	323	63 (20%)
Naylor and Schauland (1976)	346	250 (72%)
McLean and Neale (1980)	410	245 (60%)
Brightman and Harris (1982)	237	126 (53%)
Klein (1982)	204	175 (86%)

TABLE 18.2   Applications of corporate planning models

Financial forecasting	Construction scheduling
Pro forma financial statements	Tax planning
Capital budgeting	Energy requirements
Market decision-making	Labour contract negotiation fees
Mergers and acquisition analysis	Foreign currency analysis
Lease *vs* purchase decisions	*Utilities*
Production scheduling	Load forecasting
New-venture evaluation	Rate cases
Manpower planning	Generation planning
Profit planning	
Sales forecasting	
Investment analysis	

applications at most companies. The models proved to be useful tools in 'what-if' analysis, sensitivity analysis, simulations, best/worst case scenarios, goal seeking, optimization and report preparation (Klein, 1982).

A consistent finding among the surveys was the involvement of top management in successful modelling efforts. Naylor, 1976, and Klein, 1982, found that in 50–90% of the companies using models, upper managers (e.g. President, Vice-President Finance, Controller, Treasurer, Executive Vice-President) participated in the definition and implementation of the model. The background of the participants in Klein's survey was predominantly in finance, followed by computer science and accounting. Grinyer and Wooller, 1975, found a predominance of operational researchers in their sample. The end-users of the models were usually strategic planning groups, the Treasurer's department, and the Controller's department.

The only detailed figures on actual developmental costs of modelling were supplied by Naylor, 1976. The average costs (labour, computer time, materials) in 1975 for developing a model in-house with no outside assistance was $82,752. The average costs to firms that received help from outside consultants was $29,225, with markedly shorter development schedules. Ironically, most executives believed that outside consultants were too expensive and avoided hiring them (Grinyer and Wooller, 1975; Brightman and Harris, 1982; Klein, 1982). Furthermore, Ang and Chua, 1980, reported survey results showing that two-thirds of the faulty, discontinued corporate models had been developed in-house, yet only three of 31 companies hired outside consultants on subsequent efforts.

Despite the growing diversity of modelling techniques available, the vast majority of corporate models encountered in the surveys were basic, deterministic simulations. Probabilistic considerations were seldom incorporated into the models by any but the largest corporations. As recently as 1983, Naylor, 1983, found that no firms were using optimization models as a planning tool. Evidently, the accuracy of optimization models, as well as their clarity to upper management, must improve before they receive significant use.

Attitudes and problems

The reluctance of many firms to experiment with corporate planning models derives chiefly from a fear of the unknown. Confusion over what models are and how they are used precludes serious investigation of their potential benefits. Sherwood, 1977, summarized the myths that discourage managers from considering models:

1. Models are complicated – On the contrary, most effective models are fairly simple structures, incorporating only the essential processes of the problem under investigation. The maths involved is often basic algebra and modeling languages reduce complex terminology.
2. The company is not large enough – Models do not consist solely of comprehensive simulations. Some of the most frequently utilized models center on a limited number of key relationships.
3. We do not own a computer – Models are being designed for use on inexpensive personal computers, and outside time-sharing services are available.
4. We do not have any modellers – Modern planning languages have so simplified the modeling process that even a novice quickly becomes competent. Outside consultants are also available for assistance.

Attitudes of initiates towards modelling have progressed from the rather deteriorated outlook of the mid-1970s to today's more optimistic viewpoint. The past trend probably explains the general negativity of earlier results reported by Higgins and Finn, 1976, in their literature review of top management attitudes in the UK toward modelling. In summarizing the activities making up the senior executive's role, the authors concluded that most of the manager's duties involved behavioural, interpersonal communication problems requiring his direct ministering. The majority view of managers emphasized that models could not capture the essential complexity of the organization and ignored the political/behavioural issues. In the few areas where a model could prove useful, the executive had insufficient time to learn how to apply it. At that time, the picture of an executive seated at a computer and engaged in problem analysis was unrealistic. The ultimate finding, however, was not a wholesale abandonment of corporate planning models among managers but the delegation of modelling analysis to lower managers. Thus, models seemed destined to become strictly a middle-management tool.

Contemporary with that study, Grinyer and Wooller's 1975 survey showed the importance of obtaining top management's support to assure success in any model-making project. However, top managers in over 50% of the companies sampled believed their models had improved forecasts; 31% were undecided. More encouraging results followed. Wagner, 1979, reported that upper management in his survey not only requested that models be built, but participated in their development. The finished products received a high average utility rating (1 to 5, 5 best) of 3.9. A similar evaluation in 1980 by top management at 410 US firms (annual sales exceeding $100 million) yielded a 4.95 rating (7 being best) for their computer-based planning models. None of the CEOs considered the models useless. Klein, 1982, found evidence of significant cost savings through modelling, with one Vice-President of Finance reporting a $600 000 savings through use of a financial planning model.

The growing acceptance of planning models has enabled managers and technicians to identify areas requiring improvement and to formulate criteria for success. Optimization models are one technique in need of refinement. Optimization models are inscrutable 'black boxes' to those managers who have had no part in the modelling effort (Power, 1975). Naturally, top management has little confidence in forecasts produced by a model they cannot understand. The need to monitor a suite of financial and non-financial variables precludes the construction of simple optimization models.

There were no serious limitations of modelling noted by respondents in Naylor's 1975 survey. The criticisms were directed at the inflexibility of some models, poor documentation by the model builder and excessive input data requirements. Aggarwal and Khera, 1980, identified several points of inflexibility in most models. Models usually simulate only one cause-and-effect relationship, whereas multiple effects are often present. Similarly, the intended results of a control action may be accompanied by

unintended results. In that instance the desirability of the two consequences must be compared on a common utility scale. When several
consequences of a decision are separated in time, a means for making
intertemporal comparisons is required, analogous to a discount rate in
capital budgeting. Such techniques are rarely available in practice.

The reasons for discontinuation of corporate planning models in 31 of
the largest US corporations were reported by Ang and Chua, 1980. The
majority of firms sampled were industries, followed by retailers, trans-
porters, utilities, banks, finance and insurance institutions. The 31 firms
having discontinued models were only 27% of the total sample of 113
corporations. Twenty-nine of the 31 models were designed for producing
pro forma financial statements, and were discontinued within three years
following construction. The various reasons for the rejections are listed in
Table 18.3; the common justifications were model deficiencies and human
problems in implementation. Three of the prevalent reasons (inflexibility,
lack of management support, excessive input data requirements) are
familiar shortcomings discussed earlier. The need for management's
support for successful model-making cannot be over-emphasized; their
role as champion of the effort is essential for company-wide acceptance
of the final product. It is interesting to note from Table 18.3 that
excessive development time and costs were not a basis for rejection.

**TABLE 18.3   Reasons for discontinuing
models (Ang and Chua, 1980)**

Lack of sufficient flexibility
Lack of adequate management support
Excessive amounts of input data required
Replaced by a better model
The need no longer existed
The model did not perform as expected
New management de-emphasized planning
Poor documentation
Lack of user interest
Excessive development costs
Excessive operating costs
Excessive development time required

A novel insight on success factors in modelling was provided by
Simon *et al.*, 1976. The authors asserted that the modeller must
understand that management's expressed need for a particular model may
be specious; the modeller must perceive from the manager's behaviour,
rather than from his verbal request, the type of model needed. If an
incorrect determination is made, the model may never be implemented.
Two of the five categories of uses for models outlined in the study were

legitimate and straightforward: Type I models are simulation/optimiza-tion techniques and Type II models condition data for easier utilization. When the modeller perceives that management's objectives are not consistent with those of Type I or II models, one of three alternative choices is implied:

Type III: merely subterfuge for establishing a data link, forcing one part of the organization to channel information to another;
Type IV: a means of supplying formal rationale for decisions reached in the past;
Type V: a means of establishing a manager's reputation – simply a remake of a previously successful model.

A table of management behaviour was provided by the authors as a guide for modellers in determining the type of model implied in the original request and in subsequent feedback.

State-of-the-art and recommended practices

The acceptance of corporate planning models has resulted in many firms establishing planning departments, responsible for development and implementation of planning models. The structure of the typical corpor-ate financial model is an integration of smaller modules used by each department or business unit for planning purposes. Figure 18.1 shows a flowchart of a comprehensive planning model driven by a series of

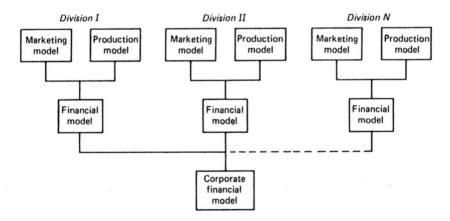

FIGURE 18.1   Typical structure of a corporate planning model (Naylor and Mansfield, 1977)

functional models which may be used either on a stand-alone basis at the business-unit level or consolidated and used by upper management (Naylor and Mansfield, 1977).

Optimal procedures for assembling effective models are still much at the discretion of the individual planning department, but useful guidelines have been published. Suggestions offered by Hammond (1974) serve as practical considerations in evaluating the timeliness of a proposed modelling project and in guiding the project. He suggested that the modelling effort could be divided into 10 stages of activities:

1. Determine which process(es) can be modelled effectively.
2. Decide whether to use a model.
3. Formalize the specifications of the model (e.g inputs/outputs, structure, etc.).
4. Prepare a proposal.
5. Conduct modelling and data gathering concurrently.
6. Debug the model.
7. Educate the prospective users.
8. Users validate the model.
9. Put model into use.
10. Update/modify the model as needed.

Hammond cautioned that several iterations between certain stages may be necessary and that several failures may be obtained before a valid model is obtained. He also provided a list of prerequisites for modelling and control factors for success (Table 18.4).

Kingston, 1977, defined the anatomy of the contemporary financial model as being composed of five parts: the documentation supporting the calculations, input assumptions regarding future periods, the projections and decision points leading to the forecasted values, managerial (financial) ratios, and graphics displaying information from decision points. The forecasting systems utilized depend upon the breadth and planning horizon of the model; typical methods include market research and Delphi method, time trends, moving averages, Box–Jenkins, and various causal methods, such as leading indicators, life-cycle analysis, regression, etc. (Naylor and Mansfield, 1977; Patterson and Walter, 1980).

Forecasting methods should be reviewed periodically by an independent party to ensure that the techniques have not become outdated. This can be determined only by maintaining a current management information system (MIS) which provides data to econometric models of the external environment. The critical importance of external data in determining company strategy is the central theorem of MIS. Thus, planners make assumptions about the business environment for a particular

TABLE 18.4   Success factors in modelling (Hammond, 1974)

Uncontrollable prerequisites
Operations understood, data plentiful
Relevant data accessible
Budgets, plans and control systems are well-defined, understood
Modellers have management's support
Management scientists accept responsibility for implementation
Similar innovative techniques used in the past
Manager and modeller share status and background

Controllable factors
Involve potential users in development process
Define model's goal explicitly
Input and output are in familiar formats
Company procedures modified little, at first
Look for common management problems to model
Start simple and keep it simple
Allow for ample judgemental inputs
Be realistic about planning time and expected results
Put a manager (not a modeller) in charge
Define roles clearly
Demonstrate part of model early on
Build model within users' organization
Develop expertise to manage and update model
Provide ample documentation

planning horizon, based upon the output from the MIS. The information is combined with internal data to prepare demand forecasts, and the results can be input to a planning model or used to check the validity of forecasts produced by current techniques (Patterson and Walter, 1980).

Planning and modelling languages (PMLs) have been a major incentive in involving higher management in modelling. General programming languages, such as FORTRAN, are seldom used in current models; oddly, COBOL, the 'business language', has never been used extensively in modelling. The advantages of PMLs are steadily edging out GPLs: models are built more easily, with shorter development and data-processing times, are more easily understood by upper management, and are periodically updated with enhancements from the vendor (Brightman and Harris, 1982). Today, over 70 PMLs are available at reasonable cost, including EMPRE, FINPLAN, VISICALC, BUDPLAN, MULTIPLAN and 1-2-3.

A further convenience offered to companies looking into modelling is pre-made planning packages sold by software vendors. The packages have often been criticized for their inflexibility, but the newer models allow for more user specificity. Analytical portfolio models are commercial packages that tell a conglomerate how to distribute resources across the portfolio of profit centres. Boston Consulting Group, Arthur D. Little and McKinsey have developed models that categorize investments into a matrix of profit potentials and recommended strategies, e.g. cash flow/ hold and collect (Naylor, 1983). A model for profit impact of market strategy (PIMS) is offered by the Strategic Planning Institute. The package is a large, multiple regression model used to identify the optimal strategy in a given business environment. Similar packages are likely to proliferate in the future as more companies are forced to use decision models to remain competitive.

MIS and personal computers

The analytic and predictive capabilities of corporate planning models depend in large part upon the supporting database. Information technology has advanced to the point that databases consist of logico-mathematical models and highly integrated collections of data, derived internally and external to the firm. The databases are now called management information systems (MIS) or decision support systems (DSS) because they store the data and decision tools utilized by management (Burch and Strater, 1974; Chacko, 1979).

A primary value of the MIS's large storage capacity for data is the potential to model more accurately the external economy and to forecast business trends. Managers are finding that effective long-range planning depends primarily upon a thorough understanding of their competitors and the forces at work in the market-place. A considerable body of data is required to develop insight into the competitive environment. Information derived from within the company has little strategic value for those purposes; thus the collection of external data should be emphasized (Young, 1981; Rucks and Ginter, 1982). As a result, the relevance of information to future conditions is the standard by which input of data to the MIS is controlled.

Once the strategic data have been stored in the mainframe computer system, managers need quick access to the database and a means for inputting alternative data sets/scenarios into the econometric models. Only recently have such activities been made possible by the development of communication links between mainframe systems and personal computers (PCs). Many of the applications of the mainframe–PC connection involve rather basic analyses, such as accounts payable, receivables, general ledger, etc. However, internal financial planning packages (e.g. EPS, IFPS and SIMPLAN) are currently available, as are external timeshare services, such as Dow Jones, Lockheed's Dialog and The Source (Ferris, 1983).

The outlook for the next few years indicates an increasing integration of the microcomputer with the mainframe. A recent survey of over 1000 organizations showed that 67% of middle management and 22% of top management of non-data-processing departments were using personal computers (Data Decisions, 1983). The results evidence significant momentum at the top of corporate management for the use of PCs. The future demand for sophisticated modelling capabilities on PCs should intensify the need for mainframe connections.

Corporate planning software packages for PCs are already proliferating. Applications now available range from cash flow analysis and budget projections to regressions, time series analysis and probabilistic analysis (Miller, 1983). Kennedy (1983) recently listed 116 software packages for financial/business analysis on the IBM, PC; many were suitable as corporate planning models. The trend in PC technology is aimed toward implementing as many mainframe, analytical capabilities onto the microcomputer as the market will support.

The future of corporate planning models

The interest in obtaining corporate models is likely to continue, and Naylor (1983) predicted some of the near-term trends. The concept of the 'strategic business unit' as an object of analysis may prove to be unviable. There has been no consistent definition of an SBU, and most models treat them as independent of one another; this may not be accurate. The SBU is typically forced into short-term profit making (rather than long-term development), eventually sapping its vitality. Consequently, an improved rationale may cause models to build around a different grouping of profit centres.

We can expect to see an increased linking of portfolio models with corporate simulation and optimization models (Naylor and Tapon, 1982). Modelling software will become more modular, in order to perform limited analyses or comprehensive projections. More software will be written for microcomputers, graphics will improve, and modelling languages will become more user-friendly. The future of modelling is somewhat assured because it is intimately linked with the continued expansion of the computer market. Though shakeouts may frequently occur among hardware manufacturers, planning models will always have a market as software writers improve their understanding of the planner's needs and produce more efficient decision-making tools.

Conclusion

The reputation of corporate planning models has improved significantly from the bad experiences of the early 1970s. As tight economic conditions and intensified competition required managers to formulate more effective strategies, the advantages of modelling became more apparent. The use of models is now less threatening to upper management, owing to the flexibility and simplicity of present techniques. As modelling success stories become more common, managers of all-sized firms can be expected more readily to lend their support to in-house modelling projects or to the purchase of ready-made systems.

References

Aggarwal, R. and Khera, I. (1980) 'Using Management Science Models: A Critique for Planners', *Managerial Planning*, **28**, pp. 12–15.

Ang, J. and Chua, J. (1980) 'Corporate Planning Models that Failed', *Managerial Planning*, **29**, pp. 34–8.

Brightman, H. J. and Harris, S. E. (1982) 'The Planning and Modeling Language Revolution: A Managerial Perspective', *Business*, **32**, pp. 15–21.

Burch, J. G. and Strater, F. R. Jr (1974) *Information Systems: Theory and Practice* (Santa Barbara, California: Hamilton).

Chacko, G. K. (1979) *Management Information Systems* (New York: Petrocelli).

Data Decisions (1983) 'Micros at Big Firms – a Survey', *Datamation*, **29**, pp. 160–75.

Ferris, D. (1983) 'The Micro-Mainframe Connection', *Datamation*, **29**, pp. 126–41.

Gershefski, G. W. (1969) 'Corporate Planning Models – the State of the Art', *Managerial Planning*, **18**, pp. 31–5.

Grinyer, P. H. and Wooller, J. (1975) 'Computer Models for Corporate Planning', *Long Range Planning*, **8**, pp. 14–25.

Hammond, J. S. (1974) 'Dos and Don'ts of Computer Models for Planning', *Harvard Business Review*, **52**, pp. 110–23.

Higgins, J. C. and Finn, R. (1976) 'Managerial Attitudes toward Computer Models for Planning and Control', *Long Range Planning*, **9**, pp. 107–12.

Kennedy, J. (1983) 'Financial Applications', *PC World – Annual Software Review*, pp. 324–40.

Kingston, P. L. (1977) 'Anatomy of a Financial Model', *Managerial Planning*, **26**, pp. 1–7.

Klein, R. (1982) 'Computer-based Financial Modeling', *Journal of Systems Management*, **33**, pp. 6–13.

McLean, E. R. and Neale, G. L. (1980) 'Computer-based Planning Models Come of Age', *Harvard Business Review*, **58**, pp. 46–54.

Miller, J. L. (1983) 'Business Management', *PC World – Annual Software Review*, pp. 368–80.

Naylor, T. H. (1976) 'Conceptual Framework for Corporate Modeling and the Results of a Survey of Current Practices', *Operational Research Quarterly*, **27**, pp. 671–82.

Naylor, T. H. (1983) 'Strategic Planning Models', *Managerial Planning*, **30**, pp. 3–11.

Naylor, T. H. and Mansfield, M. J. (1977) 'The Design of Computer-based Planning and Modelling Systems', *Long Range Planning*, **10**, pp. 16–25.

Naylor, T. H. and Schauland, H. (1976) 'A Survey of Users of Corporate Planning Models', *Management Science*, **22**, pp. 927–37.

Naylor, T. H. and Tapon, F. (1982) 'The Capital Asset Pricing Model: An Evaluation of its Potential as a Strategic Planning Tool', *Management Science*, **28**, pp. 1166–73.

Patterson, F. S. and Walter, J. D. (1980) 'Planning Models and Econometrics', *Managerial Planning*, **28**, pp. 11–15.

Power, P. D. (1975) 'Computers and Financial Planning', *Long Range Planning*, **8**, pp. 53–9.

Rucks, A. C. and Ginter, P. M. (1982) 'Strategic MIS: Promises Unfulfilled', *Journal of Systems Management*, **33**, pp. 16–19.

Sherwood, D. (1977) 'Business Computer Models – Dispelling the Myths', *Accountancy*, **88**, pp. 44–6.

Simon, L. S., Lamar, C. and Haines, G. H. Jr (1976) 'Managers' Use of Models', *Omega*, **4**, pp. 253–63.

Wagner, G. R. (1979) 'Enhancing Creativity in Strategic Planning through Computer Systems', *Managerial Planning*, **28**, pp. 10–17.

Young, R. C. D. (1981) 'A Strategic Overview of Business Information Systems', *Managerial Planning*, **29**, pp. 28–37.

CHAPTER 19

Business Ethics: two introductory questions

TOM SORELL

Introduction

It is a mistake to think that ethics is an irrelevance in business. If only because a good many ethical requirements have now been incorporated into legislation that is binding on commercial firms, morality routinely affects strategic decisions. It affects decisions about hiring and safety, advertising and debt provision, environmental protection and take-overs.

Questions in business ethics

In practice the ethical questions addressed in decision making tend to be concrete and specific. Would it be fair to make such and such a number of employees redundant given such and such an expected fall in profits? Not: how does a decline in profits ever justify a redundancy? Would it be right to store such and such a toxic chemical in a factory close to a residential area without telling anyone? Not: is it ever right for a business to withhold from people facts that could affect their safety? The more profound questions are nevertheless latent in the specific ones, and as soon as they are made explicit it is hard to ignore them. Business ethics is the field in which the more general questions are exposed and then answered with the help of systematic theories of right and wrong. These theories may be found in religion or in a personally developed code of conduct, but the richest source is moral philosophy.

Theories in moral philosophy

It is convenient to think of moral philosophy as, on the one hand, a body of thought, and, on the other, a method of analysis and argument. In the West the body of thought has a long history which is usually taken to have begun in ancient Greece more than 2000 years ago. Very elaborate theories of right and wrong were put forward by Plato and Aristotle well before the birth of Christ, and Aristotle's ethical doctrine is still very influential.[1] Other major theories derive from philosophers, a number of them British, who wrote during the eighteenth and nineteenth centuries. David Hume, a Scottish philosopher of the Enlightenment, expounded a theory of justice often embraced by those who are against meddling with market forces.[2] John Stuart Mill's moral philosophy has sometimes been thought to provide a justification for the welfare state. Mill's theory is a version of utilitarianism: it was developed in Victorian England.[3] Another enormously influential moral theory, antagonistic to both Hume's and Mill's, was formulated by the German philosopher Immanuel Kant in the eighteenth century.[4] Kant has many contemporary followers. One of the best known, the American political philosopher John Rawls, has recently adapted Kant's ideas to questions of distributive justice.[5] In the form in which they have been renewed by Rawls, Kant's views have important consequences for such matters as positive discrimination in the hiring of minorities and a system of taxation that favours the highest incomes.

Though the theories I have referred to were formulated as pieces of philosophy, their consequences have been absorbed well outside the subject. Relatively few people have read Mill's writings, but a great many are unwitting utilitarians, believing that what is morally right is what will add most to the general welfare. Not many people have read Hume, but a large number have opinions about the freedom to hold and exchange property that Hume's theory is able to justify. Many people feel strongly that there is something wrong with a society in which the poor tend mainly to be members of minorities, or in which income and jobs are concentrated in one group or in one place: Rawls' theory states principles that support and clarify these moral convictions. When concrete ethical questions are considered in the context of theories drawn from moral philosophy, it is not a case of ordinary ethical thought and real life confronting an utterly out-of-touch ivory tower − a good deal of ordinary ethical thought started out in the ivory tower and has been absorbed into the common culture, while the common culture cannot help but affect life in the ivory tower. So, although moral philosophy forms a body of thought distinguishable from ordinary thought, there is much mutual influence which blurs the differences.

Philosophical methods of analysis and argument

Moral philosophy is not just the collection of theories that have come down to us from the likes of Plato, Hume and Mill. It is also a method of analysis and argument. It is a method of analysis of very general concepts used in ethical argument, concepts such as that of a right or an obligation. It is a method for proposing principles that would justify specific moral beliefs, such as the belief that people living in the vicinity of the stored toxic chemical should know as much. Finally, it is a method for testing moral beliefs.

A moral belief that initially seems compelling, such as the belief that it is always wrong to kill, may seem less compelling when one thinks of cases of killing in self-defence or killing in a just war. One task of moral philosophy is to formulate cases that lead to the restriction or revision of principles. Sometimes this involves imagining very unusual situations that test a principle in an unexpected way. At other times it involves the discovery of analogies between situations or principles we feel morally sure about and cases that are puzzling. In business ethics it is very natural to think of a company or corporation on analogy with an individual, and to postulate corporate moral obligations similar to those an individual might be under. For example, it is plausible that each of us as an individual is under some sort of obligation not to harm others or put others in danger, and it is plausible that this obligation has to be met even if by putting others at risk one is able to obtain some benefit for oneself. If the analogy between the individual and the company is sound, then a company is under an obligation not to harm others or put others in danger, e.g. by storing a dangerous chemical. Now the question of whether the analogy is sound and the obligation of the company is genuine is a philosophical question. It could be argued that the analogy is unsound, because a company, unlike a private individual, exists solely or primarily for the purpose of trading profitably, and, this purpose being paramount, it cannot be overridden by the moral obligation. Or it could be argued that the analogy is indeed sound, and that in law the company quite commonly has the status of an individual person. These two sorts of argument illustrate the way in which the scope of moral obligation is investigated in philosophy. They are an indication of the method that operates in moral philosophy alongside the moral theories that various philosophers have proposed.

Two introductory questions

In the remainder of this article I shall illustrate the workings of business ethics by dealing at some length with two questions that could arise for practising managers. The first question asks whether it is ever morally justifiable to pay creditors late: the second concerns the permissibility of 'creative accounting'. Both questions have been chosen for their concreteness and familiarity as well as their interesting sidelines. The question of creative accounting has the further advantage of cutting across the divide between the private and public sectors, and between government and non-government bodies. As indicated at the beginning, the form in which the questions are posed will be general, and in the interest of giving the reader something definite to agree or disagree with, I shall indicate the sort of answer to each question that I find most defensible: I will not present the favoured sort of answer as the only possible one.

I How quickly should a firm pay its debts?

The question necessarily has two sides, for there is both a debtor and a creditor involved. I shall restrict attention to the case where both debtor and creditor are firms, where the creditor has already performed by supplying goods or services as demanded by the debtor, and where the debtor intends to pay, but would like for one reason or another to pay at the last possible moment. On these assumptions it seems to me to be difficult to maintain that delaying payment is all right morally. After all, the creditor has already performed, presumably conferring some benefit on the debtor, and, what is more, has usually done so on conditions about the timing of the payment known and agreed in advance.

The principle of payment at the agreed time

One reason for paying at the agreed time or during the agreed period is just that it has been agreed to: from the angle of most moral theories it is wrong to break one's agreements. Different moral theories may give different reasons *why* it is wrong. Thus utilitarianism would probably focus on the tendency of one broken agreement to foster further broken agreements and weaken trust to the disadvantage of everyone or most people. A latterday follower of Aristotle might call attention to the defect of character that the breaking of agreements expresses. A Kantian would press the question of whether it can be consistent with the intention of making an agreement that one is willing to break one when it is convenient to do so. But all three theories insist that it is wrong to break agreements. Now in general, if something seems to be the case from many different points of view, that is the reason for thinking it really is the case. The objectivity of a belief is its tendency to be confirmed however one looks at its content. So the fact that from many different points of view it seems right to keep one's agreements is good evidence that one ought to keep one's agreements, including one's agreement to pay debts at a pre-determined time.

Circumstances are nevertheless conceivable in which the straightforward principle of paying when one agrees to can be violated excusably. Suppose that due to an acquisition or a large short-term call on funds for redundancy payments a firm finds itself with a problem of liquidity at the time a payment is due; suppose further that the creditor firm, wishing to create good will and attract repeat orders, is willing to wait for its money without any penalty to the debtor; suppose finally that waiting creates no cash crisis for the creditor firm; and that given the extra time the debtor firm will pay up. In these circumstances, it seems, nothing wrong is done when the payment is made late. What excuses the debtor firm's failure to pay when it says it will? At least three things:

(i) the creditor is able to withstand the delay;
(ii) it is willing to withstand the delay; and
(iii) it makes (ii) known to the debtor firm.

Let us call a creditor that meets these conditions able and willing. Then to the uncompromising 'pay as agreed' principle we can add an escape clause that allows the payment of debt to be delayed if the creditor is able and willing.

The able and willing creditor

Though the restricted principle is more permissive than the categorical 'pay as agreed' principle, and though it fits in with the suspicion that the categorical principle can sometimes be broken excusably, the new principle is not *very* permissive. For example, it does not support a firm that considers the cash wealth of a creditor firm to be by itself a sufficient reason for postponing payment; the restricted principle requires that the cash wealthy firm be *willing* to have the payment postponed. On the other hand, the restricted principle certainly supports the debtor firm in *asking* the creditor firm to wait, given its cash wealth. Again, and more interestingly, the restricted principle does not allow debt payment to be delayed to a creditor firm that is willing to wait but is in fact unable to withstand the wait. The moral basis for prohibiting the delay in this case is easiest to grasp in the terms provided by by utilitarianism, which calculates the harms and benefits that result from different possible courses of action and always makes morally obligatory the action which produces the greatest benefit. What happens from a utilitarian perspective when a firm that is unable to wait expresses its willingness to wait for payment is that the harm that it already suffers by being kept without its money is compounded by its doing something that invites bankruptcy. A harm is aggravated. This is why a firm that offers to wait and is unable to should not be made to wait for its payment. Other things, too, are excluded by the principle on current assumptions. The debtor firm is not entitled to delay payment if it merely succeeds in convincing an able and willing creditor that it cannot pay. It must *really* be unable to pay.

There may be reasons to restrict further the principle about able and willing creditors. For what if the debtor company has an able and willing creditor, and yet finds itself in a liquidity problem because the directors have been paying themselves too much or because managers have committed themselves to a wage increase that the firm cannot afford? Perhaps in the face of these forms of mismanagement there is no justification for even an able and willing creditor to be patient.

In the face of the possibility of making the principle more restrictive someone may object that from a moral point of view it is already restrictive enough, indeed perhaps over-restrictive. For in its present form the principle prohibits delayed payments to cash-rich creditors who are unwilling to wait, and to this it might be objected that it is not right from a moral point of view for the cash-rich to be unwilling to wait; the ability to wait provides a reason for waiting.

In considering this objection we need to distinguish between what's morally right in the sense of being obligatory and what is morally right in the sense of being above and beyond the call of duty. Other things being equal the cash-rich firm does nothing immoral if it decides to be patient and wait. Other things being equal it behaves generously when it is patient. But to behave generously is to do more than morality requires. So other things being equal the cash-rich company that makes the generous gesture is doing something it is not morally obliged to do. In that sense, having the ability to wait does not provide a reason, or at least not a strong reason, for waiting. So other things being equal, it may not be morally required of even a cash-rich company that it wait for payment. And of course other things may *not* be equal. Agreeing to wait for payment may be reckless in view of the character of the debtor firm; or, without being reckless, it may break financial disciplines that shareholders would reasonably want to see upheld.

Isn't delayed payment one of the costs that a creditor company, if it is responsible, should make allowance for when it does business with a customer? If so, can't a debtor firm excuse the harm that delayed payment does by describing it as a contingency that the creditor firm should have insulated itself against? The answer seems to me to be 'No', even though it is morally right for one firm to treat another as fully responsible. For one thing, the principle behind the debtor's rationalization cuts both ways: if the creditor should have been prudent enough to make allowance for delayed payment, then by the same token the debtor should have made provision for the payment on time of the debt.

Summary The preceding discussion favours the principle of paying debts at the agreed time but implies that subject primarily to the willingness and ability of the creditor to wait, certain departures from the principle are morally permissible.

Multiple debts, relative urgency and morality

Though it does not seem to be morally right to withhold payment of a debt to a cash-rich firm that is unwilling to wait, it may nevertheless be morally better to dishonour this debt than to withhold or delay payment to a cash-poor company that is *unable* to wait. Paying the needier company first does not wipe out the wrong that one does to the rich company, but paying the rich company first does compound the wrong of disappointing the poor one. For the unpaid poor company not only has taken from it credit that it cannot afford to extend, its unpaid debts are much likelier to cause its collapse than the unpaid debts of the rich company.

Since debts are rarely owed one at a time, and since cash shortage often precludes paying all debts at once, firms with more debts than they can pay simultaneously often have to decide which are to get priority. Once things have reached this point, the firm can only avoid doing the morally wrong thing if its richer creditors are able and willing, and if there is enough left over when the debts of these firms are delayed to pay the other creditors. When these conditions are not met, a firm cannot normally avoid doing wrong; the most it can do is cut its losses and avoid doing a greater than necessary wrong, paying off first the firms who cannot survive otherwise.

It might be thought that this position is too exacting. For what about a firm that cannot afford to pay its debts because *it* is a disappointed and needy creditor? Surely *this* sort of firm cannot be expected always to try to honour its debts to the neediest of its creditors first – doing that could put *it* out of business. Surely for the neediest of companies it is too expensive to obey the principle. There is no denying that in order to stay in business a firm must sometimes pay debts first to the least or less needy of its creditors. This fact, however, is perfectly compatible with its being wrong to pay debts first to the less or least needy of its creditors. To see this, compare the case with a case of personal survival. It may be true in a given situation that to save himself from death or ruin a person has to do a particular action which, despite being necessary for his survival, is quite wrong. Consider the case where someone is accused of a murder and where conviction will lead to certain execution. The fact that the accused can avoid execution by incriminating an innocent man does not justify incriminating the innocent man, even if the accused person is also innocent. By parity of reasoning, a firm is not morally justified in causing another firm's bankruptcy to prevent its own. It is not justified in doing this even when it is a needy creditor itself and in danger of bankruptcy. Of course, not being justified morally is compatible with being justified in some other way. The point is that moral requirements do not lapse when the going gets tough.

To summarize the last few paragraphs – normally, the needier the creditor the more urgent the requirement to pay. A parallel principle, supported by the same considerations, is that normally the needier the creditor the better the reason for paying promptly.

[. . .]

II Creative accounting

A company is required by British law to present accounts that give a realistic picture of its financial position. Broadly similar requirements apply to non-commercial organizations in the public sector, whether governmental or non-governmental. Yet the Companies Acts of 1980 and 1981 seem to give firms a choice of accounting methods, and the alternatives available do not produce equivalent results. By giving latitude in this way the Companies Acts permit 'creative accounting'. Apparently similar scope is extended to such bodies as the finance departments of local governmental bodies, who are candid about using accounting to circumvent some of the central government controls on their spending.

In his recent book Ian Griffiths gives numerous examples of the use of creative accounting in private-sector as well as public-sector companies.[6] In the computer leasing industry, for example, the projected income from the sale of computers returned at the end of a lease period is sometimes included as income in the first year of the lease. At least one major retailing company has included the proceeds of sale of property in the profit and loss account when these might have been regarded as one-off transactions needing separate treatment in the accounts. Then there are the airlines that are creative in their estimates of fleet values. Griffiths gives the example of British Airways' nil-valuation of its Concorde fleet. In the public sector the latitude available in accounting has led to conclusive demonstrations both of the need and of the needlessness of price rises in the water industry. Other examples of creative accounting come from outside industry. Since 1986 certain local authorities have turned fixed assets into income in order to balance a current account. Earnings from the sale of everything from public buildings to parking meters have been invested, and the interest has been entered as income in the accounts. Meanwhile, the assets sold have been leased back, often on terms that postpone the initial payment – and the corresponding accounting entry – until a future date at which current governmental spending controls may be abolished or relaxed.

A simple judgement about all of these practices is that they are morally wrong because they deliberately misrepresent the facts, and therefore constitute a form of lying. This judgement has a good deal of initial plausibility, but perhaps it is too simple. For one thing, creative accounting is sometimes presented as precisely that: a number of local authorities that have tried to turn fixed assets into income openly admit that they are exploiting a loophole in the law and that their books reflect this. Given this public admission it is not absolutely clear that anyone reading the accounts is in danger of being misled by them, though this is clearly part of what makes lying wrong.

Another complication arises from considering what is involved in giving a full and fair picture of a firm's financial situation. On a reasonable interpretation of this requirement the accounts should provide a basis for investors to make an informed judgement about whether or not to keep a stake in the firm. It seems plausible to say that the accounts do not provide this basis unless they allow for the comparison of performances of firms in the same industrial sector. But to the extent that good accounts should allow comparison accounting practice is constrained to be consistent rather than non-creative.

Readers of a firm's accounts may be so intent on short-term profits or annually increasing profits that a report of a temporary downturn is enough to produce severe instability of share price: doesn't this sort of situation justify a sort of averaging of profits on the accounts so long as over the period being reported on the profit totals come out accurately? What is at issue is whether distortion in the accounts may sometimes be necessary to compensate for short-sightedness in readers of the accounts. There is a rough parallel between the position of the firm faced with a temporary downturn and the position of a doctor who knows that the patient's treatment will make him worse before he gets better but who has to get permission for the treatment from interested third parties who want a cure with no discomfort. It might be thought that it is in the patient's best interest for the doctor to stress the end result and pass lightly over the medium term. By analogy, it might be thought justified for the presentation of profit to disguise what is only a temporary downturn. The fact that some readers of the firm's accounts are more like the patient than third parties approving a course of treatment for a patient may not alter matters much, since it is arguable that if the treatment is absolutely the right one, even the patient should be given the positive presentation.

Rather different issues are at stake when the creative accounting consists of entering as income the indirect proceeds of sales of fixed assets in a local authority. For one thing, the object of the entry in the accounts may be to prevent the punitive withdrawal of rate support grant, and so the intended audience for the entry may be the giver of the grant, namely central government, rather than shareholders, as in the case of commercial accounts. Again, the reporting body is controlled by elected officials who have promised to implement a certain political programme: the programme may require spending that central government spending controls pre-empt. The reporting body is not a business; on the other hand, it is constrained to balance its budget and must satisfy the Audit Commission that it has 'made proper arrangements to secure economy, efficiency and effectiveness in its use of resources'. In the presence of very exacting financial controls it may not be possible for a local authority to comply with these obligations and at the same time keep its political promises. Yet the authority for the financial controls themselves may ultimately rest on an electoral mandate no stronger than that for the local programme that cannot be implemented. Against this background creative accounting may seem to be promoting the cause of local democracy. Where the local authority is short of money and the programme it is prevented from implementing relieves deprivation, creative accounting may look to the people who resort to it to be a means of protecting the poor as well.

The reasons there appear to be for resorting to creative accounting, however, derive from other reasons – reasons for spending money on housing, education, and so on – that are strong or not independently of creative accounting, and that justify spending or not independently of creative accounting. These, then, are the reasons that should be prominent in the local authority's statement of its spending plans. They should not be left implicit in its use of certain accounting or financing methods. If the reasons are strong ones the government will be morally wrong to ignore them and the Audit Commission will be morally wrong not to press independently for action in keeping with them.

Notes

1. For Plato's moral philosophy, see F. M. Cornford (trans.) *The Republic* (Oxford: University Press, 1941). For Aristotle, see the *Nicomachean Ethics*, trans. H. Tredennick (Harmondsworth: Penguin).
2. See Book Three of L. A. Selby-Bigge (ed.) *A Treatise on Human Nature* (Oxford: Clarendon Press, 1968).
3. For a good selection of Mill's works on moral philosophy, see *Mill's Ethical Writings*, J. B. Schneewind (ed.) (London: Macmillan, 1965).
4. See H. J. Paton (trans.) *The Moral Law* (London: Hutchinson University Library, 1948).
5. J. Rawls, *A Theory of Justice* (Cambridge, Mass.: Harvard University Press, 1972).
6. I. Griffiths, *Creative Accounting* (London: Waterstone, 1986).

CHAPTER 20

Strategy and Ethics: Pilkington PLC

TOM SORELL

Introduction

In the late 1950s the directors of the glass-makers Pilkington had to decide how to introduce to the world market an extremely advanced manufacturing process. The process – for making plate glass on a float line – had been developed at considerable risk and expense over most of the preceding 10 years. It enabled the firm, if it wished, to cut the costs of manufacturing high quality plate glass to such an extent that an unassailable advantage could be secured over competitors. Pilkington had the choice of keeping the process to itself or making it available under license to the rest of the glass industry in return for royalty income. It decided in favour of licensing, partly because it seemed morally the better thing to do. Lord Pilkington recalled later that during the deliberations of the Directors' Flat Glass Committee

> A great deal was said about ethics: that it was not our job to deliberately deny any existing glass competitor the opportunity of living in competition with us. I don't think we were short-sighted or rapacious. . . . There was a great deal of investment worldwide in plate, and people needed to have time to write off this plant or convert over. The alternative was chaotic disruption of a great industry.[1]

The directors of Pilkington felt a responsibility not to disrupt 'a great industry' and they considered the unilateral introduction of their own world-beating process to be disruptive.

More than 20 years after the decision to license was taken, Pilkington was criticized for failing to take full commercial advantage of the float process when it was new. An offer document distributed to Pilkington shareholders to support a BTR take-over attempt at the end of 1986 asked why Pilkington had chosen to license its flat glass technology 'for short-term gain at the cost of long-term ownership and the eventual creation of self-inflicted competition'. Pilkington replied to this question in defence documents, justifying the decision to license the float process on commercial grounds. Earnings from royalties had amounted to £400 million over 20 years, and had helped to finance the expansion of Pilkington's own plants and the acquisition of licensee companies. The ethical dimension of the decision about the float process was not revealed, but something was made of the 'social responsibility' of the firm's activities in general. Social responsibility, the Pilkington defence document said, was one of the elements that had contributed to the firm's past success.

A number of strategic decisions since the early 1960s attest to Pilkington's concern with social responsibility and ethics. How, if at all, has this sort of concern benefited the company commercially? As will emerge, it helped the company in its dealings in the 1960s with regulatory authorities, and, for a time, trade unions. It also came to Pilkington's aid in their successful defence against the BTR take-over bid. Whether its 'socially responsible' activities provide a model for other commercial firms, however, is more difficult to establish, for reasons I shall give toward the end of this paper.

I Pilkington's social responsibility in practice

Pilkington's concern with ethics has been easiest to see in its dealings with its employees and with its headquarters town of St Helens on Merseyside, but it has also been discernible in other areas. Product development is one. In 1967 its Triplex subsidiary began a decade's work on a laminated plate glass for automobile windshields specially designed to minimize laceration injuries in accidents. A high-strength, low-weight 10/20 glass was developed. 'The glass removed about 98% of the risk of lacerations or head injuries from automobile windshield accidents. When hit by an object, the glass broke into fine particles that . . . did not cut. Yet the plastic interlayer was strong enough to prevent a body going through the screen, and flexible enough to minimize brain damage.'[2] The drawback was its price, about 15% more than that of ordinary safety glass. Manufacturers were unwilling to install glass that would add significantly to the cost of automobiles in a market in which safety was not much of a selling point. Commercially the 10/20 glass was a failure, but its development was clearly in the public interest.

Competition and monopoly activity is another area in which Pilkington's concern with ethics has been visible. The directors' thoughts for other firms in the glass industry at the time of its decision to license the float process have already been mentioned. Another instance, this time arising from the dominance of Pilkington's Triplex subsidiary in the automotive safety glass market, was an agreement in the late 1960s with automobile manufacturers and the British Board of Trade. The agreement guaranteed that Pilkington would at all times (and presumably at the risk of operating plant at a loss) maintain capacity sufficient to meet all forecast demands of the main automobile manufacturers: the occasion for the agreement was the take-over by Triplex of its main competitor, BIG, and the closure of BIG's production plants.

Agreements like these, as well as public knowledge of the probity of the Pilkington family, probably justified the tribute paid to the firm after a Monopolies Commission investigation in 1968. The Commission declared that it was:

> satisfied that Pilkington is conscious of its responsibility, as a monopolist, to the public interest. This sense of responsibility may be associated to some extent with the long-established dominance of the Pilkington family within the business. There would, we think, have to be some quite unforeseen change . . . before Pilkington would deliberately set out to exploit its position of strength at the expense of the public interest.[3]

It is primarily as an employer, however, and as a philanthropic presence in the company town of St Helens, that Pilkington has demonstrated its understanding of social responsibility. The firm was a pioneer in the provision of pension funds and hospital services in British industry. Members of the Pilkington family built and endowed theatres and recreation clubs in St Helens. Retired employees received gifts of vegetable seed for their gardens and coal for heating their houses. An elaborate party for employees was mounted each year. By late 1986 specialist services funded by charities or trusts associated with the company included bereavement counselling, a victim support scheme, a transport service for old people wishing to spend a day out, a gardening and handyman scheme, and a meals on wheels service.

The Community of St Helens' Trust is perhaps the most famous of the firm's initiatives. It was formed after Pilkington began a programme of redundancies that reduced its workforce from 15 000 in 1970 to about 8000 in 1986. The purpose of the trust was to provide finance for small businesses and thereby create jobs to replace those lost in Pilkington's. By 1987 the Trust had helped to launch over 500 small firms and had created well over 6000 jobs. It is the prototype for the more than 300 local enterprise agencies that now operate in the UK. A number of the small companies that were formed by the Trust have become Pilkington suppliers or have become viable by specializing in high value-adding processes that would have been unsuitable in scale for Pilkington's own operations.

The firm has been active in industrial training in the north-west, and has directed investment in high technology into the relatively depressed regions of North Wales and Scotland. In the wider environment, Pilkington is a founder-member of Business in the Community, an association of large and medium-sized firms interested in activities that demonstrate social responsibility. It is also a founder-member of the Per Cent Club, a group of large UK firms who have pledged to make annual 'community contributions' amounting to at least half of one per cent of pre-tax profits. Finally, in at least one Third-World country, it has helped to create and fund a community school.

II The benefits

Have Pilkington's ventures in 'social responsibility' benefited the company? At first sight it seems that they have – by creating good will that Pilkington has been able to draw upon at difficult times, most recently during the period of the hostile take-over bid by BTR in the winter of 1986–7. In the company's Annual Report for 1987 the Chairman's Statement proposes the following interpretation of its success in fending off BTR:

> Our ability to demonstrate that it was possible to achieve world leadership in an industry, while maintaining that important balance between the interests of the shareholders, employees, and the wider community, was a powerful and convincing defence. Throughout the bid we were able to rely on the whole-hearted support of our employees. This support gathered momentum and widened to all of the communities in which we work, to the media, and to all three political parties. I cannot recall a similar bid where such universal support was generated by a target company.

After the BTR bid Rowntree became another much-supported target of bids by Nestlé and Suchard but, unlike Pilkington's defence, Rowntree's eventually failed, despite the fact that it had the instructive precedent of Pilkington's defence against BTR to draw upon.

Was the Chairman's Statement in the Pilkington Annual Report correct in its estimate of support for the company, and the role the support played in the defence against BTR? Statements quoted in the press during the period of the bid do not so much suggest whole-hearted support for Pilkington as whole-hearted anxiety about BTR. One local politician in St Helens, Mary Rimmer, acknowledging that Pilkington had made enemies in implementing its redundancy programme, was quoted on 11 November 1986 as saying to the *Financial Times*, 'I have not heard of one person supporting BTR, no one, I have spoken to people I know who you might expect to be anti-Pilkington and they are all against the take-over.' The *Financial Times* went on to give the reason: 'Pilks – as the company is known locally – is seen as the lesser of two evils, a practitioner of caring capitalism as opposed to potentially insensitive axemanship by decision-makers far away.' The *Financial Times* reported that one local politician, Brian Green, 'believes that Pilkington has used its reputation for industrial philanthropy as a shield when it wanted to shed jobs'.

Despite the mixed feelings, statements of strong support did come from employees, as the Annual Report said. On 7 January 1987 representatives of all 16 500 employees in the UK, as well as a few from Germany and Sweden, voted unanimous support for Pilkington at a public meeting. At about the same time, the General, Municipal and Boilermakers' Union, strongly represented in the Pilkington workforce, wrote to the trustees of its pension fund requesting opposition to the BTR bid. The *Financial Times* report of the meeting on 7 January said:

> It was soon apparent that what was happening was conditioned by Pilkington's management style and industrial relations policies. These centre on achieving co-operation, even for rationalization, which a stream of union speakers condemned per se while praising the humane approach the company had adopted.

At the same meeting on 7 January two Labour MPs and one Conservative spoke in support of Pilkington, and a message of support from the SDP leader, David Owen, was read out.

Party political support for Pilkington expressed itself not just in statements made at public meetings but in pressure from MPs urging the referral of the BTR bid to the Office of Fair Trading on public interest grounds. The issues at stake concerned the provision for research and development in Pilkington if BTR were to acquire it, the possibility of relocating the firm's headquarters away from the job-starved North West, and the possible loss of position in world markets.

III Morality with self-interest?

It seems clear that the unusually high level of support for Pilkington during the period of the BTR bid was due in part to the firm's history of good works. The good works, then, had significant benefits from the point of view of Pilkington management. Did these and other benefits – stable industrial relations, for example – justify the good works, or were they worth doing for their own sake? The question arises if one assumes that money spent on charities or trusts might otherwise have been distributed to shareholders as dividend payments, and if one assumes further that maximizing return is the overriding goal of any firm. According to this point of view, a firm should not divert into philanthropy money that would otherwise have been distributed as dividends – unless the philanthropy is commercially motivated and likely to contribute to better returns to investors itself. Were Pilkington's activities in keeping with this line of thought? And if they were, were the activities really philanthropic?

The first question concerns motivation. Did Pilkington set up charities and trusts because it would build up commercially valuable good will, or simply because it recognized a duty to its jobless former employees and the townspeople of St Helens? A statement that bears on this question was made by a retired Pilkington director involved with charities and trusts towards the beginning of the take-over episode. 'We don't like the "welfare state" tag that people have given us', the retired director said. 'We believe that doing what we do remains in our long-term self-interest.' This suggests that Pilkington's charitable activities were not purely altruistic, but a kind of prudent investment in the firm's future. A similar message seems to come through in a summary statement in the pamphlet, *The World of Glass*, issued to shareholders as part of Pilkington's defence against BTR. Under the heading 'What is different about Pilkington?' are highlighted four factors that contributed to the success of the business: 'a far-sighted approach'; 'a strategic approach'; 'co-operation with employees' and 'social responsibility'. And the 'social responsibility element' is justified in the summary by the statement that 'nothing can grow in a hostile environment'. Once again, activities that would otherwise have prompted talk of a welfare state or philanthropy are described as things necessary for the growth of the business, and therefore in its long-term interest.

A rather more subtle statement of what is involved in 'social responsibility' comes at the end of *The World of Glass*:

> We believe in the creation of wealth, not in the long-term poverty of short-term profit-taking. By wealth we mean the wealth of all those communities in which . . . we operate – shareholders, customers, suppliers and employees. If a company serves the needs of each of those communities and assists in the creation of their wealth then the environment in which it operates will be healthy and profits, and the wealth of shareholders, will follow.

This does not say that the creation of shareholder wealth is the ultimate goal or one to which all other forms of wealth-creation should bow; it says that it is one sort of wealth to be created among others, and that it is created most effectively when not pursued at the expense of other forms of wealth creation.

Though the firm's position, even as expressed on different pages of the same document, is not always perfectly consistent in emphasis and tone, it seems fair to conclude that for Pilkington social responsibility is not divorced from the goal of giving investors good returns, and is even seen as instrumental in giving good returns. But if that is so, and the company's commercial interests weigh heavily in its charitable contributions, is there really a moral aspect to its acts of social responsibility? It seems to be a requirement of acting morally that one be prepared to do good even where there is no advantage to oneself. If there are 'public relations' benefits to doing a good turn and the fact that there are makes all the difference to doing it, then there is a sense in which, arguably, the good turn lacks something required by morality. Good deeds done by stealth – that is, done with efforts to avoid publicity – are much more faithful to how moral acts ought to be done, according to this line of thought, than, say, ostentatious handings-over of big cheques on prime-time television.

Yet if moral or ethical acts must be done selflessly, can companies ever act ethically and act responsibly as commercial entities? Must there not be some self-interest in an act if it is to be the responsible act of a business, of an undertaking that exists to trade profitably? Different answers are possible. It might be argued that what makes an act moral is its helping those in need, and its being intended to help – whether or *not* it is also intended to benefit the helper in some way. With this view, any well-publicized donation to a deserving cause could count as a moral act, so long as it mattered to the donor that the deserving cause was helped. In particular, many of Pilkington's charitable activities would have had this status when they received publicity.

Another response, which again shows that there need not be a tension between corporate altruism and commercial responsibility starts from the claim that the overriding responsibility of a commercial firm like Pilkington is the maximization (let us add 'by all legal means') of returns to shareholders. Let us ask how this obligation stands when shareholders themselves have scruples about how the returns are made, or would respond sympathetically to the plight of redundant employees if it were put to them. The case need not be pure fiction. A number of large financial institutions offer portfolios to potential investors that are billed as 'ethical', and these institutions could well own blocks of stock whose sale at the disclosure of morally suspect practice could harm other shareholders. The holding of stock by these institutions can well make it prudent for companies not merely to get the biggest return allowed by the law, but the biggest return allowed by morals.

A third approach to the supposed tension between doing the moral thing and doing the financially responsible thing is to say that firms should not aim directly at, say, helping their local community, but should create wealth that allows the community to be helped through taxes or charity on the part of individuals. The idea is that firms should not consider themselves as moral agents but should leave that role to government or private individuals. A justification sometimes given for this approach is that it is likely to improve the economic position of the worst off more effectively than philanthropy. But this response turns out to be questionable. Even if it is true that the net economic gain to the worst off is higher when the better off aim at creating wealth for themselves, it does not follow that it is morally better to aim at creating wealth for oneself. The reason is that more things matter to well-being than an improvement in economic position. A sense of belonging to a community, or of living in a place in which helping the worse off comes naturally, can count for a great deal in measuring the quality of life, even the quality of life of the better off. These intangibles are not given sufficient weight by the position we are considering. Without denying that the creation of wealth matters a great deal to well-being, it is possible to hold that a too single-minded creation of wealth can also diminish well-being, e.g. by eroding feelings of community.

Two other problems with the approach under consideration can be mentioned. Although it is true that commercial firms pursue goals different from and narrower than those that private individuals can have, commercial firms must pursue their goals *through* the efforts of private individuals, whose working relationships inevitably have a personal aspect. If company policy calls for the single-minded creation of wealth and says that the welfare of redundant workers is a matter for the government and charities alone, then the good will that both manager and worker draw upon in a period of employment may have to be withdrawn when jobs are lost, withdrawn in a way that is unacceptable to both sides at a personal level.

Finally, though it may be true that the single-minded creation of wealth produces an economy in which more can be afforded in welfare payments or charitable donations to the worse off, it can also produce a climate in which those who need help are suspected of not doing enough to help themselves. In such a climate individuals or a government with the resources to help the worse off may feel justified in doing nothing. But if the facts about the worst off do not justify this feeling, then a kind of injustice is done to those who are least able to suffer it.

The upshot is not that commercial firms should aim to set up local welfare states, or invite applications for subsidy from all who might need it. The upshot is rather that in all of those areas in which good working relationships demand it, people who manage firms should be prepared to put well-being on a par with and even before maximum return to shareholders. Since working relationships do not involve the firm's management with the rest of humanity, but only with employees, suppliers, customers and regulatory authorities, it is not everyone's well-being that must be weighed. Nor is it necessarily the case that the well-being of those who have once been involved in working relationships should be given weight forever. The well-being of employees recently made compulsorily redundant may matter more than that of employees who were well-paid and worked until retirement age, for example. Finally, though working relationships may impose demands that interfere with the most efficient creation of wealth or the maximum return on investment, they do not impose demands that make the efficient creation of wealth unimportant or the maximization of return a merely secondary matter.

IV The right balance?

In the previous section it was suggested that Pilkington's good works did not lose their moral worth just because they were pursued partly out of self-interest. So long as the intention to help others is part of the reason for a firm's giving help, giving the help retains its moral aspect. It was also suggested that there is no tension between moral benevolence on the part of a firm and its commercial responsibilities. There is no tension if the benevolence is used to make and maintain good working relationships. Are Pilkington's good works a model of how benevolence and working relationships ought to be combined?

There is some evidence that, at times, working relationships in the firm have been *too* personal. A strike in 1970 sparked-off by the miscalculation of a man's wages caused management to feel hurt and shock,[4] reactions better suited to purely personal relationships than to working relationships. Again, it may be doubted that the elaborate range of services offered by the company-related trusts and charities to former employees in St Helens is really justified by the demands of present or former working relationships.

Since the withdrawal of the BTR bid for Pilkington at the beginning of 1987, the company has reduced the level of spending on activities associated with its so-called welfare state. Charitable donations, just over 0.4% of profits in 1983, rose slightly in 1986, but then declined sharply after the period of the BTR take-over bid. In an interview on the BBC current affairs programme *Panorama*, Mary Rimmer, the leader of St Helens local council, expressed no resentment at the falling-off in Pilkington's giving:

> The first time there's any dip in the economy, the private sector will be the first to stop investing in social welfare, and why shouldn't they? It isn't their responsibility – it's the government's responsibility. When that dip comes and when their investment stops in social fabric, then the people will look to the

local authority to pick up any shortfall that there may be and we will not have the money to do so.

Gordon Brown, the Labour MP and Opposition Treasury spokesman, said on the same programme that:

> the first responsibility of business in this country should be to train, to research, to do the work of innovation and to ensure a degree of personal comfort and living standards for the workforces over which they have responsibility.

He went on to deny that business had any role in running the welfare state or in making up for cuts in services offered by the welfare state. Without wishing to be seen urging a worse standard of living for workers employed by 'socially responsible' companies, Brown and Rimmer nevertheless insisted that there are limits to what can reasonably be expected of the private sector. These limits are probably exceeded – exceeded on the side of generosity – by Pilkington.

Perhaps the overstepping of the limits has been inevitable, given the intimate association of Pilkington the glass-makers with Pilkington the family. The proper limits of family philanthropy are not easy to determine, and there is no reason to think it must stop at humanely supporting working relationships, as in the case of company philanthropy. Yet for a long time Pilkington family philanthrophy and Pilkington company philanthropy tended to merge, and merge for a simple reason: from 1826 to 1970 the firm's stock was privately held by the members of the Pilkington family, and successive chairmen were descendants of the founder, William Pilkington. In 1970 10% of the stock was offered to the public. At about the same time the management structure of the company started to be decentralized and professionalized. Perhaps the definition of the firm's 'social responsibility' failed to keep up with the passage into public ownership. With a relatively new constitutency of shareholders – including some with ambitions to take over the company – future philanthropy may have to be geared more to the requirements of the business and the relationships needed to sustain the business than to the admirable generosity of the Pilkington family.

Notes

1. Quoted in the case study on Pilkington Brothers PLC in Quinn, J. B., Mintzberg, H. and James, R. M., *The Strategy Process: Concepts, Contexts and Cases* (Englewood Cliffs, New Jersey: Prentice-Hall International, 1988) p. 789.
2. Ibid, p. 791.
3. Ibid, p. 793.
4. Ibid, p. 793.

PART III

MANAGING STRATEGIC CHANGE

Introduction

Three interconnected themes in managing strategic change are developed in Part III: the selection of strategies for change; the links between strategy and structure; and strategic control processes.

Kotter and Schlesinger explore the reasons why people may resist change. They then develop a range of change strategies for dealing with anticipated resistance. They conclude with some suggestions for choosing the right strategy for a given situation.

The theme of Guth and MacMillan's chapter is overcoming resistance to change. They focus their attention on middle management motivation to implement strategy. They conclude that middle managers who believe that their self-interest is being compromised can not only redirect a strategy, delay its implementation or reduce the quality of its implementation, but also even totally sabotage the strategy. The ability to understand, anticipate and manage processes needed to secure positive commitment to strategy on the part of middle management is a critical general management implementation skill.

The first of the three articles on the relationships between strategy and structure is a lengthy chapter by Mintzberg. In this he distils the essential features of his important and influential contributions to our understanding of organization structure. Moving from the six basic parts of the organization and the basic co-ordinating mechanisms, he introduces the essential parameters of organization design: job specialization; behaviour formalization; training and indoctrination; unit grouping and unit size; planning and control systems; liaison devices and decentralization. Then the situational factors influencing the choice of these design parameters are explained: the age and size of the organization; its technical system, environment and power structure. He then pulls all these strands together to present six basic 'configurations', logically consistent groupings of design parameters, which together 'fit' the situational factors facing the organization. The six configurations are: the simple structure, the machine bureaucracy, the professional bureaucracy, the divisionalized form, the adhocracy and the missionary.

These configurations are used in turn by Miller, who suggests links between Porter's generic strategies and the Mintzberg configurations. He subdivides Porter's differentiation strategy into innovative differentiation, marketing differentiation and niche differentiation, and then draws together empirical and theoretical work which indicates matches between particular strategies and particular structures.

Greiner's chapter pre-dates Mintzberg's work, but it does suggest a developmental sequence of structural changes that an organization may go through as it pursues a growth strategy. The frequent crises which punctuate the evolutionary development of the structure, if not successfully negotiated, can lead to the stagnation or decline of the organization. Greiner's contribution emphasizes the important role the history of the organization plays in shaping present and future structures.

Alexander's research into the problem of implementing strategic change reveals a number of commonly occurring implementation problems, including unanticipated events, poor co-ordination and short-term crises distracting attention from the strategy. The clear message from his interviews with CEOs is that effective communication is at the heart of successful implementation. However, no amount of time and effort spent on implementation can rescue a strategy that is not well-formulated to begin with.

Asch presents an overview of the issues in strategic control, a vital component in the successful management of strategic change. Common strategic control problems are presented along with a consideration of 'barriers' to control stemming from the system itself, the behavioural characteristics of the management and the political acceptability of the changes proposed. Finally, he explains the crucial differences between strategic momentum control and strategic leap control, and the organizational implications of each process.

Daft and Macintosh researched management control systems in a number of organizations. They identified four common elements: budget, policies and procedures, performance appraisal system and statistical reports. Their findings and proposals enhance our understanding of the various ways in which control may be effectively utilized to aid the management of strategic change.

CHAPTER 21

Choosing Strategies for Change

JOHN P. KOTTER and LEONARD A. SCHLESINGER

Introduction

[...]

Few organizational change efforts tend to be complete failures, but few tend to be entirely successful either. Most efforts encounter problems; they often take longer than expected and desired, they sometimes kill morale, and they often cost a great deal in terms of managerial time or emotional upheaval. More than a few organizations have not even tried to initiate needed changes because the managers involved were afraid that they were simply incapable of successfully implementing them.

In this article, we first describe various causes for resistance to change and then outline a systematic way to select a strategy and set of specific approaches for implementing an organizational change effort. The methods described are based on our analyses of dozens of successful and unsuccessful organizational changes.

Diagnosing resistance

Organizational change efforts often run into some form of human resistance. Although experienced managers are generally all too aware of this fact, surprisingly few take time before an organizational change to assess systematically who might resist the change initiative and for what reasons. Instead, using past experiences as guidelines, managers all too often apply a simple set of beliefs – such as 'engineers will probably resist the change because they are independent and suspicious of top management'. This limited approach can create serious problems. Because of the many different ways in which individuals and groups can react to change, correct assessments are often not intuitively obvious and require careful thought.

Of course, all people who are affected by change experience some emotional turmoil. Even changes that appear to be 'positive' or 'rational' involve loss and uncertainty.[1] Nevertheless, for a number of different reasons, individuals or groups can react very differently to change — from passively resisting it, to aggressively trying to undermine it, to sincerely embracing it.

To predict what form their resistance might take, managers need to be aware of the four most common reasons people resist change. These include: a desire not to lose something of value, a misunderstanding of the change and its implications, a belief that the change does not make sense for the organization, and a low tolerance for change.

Parochial self-interest

One major reason people resist organizational change is that they think they will lose something of value as a result. In these cases, because people focus on their own best interests and not on those of the total organization, resistance often results in 'politics' or 'political behavior'.[2] [...]
Political behavior sometimes emerges before and during organizational change efforts when what is in the best interests of one individual or group is not in the best interests of the total organization or of other individuals and groups.

While political behavior sometimes takes the form of two or more armed camps publicly fighting things out, it usually is much more subtle. In many cases, it occurs completely under the surface of public dialogue. Although scheming and ruthless individuals sometimes initiate power struggles, more often than not those who do are people who view their potential loss from change as an unfair violation of their implicit, or psychological, contract with the organization.[3]

Misunderstanding and lack of trust

People also resist change when they do not understand its implications and perceive that it might cost them much more than they will gain. Such situations often occur when trust is lacking between the person initiating the change and the employees.[4]
[...]
Few organizations can be characterized as having a high level of trust between employees and managers; consequently, it is easy for misunderstandings to develop when change is introduced. Unless managers surface misunderstandings and clarify them rapidly, they can lead to resistance. And that resistance can easily catch change initiators by

surprise, especially if they assume that people only resist change when it is not in their best interest.

Different assessments

Another common reason people resist organizational change is that they assess the situation differently from their managers or those initiating the change and see more costs than benefits resulting from the change, not only for themselves but for their company as well.
[...]
Managers who initiate change often assume both that they have all the relevant information required to conduct an adequate organization analysis and that those who will be affected by the change have the same facts, when neither assumption is correct. In either case, the difference in information that groups work with often leads to differences in analyses, which in turn can lead to resistance. Moreover, if the analysis made by those not initiating the change is more accurate than that derived by the initiators, resistance is obviously 'good' for the organization. But this likelihood is not obvious to some managers who assume that resistance is always bad and therefore always fight it.[5]

Low tolerance for change

People also resist change because they fear they will not be able to develop the new skills and behavior that will be required of them. All human beings are limited in their ability to change, with some people much more limited than others.[6] Organizational change can inadvertently require people to change too much, too quickly.

Peter F. Drucker has argued that the major obstacle to organizational growth is managers' inability to change their attitudes and behavior as rapidly as their organizations require.[7] Even when managers intellectually understand the need for changes in the way they operate, they sometimes are emotionally unable to make the transition.

It is because of people's limited tolerance for change that individuals will sometimes resist a change even when they realize it is a good one. For example, a person who receives a significantly more important job as a result of an organizational change will probably be very happy. But it is just as possible for such a person to also feel uneasy and to resist giving up certain aspects of the current situation. A new and very different job will require new and different behavior, new and different relationships, as well as the loss of some satisfactory current activities and relationships. If the changes are significant and the individual's tolerance for change is low, he might begin actively to resist the change for reasons even he does not consciously understand.

People also sometimes resist organizational change to save face; to go along with the change would be, they think, an admission that some of their previous decisions or beliefs were wrong. Or they might resist because of peer group pressure or because of a supervisor's attitude. Indeed, there are probably an endless number of reasons why people resist change.[8]

Assessing which of the many possibilities might apply to those who will be affected by change is important because it can help a manager select an appropriate way to overcome resistance. Without an accurate diagnosis of possibilities of resistance, a manager can easily get bogged down during the change process with very costly problems.

Dealing with resistance

Many managers underestimate not only the variety of ways people can react to organizational change, but also the ways they can positively influence specific individuals and groups during a change. And, again because of past experiences, managers sometimes do not have an accurate understanding of the advantages and disadvantages of the methods with which they *are* familiar.

Education and communication

One of the most common ways to overcome resistance to change is to educate people about it beforehand. Communication of ideas helps people see the need for and the logic of a change. The education process can involve one-on-one discussions, presentations to groups, or memos and reports. For example:

● As a part of an effort to make changes in a division's structure and in measurement and reward systems, a division manager put together a one-hour audiovisual presentation that explained the changes and the reasons for them. Over a four-month period, he made this presentation no less than a dozen times to groups of 20 or 30 corporate and division managers.

An education and communication program can be ideal when resistance is based on inadequate or inaccurate information and analysis, especially if the initiators need the resistors' help in implementing the change. But some managers overlook the fact that a program of this sort requires a good relationship between initiators and resistors or that the latter may not believe what they hear. It also requires time and effort, particularly if a lot of people are involved.

Participation and involvement

If the initiators involve the potential resistors in some aspect of the design and implementation of the change, they can often forestall resistance. With a participative change effort, the initiators listen to the people the change involves and use their advice. To illustrate:

- The head of a small financial services company once created a task force to help design and implement changes in his company's reward system. The task force was composed of eight second- and third-level managers from different parts of the company. The president's specific charter to them was that they recommend changes in the company's benefit package. They were given six months and asked to file a brief progress report with the president once a month. After they had made their recommendations, which the president largely accepted, they were asked to help the company's personnel director implement them.

We have found that many managers have quite strong feelings about participation – sometimes positive and sometimes negative. That is, some managers feel that there should always be participation during change efforts, while others feel this is virtually always a mistake. Both attitudes can create problems for a manager, because neither is very realistic.

When change initiators believe they do not have all the information they need to design and implement a change, or when they need the whole-hearted commitment of others to do so, involving others makes very good sense. Considerable research has demonstrated that, in general, participation leads to commitment, not merely compliance.[9] In some instances, commitment is needed for the change to be a success. Nevertheless, the participation process does have its drawbacks. Not only can it lead to a poor solution if the process is not carefully managed, but also it can be enormously time consuming. When the change must be made immediately, it can take simply too long to involve others.

Facilitation and support

Another way that managers can deal with potential resistance to change is by being supportive. This process might include providing training in new skills, or giving employees time off after a demanding period, or simply listening and providing emotional support. For example:

- Management in one rapidly growing electronics company devised a way to help people adjust to frequent organizational changes. First, management staffed its human resource department with four counselors who spent most of their time talking to people who were feeling 'burnt out' or who were having difficulty adjusting to new jobs. Second, on a selective basis, management offered people four-week minisabbaticals that involved some reflective or educational activity away from work. And, finally, it spent a great deal of money on in-house education and training programs.

Facilitation and support are most helpful when fear and anxiety lie at the heart of resistance. Seasoned, tough managers often overlook or ignore this kind of resistance, as well as the efficacy of facilitative ways of dealing with it. The basic drawback of this approach is that it can be time consuming and expensive and still fail.[10] If time, money, and patience just are not available, then using supportive methods is not very practical.

Negotiation and agreement

Another way to deal with resistance is to offer incentives to active or potential resistors. For instance, management could give a union a higher wage rate in return for a work rule change; it could increase an individual's pension benefits in return for an early retirement. Here is an example of negotiated agreements:

● In a large manufacturing company, the divisions were very interdependent. One division manager wanted to make some major changes in his organization. Yet, because of the interdependence, he recognized that he would be forcing some inconvenience and change on other divisions as well. To prevent top managers in other divisions from undermining his efforts, the division manager negotiated a written agreement with each. The agreement specified the outcomes the other division managers would receive and when, as well as the kinds of co-operation that he would receive from them in return during the change process. Later, whenever the division managers complained about his changes or the change process itself, he could point to the negotiated agreements.

Negotiation is particularly appropriate when it is clear that someone is going to lose out as a result of a change and yet his or her power to resist is significant. Negotiated agreements can be a relatively easy way to avoid major resistance, though, like some other processes, they may become expensive. And once a manager makes it clear that he will negotiate to avoid major resistance, he opens himself up to the possibility of blackmail.[11]

Manipulation and co-optation

In some situations, managers also resort to covert attempts to influence others. Manipulation, in this context, normally involves the very selective use of information and the conscious structuring of events.

One common form of manipulation is co-optation. Co-opting an individual usually involves giving him or her a desirable role in the design or implementation of the change. Co-opting a group involves giving one of its leaders, or someone it respects, a key role in the design or implementation of a change. This is not a form of participation, however, because the initiators do not want the advice of the co-opted, merely his or her endorsement. For example:

- One division manager in a large multibusiness corporation invited the corporate human relations vice president, a close friend of the president, to help him and his key staff diagnose some problems the division was having. Because of his busy schedule, the corporate vice president was not able to do much of the actual information gathering or analysis himself, thus limiting his own influence on the diagnoses. But his presence at key meetings helped commit him to the diagnoses as well as the solutions the group designed. The commitment was subsequently very important because the president, at least initially, did not like some of the proposed changes. Nevertheless, after discussion with his human relations vice president, he did not try to block them.

Under certain circumstances co-optation can be a relatively inexpensive and easy way to gain an individual's or a group's support (cheaper, for example, than negotiation and quicker than participation). Nevertheless, it has its drawbacks. If people feel they are being tricked into not resisting, are not being treated equally, or are being lied to, they may respond very negatively. More than one manager has found that, by his effort to give some subordinate a sense of participation through co-optation, he created more resistance than if he had done nothing. In addition, co-optation can create a different kind of problem if those co-opted use their ability to influence the design and implementation of changes in ways that are not in the best interests of the organization.

Other forms of manipulation have drawbacks also, sometimes to an even greater degree. Most people are likely to greet what they perceive as covert treatment and/or lies with a negative response. Furthermore, if a manager develops a reputation as a manipulator, it can undermine his ability to use needed approaches such as education/communication and participation/involvement. At the extreme, it can even ruin his career.

Nevertheless, people do manipulate others successfully – particularly when all other tactics are not feasible or have failed.[12] Having no other alternative, and not enough time to educate, involve, or support people, and without the power or other resources to negotiate, coerce, or co-opt them, managers have resorted to manipulating information channels in order to scare people into thinking there is a crisis coming which they can avoid only by changing.

Explicit and implicit coercion

Finally, managers often deal with resistance coercively. Here they essentially force people to accept a change by explicitly or implicitly threatening them (with the loss of jobs, promotion possibilities, and so forth) or by actually firing or transferring them. As with manipulation, using coercion is a risky process because inevitably people strongly resent forced change. But in situations where speed is essential and where the changes will not be popular, regardless of how they are introduced, coercion may be the manager's only option.

Successful organizational change efforts are always characterized by the skillful application of a number of these approaches, often in very different combinations. However, successful efforts share two characteristics: managers employ the approaches with a sensitivity to their strengths and limitations (see Table 21.1) and appraise the situation realistically.

The most common mistake managers make is to use only one approach or a limited set of them *regardless of the situation*. A surprisingly large number of managers have this problem. This would include the hard-boiled boss who often coerces people, the people-oriented manager who constantly tries to involve and support his people, the cynical boss who always manipulates and co-opts others, the intellectual manager who relies heavily on education and communication, and the lawyerlike manager who usually tries to negotiate.[13]

A second common mistake that managers make is to approach change in a disjointed and incremental way that is not a part of a clearly considered strategy.

Choice of strategy

In approaching an organizational change situation, managers explicitly or implicitly make strategic choices regarding the speed of the effort, the amount of preplanning, the involvement of others, and the relative emphasis they will give to different approaches. Successful change efforts seem to be those where these choices both are internally consistent and fit some key situational variables.

TABLE 21.1 Methods for dealing with resistance to change

Approach	Commonly used in situations	Advantages	Drawbacks
Education + communication	Where there is a lack of information or inaccurate information and analysis	Once persuaded, people will often help with the implementation of the change	Can be very time-consuming if lots of people are involved
Participation + involvement	Where the initiators do not have all the information they need to design the change, and where others have considerable power to resist	People who participate will be committed to implementing change, and any relevant information they have will be integrated into the change plan	Can be very time-consuming if participators design an inappropriate change
Facilitation + support	Where people are resisting because of adjustment problems	No other approach works as well with adjustment problems	Can be time-consuming, expensive, and still fail
Negotiation + agreement	Where someone or some group will clearly lose out in a change, and where that group has considerable power to resist	Sometimes it is a relatively easy way to avoid major resistance	Can be too expensive in many cases if it alerts others to negotiate for compliance
Manipulation + co-optation	Where other tactics will not work, or are too expensive	It can be a relatively quick and inexpensive solution to resistance problems	Can lead to future problems if people feel manipulated
Explicit + implicit coercion	Where speed is essential, and the change initiators possess considerable power	It is speedy, and can overcome any kind of resistance	Can be risky if it leaves people mad at the initiators

TABLE 21.2   Strategic continuum

← ─── →

Fast	*Slower*
Clearly planned	Not clearly planned at the beginning
Little involvement of others	Lots of involvement of others
Attempt to overcome any resistance	Attempt to minimize any resistance

Key situational variables
The amount and type of resistance that is anticipated

The position of the initiators *vis-à-vis* the resistors (in terms of power, trust, and so forth)

The locus of relevant data for designing the change, and of needed energy for implementing it

The stakes involved (e.g., the presence or lack of presence of a crisis, the consequences of resistance and lack of change)

The strategic options available to managers can be usefully thought of as existing on a continuum (see Table 21.2).[14] At one end of the continuum, the change strategy calls for a very rapid implementation, a clear plan of action, and little involvement of others. This type of strategy mows over any resistance and, at the extreme, would result in a fait accompli. At the other end of the continuum, the strategy would call for a much slower change process, a less clear plan, and involvement on the part of many people other than the change initiators. This type of strategy is designed to reduce resistance to a minimum.[15]

The further to the left one operates on the continuum in Table 21.2, the more one tends to be coercive and the less one tends to use the other approaches – especially participation; the converse also holds.

Organizational change efforts that are based on inconsistent strategies tend to run into predictable problems. For example, efforts that are not clearly planned in advance and yet are implemented quickly tend to become bogged down owing to unanticipated problems. Efforts that involve a large number of people, but are implemented quickly, usually become either stalled or less participative.

Situational factors

Exactly where a change effort should be strategically positioned on the continuum in Table 21.2 depends on four factors:

1. The amount and kind of resistance that is anticipated. All other factors being equal, the greater the anticipated resistance, the more difficult it will be simply to overwhelm it, and the more a manager will need to move toward the right on the continuum to find ways to reduce some of it.[16]
2. The position of the initiator *vis-à-vis* the resistors, especially with regard to power. The less power the initiator has with respect to others, the more the initiating manager *must* move to the left on the continuum.[17] Conversely, the stronger the initiator's position, the more he or she can move to the right.
3. The person who has the relevant data for designing the change and the energy for implementing it. The more the initiators anticipate that they will need information and commitment from others to help design and implement the change, the more they must move to the right.[18] Gaining useful information and commitment requires time and the involvement of others.
4. The stakes involved. The greater the short-run potential for risks to organizational performance and survival if the present situation is not changed, the more one must move to the left.

Organizational change efforts that ignore these factors inevitably run into problems. A common mistake some managers make, for example, is to move too quickly and involve too few people despite the fact that they do not have all the information they really need to design the change correctly.

Insofar as these factors still leave a manager with some choice of where to operate on the continuum, it is probably best to select a point as far to the right as possible for both economic and social reasons. Forcing change on people can have just too many negative side effects over both the short and the long term. Change efforts using the strategies on the right of the continuum can often help develop an organization and its people in useful ways.[19]

In some cases, however, knowing the four factors may not give a manager a comfortable and obvious choice. Consider a situation where a manager has a weak position *vis-à-vis* the people whom he thinks need a change and yet is faced with serious consequences if the change is not implemented immediately. Such a manager is clearly in a bind. If he somehow is not able to increase his power in the situation, he will be forced to choose some compromise strategy and to live through difficult times.

Implications for managers

A manager can improve his chance of success in an organizational change effort by:

1. Conducting an organizational analysis that identifies the current situation, problems, and the forces that are possible causes of those problems. The analysis should specify the actual importance of the problems, the speed with which the problems must be addressed if additional problems are to be avoided, and the kinds of changes that are generally needed.
2. Conducting an analysis of factors relevant to producing the needed changes. This analysis should focus on questions of who might resist the change, why, and how much; who has information that is needed to design the change, and whose co-operation is essential in implementing it; and what is the position of the initiator *vis-à-vis* other relevant parties in terms of power, trust, normal modes of interaction, and so forth.
3. Selecting a change strategy, based on the previous analysis, that specifies the speed of change, the amount of preplanning, and the degree of involvement of others; that selects specific tactics for use with various individuals and groups, and that is internally consistent.
4. Monitoring the implementation process. No matter how good a job one does of initially selecting a change strategy and tactics, something unexpected will eventually occur during implementation. Only by carefully monitoring the process can one identify the unexpected in a timely fashion and react to it intelligently.

Interpersonal skills, of course, are the key to using this analysis. But even the most outstanding interpersonal skills will not make up for a poor choice of strategy and tactics. And in a business world that continues to become more and more dynamic, the consequences of poor implementation choices will become increasingly severe.

Notes

1. For example, see Robert A. Luke, Jr., 'A Structural Approach to Organizational Change', *Journal of Applied Behavioral Science*, September–October 1973, p. 611.
2. For a discussion of power and politics in corporations, see Abraham Zaleznik and Manfred F. R. Kets de Vries, *Power and the Corporate Mind* (Boston: Houghton Mifflin, 1975) ch. 6; and Robert H. Miles, *Macro Organizational Behavior* (Pacific Palisades, Calif.: Goodyear, 1978) ch. 4.
3. See Edgar H. Schein, *Organizational Psychology* (Englewood Cliffs, N.J.: Prentice-Hall, 1965) p. 44.
4. See Chris Argyris, *Intervention Theory and Method* (Reading, Mass.: Addison-Wesley, 1970) p. 70.
5. See Paul R. Lawrence, 'How to Deal with Resistance to Change', *HBR*, May–June 1954, p. 49; reprinted as HBR Classic, January–February 1969, p. 4.
6. For a discussion of resistance that is personality based, see Goodwin

Watson, 'Resistance to Change', in *The Planning of Change*, Warren G. Bennis, Kenneth F. Benne, and Robert Chin (eds) (New York: Holt, Rinehart, and Winston, 1969) p. 489.

7. Peter F. Drucker, *The Practice of Management* (New York: Harper & Row, 1954).
8. For a general discussion of resistance and reasons for it, see Chapter 3 in Gerald Zaltman and Robert Duncan, *Strategies for Planned Change* (New York: John Wiley, 1977).
9. See, for example, Alfred J. Marrow, David F. Bowers, and Stanley E. Seashore, *Management by Participation* (New York: Harper & Row, 1967).
10. Zaltman, G. and Duncan, R. (1977) *Strategies for Planned Change*, ch. 4.
11. For an excellent discussion of negotiation, see Gerald I. Nierenberg, *The Art of Negotiating* (Birmingham, Ala.: Cornerstone, 1968).
12. See John P. Kotter, 'Power, Dependence, and Effective Management', *HBR*, July–August 1977, p. 125.
13. Ibid, p. 135.
14. See Larry E. Greiner, 'Patterns of Organization Change', *HBR*, May–June 1967, p. 119; and Larry E. Greiner and Louis B. Barnes, 'Organization Change and Development', in *Organizational Change and Development*, Gene W. Dalton and Paul R. Lawrence (eds) (Homewood, Ill.: Irwin, 1970) p. 3.
15. For a good discussion of an approach that attempts to minimize resistance, see Renato Tagiuri, 'Notes on the Management of Change: Implication of Postulating a Need for Competence', in John P. Kotter, Vijay Sathe, and Leonard A. Schlesinger, *Organization* (Homewood, Ill.: Irwin, 1979).
16. Jay W. Lorsch, 'Managing Change', in *Organizational Behavior and Administration*, Paul R. Lawrence, Louis B. Barnes, and Jay W. Lorsch (eds) (Homewood, Ill.: Irwin, 1976) p. 676.
17. Ibid.
18. Ibid.
19. Michael Beer, *Organization Change and Development: A Systems View* (Pacific Palisades, Calif.: Goodyear, 1979).

CHAPTER 22

Strategy Implementation versus Middle Management Self-interest

WILLIAM D. GUTH and IAN C. MACMILLAN

Introduction

[...]
This article suggests that middle managers with low or negative commitment to the strategies formulated by senior management create significant obstacles to effective implementation.

Middle managers are motivated more by their perceived self-interest than by the organizational interest unless they coincide, so the possibility of divergence between the self-interest of middle managers, and organization interest (as perceived by senior management) makes the management of those processes that create middle management commitment a critical prerequisite for effective strategy implementation.

Commitment theory and strategy implementation

Discussions of commitment in the management literature tend to vary, but two common themes are associated with commitment: a willingness by individuals to exert high levels of effort on behalf of the organization, and a sense of identification with the organization's objectives, so that individual and organizational goals are closely aligned (Buchanan, 1974, 1975; Hrebiniak, 1974; Cook and Wall, 1980; Morris and Steers, 1980). Empirical studies indicate that individuals in organizations vary in their levels of commitment, and that the average level of commitment of individuals varies between organizations (Buchanan, 1974, 1975; Porter, Crampon and Smith, 1976). These studies have also indicated that there is an association between levels of individual commitment and various organizational and individual characteristics. Some characteristics that are associated with a high level of commitment are trust in senior management, satisfaction with degree of participation in decision-making, higher degrees of organizational decentralization, and positive attitudes toward the organization among other individuals worked with in the first year after joining the organization (Alutto and Acito, 1974; Cook and Wall, 1980; Buchanan, 1975).

One particularly interesting finding from this stream of research is presented by Mohrman (1979). Mohrman found that a key factor related to commitment is 'political access', that is, being able to raise issues and to secure serious attention to those issues. According to Mohrman's analysis, being able to participate in a wide range of decisions is not what makes for commitment. Rather, what matters is the possibility of gaining an appropriate forum on those issues that are important to the individual.

Although none of the studies mentioned explicitly document a relationship between commitment and organizational performance, their authors all imply that such a relationship exists: there is a relationship between commitment and willingness to exert high levels of effort on behalf of the organization so that, all other things being equal, the inference is that an organization with a high level of commitment from the individuals in it should perform better than one with indifferent individuals.

Commitment theory provides a relatively simple explanation for the level of an individual manager's commitment to the implementation of a strategy. If the perceived degree of goal alignment is low, the individual's commitment to the strategy will be low, so the amount of effort a middle manager would be willing to put forward to implement the strategy will be low.

Expectancy theory and strategy implementation

A richer, if more complex, explanation for individual managers' commitment to a strategy comes from the expectancy theory of motivation. According to this theory, close alignment of individual and organizational goals is but one of several factors related to individual effort.

A number of authors have proposed expectancy theories that, for our purposes, differ in relatively minor ways. All emphasize that individuals in organizations are concerned with the outcomes their behaviors will produce. We drew on an expectancy model developed by Lawler that has wide support (1976: 1252):

$$\text{Motivation} = \sum \left[(E \to P) \times [\Sigma(P \to O \times V(O)] \right]^1$$

The first factor in the model, $E \rightarrow P$, refers to the individual's subjective estimate of the probability that effort E on their part will lead to successful performance P. This factor can be thought of as varying from zero to one. The second factor is the product of $P \rightarrow O$ (or the individual's subjective estimate of the probability that performance P will lead to an outcome O) and $V(O)$ (or the valence, or degree of attractiveness, the individual places on outcome O). (Outcomes gain their valence from their ability to satisfy the needs and/or goals of the individual.) The value of $P \rightarrow O$ in the model varies from $+$ one (performance sure to lead to outcome) to zero (performance sure not to lead to outcome). The value of $V(O)$ varies from $+$ one (very desirable) to $-$ one (very undesirable). The products of all probability times valence combinations [i.e. $P \rightarrow O \times V(O)$] are summed for all the possible outcomes that are seen to be related to that performance.

The level of effort that an individual middle manager will apply to the implementation of a particular strategy depends on his/her perception of his/her and the organization's potential to perform (i.e. successfully execute the strategy) and his/her perception of the likelihood that successful performance will lead to an outcome he/she desires. The degree of alignment between the middle manager's goals and the organizational goals toward which a particular strategy is directed is captured in the valence factor in expectancy theory. So according to the expectancy theory, individual middle managers may decide to put very little effort into the implementation of a particular strategy if:

1. they believe that they have a low probability of performing successfully in implementing that strategy; or
2. they believe that even if they do perform successfully individually, that performance has low probability of achieving the organizationally desired outcome; or
3. the organizationally desired outcome does not satisfy their individual goals (and hence needs).

Consider the following examples:

Example 1
First assume that the relevant middle managers are highly confident that they could successfully implement a particular strategy being advocated by general management ($E \rightarrow P = 1.0$), but they feel that the strategy itself has a low probability of generating the outcomes predicted by general management ($P \rightarrow O = 0.1$). Further assume that the outcomes predicted by general management in its advocacy of the strategy are judged by the middle managers to have high ability to satisfy their goals ($V(O) = 1.0$). The product of the probabilities times the valence is 0.1,

which according to the theory would predict that the middle managers in this illustration would each put a low level of individual effort into implementing the strategy.

Example 2
Next assume that the relevant middle managers are highly confident of their ability to perform successfully in implementing the strategy ($E \rightarrow P = 1.0$), are this time highly confident that the strategy will result in the outcome predicted by general management ($P \rightarrow O = 1.0$), but believe that the outcome will have a negative impact on their individual goals ($V(O) = -1.0$). The product of the probabilities times the valence is -1.0. So expectancy theory would predict that a high degree of effort would be applied by the relevant middle managers to counter the implementation of the strategy.

Example 3
To develop the notion of 'counter effort' further, let us return to and modify the first example. Assume that a new strategy is being advocated by general management. The new strategy is a significant departure from the present strategy. For a particular middle manager this new strategy has a product of probabilities times valence that equals 0.1. In addition, assume that the middle manager is already applying high effort to the implementation of the *present* strategy, because in his/her view it has a product of probabilities times valence that equals 0.9. For this middle manager, switching from his/her implementation of the current strategy to implementation of the new strategy has a net impact of -0.8, the difference between the 0.1 product associated with the new strategy, and the 0.9 product associated with the current strategy.

   In both the second and third examples, the middle managers' self-interest would dictate that they apply high counter effort. In other words, expectancy theory suggests that there are conditions under which middle managers may actively intervene in strategy implementation in order to inhibit or redirect it. The next section discusses how and when this could take place.

Middle management intervention in strategy implementation

In attempting to shape how and what strategy will actually be implemented, middle managers can intervene in two ways, at two different stages in the decision-making process:

1. *Taking a position* – During the decision-making process, the manager takes a position on the alternatives being considered.
2. *Resisting decisions* – After the decision has already been made, the manager resists it.

Expectancy theory provides us with some guidelines to predict whether a manager is likely to undertake one or the other of these timing options. Self-interested intervention in organizational decision processes carries with it some risk of sanctions, if those in the organization who have the power to sanction (i.e. general management) see the intervention as inimical to the organization's interests. A middle manager's decision to intervene must take this risk of sanction into account.

Extending expectancy theory to accommodate assessment of this risk, we reason that the perceived risk of being sanctioned for self-interested intervention will reduce the motivation to apply counter effort against a decision with an otherwise negative product. The significance of the potential sanctions to the individual multiplied by the probability of them being administered must be weighed against the probability of being successful at the intervention multiplied by the net benefit to the individual associated with stopping or reshaping the decision.

We further reason that the timings of interventions carry different degrees of risk of organizational sanction. We hypothesize that resisting decisions after they are made carries higher risk of organizational sanctions than taking a position during the decision-making process. Even in organizations in which taking a position is discouraged (e.g. under a highly authoritarian management style), doing so can at least be rationalized as an effort to contribute to the organization's interests. On the other hand, resisting a decision after it is made is a clear and unequivocal challenge to the legitimacy of the organization's decision-making process (assuming such resistance can be accurately observed). Thus, all other things being equal, it would take a greater negative product of our model, $(E \rightarrow P) \times [(P \rightarrow O) \times V(O)]$, to motivate resisting a decision than it would to motivate taking a position. Resisting a decision is thus likely to be the less frequently exercised of the intervention options, and also the less likely to be successful.

Unfortunately, no substantive emperical work has been published in the strategic management literature that documents and analyses middle management behavior in the strategy implementation process when their self-interest is at stake. However it is possible to use a data base which codified behavior of middle managers who intervened in their organizational decision process to support their own interests (MacMillan and Guth, 1985), and this can be done in such a way as to provide strong, if indirect, supporting evidence for the above arguments.

Study of middle managers' interventions in organization decisions

While this study did not specifically address strategy implementation issues, it did focus on the degree to which managers intervened in organization decision-making processes when their interests were at stake. It provides strong evidence of the middle manager's ability to intervene successfully in decisions that impact beyond their departments, and since new strategies and strategy changes usually have substantive impact on more than one department in the organization, the study provides powerful, if indirect, evidence of how and how much middle management interventions could influence the implementation of strategy.

In this study middle managers who were taking a part-time masters degree in business were asked to participate. These managers represented firms in a wide diversity of industries and of widely varying size.

The final sample of 90 middle managers reported the most recent cases in which they intervened, in their own self-interest, in the decision processes of their firms. They were asked to provide short written descriptions of the most recent cases, *if any*, in which they took a position on a decision issue, and in which they resisted a decision. Note that the study was not focused on the conditions under which the managers might or might not intervene. It was focused on descriptions of those occasions, if any, when they did intervene. Also note that the study did not attempt to determine the frequency of interventions in any particular time frame.

Approximately 330 written reports of such interventions were received. For the purposes of this paper this data base was reanalysed along two dimensions:

1. Interventions were classified according to whether the issue over which the managers intervened had an impact that was confined to their department, or whether the impact went beyond the departmental level, i.e. organizational level. If the decision had an impact on members of the organization which were outside the authority of the respondent's immediate superior, or on members of other organizations, the impact was classified as organizational. The rationale for this classification is that strategic decisions usually affect more than one department, so if we can show from the data base that managers can successfully resist decisions and successfully take positions that support their interest, all on issues that have an impact beyond their departments, then we have strong indirect evidence that strategy implementation can be significantly affected by middle management intervention.

2. Second, actions were classified according to whether the intervention was perceived as successful or not, since respondents had been asked to report whether they had been successful or not.

In the original study a follow-up subsample (25 per cent) of respondents themselves had been asked to categorize the decisions according to level of issue. The coefficient of association between their categories and ours was 0.75, indicating a satisfactory correlation between the classification done by the researchers and that done by respondents themselves.

The original study has all the problems of any self-report study. Respondents could tend to bias their responses: they might be inclined to create nonexistent interventions, or inflate the level of the issue, or overstate the success of their attempts, so all *absolute* results should be viewed with circumspection. However, comparisons of the results *between* different intervention options (taking a position and resisting a decision) would to some extent compensate for such bias, assuming that the respondents were equally inclined to over-report the level of intervention and degree of success.

From the above arguments it was possible to develop a number of propositions regarding middle management's propensity for, and success at, intervening in decisions that have an impact on the organization beyond the department of the middle managers themselves.
[...]
First, since there may be significant sanctions associated with resisting decisions, particularly those that cross departmental boundaries, one would expect that middle managers would confine such interventions to intradepartmental issues. Therefore *compared to taking a position* we would expect middle managers to report a much lower proportion of resisting decision interventions on decisions that have an impact beyond their departments.
[...]
Second, we expect that irrespective of the type of intervention, the middle managers will report significant success at intervening.
[...]
Finally, given the relative clarity of challenge to the legitimacy of organizational decision processes between the two intervention options, one would expect middle managers to report a higher success rate for taking a position than for resisting decisions.
[...]
The following summarizes the results of our findings.

First it is clear that middle managers were prepared to intervene in organization decision processes to protect their self-interest, even when such decisions had an impact beyond their own departments, *as do most strategic decisions*. Intervention actually was reported at both stages of the decision process – by resisting decisions, where 38.9 per cent of the cases reported had an organizational level impact; and by taking a position on a decision in progress, where 60.0 per cent of the cases reported had an organizational level impact. We take this as strong supportive evidence that any strategy implementation decision which is seen as compromising middle management's interests can meet with active intervention by these managers, and at both stages of the decision-making process.

Second it was clear from the results that the middle managers perceived that they had been frequently successful in their intervention attempts. Not only this, but middle managers reported being no less successful at the more organizationally challenging intervention option (resisting extant decision) than at the less organizationally challenging option (taking a position). We take this as strong, if indirect, evidence that middle managers who feel that their goals are compromised can not only redirect the strategy, delay implementation or reduce the quality of implementation, but they could also even totally sabotage the strategy.

Furthermore, MacMillan and Guth (1985) found that middle managers participate extensively in organizational coalitions. Forming or joining a coalition is an attractive alternative option to 'going it alone' because a coalition usually will have greater leverage and chances of success than the individual manager for any intervention option. Groups of middle managers opposed to a strategy are even more likely to successfully subvert it.

Implications for general management

In the light of this evidence it is clear that there is a real imperative for general managers to systematically address the problem of securing pervasive (though not necessarily unanimous) commitment to the implementation of strategy. Implications of this evidence for the management of strategy implementation are discussed in the following four sections.

Recognize the political realities and manage them

Political activity in organizations, such as individual and coalition intervention behavior, is the natural and spontaneous result of competing demands from inside and outside the organization on the allocation of its resources. In fact, political processes are essential to the articulation of these demands, and constructively influence how the final trade-offs between the many demands are actually made. A major way that the dislocations between what the firm offers and what its current task environment currently demands is articulated via political processes – individuals and groups operating on the interface experience these dislocations as external pressures and transmit them back to the firm via political behavior.

For instance, a sales manager who supports various customers' demands about desired product characteristics and who attempts to get the current product policy modified, is responding (in his/her own self-interest in increasing a bonus tied to sales volume) to what could be unrecognized or emerging demand shifts in the market place. So is a purchasing manager who finds ways of 'circumventing' the firm's purchasing power in order to secure loyalty of suppliers. Admittedly, these middle managers are acting in their own interest, but they are also acting in the interest of their organizations, as they see it. [. . .]

Since intervention and coalition behavior exist in organizations, perform a necessary function, and influence decision outcomes, general management must recognize them, understand them, and learn to manage them.

Recognize the essentiality of middle management commitment

General management is not omnipotent. It is, in varying degrees, dependent on middle management for technical knowledge and functional skills. So, in reality, general management is rarely as free as it would like to be to 'find somebody else (or a number of others, in the case of a coalition) if they don't like it'. This results in the need, much of the time, to take the demands of middle-level managers seriously and to find solutions to conflicts over strategy and policy. There is an imperative to seek strategies that are both competitively effective and capable of gaining organizational commitment.

If general management decides to go ahead and impose its decisions in spite of lack of commitment, resistance by middle management can drastically lower the efficiency with which the decisions are implemented, if it does not completely stop them from being implemented. Particularly in dynamic, competitive environments, securing commitment to the strategy is crucial because rapid implementation is so important. ·

Learn to use classical political tools

Accepting that strategy and its related policy decisions must be both effective in the competitive market place and capable of gaining commitment from organizational members, the following political tools, used by politicians for centuries, can be helpful to general management in managing the implementation of strategy (Cyert and March, 1963; Katz and Kahn, 1978).

Equifinality

Since it is often possible to achieve very similar results using different means or paths, general management should accept that achieving a successful outcome is more important than imposing the method of achieving it. When confronted with obvious lack of organizational commitment to a particular strategy or related policy, it may be possible to generate new alternatives in search of one that gives equal results but with far greater potential for gaining commitment.

Satisficing

Politicians learn that achieving satisfactory results is far better than failing to achieve 'optimal' results via an unpopular strategy. If it tries to pursue the 'best' course without essential commitment from the organization, general management might actually achieve far less than what it would find satisfactory.

Generalization

Shifting focus from specific issues to more general ones may increase general management's options in its search for strategy and related policies that are both effective and capable of gaining organizational commitment. For example, shifting focus from how to cut costs to how to improve productivity may generate new alternatives that both lower the average unit cost of output, and gain higher commitment from middle management.

Focus on higher-order issues

By raising an issue to a higher level, many shorter-term interests can be postponed in favor of longer-term but more fundamental interests. For instance, the auto and steel industries, by focusing on issues of survival, were able to persuade unions to make concessions on wage increases.

Provide political access on important issues

Strategy and related policy decisions with significant negative consequences for middle managers will motivate intervention behavior from them. If middle managers do not have an opportunity to take a position on such decisions in appropriate political forums, they are capable, as our study shows, of successfully resisting the decisions after they are made. Providing such political access provides general management with information that might otherwise not be available to them and that could be useful in managing intervention behavior.

Manage intervention behavior

The application of expectancy theory above suggests that there are three fundamentally different sources of low to negative individual manager commitment to implementing a particular strategy: low perceived ability to perform successfully in implementing that strategy; low perceived probability that the proposed outcomes will result, even if individual performance is successful; and low capacity of the outcome to satisfy individual goals/needs.

Each of these sources requires a different approach, if implementation is to be effective. Thus the first problem that general management faces is in *anticipating* sources of low to negative commitment.

Source I: perceived inability to execute strategy

The skills and experience required to implement a particular strategy may be perceived by the relevant middle managers as being significantly different from those they have. So they perceive a risk that they will not be able to perform successfully at implementing the strategy. This perceived risk can, by itself, be the cause of low commitment.

If general management can determine that this is a cause of low commitment, it still must diagnose the basis of the relevant manager's concerns and remedy the problem as appropriate: either by increasing the middle managers' self-confidence that they can perform successfully; or by providing additional training and development; or by providing additional resource support (such as consultant or staff expertise) to supplement missing skills and expertise.

If the middle manager has low self-confidence (perhaps due to recent difficulties in performance), general management might be able to build commitment relatively easily, simply by providing the necessary moral support and encouragement, followed by rapid positive reinforcement of any successful performance.

If the middle managers actually need to develop new skills and experience, building self-esteem will not be enough. Formal training and development is necessary, or their skill shortfalls need to be supplemented.

Source II: low perceived probability that strategy will work

When middle managers feel that the outcomes predicted by general management are unlikely to occur, or in other words, they do not believe that the proposed strategy will work, the general manager has a particular responsibility not to let ego get in the way of an organizationally sound decision. Here the critical issue is not *who* is right, but *what* is right for the organization. It is far better for the organization to pursue the *right* strategy than to insist on pursuing general management's strategy. At issue here is a *disagreement between the judgements* of general management and middle management, on a highly important but uncertain decision. And since one of the main reasons that middle managers are employed is to contribute such judgements to the organization, they deserve a careful hearing.

In management decision-making, alternative decisions or courses of actions are evaluated in relation to their expected outcomes. Each manager uses his or her own theories or 'causal maps' about the relationship between alternative courses of actions and their outcomes in this evaluation (Argyris, 1982). However, managers are often not very explicit about the theories or 'causal maps' they are using in this evaluation of alternatives. Often they themselves are not sure about the strength of their beliefs in the theories or 'causal maps' they are in fact using (Starbuck, 1984).

[...]

Such cases, where low commitment stems from disagreement on judgements about causality, can have particular challenges when the subordinates do not agree that the strategy will work but fail to say so. Because general management has not experienced significant opposition, they can easily assume that there is high commitment to the strategy they are promulgating. Then the strategy just does not get implemented due to simple lack of commitment. Unfortunately, if they do not anticipate this source of low commitment, general management only discovers the problem after implementation failure occurs. This is particularly serious in situations where time is of the essence due to high competitiveness or rapidly changing conditions.

Two techniques are available to general managers who suspect that this type of strategy implementation problem may occur.

First, general management should commit to listening to and understanding middle management positions well enough to be able to restate them to the satisfaction of middle management. They should then insist that middle managers in turn describe *general management's* position (or 'causal map') to the satisfaction of general management. This discipline, which forces both parties to fully understand each other's position, will usually achieve full articulation of the implicit theories of the cause/effect relationships that lay behind each party's conclusions (Rapoport, 1960). Once this is accomplished, it becomes possible to develop hypotheses to test which theory is most applicable to the situation. So at minimum, this technique forces a clear understanding of the basis of any disagreement, and significantly increases the chances that the focus is kept on what the right strategy is, rather than whose strategy is right.

The second technique is to insist upon fully identifying the risks associated with any strategy being advocated. Doing so also exposes and makes explicit the cause/effect theories in use, the strength of each party's belief in those theories, and so prevents the phenomenon of convincing oneself that the risk is not as great as it rationally is. This shifts the focus of managerial attention from the choice between alternatives, to the management of the risks inherent in the different alternatives. Once again, the use of this technique leads to a more careful consideration of what is the right strategy rather than whose strategy is right.

Source III: perception that outcomes will not satisfy individual goals

It is not surprising for middle managers to have goals (and hence desired outcomes) which are different from general management goals. After all, middle management's decision-making is made in the context of sub-unit goals and personal goals rather than corporate goals, while general management pursues overall organizational goals (and personal goals).

In confronting the problem of low middle management valence on strategy outcomes, general management has four general ways of obtaining the support necessary to implement its strategy (MacMillan, 1978).

Inducement In this approach, general management adds additional payoffs to the strategy it favors for those middle managers with low valence on the outcomes. It is important to remember that these additional payoffs must have positive valence to the middle managers – it may be easier to identify salient inducements from the point of view of general management than to find inducements that actually work in relation to middle manager personal and sub-unit goals.

Persuasion In this approach, general management attempts to help middle managers with low valence on outcomes to perceive payoffs that they had not seen before. Persuasion efforts will fail, of course, if general management confuses its goal structure with that of the middle managers evidencing low to negative commitment.

Coercion The objective of this approach is to decrease the valence of the alternative strategies favored by those middle managers who see low valence in the general management strategy. If successful, this approach reduces the payoff of the alternatives favored by middle management to below that of the alternative favored by general management. Threats of sanctions for failure to implement general management's strategy, for example, may result in a middle manager concluding that the payoff associated with general management's strategy, while initially not seen as great as the payoff associated with his/her alternative, is in fact and on balance the greater of the two.

Obligation   In this approach, general management attempts to connect implementing the desired strategy to a sense of obligation on the part of the middle managers whose personal and sub-unit goals result in low valence on the outcomes associated with the desired strategy. For example, a general manager who is perceived by an unmotivated middle manager as having been very helpful in advancing the middle manager's career to date might be able to obtain commitment to implementing his strategy from the middle manager's sense of obligation (if he has such a sense) to repay the help given in the past. In effect, this approach reduces the net payoff to the middle manager of the alternative previously favored, by requiring that the cost of violating a sense of obligation be deducted from the positive returns perceived to be associated with the alternative.

Note that all the above techniques require a thorough understanding of the goal structure and needs of the middle managers who will be responsible for implementation.

[...]

Note

1. The full model also links actual ability to performance, and in the 'extrinsic motivation' version, links performance to rewards and rewards to valence. Our study focuses only on the relationships depicted here.

References

Alutto, J. A. and Acito, F. (1974) 'Decisional participation and sources of job satisfaction: a study of manufacturing personnel', *Academy of Management Journal*, March, pp. 160–7.

Argyris, C. (1982) 'The executive mind and double-loop learning', *Organizational Dynamics*, Autumn, pp. 5–22.

Buchanan, B. (1974) 'Building organizational commitment: the socialization of managers in work organizations', *Administrative Science Quarterly*, December, pp. 533–46.

Buchanan, B. (1975) 'To walk an extra mile – the whats, whens, and whys of organizational commitment', *Organizational Dynamics*, Spring, pp. 67–80.

Cook, J. and Wall, T. (1980) 'New work attitude measures of trust, organizational commitment, and personal need non-fulfilment', *Journal of Occupational Psychology*, March, pp. 39–52.

Cyert, R. M. and March, J. G. (1963) *A Behavioral Theory of the Firm*. (Engelwood Cliffs, NJ: Prentice-Hall).

Hrebiniak, L. G. (1974) 'Effects of job level and participation on employee attitudes and perceptions of influence', *Academy of Management Journal*, December, pp. 647–62.

Katz, D. and Kahn, R. (1978) *The Social Psychology of Organizations*. (New York: Wiley).

Lawler, E. E. (1976) 'Control systems in organizations', in Dunnett, M. D. (ed.) *Handbook of Industrial and Organizational Psychology*. (Chicago, IL, Rand McNally).

MacMillan, I. C. (1985) *Strategy Formulation: Political Concepts*. (St Paul, MN: West).

MacMillan, I. C. and Guth, W. D. (1985) 'Strategy implementation and middle management coalitions', in Lamb, R. (ed.) *Advances in Strategic Management*, Vol. 3 (Greenwich, CN: JAI Press).

Mohrman, S. A. (1979) 'A new look at participation in decision making: the concept of political access', *Academy of Management Proceedings*, pp. 200–4.

Morris, J. H. and Steers, R. M. (1980) 'Structural influences on organizational commitment', *Journal of Vocational Behavior*, August, pp. 50–7.

Porter, L. W., Crampon, W. J. and Smith, F. J. (1976)'Organizational commitment and managerial turnover: a longitudinal study', *Organizational Behavior and Human Performance*, February, pp. 87–98.

Rapoport, A. (1960) *Fights, Games, and Debates*. (Ann Arbor: University of Michigan Press).

Starbuck, W. H. (1984) 'Acting first and thinking later: finding decisions and strategies in the past'. Working Paper, School of Business Administration, University of Wisconsin-Milwaukee.

CHAPTER 23

The Structuring of Organizations

HENRY MINTZBERG

Introduction

[...]
This [reading] argues that [...] spans of control, types of formalization and decentralization, planning systems, and matrix structures should not be picked and chosen independently, the way a shopper picks vegetables at the market or a diner a meal at a buffet table. Rather, these and other parameters of organizational design should logically configure into internally consistent groupings. Like most phenomena – atoms, ants, and stars – characteristics of organizations appear to fall into natural clusters, or configurations.

We can, in fact, go a step farther and include in these configurations not only the design parameters but also the so-called contingency factors. In other words, the organization's type of environment, its production system, even its age and its size, can in some sense be 'chosen' to achieve consistency with the elements of its structure. The important implication of this conclusion, in sharp contrast to that of contingency theory, is that organizations can select their situations in accordance with their structural designs just as much as they can select their designs in accordance with their situations. Diversified firms may divisionalize, but there is also evidence that divisionalized firms have a propensity to further diversify [...] Stable environments may encourage the formalization (bureaucratization) of structure, but bureaucracies also have a habit of trying to stabilize their environments. And in contrast, entrepreneurial firms, which operate in dynamic environments, need to maintain flexible structures. But such firms also seek out and try to remain in dynamic environments in which they can outmaneuver the bureaucracies. In other words, no one factor – structural or situational – determines the others; rather, all are often logically formed into tightly knit configurations.

When the enormous amount of research that has been done on organizational structuring is looked at in the light of this conclusion, much of its confusion falls away, and a convergence is evident around several configurations, which are distinct in their structural designs, in the situations in which they are found, and even in the periods of history in which they first developed.

To understand these configurations, we must first understand each of the elements that make them up. Accordingly, the first four sections of this [reading] discuss the basic parts of organizations, the mechanisms by which organizations co-ordinate their activities, the parameters they use to design their structures, and their contingency, or situational, factors. The final section of this reading introduces the structural configurations. [...]

I Six basic parts of the organization

Different parts of the organization play different roles in the accomplishment of work and of these forms of co-ordination. Our framework introduces six basic parts of the organization, shown in Figure 23.1 and listed below:

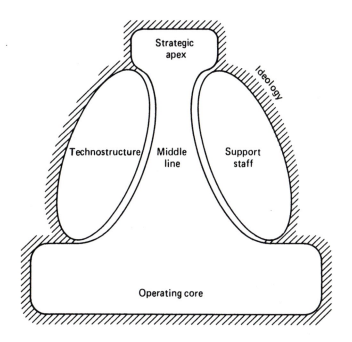

FIGURE 23.1 The six basic parts of the organization

1. The *operating core* is where the basic work of producing the organization's products and services gets done, where the workers assemble
   automobiles and the surgeons remove appendices.
2. The *strategic apex* is the home of top management, where the
   organization is managed from a general perspective.
3. The *middle line* comprises all those managers who stand in direct line
   relationship between the strategic apex and the operating core.
4. The *technostructure* includes the staff analysts who design the systems
   by which work processes and outputs of others in the organization are
   formally designed and controlled.
5. The *support staff* comprises all those specialists who provide support
   to the organization outside of its operating workflow – in the typical
   manufacturing firm, everything from the cafeteria staff and the
   mailroom to the public relations department and the legal counsel.
6. The *ideology* forms the sixth part, a kind of halo of beliefs and
   traditions that surrounds the whole organization.

II   Six basic co-ordinating mechanisms

Six mechanisms of co-ordination seem to describe the fundamental ways
in which organizations co-ordinate their work. Two are *ad hoc* in nature;
the other four involve various forms of standardization.

1. *Mutual adjustment* achieves co-ordination of work by the simple
   process of informal communication. The people who do the work
   interact with one another to co-ordinate, much as two canoeists in the
   rapids adjust to one another's actions. Figure 23.2a shows mutual
   adjustment in terms of an arrow between two operators. Mutual
   adjustment is obviously used in the simplest of organizations – it is
   the most obvious way to co-ordinate. But, paradoxically, it is also
   used in the most complex, because it is the only means that can be
   relied upon under extremely difficult circumstances, such as trying to
   figure out how to put a man on the moon for the first time.
2. *Direct supervision* in which one person co-ordinates by giving orders
   to others, tends to come into play after a certain number of people
   must work together. Thus, fifteen people in a war canoe cannot co-
   ordinate by mutual adjustment; they need a leader who, by virtue of
   his instructions, co-ordinates their work, much as a football team
   requires a quarterback to call the plays. Figure 23.2b shows the leader
   as a manager with his instructions as arrows to the operators.

Co-ordination can also be achieved by *standardization* – in effect,
automatically – by virtue of standards that predetermine what people do

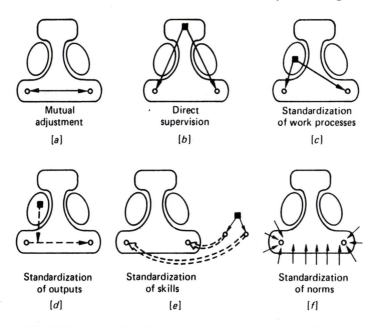

FIGURE 23.2 The basic mechanisms of co-ordination

and so ensure that their work is co-ordinated. We can consider four forms – the standardization of the work processes themselves, of the outputs of the work, of the knowledge and skills that serve as inputs to the work, or of the norms that more generally guide the work.

3. *Standardization of work processes* means the specification – that is, the programming – of the content of the work directly, the procedures to be followed, as in the case of the assembly instructions that come with many children's toys. As shown in Figure 23.2c, it is typically the job of the analyst to so program the work of different people in order to co-ordinate it tightly.
4. *Standardization of outputs* means the specification not of what is to be done but of its results. In that way, the interfaces between jobs is predetermined, as when a machinist is told to drill holes in a certain place on a fender so that they will fit the bolts being welded by someone else, or a division manager is told to achieve a sales growth of 10% so that the corporation can meet some overall sales target. Again, such standards generally emanate from the analyst, as shown in Figure 23.2d.
5. *Standardization of skills*, as well as knowledge, is another, though looser way to achieve co-ordination. Here, it is the worker rather than the work or the outputs that is standardized. He or she is taught a

body of knowledge and a set of skills which are subsequently applied to the work. Such standardization typically takes place outside the organization – for example in a professional school of a university before the worker takes his or her first job – indicated in Figure 23.2e. In effect, the standards do not come from the analyst; they are internalized by the operator as inputs to the job he takes. Co-ordination is then achieved by virtue of various operators' having learned what to expect of each other. When an anesthetist and a surgeon meet in the operating room to remove an appendix, they need hardly communicate (that is, use mutual adjustment, let alone direct supervision); each knows exactly what the other will do and can co-ordinate accordingly.

6. *Standardization of norms* (Figure 23.2f) means that the workers share a common set of beliefs and can achieve co-ordination based on it, as implied in Figure 23.2d. For example, if every member of a religious order shares a belief in the importance of attracting converts, then all will work together to achieve this aim.

Bear these six co-ordinating mechanisms in mind; we shall be returning to them repeatedly. Every organization must divide up its work among individuals (known as 'division of labor') to get it done. These co-ordinating mechanisms, as the basic means to knit together the divided labor of the organization, serve as the most basic elements of structure – the glue that holds the organization together.

III   The essential parameters of design

In the structuring of organizations, design means turning those knobs that influence the division of labor and co-ordination. In this section we shall be discussing ten such knobs or 'design parameters', which fall into four basic groups. The first deals with the design of individual positions in the organization and includes the specialization of jobs, the formalization of behavior, and the establishment of requirements for the training and indoctrination associated with each job. The second concerns the design of the 'superstructure', or skeleton of the organization, and includes the determination of the bases on which positions and units are grouped, as well as establishment of the size of units. The third deals with the design of lateral linkages to flesh out the superstructure, and includes two design parameters called planning and control systems and liaison devices. The last concerns the design of the decision-making system in the organization, and includes the design parameters we call vertical decentralization and horizontal decentralization.

Job specialization

The first order of business in organizational design is to decide what each person will do. Key here is the determination of how specialized each job is to be – how many distinct tasks it is to contain – and how much control over those tasks the person who does the job should have. In determining these aspects of job specialization, the organization designer is essentially establishing the division of labor in the organization.

Jobs that have few and 'narrow' tasks are generally referred to as *horizontally specialized,* those with many and 'broad' ones as *horizontally enlarged.* A worker bolts on a bumper every few seconds all day long; a maintenance man nearby is a jack-of-all-trades, shifting from one problem to another. Jobs that involve little control by those who do them – carried out without thinking how or why – are called *vertically specialized;* those which are thoroughly controlled by the worker are referred to as *vertically enlarged.*
[. . .]

Jobs must often be specialized vertically because they are specialized horizontally: the work is so narrow that worker control of it would preclude the necessary co-ordination. These are generally *unskilled* jobs. On the other hand, many so-called *professional* jobs are horizontally specialized yet vertically enlarged – the worker has a narrow repertoire of programs, but because these are highly complex, he must have a good deal of control over them.

Behavior formalization

The next issue in the design of individual positions is the determination of the extent to which the work content of tasks will be specified – in other words, the behavior or the job 'formalized.'

Organizations formalize the behavior of their workers in order to reduce its variability, ultimately to predict and control it. Thus behavior formalization is also a means to achieve specialization in the vertical direction. A prime motive for formalizing behavior is, of course, to co-ordinate work very tightly, specifically through the mechanism we have called standardization of work processes. Airline pilots, for example, cannot figure out emergency landing procedures when the need arises and then co-ordinate by mutual adjustment with the ground staff; those have to be very carefully prescribed in advance.

Organizations that rely primarily on the formalization of behavior to achieve co-ordination are generally referred to as 'bureaucracies,' a word that has become highly charged in everyday speech. We shall, however, use a neutral definition here. A structure is *bureaucratic* to the extent that it relies on standardization for co-ordination. Note that this definition includes any form of standardization, not just that of work processes. [...]

Training

The behavior required of some tasks is too complex to be rationalized and then formalized directly by the analysts of the technostructure. And so the people who are to do the tasks must be extensively trained before they begin their work. In other words, they must acquire some standardized body of knowledge and set of skills. Such training can, of course, be designed in the organization itself, but more often it must take place in some formal institution (unless it must be learned under an apprenticeship system, as a craft). And so this third aspect of position design entails deciding what formal training the organization will require in its different positions and then selecting the appropriately trained 'professionals' to fill them (or establishing its own training programs where it can).

We noted above that formalization and training are basically substitutes for one another. [...] Both are designed to program the work of the individual, but one focuses on unskilled work, while the other is oriented toward complex, professional work. And herein lies the essential difference between the two, for while one takes power from the worker and puts it into the technostructure, the other takes power from all the other parts of the organization and puts it into the hands of the professional workers themselves. In other words, professional tasks must be controlled by those who actually perform them.
[...]

Indoctrination

Socialization refers to the process by which a new member learns the value system, the norms, and the required behavior patterns of the society, organization, or group which he is entering [...] A good deal of socialization takes place informally and unofficially in the organization, as new members interact with old. But some also takes place more formally, for the organization's own benefit, through the process known as *indoctrination*. As a parameter in the design of individual positions, indoctrination resembles training in many ways. It too takes place largely outside the job — often before it begins — and is also designed for the internalization of standards. But the standards differ. They relate not to formal bodies of knowledge and sets of skills, but to the norms of the organization itself — its values, beliefs, manners of doing things, what is generally referred to as its internal 'culture'. And because these standards are unique to each organization, indoctrination must take place within its own walls under full control of its own personnel.

[...]

Unit grouping

Given a set of positions duly designed in terms of specialization, formalization, training, and indoctrination, the next issue in organization design relates to the establishment of a managerial 'superstructure' to knit it all together. In other words, positions are grouped into units, each under its own manager, and units clustered into ever larger units under their own managers, until the whole organization comes under a single manager – the chief executive officer at the strategic apex. Thus, a hierarchy of authority is constructed through which flows the *formal* power to control decisions and actions.

That hierarchy is generally represented by an organizational chart, what we shall call (borrowing from the French) an *organigram* [...] The organigram is a much maligned document, rejected by many as an inadequate picture of what really takes place in organizations. True enough, since it represents the flow of official power – formal authority – which is often superseded by informal power. Yet the organigram is inevitably the first thing asked for by anyone interested in the organization, and for good reason: like a map, it is a useful portrayal of certain surface features of the organization and their linkages. In particular, it tells at a glance how labor is divided into positions in the organization, who fills these positions, how they are grouped into units, and how formal authority flows among these units.

Two major questions arise in the design of the superstructure which are dealt with by our next two design parameters. First, on what basis are positions and units grouped into larger units, and second, what size should each of the units be?

Grouping is not simply a convenience for the sake of creating an organigram, a handy way to keep track of everyone who works for the organization. Rather, it is a fundamental way to co-ordinate work in the organization, for four reasons: (a) it establishes a system of common supervision among positions and units, (b) it typically requires positions and units to share common resources and (c) to be assessed on common measures of performance (i.e., output standards), and (d) as a result of the tendency to put the members of given units into close physical proximity with one another, it encourages mutual adjustment amor.g them.

Positions and units can be grouped [...] by *function* (including knowledge, skill, work process work function), and by *market* (output, client, and place). In one we have grouping by *means*, by the intermediate

functions the organization uses to produce or support the production of its final outputs, in the other, grouping by *ends*, by the features of the markets served by the organization – the products or services it markets, the clients it serves, the places where it serves them.
[. . .]

In designing the superstructure, the question is often not so much *which* basis of grouping, but in what *order*. Much as fires are built by stacking logs first one way and then the other, so too are superstructures often built by varying the different bases for grouping to take care of various interdependencies.

Unit size

On the question of the size of units – historically described in terms of the 'span of control' of their managers – the classical literature was clear: [. . .] 'No supervisor can supervise directly the work of more than five or, at the most, six subordinates whose work interlocks.' Yet effective units containing dozens – sometimes even hundreds – of people or subunits have been reported. The problem as we shall see, seems to stem from the assumption in the classical literature that co-ordination was synonymous with direct supervision, in other words, that mutual adjustment and the various forms of standardization did not exist as co-ordinating mechanisms. Thus, the focus was on the span of 'control' of the manager, instead of the size of the unit, as if managerial control were the only factor in determining the size of units.

When we turn to an analysis of the co-ordinating mechanisms other than direct supervision, we get the clearest explanation of variation in unit size. Two relationships in particular explain a good deal. First, the greater the use of standardization (of any kind) for co-ordination, the larger the size of the work unit. It stands to reason that the more co-ordination within a unit can be achieved by standardization – in effect, automatically, without direct managerial intervention – the less time its manager need spend on direct supervision and so the greater the number of employees that can report to him. Thus we find examples of 50 and 100 assembly line workers reporting to a single foreman; similarly, I report together with fifty colleagues directly to one dean.

The second relationship is that the greater the need for mutual adjustment, the smaller must be the size of the work unit. When tasks are rather complex yet tightly coupled, neither direct supervision nor any form of standardization suffices to effect the necessary co-ordination. The specialists who perform the various tasks must co-ordinate by virtue of informal, face-to-face communication among themselves. As we noted at the very outset of this [reading], mutual adjustment is the favored co-ordinating mechanism for the most complex of endeavors, like putting a

man on the moon for the first time. Now, what effect does reliance on mutual adjustment have on unit size? For mutual adjustment to work effectively, the work unit must be small enough to encourage convenient, frequent, and informal interaction among all its members – typically less than ten people and often of the order of five, six, or seven.
[...]

Planning and control systems

With the establishment of positions and the construction of the super-structure, we have the skeleton of the organizational structure. But the design is still not complete. We need other parameters to flesh it out, to create other kinds of linkages among the component parts. Specifically, we need planning and control systems to standardize outputs and liaison devices to encourage mutual adjustment.

The purpose of formal planning is to specify – standardize – outputs ahead of time, and the purpose of formal control is to determine later whether or not the standards have in fact been met. The two go together, like the proverbial horse and carriage. Nevertheless, we can distinguish *action planning systems* – which focus on before-the-fact determination of outputs – from *performance control systems* – which are more oriented to after-the-fact monitoring of results.
[...]

Action planning, by focusing on specific actions, like behavior formalization, tends to be used to co-ordinate work across functional structures, but often at a higher level in the hierarchy. Performance control, in contrast, is less tightly regulating, more respectful of unit autonomy. Thus, whereas it says 'Increase sales by 10% this year (in any way you care to)', action planning specifies who, when, where. Thus, performance control tends to be associated with the market bases for grouping, to control the performance of self-contained units while leaving the details of how to do so to each of them.
[...]

Liaison devices

Mutual adjustment may occur naturally in the small, face-to-face work unit. But how to encourage it across units, when grouping has the known tendency to discourage *inter*unit communication even as it encourages *intra*unit communication? In the past, the resolution of this problem was left to chance. But in recent years, as it has become more and more serious, a whole series of what we shall call *liaison devices* – formal parameters of structural design – have developed to stimulate mutual adjustment across units. These, in fact, represent the most significant –

perhaps the only significant – development in structural design in the past fifteen or twenty years. Four are of particular importance, presented in ascending order of their capacity to encourage mutual adjustment.

- *Liaison positions* are jobs created to co-ordinate the work of two units directly, without having to pass through vertical, managerial channels. They carry no formal authority *per se*; rather, those who serve in them must use their powers of persuasion, negotiation, etc. to bring the two sides together. Typical liaison positions are the purchasing engineer who sits between purchasing and engineering or the sales liaison person who mediates between the sales force and the factory.
- *Task forces and standing committees* are institutionalized forms of meetings which bring members of a number of different units together on a more intensive basis, in the first case to deal with a temporary issue, in the second, in a more permanent and regular way to discuss issues of common interest. Thus a task force may be formed of engineering, sales, and production personnel to redesign a given product and then disband, while line and technocratic personnel may form a standing committee to meet weekly to plan production.
- *Integrating managers* – essentially liaison personnel with formal authority – provide for stronger co-ordination by mutual adjustment than either of the first two devices. These 'managers' are not given authority over the units they link – each of these still has its own manager. But they are given authority over something important to those units, for example, approval of certain of their decisions or control over their budgets. One example is the unit manager in the hospital, responsible for integrating the efforts of doctors, nurses, and support staff in a particular ward; another is the brand manager in a consumer goods firm who is responsible for a certain product but who must negotiate its production and marketing with different functional departments.
- *Matrix structure* carries liaison to its natural conclusion. No matter what the bases of grouping at one level in an organization, some interdependencies always remain. Functional groupings pose work-flow problems; market-based ones impede contacts among like specialists. Standardization may help, but problems often remain. As shown in Figure 23.3, we have seen three ways to deal with the 'residual interdependencies': a different type of grouping can be used at the next level in the hierarchy; staff units can be formed next to line units to advise on the problem; or one of the liaison devices already discussed can be overlaid on the grouping. But in each case, one basis of grouping is favored over the others. The concept of matrix structure is to balance two (or more) bases of grouping, for example functional with market (or for that matter, one kind of market with

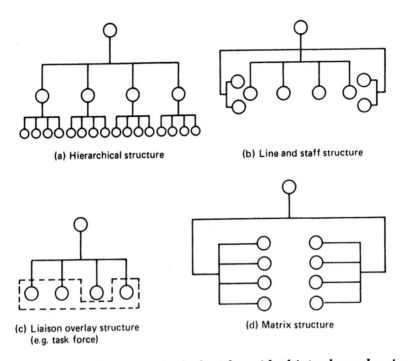

(a) Hierarchical structure

(b) Line and staff structure

(c) Liaison overlay structure
(e.g. task force)

(d) Matrix structure

FIGURE 23.3   Structures to deal with residual interdependencies

another – say, regional with product). This is done by the creation of a dual authority structure – two (or more) managers, units, or individuals are made jointly and equally responsible for the same decisions. We can distinguish a *permanent* form of matrix structure, where the units and the people in them remain more or less in place, as shown in the example of a whimsical multinational firm in Figure 23.4, and a *shifting* form, suited to project work, where the units and the people in them move around frequently. Shifting matrix structures are common in high technology industries, which group specialists in functional departments for housekeeping purposes (process interdependencies, etc.) but deploy them from various departments in project teams to do the work, as shown in Figure 23.5.

How do these liaison devices relate to the other design parameters we have already discussed? One point seems clear. As means to encourage mutual adjustment, these are most logically used with work that is: (a) horizontally specialized, since specialization impedes natural co-ordination, (b) complex, in other words, professional, and (c) interdependent, so that co-ordination is in fact necessary. Thus, the liaison devices – especially the stronger ones, such as task forces, integrating managers

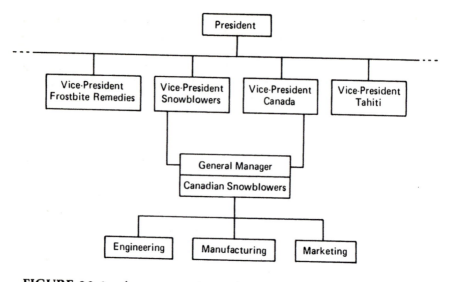

FIGURE 23.4   A permanent matrix structure in an international firm

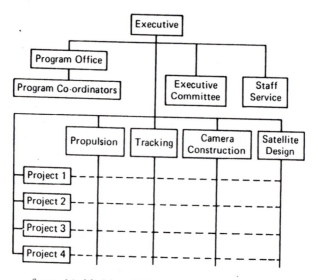

Source: Modified from Delbecq and Filley, 1974: 16.

FIGURE 23.5   Shifting matrix structure in the NASA weather satellite program

and matrix structure — seem most appropriate to the second kind of professional work we discussed earlier, where the professionals must work together in small units. These liaison devices, as agents of mutual adjustment instead of standardization, are obviously associated with organic structures — indeed, in overriding formal authority or bifurcating it, they tend to destroy bureaucratic priority.

Vertical and horizontal decentralization

Finally we come to the most extensively discussed yet least understood of the parameters of structural design, those related to *decentralization*. What does the word really mean? To some, it describes the physical location of facilities: a library is 'centralized' in one location or 'decentralized' to many. To others, it describes the delegation of formal power down the hierarchy of authority. We shall use a broader definition than the second one, but different from the first, associating the term with the sharing of decision making power. When all the power rests at a single point in the organization, we shall call the structure centralized; to the extent that the power is dispersed among many individuals, we shall call the structure relatively decentralized. Notice that our definition of decentralization is not restricted to formal power. In fact we shall distinguish *vertical decentralization* — the delegation of *formal* power down the hierarchy to line managers — from *horizontal decentralization* — the extent to which *formal or informal* power is dispersed out of the line hierarchy to non-managers (operators, analysts, and support staffers). We also introduce another distinction: between *selective* decentralization — the dispersal of power over one or a few kinds of decisions to the same place in the organization — from *parallel* decentralization — the dispersal of power for many kinds of decisions to the same place.

Centralization has one great advantage in the organization. By keeping all the power in one place, it ensures the very tightest form of co-ordination. All the decisions are made in one head, and then implemented through direct supervision. So then why bother to decentralize? Primarily because one brain is often not big enough. It cannot understand all that must be known. Also, decentralization allows the organization to respond quickly to local conditions in many different places, and it can serve as a stimulus for motivation, since capable people require considerable room to maneuver if they are to perform at full capacity.
[...]

Let us consider decentralization in terms of the six co-ordinating mechanisms because, as we shall see, each inherently leads to a different form and a different degree of decentralization. By considering them all together, in the context of our preceding discussion, we can derive six basic types of decentralization.

Direct supervision clearly constitutes full horizontal centralization, since all the power rests with the managers. In fact, it also constitutes vertical centralization since a dependence on direct supervision for co-ordination means that each manager tightly controls those below him such that all the power eventually rises to the top of the hierarchy, where it rests in the hands of the chief executive at the strategic apex. What we call *centralization* – in effect, horizontal and vertical as well as parallel – is shown as Type I decentralization in Figure 23.6 (where the size of the shaded parts designate their influence in decision making).

The various forms of standardization can, as we have seen, lead to different degrees of decentralization. When the organization relies on the standardization of work processes for co-ordination, as we have seen, the unskilled operators and lower level line managers lose power to the managers higher up in the hierarchy, and also to some extent to the analysts of the technostructure who design the systems of behavior formalization that control others. The result is centralization in the vertical dimension, with a limited and selective degree of decentralization in the horizontal dimension (to the analysts, who control only the design of the systems of standardization). What we call *limited horizontal decentralization* (selective) is shown as Type II in Figure 23.6.

We have also seen that a reliance on standardization of output goes with the delegation of power over many decisions to the managers of market-based units. This is a form of vertical decentralization, but as we noted earlier, only a very limited form, since a few division managers can retain the lion's share of the power. Thus our Type III decentralization is referred to as *limited vertical decentralization (parallel)*. (Some power is shown in the technostructure, because it is the analysts who design the planning and control systems to standardize outputs.)

Next, we have decentralization based on the two kinds of professional work. Because, as noted earlier, experts who do complex work must control it to a large degree, these represent – in contrast to our first three types – rather extensive forms of decentralization.

In the first, the standardization of skills (based on extensive training) is relied upon for co-ordination. As a result, the professionals can work rather autonomously in large units, relatively free of the control of line managers and in control of most of the decisions that affect their work directly. In other words, here we have an extreme form of *horizontal decentralization (parallel)*, shown as Type IV in Figure 23.6, with much of the power residing at the bottom of the hierarchy. Note that we have in Types II and IV our two kinds of bureaucracies, the first relatively centralized, the second relatively decentralized.

In the second kind of professional work, the experts work in small units and co-ordinate by mutual adjustment (encouraged by use of the liaison devices), which gives them a good deal of power. Here we have a

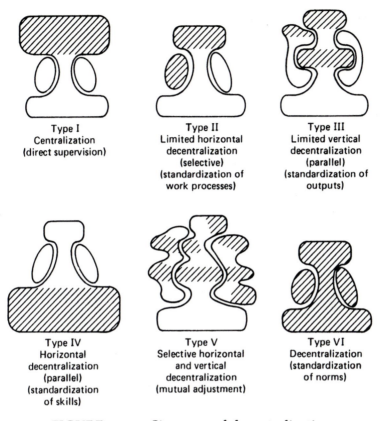

Type I Centralization (direct supervision)	Type II Limited horizontal decentralization (selective) (standardization of work processes)	Type III Limited vertical decentralization (parallel) (standardization of outputs)
Type IV Horizontal decentralization (parallel) (standardization of skills)	Type V Selective horizontal and vertical decentralization (mutual adjustment)	Type VI Decentralization (standardization of norms)

FIGURE 23.6   Six types of decentralization

combination, in both cases selective, of vertical decentralization – delegation to work groups at different levels in the hierarchy – and horizontal decentralization – a varying distribution of power within each group, of managers and non-managers, with the different decisions being controlled by whoever happens to have the necessary expertise. We end up with *selective horizontal and vertical decentralization*, Type V in Figure 23.6. Note that in Types I and V we have essentially two kinds of organic structures, one based on direct supervision for co-ordination, the other on mutual adjustment.

Finally, we come to the form of decentralization dictated by a reliance on the standardization of norms for co-ordination. As noted earlier, when an organization socializes and indoctrinates its members to believe in its strong ideology, it can then allow them considerable freedom to act, since they will in fact act in accordance with the prevailing norms. The result can be the purest form of decentralization – in one sense, the most democratic form of structure. Everyone shares power more or less equally

– manager, staff person, operator – hence we have just plain *decentralization*.

IV   The situational factors

A number of contingency or situational factors influence the choice of these design parameters, and vice versa. These include the age and size of the organization; its technical system of production; various characteristics of its environment, such as stability and complexity; and its power system, for example, whether or not it is tightly controlled from the outside. Some of their influences on the design parameters as found in an extensive body of research are summarized below as hypotheses.

Age and size

Five hypotheses seem to cover a good deal of the findings in the research on the effects of the age and size of the organization itself on its own structure.

H1. The older the organization, the more formalized its behavior   What we have here is the 'we've-seen-it-all-before' syndrome. As organizations age, they tend to repeat their behaviors; as a result, these become more predictable and so more amenable to formalization.

H2. The larger the organization, the more formalized its behavior   Just as the older organization formalizes what it has seen before, so the larger organization formalizes what it sees often. ('Listen mister, I've heard that story at least five times today. Just fill in the form like it says.')

H3. The larger the organization, the more elaborate its structure; that is, the more specialized its tasks, the more differentiated its units, and the more developed its administrative components   As organizations grow in size, they are able to specialize their tasks more finely. (The big barbershop can afford a specialist to cut children's hair; the small one cannot.) As a result, they can also specialize – or 'differentiate' – the work of their units more extensively. This leads to greater homogeneity of work within units, but greater diversity between them, which necessitates more efforts at co-ordination. And so the larger organization tends also to enlarge its hierarchy to effect direct supervision or its technostructure to co-ordinate by standardization, or to include more liaison or integrating positions to encourage co-ordination by mutual adjustment.

H4. The larger the organization, the larger the size of its average unit   This finding relates to the previous two, the size of units growing larger as organizations themselves grow larger because: (a) as behavior becomes more formalized, and (b) as the work of each unit becomes more homogeneous, managers are able to supervise more employees.

H5. Structure reflects the age of founding of the industry   This is a curious finding, but one that we shall see holds up remarkably well. Organizational structure seems to reflect not just the age of the organization itself, but the age of the industry in which it operates, no matter what its own age. Industries that predate the industrial revolution seem to favor one kind of structure, those of the age of the early railroads another, and so on. We should obviously expect different structures in different periods; the surprising thing is that these structures seem to carry through to new periods, old industries remaining relatively unaffected by innovations in structural design.

Technical system

Technical system refers to the instruments used in the operating core to produce the outputs. (This should be distinguished from 'technology', which refers to the knowledge base of the organization.) Three hypotheses are especially important here.

H6. The more regulating the technical system – that is, the more it controls the work of the operators – the more formalized the operating work and the more bureaucratic the structure of the operating core   Technical systems that regulate the work of the operators – for example, mass production assembly lines – render that work highly routine and predictable, and so encourage its specialization and formalization, which in turn create the conditions for bureaucracy in the operating core.

H7. The more complex the technical system, the more elaborate the administrative structure, especially the larger and more professional the support staff, the greater the selective decentralization (to that staff), and the greater the use of liaison devices to co-ordinate the work of that staff   Essentially, if an organization is to use complex machinery, it must hire staff experts who can understand that machinery – who have the capability to design, select, and modify it. And then it must give them considerable power to make decisions concerning that machinery, and encourage them to use the liaison devices to ensure mutual adjustment among them.

H8. The automation of the operating core transforms a bureaucratic administrative structure into an organic one   When unskilled work is co-ordinated by the standardization of work processes, we get bureaucratic structure,

But it is not only the operating core that gets bureaucratized. The whole organization tends to take on characteristics of bureaucracy, because an obsessive control mentality pervades the system. But when the work of the operating core gets automated, social relationships change. Now it is machines, not people, that are regulated. So the obsession with control disappears – machines do not need to be watched over – and with it go many of the managers and analysts who were needed to control the operators. In their place come the support specialists, to look after the machinery. And they, as described in the last hypothesis, gain a good deal of power and co-ordinate by mutual adjustment. In other words, the result of automation is a reduction of line authority in favor of staff expertise and a tendency to rely less on standardization for co-ordination, more on mutual adjustment. Thus, ironically, organizations tend to get humanized by the automation of their operating work.

Environment

Environment is a catch-all term that has been used in the literature to describe the general conditions that surround an organization. We shall discuss five hypotheses here, each one dealing with a different condition.

H9. The more dynamic the environment, the more organic the structure It stands to reason that in a stable environment – when nothing changes – an organization can predict its future conditions and so, all other things being equal, can easily rely on standardization for co-ordination. But when conditions become dynamic – when sources of supply are uncertain, the need for product change frequent, labor turnover high, political conditions unstable – the organization cannot standardize, but must instead remain flexible through the use of direct supervision or mutual adjustment for co-ordination. In other words, it must have organic structure. Thus, for example, armies, which tend to be highly bureaucratic institutions in peacetime, can become rather organic when engaged in highly dynamic, guerrilla-type warfare.

H10. The more complex the environment, the more decentralized the structure We saw earlier that the prime reason to decentralize a structure is that all the information needed to make decisions cannot be comprehended in one head. For example, when the operations of the organization are based on a complex body of technical knowledge (as in a hospital), then the organization must engage professionals (the physicians) and grant them a good deal of power over their own work. Note that Hypotheses 9 and 10 are independent of one another. A simple environment can be stable or dynamic (the manufacturer of dresses faces a simple environment yet cannot predict style from one season to another). A complex one likewise can be stable or dynamic (the specialist in perfected open heart surgery faces a complex task, yet knows exactly what to expect).

H11. The more diversified the organization's markets, the greater the propensity to split it into market-based units, or divisions, given favorable economies of scale When an organization can identify distinct markets – geographical regions, clients, but especially products and services – it will be predisposed to split itself into high-level units on that basis, and to give each a good deal of control over its own operations (that is, to use what we called 'limited vertical decentralization'). In simple terms, diversification breeds divisionalization. In this way, the organization can reduce the co-ordination needed across units: each has all the functions associated with its own markets. But this assumes favorable economies of scale. If the operating core cannot be divided (as in the case of an aluminum smelter), or if some critical function must be centrally co-ordinated (as in purchasing in a retail chain), then full divisionalization may simply be impossible.

H12. Extreme hostility in its environment drives any organization to centralize its structure temporarily Evidence from the social psychological laboratory suggests that when threatened by extreme hostility in its environment, the tendency for groups (and, presumably, organizations) is to centralize power, in other words, to fall back on the tightest co-ordinating mechanism they know, direct supervision. Here a central leader can ensure fast and highly co-ordinated response to the threat (at least temporarily).

H13. Disparities in the environment encourage the organization to decentralize selectively to differentiated work constellations When an organization faces very different kinds of environments – one dynamic, requiring organic structure, another stable, requiring bureaucratic structure, and so on – the natural tendency is to differentiate the structure, to create different pockets, or 'work constellations', to deal with each. Each constellation is given the power to make the decisions related to its own 'subenvironment', with the result that the structure becomes decentralized selectively.

Power

Our fourth set of situational factors relates to power. The impact of external control of the organization, the power needs of the members, and fashion are discussed below.

H14. The greater the external control of the organization, the more centralized and formalized its structure   This important hypothesis claims that to the extent that an organization is controlled externally – for example, by a parent firm or a government – it tends to centralize power at the strategic apex and to formalize its behavior. The reason is that the two most effective ways to control an organization from the outside are to hold its chief executive officer responsible for its actions and to impose clearly defined standards on it. Moreover, external control forces the organization to be especially careful about its actions; because it must justify its behaviors to outsiders, it tends to formalize them. Finally, external control can further formalize the structure when it imposes special demands for rationalization, for example, when a parent firm insists that all its subsidiaries use a common set of purchasing procedures. The important point about this hypothesis is that the centralization of power in society – as independent organizations lose their power to larger systems – means centralization of power at the organizational level, and bureaucratization in the use of that power.

H15. The power needs of the members tend to generate structures that are excessively centralized   All members of the organization – operators, support staffers, analysts, managers – seek to enhance their own power, or at least to keep others from having power over them. But the dice are loaded in this game, the line managers and especially those at the strategic apex being favored by the existence of an authority structure that aggregates formal power up the hierarchy of command. And so we would expect that to the extent that the members seek personal power, excessively centralized structures would tend to be the most common result.

H16. Fashion favors the structure of the day, (and of the culture), sometimes even when inappropriate   Ideally, the design parameters are chosen according to the dictates of age, size, technical system, and environment. In fact, however, fashion seems to play a role too, encouraging many organizations to adopt currently popular design parameters that are inappropriate for themselves. Paris has its salons of haute couture; likewise New York has its offices of 'haute structure', the consulting firms that sometimes tend to oversell the latest in structural fashion.

V The configurations

This completes our discussion of the elements of structure. So far – and especially in our presentation of the situational factors – we have tended to look at structure the way a diner looks at a buffet table. But in fact these elements seem to cluster naturally in a certain number of ways, which we have called configurations. A number may have been evident to the reader in the discussion. In particular, we have six basic parts of the organization, six basic mechanisms of co-ordination, six basic types of decentralization. These in fact all fit together, to describe the essence of six basic configurations, as can be seen in Table 23.1, which also lists the design parameters and situational factors associated with each configuration.

We can explain this correspondence by considering the organization as being pulled in six different directions, one by each of its parts, as shown in Figure 23.7. When conditions favor one of these pulls over the others, a particular organization is drawn to structure itself as one of the configurations, as described below.

The simple structure

The name tells it all. And Figure 23.8 shows it all. The structure is simple, not much more than one large unit consisting of one or a few top managers, one of whom dominates by the pull to centralize, and a group of operators who do the basic work. Little of the behavior in the organization is formalized and minimal use is made of planning, training, or the liaison devices. The absence of standardization means that the structure is organic and has little need for staff analysts. Likewise there are few middle line managers because so much of the co-ordination is handled at the top. Even the support staff is minimized, in order to keep the structure lean, the organization flexible.

The organization must be flexible because it operates in a dynamic environment, often by choice since that is the only place where it can outsmart the bureaucracies. But that environment must be simple, as must the production system, or else the chief executive could not for long hold on to the lion's share of the power. The organization is often young, in part because time drives it toward bureaucracy, in part because the vulnerability of simple structures causes many of them to fail. And many are often small, since size too drives the structure toward bureaucracy. Not infrequently the chief executive purposely keeps the organization small in order to retain his personal control.

The classic simple structure is of course the entrepreneurial firm, controlled tightly and personally by its owner. Sometimes, however, under the control of a very clever autocratic leader who refuses to let go of the reins, a simple structure can grow large. Sometimes under crisis conditions, large organizations also revert temporarily to simple structures to allow forceful leaders to try to save them.

The machine bureaucracy

The machine bureaucracy is the offspring of the Industrial Revolution, when jobs became highly specialized and work became highly standard-

TABLE 23.1 Basic dimensions of the six configurations*

	Simple structure	Machine bureaucracy	Professional bureaucracy	Divisionalized form	Adhocracy	Missionary
Key co-ordinating mechanism	Direct supervision	Standardization of work	Standardization of skills	Standardization of outputs	Mutual adjustment	Standardization of norms
Key part of organization	Strategic apex	Technostructure	Operating core	Middle line	Support staff	Ideology
Design parameters: Specialization of jobs	Little specialization	Much horizontal and vertical specialization	Much horizontal specialization	Some horizontal and vertical specialization (between divisions and HQ)	Much horizontal specialization	Little specialization
Training	Little	Little	Much	Little	Much	Little
Indoctrination	Little	Little	Little	Some of divisional managers	Some	Much
Formalization of behavior, bureaucratic/organic	Little formalization, organic	Much formalization, bureaucratic	Little formalization, bureaucratic	Much formalization (within divisions), bureaucratic	Little formalization, organic	Little formal, bureaucratic
Grouping	Usually functional	Usually functional	Functional and market	Market	Functional and market	Market
Unit size	Wide	Wide at bottom, narrow elsewhere	Wide at bottom, narrow elsewhere	Wide (at top)	Narrow throughout	Wide (in enclaves of limited size)

Planning and control systems	Little planning and control	Action planning	Little planning and control	*Much perf. control*	Limited action planning	Little planning and control
Liaison devices	Few liaison devices	Few liaison devices	Liaison devices in administration	Few liaison devices	*Many liaison devices throughout*	Few liaison devices
Decentralization	*Centralization*	*Limited horizontal decentralization*	*Horizontal decentralization*	*Limited vertical decentralization*	*Selective decentralization*	*Decentralization*
Situational factors:						
Age and size	Typically young and small (first stage)	Typically old and large (second stage)	Varies	Typically old and very large (third stage)	Often young	Typically neither very young nor very old; large only through many small enclaves
Technical system	Simple, not regulating	Regulating but not automated, not very sophisticated	Not regulating or sophisticated	Divisible, otherwise typically like Mach. Bur.	Very sophisticated, often automated, or else not regulating or sophisticated	Simple, not regulating
Environment	Simple and dynamic; sometimes hostile	Simple and stable	Complex and stable	Relatively simple and stable; diversified markets (esp. products and services)	Complex and dynamic; sometimes disparate	Simple and usually stable
Power	Chief executive control; often owner-managed; not fashionable	Technocratic and external control; not fashionable	Professional operator control; fashionable	Middle-line control; fashionable (esp. in industry)	Expert control; very fashionable	Ideological control; coming fashion?

*Italic type within columns designates key design parameter.

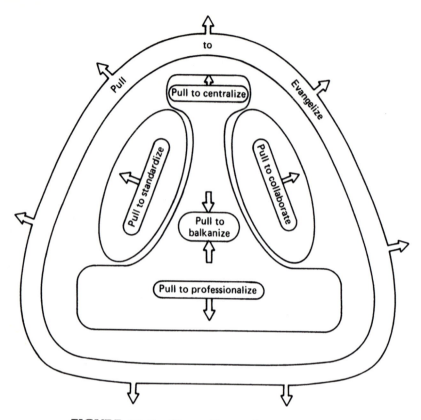

FIGURE 23.7   Six pulls on the organization

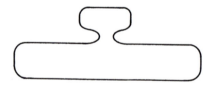

FIGURE 23.8   The simple structure

ized. As can be seen in Figure 23.9, in contrast to simple structure, the machine bureaucracy elaborates its administration. First, it requires a large technostructure to design and maintain its systems of standardization, notably those that formalize its behaviors and plan its actions. And by virtue of the organization's dependence on these systems, the technostructure gains a good deal of informal power, resulting in a limited amount of horizontal decentralization, reflecting the pull to standardize. A large hierarchy of middle line managers emerges to control the highly specia-

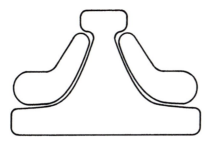

FIGURE 23.9   The machine bureaucracy

lized work of the operating core. But that middle line hierarchy is usually structured on a functional basis all the way up to the top, where the real power of co-ordination lies. So the structure tends to be rather centralized in the vertical sense.

To enable the top managers to maintain centralized control, both the environment and the production system of the machine bureaucracy must be fairly simple, the latter regulating the work of the operators but not itself automated. In fact, machine bureaucracies fit most naturally with mass production. Indeed it is interesting that this structure is more prevalent in industries that date back to the period from the Industrial Revolution to the early part of this century.

The professional bureaucracy

There is another bureaucratic configuration, but because this one relies on the standardization of skills rather than of work processes or outputs for its co-ordination, it emerges as dramatically different from the machine bureaucracy. Here the pull to professionalize dominates. In having to rely on trained professionals – people highly specialized, but with considerable control over their work, as in hospitals or universities – to do its operating tasks, the organization surrenders a good deal of its power not only to the professionals themselves but also to the associations and institutions that select and train them in the first place. So the structure emerges as highly decentralized horizontally; power over many decisions, both operating and strategic, flows all the way down the hierarchy, to the professionals of the operating core.

Above the operating core we find a rather unique structure, as can be seen in Figure 23.10. There is little need for a technostructure, since the main standardization occurs as a result of training that takes place outside the organization. Because the professionals work so independently, the size of operating units can be very large, and few first line managers are needed. The support staff is typically very large too, in order to back up the high priced professionals.

FIGURE 23.10   The professional bureaucracy

Professional bureaucracy is called for whenever an organization finds itself in an environment that is stable yet complex. Complexity requires decentralization to highly trained individuals, and stability enables them to apply standardized skills and so to work with a good deal of autonomy. To ensure that autonomy, the production system must be neither highly regulating, complex, nor automated.

The divisionalized form

Like the professional bureaucracy, the divisionalized form is not so much an integrated organization as a set of rather independent entities coupled together by a loose administrative structure. But whereas those entities of the professional bureaucracy are individuals, in the divisionalized form they are units in the middle line, generally called 'divisions', exerting a dominant pull to Balkanize. The divisionalized form differs from the other four configurations in one central respect: it is not a complete structure, but a partial one superimposed on others. Each division has its own structure.

An organization divisionalizes for one reason above all, because its product lines are diversified. And that tends to happen most often in the largest and most mature organizations, the ones that have run out of opportunities – or have become bored – in their traditional markets. Such diversification encourages the organization to replace functional by market-based units, one for each distinct product line (as shown in Figure 23.11), and to grant considerable autonomy to each to run its own business. The result is a limited form of decentralization down the chain of command.

How does the central headquarters maintain a semblance of control over the divisions? Some direct supervision is used. But too much of that interferes with the necessary divisional autonomy. So the headquarters relies on performance control systems, in other words the standardization of outputs. To design these control systems, headquarters creates a small technostructure. This is shown in Figure 23.11, across from the small central support staff that headquarters sets up to provide certain services common to the divisions such as legal counsel and public relations.

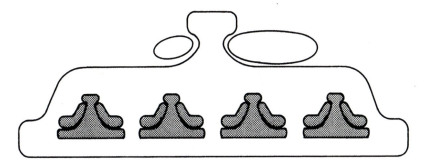

FIGURE 23.11   The divisionalized form

The adhocracy

None of the structures so far discussed suits the industries of our age, industries such as aerospace, petrochemicals, think tank consulting, and film making. These organizations need above all to innovate in very complex ways. The bureaucratic structures are too inflexible, and the simple structure too autocratic. These industries require 'project structures', structures that can fuse experts drawn from different specialties into smoothly functioning creative teams. That is the role of our fifth structural configuration, adhocracy, dominated by the experts' pull to collaborate.

Adhocracy is an organic structure that relies for co-ordination on mutual adjustment among its highly trained and highly specialized experts, which it encourages by the extensive use of the liaison devices – integrating managers, standing committees, and above all task forces and matrix structure. Typically the experts are grouped in functional units for housekeeping purposes but deployed in small market based project teams to do their work. To these teams, located all over the structure in accordance with the decisions to be made, is delegated power over different kinds of decisions. So the structure becomes decentralized selectively in the vertical and horizontal dimensions, that is, power is distributed unevenly, all over the structure, according to expertise and need.

All the distinctions of conventional structure disappear in the adhocracy, as can be seen in Figure 23.12. With power based on expertise, the line-staff distinction evaporates. With power distributed throughout the structure, the distinction between the strategic apex and the rest of the structure blurs.

Adhocracies are found in environments that are both complex and dynamic, because those are the ones that require sophisticated innova-

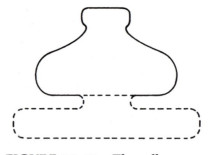

FIGURE 23.12   The adhocracy

tion, the type of innovation that calls for the co-operative efforts of many different kinds of experts. One type of adhocracy is often associated with a production system that is very complex, sometimes and so requires a highly skilled and influential support staff to design and maintain the technical system of the operating core. (The dotted lines of Figure 23.12 designate the separation of the operating core from the adhocratic administrative structure.) Here the projects take place in the administration to bring new operating facilities on line (or when a new complex is designed in a petro-chemical firm). Another type of adhocracy produces its projects directly for its clients (as in a think tank consulting firm or a manufacturer of engineering prototypes). Here, as a result, the operators also take part in the projects, bringing their expertise to bear on them; hence the operating core blends into the administrative structure (as indicated in Figure 23.12 above the dotted line). This second type of adhocracy tends to be young on average, because with no standard products or services, many tend to fail while others escape their vulnerability by standardizing some products or services and so converting themselves to a form of bureaucracy.

The missionary

Our sixth configuration forms another rather distinct combination of the elements we have been discussing. When an organization is dominated by the pull to evangelize, its members are encouraged to pull together, and so there tends to be loose division of labor, little job specialization as well as a reduction of the various forms of differentiation found in the other configurations – of the strategic apex from the rest, of staff from line or administration from operations, between operators, between divisions, and so on.

What holds the missionary together – that is, provides for its co-ordination – is the standardization of norms, the sharing of values and beliefs among all its members. And the key to ensuring this is their socialization, effected through the design parameter of indoctrination. Once the new member has been indoctrinated into the organization — once he or she identifies strongly with the common beliefs — then he or she can be given considerable freedom to make decisions. Thus the result of effective indoctrination is the most complete form of decentralization. And because other forms of co-ordination need not be relied upon, the missionary formalizes little of its behavior as such and makes minimal use of planning and control systems. As a result, it has virtually no technostructure. Likewise, external professional training is not relied upon, because that would force the organization to surrender a certain control to external agencies.

Hence, the missionary ends up as an amorphous mass of members, with little specialization as to job, differentiation as to part, division as to status. Beyond a certain size, however, as indicated in Figure 23.13, it tends to divide itself, like the amoeba, into smaller units, best thought of as 'enclaves', with perhaps a nominal headquarters in one of the enclaves — a loose strategic apex to serve as the depository of the official manifestations of the ideology (the 'archives').

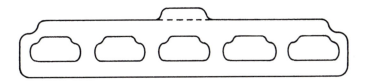

FIGURE 23.13   The missionary

Missionaries tend not to be very young organizations — it takes time for a set of beliefs to become institutionalized as an ideology. Many missionaries do not get a chance to grow very old either (with notable exceptions, such as certain long-standing religious orders). Size, as we saw, is also not very clear-cut. On one hand, there is a clear limit to the size of each enclave; on the other hand, nothing stops the organization from spinning off enclave after enclave, since each is a rather independent entity. Neither the environment nor the technical system of the missionary can be very complex, because that would require the use of highly skilled specialists, who would hold a certain power and status over others and thereby serve to differentiate the structure. Nor can the technical system be regulating, because that would lead to the formalizing of the operating work. Thus we would expect to find the simplest technical systems in missionaries, usually hardly any at all, as in religious orders or in the primitive farm co-operatives. And the environment of the missionary, in addition to being simple, can also typically be described as stable, in that the organization tends to function in a placid environment that makes few demands on it.

This completes a rather lengthy discussion of the structuring of organizations. As we have seen, what appears to be an enormously complex subject – comprising organizational parts, co-ordinating mechanisms, design parameters, and situational factors – can be made manageable by considering how all these many dimensions cluster to form distinct types of organizations. This may seem like an artificial reduction of the complexity, but in important ways it is far more realistic than trying to consider all of the permutations and combinations of these dimensions (an impossible, or at least awfully confusing task, in any event), or of giving up and dealing with this material in a fragmented way (as has been done in much of the traditional academic literature).

In fact, a good deal of experience with this 'typology' (the common label for a set of types developed logically) in both university teaching and business practice has suggested much use for it. In no way do all organizations fit one type or another. But having the set of them as a conceptual framework can help enormously to cut through, not only the complexities of structure, but of strategy and power and almost any other factor associated with organizations.

[...]

CHAPTER 24

Configurations of Strategy and Structure: towards a synthesis

DANNY MILLER

Introduction

[...]

In recent years the field of business strategy/policy has made some very significant advances. The conceptual work of Porter (1980) and the empirical studies of the PIMS data by Hambrick and his collaborators (1983, 1983a) are among the most interesting. These authors have derived extremely suggestive conceptual typologies and empirical taxonomies of strategy, focusing on variables that have enjoyed much attention from industrial economists – variables that were shown repeatedly to influence performance; those that can often be manipulated by managers. These include *differentiation* (e.g. innovation, advertising, product quality); *cost leadership* (capacity utilization, relative direct costs); *focus* (breadth of product lines, heterogeneity of clientele); and *asset parsimony* (fixed assets to revenue). Dimensions of market power are also considered (market share rank, barriers to entry, dependence on suppliers and customers), as are performance variables (ROI, earnings variability, growth in market share). The importance of some of these dimensions had already been suggested by Hofer and Schendel (1978) and Henderson (1979).

A central gap in the literature to date is that the rich content of strategies has never been related to structure. It may be, for example, that strategies of differentiation through innovation would not be easy to implement within a bureaucratic or mechanistic structure (Burns and Stalker, 1961). It also seems incongruous that bureaucratic structures could give rise to differentiation through innovation. By the same token, organizations that have embraced a cost leadership strategy pursue

353

extremely efficient, low cost production to lower prices. They might then require bureaucratic, 'mechanistic' structures that place a great deal of emphasis on sophisticated cost controls; standard, repetitive procedures; cost information systems, etc. Organic structures could be too flexible and inefficient to appropriately serve cost leaders. These conjectures are worthy of further study as the match between strategy and structure may vitally influence performance.

The theme we wish to pursue here is that there are ties that unite strategy and structure; that given a particular strategy there are only a limited number of suitable structures and vice versa. The theme is, of course, anything but novel. But it seems to require development in its particulars. Specifically, it would be useful to relate the rather sophisticated conceptions of recent strategic theorists – particularly those of Porter (1980), Hambrick (1983a,b), and Miles and Snow (1978) – to those of the major structural theorists – notably Lawrence and Lorsch (1967), Burns and Stalker (1961), Woodward (1965), Thompson (1967), Galbraith (1973) and Mintzberg (1979). A guiding philosophy that motivates the integration is that all of these authors, whose works have been so very well received, have identified extremely crucial slices of organizational reality. Also, most have tended to do so in terms of ideal or common types. That is, they have isolated frequently occurring configurations of organizational elements. The elements seem to form common gestalts such that each can best be understood in relation to the other elements in the configuration. It is the very fact that we conceive of such configurations that makes it possible for us to order our world of organizations in a rich and holistic way.
[. . .]

The case for configuration

[. . .]
There are three interrelated arguments for configuration. Recent literature on the population ecology of organizations (Hannan and Freeman, 1977; Aldrich, 1979; McKelvey, 1981) contends that the environment selects out various common organizational forms. There are only a rather limited number of possible strategies and structures feasible in any type of environment. A few favored strategies and structures cause the organizations pursuing them to thrive at the expense of competing organizations. Competitors must therefore either begin to move toward the superior strategies, or perish. In either event the repertoire of viable strategic and structural configurations is reduced. Miller (1982), Astley (1983), Tushman and Romanelli (1983) and Hinings *et al.*, 1984 argue that this convergence upon viable configurations will tend to happen rela-

tively quickly – in short bursts – and that, once reached, a fairly stable set of configurations will exist over a long period.

A second, related argument for the existence of configurations is that organizational features are interrelated in complex and integral ways. In other words the organization may be driven toward a common configuration to achieve internal harmony among its elements of strategy, structure and context. A central theme is pursued which marshals and orders the individual elements. Consider Miller and Mintzberg's (1984:21) description of the machine bureaucracy:

> The organization has highly specialized, routine operating tasks, very formalized procedures, and large units in its operations. The basis for grouping tasks ... is by function and co-ordination is effected by rules and hierarchy. Power for decision making is quite centralized, and there exists an elaborate administrative structure with a clear hierarchy of line authority.

Here standardization, rules and regulations, formal communications, and tight controls are emphasized. These large organizations can only function in stable and simple environments in which their inflexibility is not overly limiting.

Clearly many of these attributes are complementary and mutually reinforcing. The stable environment enables the operating procedures to be routinized and formalized, but the procedures in turn cause the organization to seek out a stable environment. Large size encourages standardization since procedures repeat and controls must be impersonal – but standardization in turn encourages growth to boost economies of scale. Cost leadership strategies (Porter, 1980) come to be favored. Large size causes inflexibility which then prompts the search for stability in the environment. But the reverse causal direction may also apply since stability encourages growth to a scale that can optimally exploit opportunities. Thus each element makes sense in terms of the whole – and together they form a cohesive system (Miller and Friesen, 1984b:22). Cohesive configurations reduce the number of possible ways in which the elements combine. They make it that much more likely that common configurations will account for a sizeable proportion of organizations.

This brings us to our third argument for the prevalence of common configurations: that organizations tend to change their elements in a manner that either extends a given configuration, or moves it quickly to a new configuration that is preserved for a very long time. Piecemeal changes will often destroy the complementarities among many elements of configuration and will thus be avoided. Only when change is absolutely necessary or extremely advantageous will organizations be tempted to move concertedly and rapidly (to shorten the disruptive interval of transition) from one configuration to another that is broadly different. Such changes, because they are so expensive, will not be undertaken very frequently. Consequently organizations will adhere to their configurations for fairly long periods. Astley (1983), Miller (1982), Miller and Friesen (1984b) and Tushman and Romanelli (1983), have given more detailed arguments for this quantum view of change. Miller and Friesen (1980, 1982) have found corroborating empirical evidence.

So much for the conceptual arguments in favor of configurations. But there is also strong empirical evidence to support the existence of configurations. This is to be found in the well-known works by Woodward (1965), Lawrence and Lorsch (1967), Burns and Stalker (1961) and others, all of whom found integral structural configurations in their data. Hambrick (1983b) and Miller and Friesen (1984a) have also found configurations among elements of strategy in the PIMS data – largely corresponding to Porter's (1980) strategies and appearing in different environments. Dess and Davis (1984) and Miller and Friesen (1984a) showed that firms pursuing Porter's three generic strategies are quite common, and also that they outperform firms that are 'stuck in the middle'.

One of the most heartening developments is that there is considerable overlap between the structural and strategic typologies and taxonomies. Even though the authors were looking at different parts of the proverbial elephant, their work seems to converge considerably so that it is becoming increasingly possible to construct pictures of the whole beast. For example, our bureaucracy described earlier seems to be reflected by Lawrence and Lorsch's (1967) container firms, Burns and Stalker's (1961) mechanistic organizations, Woodward's (1965) mass producers, Perrow's (1971) routine manufacturers, and Mintzberg's (1979) machine bureaucracy. The adhocracy of Mintzberg (1979) recalls Lawrence and Lorsch's (1967) plastics firms, Burns and Stalker's (1961) organic organizations, Perrow's (1971) nonroutine manufacturers, and so on.

Turning to the literature on strategic types there are notable similarities among Porter's (1980) differentiators, Miller and Friesen's (1978) adaptive firms, and Miles and Snow's (1978) prospectors. By the same token, Porter's (1980) cost leaders roughly recall Miles and Snow's (1978) defenders and Miller and Friesen's (1978) giants under fire.

We do not wish to argue that these typologies are substitutes for one another. They do indeed have different emphases. But there seem to be important areas of commonality that suggest some natural links between types of structures and types of strategies.

Selection of strategic configurations

[...]

The conceptual work by Porter (1980), Scherer (1980), Miles and Snow

(1978) and MacMillan and Hambrick (1983) suggests four broad categories of variables or 'dimensions' that reflect important competitive strategies. They are *differentiation, cost leadership, focus* and *asset parsimony*. These dimensions can be used to compare firms' competitive advantages within and across industries. Table 24.1 shows some of the many representative variables that are subsumed by each dimension. The empirical work by Hambrick (1983b), Miller and Friesen (1984a) and Dess and Davis (1984) shows how reliably the individual variables cluster together to form the fundamental dimensions. The dimensions do not exhaust the concept of strategy – but they do reflect many of its important elements. We shall discuss each dimension in turn.

Differentiation aims to create a product that is perceived as uniquely attractive. It emphasizes strong marketing abilities, creative, well-

TABLE 24.1   Representative strategic variables within each dimension

Differentiation
Innovation
  Percentage of sales from products introduced over last 2 or 3 years
  R&D as a percentage of sales
  Average age of products
  Frequency of major product changes

Marketing
  Product quality
  Product image
  Marketing expenses
  Advertising and promotion
  Sales force
  Services quality

Focus
  Product line breadth
  Breadth of customer types
  Geographic coverage

Cost leadership
  Relative directive costs/unit
  Newness of plant and equipment
  Product pricing
  Capacity utilization
  Backward vertical integration
  Process R&D

Asset parsimony
  Fixed asset intensity (gross book value of plant and equipment revenues)
  Current asset intensity (current assets/revenues)

designed products, a reputation for quality, a good corporate image, and strong cooperation from marketing channels.

Notwithstanding Porter's (1980) discussion, there appear to be at least two varieties of differentiators – each, as we shall see, with different structural and environmental co-requisites. The *innovating* differentiators are really much like Miles and Snow's (1978) prospectors, and Miller and Friesen's (1984b) S_{1B} adaptive firms. They differentiate by coming out with new products and new technologies. They lead their competitors in innovation and can charge fairly high prices. There is a strong emphasis on R&D and pioneering. In contrast, the *marketing* differentiators are more like Miller and Friesen's (1984b) S_{1A} firms which offer an attractive package, good service, convenient locations, and good product/service reliability. These firms are very forceful marketers – spending large sums on advertising, salesmen, promotion, and distribution. They are rarely the first out with new products.

Cost leadership is a strategy that strives to produce goods or services more cheaply than competitors. It stresses efficient scale facilities, the pursuit of cost reductions in manufacture, and the minimization of expenses of product R&D, services, selling and advertising. Cost leaders try to supply a standard, no-frills, high-volume product at the most competitive possible price. They do very little product innovation since this is disruptive of efficiency. The innovations of competitors will only be imitated after a considerable risk-reducing lag. Process R&D, backward vertical integration, and production automation may be pursued to reduce costs. Variants of the cost leadership strategy have been discussed by Buzzell, Gale and Sultan (1975), Henderson (1979), Miles and Snow (1978) and Miller and Friesen (1984b). Porter (1980) claims that differentiation and cost leadership do not usually go well together – that their joint pursuit could lead to a 'stuck-in-the-middle position' which fails to realize the advantages of either strategy.

Focus has been used by Porter (1980) to designate a niche strategy that concentrates the firm's attention on a specific type of customer, product or geographic locale. The firm uses either a differentiation or a cost leadership strategy (or some combination of the two) within a specialized part of the industry. We believe that focus can best be treated as a dimension with both ends of the continuum – very highly focused and very *un*focused – having rather different implications. The highly focused firms pursue Miller and Friesen's (1978) niche strategy. The highly diversified firms recall Miller and Friesen's (1984b) conglomerate strategy, and Rumelt's (1974) unrelated diversification strategy. In all cases focus complements, but does not substitute for, differentiation and cost leadership.

It is worthwhile noting that the focus dimension can refer to a business-level strategy or a corporate-level strategy. In the first instance focus measures the degree to which a firm covers one specific industry.

At the corporate level, however, focus describes the extent to which the firm has diversified into different industries. In fact, the same firm may employ highly focused business strategies in two very different industries. It could then be said to have an unfocused (diversified) corporate strategy and two focused business strategies. Although our typology will deal with strategy at the business level, we shall make a single exception in the case of the discussion of Divisionalized Conglomerates that pursue an unfocused corporate strategy. This common corporate strategy has important implications both for structure and for business-level strategies, and this warrants some discussion.

Asset parsimony is our final strategic category. It refers to the fewness of assets per unit output (MacMillan and Hambrick, 1983). Initially, the literature on strategy showed that capital intensity seemed to impede performance in many different industries (Schoeffler, Buzzell and Heany, 1974; Gale, 1980; MacMillan, Hambrick and Day, 1982). It tends to reduce flexibility and increase competition when an industry reaches overcapacity. But MacMillan and Hambrick (1983) discovered that asset intensity, because it can provide for greater efficiency, may be quite suitable for cost leaders operating in stable environments. In contrast, where the organization must be flexible, as is often the case with differentiators, asset parsimony is most necessary (MacMillan and Hambrick, 1983).

How do these four strategic dimensions interact to produce effective strategic types or configurations? There are probably many ways, so just a few important ones will be isolated. Three rules of thumb were used as guides in deriving five common strategic configurations. The first rule has already been referred to. It is that successful firms tend to pursue either cost leadership or differentiation strategies, but usually not both (Porter, 1980). The second rule is that asset parsimony is desirable for differentiators who must remain flexible, but less suitable for cost leaders who must pursue efficiency (MacMillan and Hambrick, 1983). The third rule is that most strategies can have various degrees of focus, subject, of course, to a few constraints: most cost leaders cannot be too narrowly focused because of their need for economies of scale (Scherer, 1980); innovators cannot be too broadly focused or they will deplete their resources trying to lead in too many markets; but they also should not be too narrowly focused as their innovations can take them into new and profitable markets (Miles and Snow, 1978); conglomerates that are completely unfocused at the *corporate* level can have divisions that pursue most other business-level strategies – but our subsequent analysis will indicate that they will often do best with marketing differentiation and cost leadership strategies.

In light of the above, our five strategic configurations are presented in Figure 24.1.

[...]

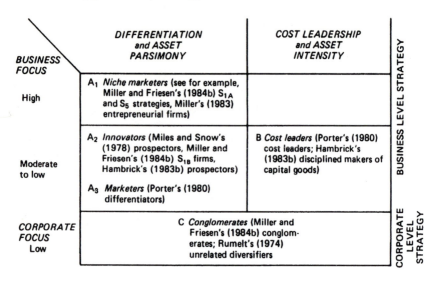

FIGURE 24.1   Five successful configurations of strategy

.Having identified some common strategic types we shall proceed to examine the structures which can adequately support them, and the environments in which they may thrive.

Bridging strategy and structure

The literature has shown that there are very many types of organization structures and environments. There are also many elements or variables that can be used to characterize them. So we shall again concentrate on only a selection of elements that has already been shown to be important in its possible consequences for strategy. We shall, using the literature, synthesize these elements into common types, and relate each to our five strategic configurations. We must stress at the outset that we do not by any means believe that there are only five successful matches between strategy and structure. These are to be taken as representative, not exhaustive.

Mintzberg's (1979) five structural types provide an excellent synthesis of the literature on structure. While his professional bureaucracies are usually not business firms and therefore are beyond our scope, his other types are quite relevant: they are the simple structure, the machine bureaucracy, the divisionalized form and the adhocracy. We shall adapt and extend Mintzberg's framework somewhat to make it more easy to relate it to the common strategies. The dimensions of each type are summarized in Table 24.2.

Simple niche marketers

Simple structure

The simple structure is used by small firms run by a dominating chief executive, often an owner–manager. The structure is highly informal with co-ordination of tasks accomplished via direct supervision, and all strategies made at the top. There is little specialization of tasks, a low degree of bureaucratization and formalization (few programs, rules or regulations) (Pugh, Hickson and Hinings, 1969), and information systems are extremely primitive. Because there is a low level of differentiation in the goals, interpersonal orientations, methods and time horizons of the various departments, there is little need for sophisticated integrative or 'liaison' devices (Lawrence and Lorsch, 1967). Power is centralized at the top. Technology is often of Perrow's (1971) engineering or nonroutine manufacturing, or Woodward's (1965) custom variety.

Clearly, simple structures cannot be appropriate in all environments and industries. They typically exist where the industry is fragmented (low concentration) and comprised of small highly competitive firms. Competitive rivalry restricts the munificence of the environment and boosts firms' vulnerability. Because simple technologies are often used to produce products, barriers to entry are very low. Market share instability and cost–price squeezes can therefore be major threats. Firms usually have very little bargaining power over their customers in such a competitive setting (see Table 24.2). Indeed, the environment recalls Hambrick's (1983a) 'unruly mob'.

Niche marketing strategy

Given the simple structure and the competitive environment, which of our five strategic types would be most suitable? Typically, simple firms must pursue some sort of differentiation strategy in order to succeed. They are too small and vulnerable to become fixed asset intensive. This would be extremely risky in the light of the substantial industry instability (MacMillan and Hambrick, 1983). Also, simple technologies and small size generally do not allow for cost leadership. Finally, structures are too primitive, too undifferentiated, and too centralized to support *complex* innovation (although very simple, CEO-driven innovations can be common). Thus firms with simple structures must generally pursue a niche or a marketing differentiation strategy. They may flourish by producing a somewhat distinctive product for a niche of the market that is the least competitive. This minimizes some of the disadvantages of smallness. To defend their niche these firms may differentiate their offerings by providing greater convenience, more reliable service, or a

TABLE 24.2 Structures, environments and strategies

Structural dimensions	Simple structure	Machine bureaucracy	Organic	Divisionalized
Power centralization	All at the top	CEO and designers of workflow	Scientists, technocrats and middle managers	Divisional executives
Bureaucratization	Low–informal	Many formal rules, policies and procedures	Organic	Bureaucratic
Specialization	Low	Extensive	Extensive	Extensive
Differentiation	Minimal	Moderate	Very high	High
Integration and co-ordination of effort	By CEO via direct supervision	By technocrats via formal procedures	By integrating personnel, task forces via mutual adjustment	By formal committees via plan and budgets
Information Systems	Crude, informal	Cost controls and budgets	Informal scanning, open communications	Management information systems and profit centers
Evironmental dimensions Technology	Simple, custom	Mass production, large batch/line	Sophisticated product, automated or custom	Varies

	Business-level strategies			Corporate-level strategy
Favored strategy	Niche differentiation	Cost leadership	Innovative differentiation	Conglomeration
Competition	Extreme	High	Moderate	Varies
Dynamism/uncertainty	Moderate	Very low	Very high	Varies
Growth	Varies	Slow	Rapid	Varies
Concentration ratio	Very low	High	Varies	Varies
Barriers to Entry	None	Scales barriers	Knowledge barriers	Varies
Marketing emphasis	Quality, service, convenience	Low price	New products, high quality	Image
Production emphasis	Economy	Efficiency	Flexibility	Vertical integration
Asset management	Parsimony	Intensity	Parsimony	Varies
Innovation and R&D	Little	Almost none	Very high	Low to moderate
Product-market scope	Very narrow	Average	Average	Very broad

TABLE 24.3   Matching strategy and structure

Structure and rationale	Match/ conflict	Strategy
Simple structure		
Can offer quality, convenience, and better service since this will not tax the structure	M	Marketing differentiation
Avoids some competition in hostile environment; reduces liability of being small	M	Niche differentiation
Complex innovation impossible in centralized, monolithic structure	C	Innovative differentiation
Insufficient scale; overly primitive structure	C	Conglomeration
Insufficient scale	C	Cost leadership
Machine bureaucracy		
Substantial scale economies possible; emphasis on efficiency good in stable setting	M	Cost leadership
Suitable only if differentiation does not upset production regularity and efficiency (e.g. advertising, good service)	M	Marketing differentiation
Structure too inflexible	C	Innovative differentiation
Functional–departmental structure inappropriate	C	Conglomeration
Inflexibility, capital intensity	C	Niche differentiation
Organic structure		
Flexible, innovative structure	M	Innovative differentiation
May be suitable if niche wide enough to make use of innovation potential; need for caution	M	Niche differentiation
Should not squander resources on selling since state-of-art product is already highly desirable to customers	C	Marketing differentiation
Structure is too inefficient	C	Cost leadership
Would spread innovative efforts too thinly; also, structure is not divisionalized	C	Conglomeration
Divisionalized structure		
Divisions, profit centers, head office controls, formal plans, etc. suitable for diversification	M	Cost leadership

TABLE 24.3 *cont.*   **Matching strategy and structure**

Structure and rationale	Match/ conflict	Strategy
Consistent with bureaucratic tendency; scale economies and vertical integration if divisions use related inputs	M	Cost leadership
Where cost leadership contraindicated marketing differentiation may be suitable for intermediate level of bureaucracy	M	Marketing differentiation
Generally, divisions are forced by head office to be too bureaucratic to be innovative	C	Innovative differentiation

more appealing – higher visibility or better quality – product to a select group of customers (strategies A_1 or A_3 on Figure 24.1). None of these competitive strengths require much structural complexity. To conclude, niche or marketing differentiation strategies and simple structures should probably go together (see Table 24.2). Table 24.3 summarizes some of the reasons for the matches and mismatches between the simple structure, its setting, and the five strategic types.

Mechanistic cost leaders

Machine bureaucracy structure

The mechanistic (Burns and Stalker, 1961) or machine bureaucracy structure has been alluded to earlier. It is a very rigid structure in which the co-ordination of tasks is done via standardization of work. A key part of the organization is the technostructure (Mintzberg, 1979) which designs the production system. The technology is somewhat automated and integrated and is normally of the line or large batch variety (Woodward, 1965). The firm is highly specialized as tasks are finely broken down. As its name implies, the structure is exceedingly bureaucratic and hierarchical with its many formal rules, programs and procedures (Burns and Stalker, 1961; Pugh, Hickson and Hinings, 1969). The information systems are quite well developed – but mainly for reporting cost and output rather than market information. The departmental, functionally organized structure is only moderately differentiated as the emphasis throughout is on following programs and plans. Integration is effected mainly through these programs (Lawrence and Lorsch, 1967).

Power rests in the hands of the top executives and the designers of workflow processes. Very little authority resides at lower or middle management levels.

The environments of these firms are quite different from those of the niche marketers. Mechanistic firms can thrive only in stable settings. Industries are often highly concentrated and mature, and all the firms are quite large. There is relatively little uncertainty since competitor and customer behavior is fairly predictable. Demand is quite stable, as are market shares. Hambrick's (1983a) 'orderly producers' environments are recalled (see Table 24.2).

Cost leadership strategy

Clearly the strategic options open to these firms are quite limited. The structures are extremely inflexible and geared to efficiency; so strategies of innovation are out of the question. Also, because markets are not growing much (due to maturity) and because firms are large, it is unwise to focus on too small a segment of the industry. This would increase the risk of declines in demand and under-utilization of facilities. There are thus only two possible strategies that remain promising – marketing differentiation and cost leadership. The second is very natural since it requires the least flexibility and the greatest production efficiency – characteristics which inhere in these structures. Some firms are able to make excellent use of their machine-like structures. They cut costs to the bone and either earn margins superior to the competition or else build up market share by selling very cheaply. Although it is less likely that mechanistic structures can support a marketing differentiation strategy, this is not totally out of the question. This might happen when the firm sells a fairly standard product in high volume but offers services, convenience or quality that exceed the competition's. It is important that this firm not be placed in a position of having to react quickly to competitors. It must therefore differentiate in a way that does not interfere with efficient and mechanical operations, and is not easy to imitate. For example, a poor differentiation tactic would be to fragment the product line by customizing products. This would immediately boost costs and invite retaliation. Better alternatives might be to integrate forward (perhaps by buying distributorships), to improve quality, or to boost brand image through advertising. None of these tactics requires structural flexibility and all are facilitated by large size. The theme is clear: these structures and settings favor cost leadership. Only under special conditions can they support a strategy of marketing differentiation (see Table 24.3).

Innovating adhocracies

Organic structure

The organic form (Burns and Stalker, 1961) or adhocracy (Mintzberg, 1979) is a structure that is extremely different from – one might almost say opposite to – the machine bureaucracy. It is ideal for performing unusual and complex tasks which tend to change continually. Such tasks confront Perrow's (1971) R&D firms where there are 'many exceptions' in production and no obvious way of accomplishing the job. Typically, groups of highly trained specialists from a variety of areas work together intensively to design and produce complex and rapidly changing products. Representatives from R&D, marketing and production departments, collaborate face-to-face, via mutual adjustment (Thompson, 1967) in order to co-ordinate their contributions. A high degree of differentiation prevails as people with different skills, goals and time horizons work together (Lawrence and Lorsch, 1967). Frequent meetings, integrating personnel, committees, and other liaison devices are used to ensure effective collaboration (Galbraith, 1973). Power is decentralized as much of it resides with the technocrats and scientists responsible for innovation. Authority is thus situational and based on expertise (Burns and Stalker, 1961). There are few bureaucratic rules or standard procedures since these are too confining and would in any event rapidly become obsolete. Sensitive information gathering systems are developed for analysing the environment, and vertical and horizontal communications are open and frequent. Production technology varies both in its degree of automation and its complexity. It is, for example, highly automated and complex in the semiconductor industry, but of a job shop, custom nature in some aerospace firms.

The environment tends to be very complex and dynamic. Technologies change rapidly, as do product designs and customer needs. A high percentage of production may be exported. Advanced industry capabilities create 'knowledge barriers' to entry (Scherer, 1980). As a result, competitive rivalry is usually not quite as intensive as for the simple structures. Competition is further reduced by a fairly brisk rate of demand growth. But market share instability may arise as firms leapfrog one another with their new creative advances. Product sophistication is often substantial. To summarize, the environment is dynamic, uncertain and moderately competitive (see Table 24.3).

Innovative differentiation strategy

One of our strategies immediately comes to mind as a fine match for this structure and environment. It is differentiation through innovation (A_2). The structure is flexible and allows for the collaboration among specialists so necessary to create new products. Burns and Stalker (1961), Lawrence and Lorsch (1967) and Mintzberg (1979), have already stressed this theme. The information and scanning systems keep managers and technocrats up to date with scientific and competitive developments. Intensive collaboration and liaison devices, open communications, and decentralization of power (in fact, the reliance on expertise-based power) facilitate complex and continual innovation. Rapid adaptation to the dynamic environment is essential, and this can only be accomplished with a strategy of innovation. Asset parsimony may be useful as high capital intensity dramatically reduces flexibility (MacMillan and Hambrick, 1983). (The cost leadership strategy is clearly inappropriate since it impedes innovation and inhibits adaptiveness. See Table 24.3.)

Innovating adhocracies would do well not to focus too broadly or too narrowly in their selection of markets. While geographic expansion and exporting may be advisable because of barriers to entry and product sophistication, other types of broadening should probably be restricted. For example, if the firm enters too many markets which have different competitive conditions and customer requirements, it may find its efforts spread too thin to do very well in any one of them. Recall that market dynamism places a premium on flexibility, innovation and product sophistication. This entails a large administrative and structural burden even in a limited market. On the other hand, firms probably should not focus as narrowly as the simple niche marketers. This might increase their dependence on a small cyclical market and prevent them from commercializing their discoveries in a new and growing domain. Diversification could allow firms to more easily shift into safer niches when attacked.

We have discussed only the innovation aspects of differentiation as these can best be exploited by adhocracies. The marketing differentiation variables generally should play a smaller role. Customers want state-of-the-art, sophisticated products. If these are not supplied, no amount of advertising or promotion will help. In fact, firms may benefit from holding down their marketing expenses to conserve the resources necessary for innovation. One marketing differentiation strategy that might succeed here stresses high quality. Some customers might be willing to trade off novelty for reliability.

Divisionalized conglomerates

Divisional structure

An organization may be split into divisions that are responsible for producing and marketing a discrete type of product. Usually these divisions are self-contained profit centers run by an executive whose responsibilities are similar to those of the chief executives of most independent enterprises. The individual divisions may in fact be quite different from one another – a few employing organic structures, many more using bureaucratic structures. Therefore we must shift our focus from business-level structures and strategies to those that apply at the corporate level.

Mintzberg (1979) argues that most divisions in his 'divisionalized form' are driven to become somewhat bureaucratic and formalized. The head office standardizes procedures and methods wherever possible to improve control over the divisions (Chandler, 1962; Channon, 1973). It emphasizes performance control through sophisticated management information systems, cost centers, and profit centers. However, a good deal of decision-making power remains in the hands of the divisional managers who know the most about their markets. The divisions tend to operate fairly independently of one another, with company-wide issues being handled by interdivisional committees and head office staff departments (see Table 24.2).

Environments vary from one division to the next. Mintzberg (1979) believes that the bureaucratic orientations of the divisions require that the environment be stable and simple. Clearly, however, there are exceptions as some divisionalized firms operate in rather turbulent sectors of the economy.

Conglomeration and diversification strategy

The literature agrees overwhelmingly that corporate-level conglomerate strategies that embrace very different industries require divisionalized structures. The administrative complexity caused by diversification gets divided up so that each significant market is dealt with by its own specialist and generalist managers. The head office is concerned only with controlling and appraising the divisions, allocating capital, and scouting out new diversification ventures.

This relationship between diversification and divisionalization has given rise to Chandler's (1962) famous dictum that 'structure follows strategy'. We are not at all sure, however, that this is always true. A corporate strategy of conglomeration and a divisional structure may well be part of the same gestalt – diversification creates the need for divisionalization; but divisionalized structures, with their head office venture groups and planning departments, seek out new acquisitions. Often, then, strategy may follow structure. One thing, however, is certain: divisionalized structures tend to be matched by corporate strategies that are the least focused – irrespective of the source of the match (see Table 24.3).

We mentioned earlier that the divisions experience pressures of control from the head office, which often induce bureaucratization, formalization, and a loss of flexibility. This precludes business-level strategies of differentiation through innovation. But marketing differentiation strategies and cost leadership business strategies may be quite useful. Their appropriateness will be a function of the degree of stability in the environment, the prospects of economies of scale, and, of course, the degree of bureaucratization in the divisions. The more prevalent these qualities, the greater the appropriateness of cost leadership. The less prevalent the qualities (all other things being equal) the more suitable the strategy of marketing or even niche differentiation. Of course different divisions may pursue different business strategies.

One element of cost leadership – backward vertical integration at the corporate level – may be quite appropriate for some conglomerates. In cases where divisions use similar raw material inputs, their collective demand for supplies may warrant backward integration. This can allow economies of manufacture for the total organization without reducing the possibilities of differentiation for the division. The same argument might hold for integration forward.

Conclusion

Our arguments throughout have been somewhat crude, the principal aim having been to propose a new method of relating strategy to structure and to suggest some illustrative configurations and linkages. No doubt there are many effective matches between strategies and structures other than the ones we have discussed. Also, the appropriateness of a strategy in general, as well as the relative effectiveness of its various elements, will be a function of much more than structure. It will depend on economic, competitive and customer factors, as well as conditions in international markets. Our arguments, therefore, must be viewed as tentative because we still know so little about the subject. We very much hope that this does not alienate readers but rather spurs them on to more thoroughly investigate the relationships between common structural and strategic configurations and their implications for performance in different environments. More encompassing empirical taxonomies should be of considerable help in this quest.

References

Aldrich, H. E. (1979) *Organizations and Environments* (Englewood Cliffs, NJ: Prentice-Hall).
Astley, W. G. (1983) 'The dynamics of organizational evolution: critical reflec-

tions on the variation–selection–retention model'. Working Paper, The Wharton School, Philadelphia.

Burns, T. and Stalker, G., (1961) *The Management of Innovation* (London: Tavistock).

Buzzell, R. D., Gale, B. and Sultan, R. (1975) 'Market share: a key to profitability', *Harvard Business Review*, **51**(1), pp. 97–106.

Chandler, A. (1962) *Strategy and Structure* (Cambridge, MA: MIT Press).

Channon, D. (1973) *Strategy and Structure in British Enterprise* (Boston, MA: Harvard University Press).

Dess, G. and Davis, P. (1984) 'Porter's generic strategies as determinants of strategic group membership and organizational performance', *Academy of Management Journal*, **27**, pp. 467–88.

Galbraith, J., (1973) *Designing Complex Organizations* (Reading, MA: Addison–Wesley).

Gale, B. (1980) 'Can more capital buy higher productivity?', *Harvard Business Review*, **58**(4), pp. 67–77.

Hambrick, D. C. (1983a) 'An empirical typology of mature industrial product environments', *Academy of Management Journal*, **26**, pp. 213–30.

Hambrick, D. C. (1983b) 'High profit strategies in mature capital goods industries: a contingency approach', *Academy of Management Journal*, **26**, pp. 687–707.

Hambrick, D. and Schecter, S. (1983) 'Turnaround strategies for mature industrial-product business units', *Academy of Management Journal*, **26**, pp. 231–48.

Hannan, M. and Freeman, J. (1977) 'The population ecology of organizations', *American Journal of Sociology*, **83**, pp. 929–64.

Henderson, B. (1979) *Henderson on Corporate Strategy* (Cambridge, MA: Abt Books).

Hinings, C. R., Greenwood, R., Ranson, S. and Walsh, K. (1984). 'Reform reorientation and change: the designing of organizational change', unpublished manuscript, Department of Commerce, University of Alberta, Edmonton.

Hofer, C. and Schendel, D. (1978) *Strategy Formulation: Analytical Concepts* (St Paul, MN: West).

Lawrence, P. R. and Lorsch, J. W. (1967) *Organization and Environment* (Boston, MA: Harvard University Press).

MacMillan, I. C. and Hambrick, D. (1983) 'Capital intensity, market share instability and profits – the case for asset parsimony', working paper, Columbia University Strategy Research Center, New York.

MacMillan, I. C., Hambrick, D. C. and Day, D. (1982) 'The product portfolio and profitability – a PIMS-based analysis of industrial-product businesses', *Academy of Management Journal*, **25**, pp. 733–55.

McKelvey, W. (1981) *Organizational Systematics* (Los Angeles, CA: University of California Press).

Miles, R. and Snow, C. (1978) *Organizational Strategy, Structure and Process* (New York: McGraw-Hill).

Miller, D. (1982) 'Evolution and revolution: a quantum view of structural change in organizations', *Journal of Management Studies*, **19**, pp. 131–51.

Miller, D. (1983) 'The correlates of entrepreneurship in three types of firms', *Management Science*, **29**, pp. 770–91.

Miller, D. and Friesen, P. H. (1978) 'Archetypes of strategy formulation', *Management Science*, **24**, pp. 921–33.

Miller, D. and Friesen, P. H. (1980) 'Momentum and revolution in organizational adaptation', *Academy of Management Journal*, **23**, pp. 591–614.

Miller, D. and Friesen, P. H. (1982) 'Structural change and performance: quantum vs. piecemeal–incremental approaches', *Academy of Management Journal*, **25**, pp. 867–92.

Miller, D. and Friesen, P. H. (1984a) 'Porter's generic strategies and performance', working paper, McGill University, Montreal.

Miller, D. and Friesen, P. H. (1984b) *Organizations: A Quantum View* (Englewood Cliffs, NJ: Prentice Hall).

Miller, D. and Mintzberg, H. (1984) 'The case for configuration', in D. Miller and P. Friesen (eds) *Organizations: A Quantum View* (Englewood Cliffs, NJ: Prentice Hall) pp. 10–30.

Mintzberg, H. (1979) *The Structuring of Organizations* (Englewood Cliffs, NJ: Prentice Hall).

Perrow, C. (1971) *Organizational Analysis: A Sociological View* (Belmont, CA: Wadsworth).

Porter, M. (1980) *Competitive Strategy* (New York: Free Press).

Pugh, D. S., Hickson, D. J. and Hinings, C. R. (1969) 'An empirical taxonomy of structures of work organizations', *Administrative Science Quarterly*, **14**, pp. 115–26.

Rumelt, R. P. (1974) *Strategy, Structure, and Economic Performance* (Division of Research, Graduate School of Business Administration, Harvard University, Cambridge, MA).

Scherer, F. (1980) *Industrial Market Structure and Economic Performance* (Chicago, IL: Rand McNally).

Schoeffler, S., Buzzell, R. D., and Heany, D. F. (1974) 'Impact of strategic planning on profit performance', *Harvard Business Review*, **52**(2), pp. 137–45.

Thompson, J. (1967) *Organizations in Action* (New York: McGraw-Hill).

Tushman, M. L. and Romanelli, E. (1983) 'Organizational evolution: a metamorphosis model of convergence and reorientation', working paper, Columbia University Center for Strategy Research, New York.

Woodward, J. (1965) *Industrial Organization: Theory and Practice* (Oxford: Oxford University Press).

CHAPTER 25

Evolution and Revolution as Organizations Grow

LARRY E. GREINER

Reprinted by permission of *Harvard Business Review*. Extracts from 'Evolution and Revolution as Organisations Grow' by Larry E. Greiner, July/August 1972. Copyright © 1972 by the President and Fellows of Harvard College; all rights reserved.

[. . .]

Introduction

A small research company chooses too complicated and formalized an organization structure for its young age and limited size. It flounders in rigidity and bureaucracy for several years and is finally acquired by a larger company.

Key executives of a retail store chain hold on to an organizational structure long after it has served its purpose, because their power is derived from this structure. The company eventually goes into bankruptcy.

A large bank disciplines a 'rebellious' manager who is blamed for current control problems, when the underlying cause is centralized procedures that are holding back expansion into new markets. Many younger managers subsequently leave the bank, competition moves in, and profits are still declining.

The problems of these companies, like those of many others, are rooted more in past decisions than in present events or outside market dynamics. Historical forces do indeed shape the future growth of organizations. Yet management, in its haste to grow, often overlooks such critical developmental questions as: Where has our organization been? Where is it now? And what do the answers to these questions mean for where we are going? Instead, its gaze is fixed outward toward the environment and the future — as if more precise market projections will provide a new organizational identity.

Companies fail to see that many clues to their future success lie within their own organizations and their evolving states of development. Moreover, the inability of management to understand its organization development problems can result in a company becoming 'frozen' in its present stage of evolution or, ultimately, in failure, regardless of market opportunities.

My position in this article is that the future of an organization may be less determined by outside forces than it is by the organization's history. In stressing the force of history on an organization, I have drawn from the legacies of European psychologists (their thesis being that individual behavior is determined primarily by previous events and experiences, not by what lies ahead). Extending this analogy of individual development to the problems of organization development, I shall discuss a series of developmental phases through which growing companies tend to pass. But, first, let me provide two definitions:

1. The term *evolution* is used to describe prolonged periods of growth where no major upheaval occurs in organization practices.
2. The term *revolution* is used to describe those periods of substantial turmoil in organization life.

As a company progresses through developmental phases, each evolutionary period creates its own revolution. For instance, centralized practices eventually lead to demands for decentralization. Moreover, the nature of management's solution to each revolutionary period determines whether a company will move forward into its next stage of evolutionary growth. As I shall show later, there are at least five phases of organization development, each characterized by both an evolution and a revolution.

Key forces in development

During the past few years a small amount of research knowledge about the phases of organization development has been building. Some of this research is very quantitative, such as time-series analyses that reveal patterns of economic performance over time.[1] The majority of studies, however, are case-oriented and use company records and interviews to reconstruct a rich picture of corporate development.[2] Yet both types of research tend to be heavily empirical without attempting more generalized statements about the overall process of development.

A notable exception is the historical work of Alfred D. Chandler, Jr., in his book *Strategy and Structure*.[3] This study depicts four very broad and general phases in the lives of four large US companies. It proposes that outside market opportunities determine a company's strategy, which in turn determines the company's organization structure. This thesis has a valid ring for the four companies examined by Chandler, largely because they developed in a time of explosive markets and technological advances. But more recent evidence suggests that organization structure may be less malleable than Chandler assumed; in fact, structure can play a critical role in influencing corporate strategy. It is this reverse emphasis on how organization structure affects future growth which is highlighted in the model presented in this article.

From an analysis of recent studies,[4] five key dimensions emerge as essential for building a model of organization development:

1. Age of the organization.
2. Size of the organization.
3. Stages of evolution.
4. Stages of revolution.
5. Growth rate of the industry.

I shall describe each of these elements separately, but first note their combined effect as illustrated in Figure 25.1. Note especially how each dimension influences the other over time; when all five elements begin to interact, a more complete and dynamic picture of organizational growth emerges.

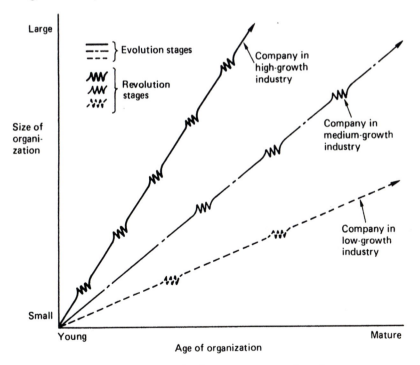

FIGURE 25.1 Model of organization development

After describing these dimensions and their interconnections, I shall discuss each evolutionary/revolutionary phase of development and show (a) how each stage of evolution breeds its own revolution, and (b) how management solutions to each revolution determine the next stage of evolution.

Age of the organization

The most obvious and essential dimension for any model of development is the life span of an organization (represented as the horizontal axis in Figure 25.1). All historical studies gather data from various points in time and then make comparisons. From these observations, it is evident that the same organization practices are not maintained throughout a long time span. This makes a most basic point: management problems and principles are rooted in time. The concept of decentralization, for example, can have meaning for describing corporate practices at one time period but loses its descriptive power at another.

The passage of time also contributes to the institutionalization of managerial attitudes. As a result, employee behavior becomes not only more predictable but also more difficult to change when attitudes are outdated.

Size of the organization

This dimension is depicted as the vertical axis in Figure 25.1. A company's problems and solutions tend to change markedly as the number of employees and sales volume increase. Thus, time is not the only determinant of structure; in fact, organizations that do not grow in size can retain many of the same management issues and practices over lengthy periods. In addition to increased size, however, problems of co-ordination and communication magnify, new functions emerge, levels in the management hierarchy multiply, and jobs become more interrelated.

Stages of evolution

As both age and size increase, another phenomenon becomes evident: the prolonged growth that I have termed the evolutionary period. Most growing organizations do not expand for two years and then retreat for one year; rather, those that survive a crisis usually enjoy four to eight years of continuous growth without a major economic setback or severe internal disruption. The term evolution seems appropriate for describing these quieter periods because only modest adjustments appear necessary for maintaining growth under the same overall pattern of management.

Stages of revolution

Smooth evolution is not inevitable; it cannot be assumed that organization growth is linear. *Fortune's* '500' list, for example, has had significant turnover during the last 50 years. Thus we find evidence from numerous case histories which reveals periods of substantial turbulence spaced between smoother periods of evolution.

I have termed these turbulent times the periods of revolution because they typically exhibit a serious upheaval of management practices. Traditional management practices, which were appropriate for a smaller size and earlier time, are brought under scrutiny by frustrated top managers and disillusioned lower-level managers. During such periods of crisis, a number of companies fail — those unable to abandon past practices and effect major organization changes are likely either to fold or to level off in their growth rates.

The critical task for management in each revolutionary period is to find a new set of organization practices that will become the basis for managing the next period of evolutionary growth. Interestingly enough, these new practices eventually sow their seeds of decay and lead to another period of revolution. Companies therefore experience the irony of seeing a major solution in one time period become a major problem at a later date.

Growth rate of the industry

The speed at which an organization experiences phases of evolution and revolution is closely related to the market environment of its industry. For example, a company in a rapidly expanding market will have to add employees rapidly; hence, the need for new organization structures to accommodate large staff increases is accelerated. While evolutionary periods tend to be relatively short in fast-growing industries, much longer evolutionary periods occur in mature or slowly growing industries.

Evolution can also be prolonged, and revolutions delayed, when profits come easily. For instance, companies that make grievous errors in a rewarding industry can still look good on their profit and loss statements; thus they can avoid a change in management practices for a longer period. The aerospace industry in its infancy is an example. Yet revolutionary periods still occur, as one did in aerospace when profit opportunities began to dry up. Revolutions seem to be much more severe and difficult to resolve when the market environment is poor.

Phases of growth

With the foregoing framework in mind, let us now examine in depth the five specific phases of evolution and revolution. As shown in Figure 25.2, each evolutionary period is characterized by the dominant *management style* used to achieve growth, while each revolutionary period is characterized by the dominant *management problem* that must be solved before growth can continue. The patterns presented in Figure 25.2 seem to be typical for companies in industries with moderate growth over a long time period; companies in faster growing industries tend to experience all five phases more rapidly, while those in slower growing industries encounter only two or three phases over many years.

It is important to note that *each phase is both an effect of the previous phase and a cause for the next phase.* For example, the evolutionary management style in Phase 3 of Figure 25.2 is 'delegation', which grows out of, and becomes the solution to, demands for greater 'autonomy' in the preceding Phase 2 revolution. The style of delegation used in Phase 3,

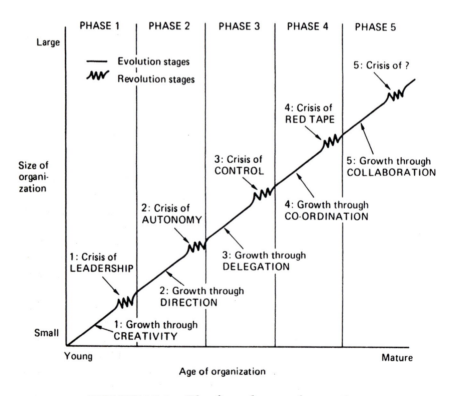

FIGURE 25.2   The five phases of growth

however, eventually provokes a major revolutionary crisis that is characterized by attempts to regain control over the diversity created through increased delegation.

The principal implication of each phase is that management actions are narrowly prescribed if growth is to occur. For example, a company experiencing an autonomy crisis in Phase 2 cannot return to directive management for a solution – it must adopt a new style of delegation in order to move ahead.

Phase 1: Creativity ...

In the birth stage of an organization, the emphasis is on creating both a product and a market. Here are the characteristics of the period of creative evolution:

- The company's founders are usually technically or entrepreneurially oriented, and they disdain management activities; their physical and mental energies are absorbed entirely in making and selling a new product.
- Communication among employees is frequent and informal.
- Long hours of work are rewarded by modest salaries and the promise of ownership benefits.
- Control of activities comes from immediate marketplace feedback; the management acts as the customers react.

... & the leadership crisis All of the foregoing individualistic and creative activities are essential for the company to get off the ground. But therein lies the problem. As the company grows, larger production runs require knowledge about the efficiencies of manufacturing. Increased numbers of employees cannot be managed exclusively through informal communication; new employees are not motivated by an intense dedication to the product or organization. Additional capital must be secured, and new accounting procedures are needed for financial control.

Thus the founders find themselves burdened with unwanted management responsibilities. So they long for the 'good old days', still trying to act as they did in the past. And conflicts between the harried leaders grow more intense.

At this point a crisis of leadership occurs, which is the onset of the first revolution. Who is to lead the company out of confusion and solve the managerial problems confronting it? Quite obviously, a strong manager is needed who has the necessary knowledge and skill to introduce new business techniques. But this is easier said than done. The founders often hate to step aside even though they are probably temperamentally unsuited to be managers. So here is the first critical developmental choice

— to locate and install a strong business manager who is acceptable to the founders and who can pull the organization together.

Phase 2: Direction ...

Those companies that survive the first phase by installing a capable business manager usually embark on a period of sustained growth under able and directive leadership. Here are the characteristics of this evolutionary period:

- A functional organization structure is introduced to separate manufacturing from marketing activities, and job assignments become more specialized.
- Accounting systems for inventory and purchasing are introduced.
- Incentives, budgets, and work standards are adopted.
- Communication becomes more formal and impersonal as a hierarchy of titles and positions builds.
- The new manager and his key supervisors take most of the responsibility for instituting direction, while lower-level supervisors are treated more as functional specialists than as autonomous decision-making managers.

... & the autonomy crisis   Although the new directive techniques channel employee energy more efficiently into growth, they eventually become inappropriate for controlling a larger, more diverse and complex organization. Lower-level employees find themselves restricted by a cumbersome and centralized hierarchy. They have come to possess more direct knowledge about markets and machinery than do the leaders at the top; consequently, they feel torn between following procedures and taking initiative on their own.

Thus the second revolution is imminent as a crisis develops from demands for greater autonomy on the part of lower-level managers. The solution adopted by most companies is to move toward greater delegation. Yet it is difficult for top managers who were previously successful at being directive to give up responsibility. Moreover, lower-level managers are not accustomed to making decisions for themselves. As a result, numerous companies flounder during this revolutionary period, adhering to centralized methods while lower-level employees grow more disenchanted and leave the organization.

Phase 3: Delegation ...

The next era of growth evolves from the successful application of a decentralized organization structure. It exhibits these characteristics:

- Much greater responsibility is given to the managers of plants and market territories.
- Profit centers and bonuses are used to stimulate motivation.
- The top executives at headquarters restrain themselves to managing by exception, based on periodic reports from the field.
- Management often concentrates on making new acquisitions which can be lined up beside other decentralized units.
- Communication from the top is infrequent, usually by correspondence, telephone, or brief visits to field locations.

The delegation stage proves useful for gaining expansion through heightened motivation at lower levels. Decentralized managers with greater authority and incentive are able to penetrate larger markets, respond faster to customers, and develop new products.

... & the control crisis A serious problem eventually evolves, however, as top executives sense that they are losing control over a highly diversified field operation. Autonomous field managers prefer to run their own shows without co-ordinating plans, money, technology, and manpower with the rest of the organization. Freedom breeds a parochial attitude.

Hence, the Phase 3 revolution is under way when top management seeks to regain control over the total company. Some top managements attempt a return to centralized management, which usually fails because of the vast scope of operations. Those companies that move ahead find a new solution in the use of special co-ordination techniques.

Phase 4: Co-ordination ...

During this phase, the evolutionary period is characterized by the use of formal systems for achieving greater co-ordination and by top executives taking responsibility for the initiation and administration of these new systems. For example:

- Decentralized units are merged into product groups.
- Formal planning procedures are established and intensively reviewed.
- Numerous staff personnel are hired and located at headquarters to initiate company-wide programs of control and review for line managers.
- Capital expenditures are carefully weighed and parceled out across the organization.
- Each product group is treated as an investment center where return on invested capital is an important criterion used in allocating funds.

- Certain technical functions, such as data processing, are centralized at headquarters, while daily operating decisions remain decentralized.
- Stock options and companywide profit sharing are used to encourage identity with the firm as a whole.

All of these new co-ordination systems prove useful for achieving growth through more efficient allocation of a company's limited resources. They prompt field managers to look beyond the needs of their local units. While these managers still have much decision-making responsibility, they learn to justify their actions more carefully to a 'watchdog' audience at headquarters.

... & the red-tape crisis   But a lack of confidence gradually builds between line and staff, and between headquarters and the field. The proliferation of systems and programs begins to exceed its utility; a red-tape crisis is created. Line managers, for example, increasingly resent heavy staff direction from those who are not familiar with local conditions. Staff people, on the other hand, complain about unco-operative and uninformed line managers. Together both groups criticize the bureaucratic paper system that has evolved. Procedures take precedence over problem solving, and innovation is dampened. In short, the organization has become too large and complex to be managed through formal programs and rigid systems. The Phase 4 revolution is under way.

Phase 5: Collaboration ...

The last observable phase in previous studies emphasizes strong interpersonal collaboration in an attempt to overcome the red-tape crisis. Where Phase 4 was managed more through formal systems and procedures, Phase 5 emphasizes greater spontaneity in management action through teams and the skillful confrontation of interpersonal differences. Social control and self-discipline take over from formal control. This transition is especially difficult for those experts who created the old systems as well as for those line managers who relied on formal methods for answers.

The Phase 5 evolution, then, builds around a more flexible and behavioral approach to management. Here are its characteristics:

- The focus is on solving problems quickly through team action.
- Teams are combined across functions for task-group activity.
- Headquarters staff experts are reduced in number, reassigned, and combined in interdisciplinary teams to consult with, not to direct, field units.

- A matrix-type structure is frequently used to assemble the right teams for the appropriate problems.
- Previous formal systems are simplified and combined into single multipurpose systems.
- Conferences of key managers are held frequently to focus on major problem issues.
- Educational programs are utilized to train managers in behavioral skills for achieving better teamwork and conflict resolution.
- Real-time information systems are integrated into daily decision-making.
- Economic rewards are geared more to team performance than to individual achievement.
- Experiments in new practices are encouraged throughout the organization.

. . . & the ? crisis What will be the revolution in response to this stage of evolution? Many large US companies are now in the Phase 5 evolutionary stage, so the answers are critical. While there is little clear evidence, I imagine the revolution will center on the 'psychological saturation' of employees who grow emotionally and physically exhausted by the intensity of teamwork and the heavy pressure for innovative solutions.

My hunch is that the Phase 5 revolution will be solved through new structures and programs that allow employees to periodically rest, reflect, and revitalize themselves. We may even see companies with dual organization structures: a 'habit' structure for getting the daily work done, and a 'reflective' structure for stimulating perspective and personal enrichment. Employees could then move back and forth between the two structures as their energies are dissipated and refueled.
[. . .]

Implications of history

Let me now summarize some important implications for practicing managers. First, the main features of this discussion are depicted in Table 25.1, which shows the specific management actions that characterize each growth phase. These actions are also the solutions which ended each preceding revolutionary period.

In one sense, I hope that many readers will react to my model by calling it obvious and natural for depicting the growth of an organization. To me this type of reaction is a useful test of the model's validity.

But at a more reflective level I imagine some of these reactions are more hindsight than foresight. Those experienced managers who have

TABLE 25.1 Organization practices during evolution in the five phases of growth

Category	Phase 1	Phase 2	Phase 3	Phase 4	Phase 5
Management focus	Make and sell	Efficiency of operations	Expansion of market	Consolidation of organization	Problem solving and innovation
Organization structure	Informal	Centralized and functional	Decentralized and geographical	Line-staff and product groups	Matrix of teams
Top management style	Individualistic and entrepreneurial	Directive	Delegative	Watchdog	Participative
Control system	Market results	Standards and cost centers	Reports and profit centers	Plans and investment centers	Mutual goal setting
Management reward emphasis	Ownership	Salary and merit increases	Individual bonus	Profit sharing and stock options	Team bonus

been through a developmental sequence can empathize with it now, but how did they react when in the middle of a stage of evolution or revolution? They can probably recall the limits of their own developmental understanding at that time. Perhaps they resisted desirable changes or were even swept emotionally into a revolution without being able to propose constructive solutions. So let me offer some explicit guidelines for managers of growing organizations to keep in mind.

Know where you are in the developmental sequence

Every organization and its component parts are at different stages of development. The task of top management is to be aware of these stages; otherwise, it may not recognize when the time for change has come, or it may act to impose the wrong solution.

Top leaders should be ready to work with the flow of the tide rather than against it; yet they should be cautious, since it is tempting to skip phases out of impatience. Each phase results in certain strengths and learning experiences in the organization that will be essential for success in subsequent phases. A child prodigy, for example, may be able to read like a teenager, but he cannot behave like one until he ages through a sequence of experiences.

I also doubt that managers can or should act to avoid revolutions. Rather, these periods of tension provide the pressure, ideas, and awareness that afford a platform for change and the introduction of new practices.

Recognize the limited range of solutions

In each revolutionary stage it becomes evident that this stage can be ended only by certain specific solutions; moreover, these solutions are different from those which were applied to the problems of the preceding revolution. Too often it is tempting to choose solutions that were tried before, which makes it impossible for a new phase of growth to evolve.

Management must be prepared to dismantle current structures before the revolutionary stage becomes too turbulent. Top managers, realizing that their own managerial styles are no longer appropriate, may even have to take themselves out of leadership positions. A good Phase 2 manager facing Phase 3 might be wise to find another Phase 2 organization that better fits his talents, either outside the company or with one of its newer subsidiaries.

Finally, evolution is not an automatic affair; it is a contest for survival. To move ahead, companies must consciously introduce planned structures that not only are solutions to a current crisis but also are fitted to the *next* phase of growth. This requires considerable self-awareness on the part of top management, as well as great interpersonal skill in persuading other managers that change is needed.

Realize that solutions breed new problems

Managers often fail to realize that organizational solutions create problems for the future (i.e. a decision to delegate eventually causes a problem of control). Historical actions are very much determinants of what happens to the company at a much later date.

An awareness of this effect should help managers to evaluate company problems with greater historical understanding instead of 'pinning the blame' on a current development. Better yet, managers should be in a position to *predict* future problems, and thereby to prepare solutions and coping strategies before a revolution gets out of hand.

A management that is aware of the problems ahead could well decide *not* to grow. Top managers may, for instance, prefer to retain the informal practices of a small company, knowing that this way of life is inherent in the organization's limited size, not in their congenial personalities. If they choose to grow, they may do themselves out of a job and a way of life they enjoy.

And what about the managements of very large organizations? Can they find new solutions for continued phases of evolution? Or are they reaching a stage where the government will act to break them up because they are too large?

Concluding note

Clearly, there is still much to learn about processes of development in organizations. The phases outlined here are only five in number and are still only approximations. Researchers are just beginning to study the specific developmental problems of structure, control, rewards, and management style in different industries and in a variety of cultures.

One should not, however, wait for conclusive evidence before educating managers to think and act from a developmental perspective. The critical dimension of time has been missing for too long from our management theories and practices. The intriguing paradox is that by learning more about history we may do a better job in the future.
[...]

Notes

1. See, for example, William H. Starbuck, 'Organizational Metamorphosis', in *Promising Research Directions*, edited by R. W. Millman and M. P. Hottenstein (Tempe, Arizona, Academy of Management, 1968) p. 113.

2. See, for example, the *Grangesberg* case series, prepared by C. Roland Christensen and Bruce R. Scott, Case Clearing House, Harvard Business School.

3. *Strategy and Structure: Chapters in the History of the American Industrial Enterprise* (Cambridge, Massachusetts: MIT Press, 1962).

4. I have drawn on many sources for evidence: (a) numerous cases collected at the Harvard Business School; (b) *Organization Growth and Development*, edited by William H. Starbuck (Harmondsworth: Penguin, 1971), where several studies are cited, and (c) articles published in journals, such as Lawrence E. Fouraker and John M. Stopford, 'Organization Structure and the Multinational Strategy', *Administrative Science Quarterly*, vol. 13, no. 1, 1968, p. 47; and Malcolm S. Salter, 'Management Appraisal and Reward Systems', *Journal of Business Policy*, vol. 1, no. 4, 1971.

CHAPTER 26

Successfully Implementing Strategic Decisions

LARRY D. ALEXANDER

Introduction

Although strategy implementation is viewed as an integral part of the strategic management process, little has been written or researched on it. The overwhelming majority of the literature so far has been on the long-range planning process itself or the actual content of the strategy being formulated. We have so far been giving lip service to the other side of the coin, namely strategy implementation. Consequently, it is not surprising that after a comprehensive strategy or single strategic decision has been formulated, significant difficulties are often encountered during the subsequent implementation process.

This study surveyed 93 private sector firms through a questionnaire to determine which implementation problems occurred most frequently as they tried to put strategic decisions into effect. Later on, in-depth telephone interviews with chief executive officers of 21 of these firms were conducted to comprehend these problems more fully. These interviews, combined later on with another 25 interviews with governmental agency heads in another study of implementation in the public sector by this researcher, help to identify factors which promote successful implementation.

[...]

Companies surveyed

The 93 firms participating in this survey were strategic business units of medium and large sized firms. Some 72 firms (77 per cent) were listed in the Fortune 500 list of leading industrials. If Fortune's second 500 list of industrials is included along with Fortune's top 50 listings for utilities, retailing and services, then 89 firms (96 per cent) responding were included on one Fortune list or another.

The firms' SBUs (strategic business units) sampled differed with respect to their size, industry and geographical location within the US. For example, 26 (28 per cent) of the SBUs had less than 400 employees, 23 (25 per cent) had 400–999 employees, 29 (31 per cent) had 1000–4999 employees, 13 (14 per cent) had over 5000 employees, and 2 (2 per cent) were unidentified. While most of the corporations operated within a number of different businesses, this study was focused on implementing strategic decisions within individual SBUs.

The strategic decisions evaluated

In the questionnaire, each responding company president (or division general manager) was asked to select one recent strategic decision that had been implemented in his SBU. He was asked to select one in which he had a great deal of personal knowledge about its subsequent implementation. Table 26.1 shows the types of strategic decisions that were evaluated. The main part of the questionnaire then asked the participants to evaluate the extent to which some 22 possible implementation problems actually were a problem in its subsequent implementation using a five-point Likert-type response scale. Finally, questions were asked to evaluate the overall success of the strategy implementation effort itself.

Most frequently occurring problems

The 10 most commonly occurring strategy implementation problems are shown in Table 26.2 in descending order according to mean ratings. Two adjacent pairs of numbers on the five-point Likert response scale are

TABLE 26.1 Types of strategic decisions implemented

Type of strategic decision	*No*	*%*
Introducing a new product or service	29	31
Opening and starting up a new plant or facility	17	18
Expanding operations to enter a new market	15	16
Discontinuing a product or withdrawing from a market	11	12
Acquiring or merging with another firm	10	11
Changing the strategy in functional departments	6	7
Other	5	5
	93	100

TABLE 26.2 Ten most frequent strategy implementation problems

Potential strategy implementation problem	Mean	Frequency of any degree of problem	Frequency of minor/ moderate problems	Frequency of substantial/ major problems
			=	+
Implementation took more time than originally allocated	2.71	71 (76%)	45 (48%)	26 (28%)
Major problems surfaced during implementation that had not been identified beforehand	2.63	69 (74%)	45 (48%)	24 (26%)
Co-ordination of implementation activities was not effective enough	2.34	62 (66%)	45 (48%)	17 (18%)
Competing activities and crises distracted attention from implementing this decision	2.29	60 (64%)	41 (44%)	19 (20%)
Capabilities of employees involved were not sufficient	2.28	59 (63%)	40 (43%)	19 (20%)
Training and instruction given to lower level employees were not adequate	2.14	58 (62%)	47 (50%)	11 (12%)
Uncontrollable factors in the external environment had an adverse impact on implementation	2.28	56 (60%)	40 (43%)	16 (17%)
Leadership and direction provided by departmental managers were not adequate enough	2.23	55 (59%)	39 (42%)	16 (17%)
Key implementation tasks and activities were not defined in enough detail	2.09	52 (56%)	36 (39%)	16 (17%)
Information systems used to monitor implementation were not adequate	1.94	52 (56%)	43 (46%)	9 (10%)

combined for display purposes only as follows: minor and moderate problems (points 2 and 3), and substantial and major problems (points 4 and 5). The 10 listed items are the only ones rated as problems by over half of the sample group.

The first seven listed implementation problems occurred to at least 60 per cent of the firms. They are:

1. implementation took more time than originally allocated by 76 per cent;
2. major problems surface during implementation that had not been identified beforehand by 74 per cent;
3. co-ordination of implementation activities (e.g. by task force, committees, superiors) was not effective enough by 66 per cent;
4. competing activities and crises distracted attention from implementing this strategic decision by 64 per cent;
5. capabilities (skills and abilities) of employees involved with the implementation were not sufficient by 63 per cent;
6. training and instruction given to lower level employees were not adequate by 62 per cent; and
7. uncontrollable factors in the external environment (e.g. competitive, economic, governmental) had an adverse impact on implementation by 60 per cent.

Three additional implementation problems listed in Table 26.2 occurred to somewhat fewer firms but still experienced by over 50 per cent of the sample firms.

Three-quarters (76 per cent) of the sampled firms found that their implementation efforts took more time than originally allocated. A number of explanations were given by CEOs in the follow-up telephone interviews. As one executive put it, 'In retrospect, we were overly optimistic in thinking how much time it would take to implement a new strategic decision. We thought that everything would work fine which it never does'. From the interviews, this problem seems to occur because top management:

1. understands how long various implementation tasks will take to complete,
2. downplays the likelihood of potential problems that may or may not occur, and
3. is blind to other problems occurring altogether.

Obviously, when all three of these occur during implementation, it can greatly lengthen the time it will take to implement the decision effectively.

Solutions to the problem of taking too much time are numerous. More time should initially be allocated from the start to handle unexpected problems and, in general, the unknown. More manpower initially can be put on important strategic decisions, and particularly later on when unexpected problems emerge. In addition, rewards and penalties can also be used to bring about the desired results.

[...]

Major problems (and obstacles) surfaced during implementation that had not been identified beforehand were experienced by almost as many firms, specifically 74 per cent. These can be internally oriented problems brought on by the firm trying something new, insufficient advance planning, and strategy formulators not getting actively involved in implementation to name a few. Or they can be caused by externally oriented factors such as the uncertainty involved with a new product or new market, uncontrollable events in the external environment, or legal/ political complications introduced by new legislation or regulations among others.

[...]

The presence of competing activities and crises that distracted attention from implementing the strategic decision was yet another frequently occurring problem. Some 64 per cent of the firms experienced this implementation problem. One aerospace components firm was starting to implement one strategic decision when along came one order from an airline firm that amounted to 25 per cent of its total sales in a typical year. Obviously, considerable time and attention had to be given to this major order for about 3 months which clearly had priority over the other strategic decision. Actually, the firm decided to forget trying to implement the new strategic decision for a while and put it on hold. Given the size of the customer order, this seemed the best way to handle these competing events.

[...]

One of three things typically occurs when competing events exist. Time and attention are taken away from implementing the new strategic decision. They are taken away from other existing programs which suffer. Or often, some time and attention are taken away from the new and existing programs.

Some 60 per cent of the firms experienced uncontrollable factors in the external environment that had an adverse impact on implementation. Some of these problems are truly surprise events. Examples of these include:

1. a hurricane tearing off a roof of a new plant which damaged equipment;
2. the Professional Airline Traffic Controllers strike and the 25 per cent

reduction in flights which reduced the demand for a firm's new jet-pull-out tractor; and
3. a surprising upturn in an industry's sales when a firm was trying to move three plants into one new modern facility.

[. . .]

While most uncontrollable problems in the external environment cannot be anticipated, contingency plans can be developed for some of them. Then, if that problem does occur, at least the firm will be in a better position to take corrective action to minimize its impact on the firm.

Two somewhat lower rated items, which are:

1. advocates and supporters of the strategic decision left (the division or company) during implementation (experienced by only 27 per cent of the firms) and
2. the key people who developed and made the strategic decision, did not play an active enough role in its subsequent implementation (40 per cent),

illustrate how two problems can combine to make things even worse. One company president put it this way:

> Our company was acquired by another parent firm with no background in this business. A new group vice president was installed to straighten out the mess here. He and I developed a strategy to break even in about 15 months with proper equipment, but then 6 months later, this group vice president was replaced for reasons beyond my knowledge. His replacement was not familiar with our operations, wants us now to go in about a 180 degree different direction, and only looks at bottom line results.

[. . .]

Promoting successful strategy implementation

In the followup telephone interviews with CEOs, one major purpose was to understand better various implementation problems that did hinder the implementation effort. However, another reason for these interviews was to get these executives to draw on their extensive experience and speculate on the things that help to promote successful strategy implementation. Although these generalizations are not statistically valid, they were mentioned most frequently by 21 CEOs plus 25 additional interviews with agency heads from federal and state governments in a comparison study.

Communication, communication, communication

This seemingly simple suggestion was mentioned more frequently by CEOs than any other single item. The reason it is repeated is to reflect exactly what was said by a number of these company presidents. They felt that top management must first of all clearly communicate with all employees what the new strategic decision is all about. Hopefully, it involves two-way communication that permits and solicits questions from affected employees about the formulated strategy, issues to be considered, or potential problems that might occur. In addition, communication includes clearly explaining what new responsibilities, tasks, and duties need to be performed by the affected employees. It also includes the why behind changed job activities, and more fundamentally the reasons why the new strategic decision was made in the first place. Finally, CEOs mentioned that two-way communication is needed throughout the implementation process to monitor what is actually happening, analyse how to deal with emerging problems, and in deciding what modifications might be needed in the program to make it work.

Start with a good concept or idea

The need to start with a formulated strategy that involves a good idea or concept was mentioned next most often in helping promote successful implementation. In a nut shell, what this idea suggests is that no amount of time and effort spent on implementation can rescue a strategic decision that is not well formulated to begin with. More than being thoroughly planned out, the idea must be fundamentally sound. Thus, this suggests that strategy implementation can fail for one of two reasons. One is caused by a failure to do the things required during implementation to insure that a well-formulated strategy is successful. The other cause of failure is due to a poorly conceived formulated plan that no amount of implementation effort can help rescue.

Obtain employee commitment and involvement

This third suggestion builds on the first two and interrelates with them. CEOs suggested that one way to accomplish this is to involve affected employees and managers right from the start in the strategy formulation process. On the contrary, when a strategic decision has been developed in a vacuum by a few people, top management should not be surprised that it is resisted during implementation by the affected employees. Top management should not be surprised if the formulated plan has major flaws in it because key employees and affected groups did not participate in its formulation. In fact, just the opposite may be true. Top management ought to be surprised if a formulated strategy, developed pretty much without key employee involvement, is implemented successfully.

Involvement and commitment should also be developed and maintained throughout the implementation process. If middle and lower level managers and key subordinates are permitted to be involved with the detailed implementation planning, their commitment typically will tend to increase. The workability of the specific action plan should also be improved simply by getting the affected employees involved – and committed – early on as well as throughout the implementation process.

Provide sufficient resources

CEOs mentioned at least four different kinds of resources. The obvious one is money, which, considering the sizeable scope of many strategic decisions, is a bottom line requirement. Conversely, failure to provide adequate funding may contribute to limited success or outright failure. Manpower is another key resource which can have either a positive or a negative effect on implementation. Technical expertise (or knowledge), as related to the new strategic decision, is still another resource mentioned by some CEOs. The idea suggested here is that firms need to have in-house expertise or hire a few new employees who possess it in order to implement strategic decisions involving new endeavors. A final resource mentioned is time. Sufficient time to accomplish the implementation, adequate time and attention given by top management to the new effort, and hopefully not too many other competing programs demanding the time of affected employees who will implement this one.

Develop an implementation plan

This final suggestion is a plea to develop many of the specifics to be done during implementation. In essence, this details who is to do what and when it is to be accomplished. A few CEOs mentioned that this plan must strike the right balance. If the implementation plan is too vague, it is of little practical use. Conversely, if the plan is too detailed, it may tend to force various functional departments to follow it precisely, even when it clearly needs to be modified.

Several CEOs also mentioned that a part of that plan should be to identify likely implementation problems. Instead of being blindly optimistic that nothing will go wrong while implementing a strategic decision, do just the opposite. Try to identify the most likely problems that might occur and then develop contingency responses for those eventualities.

Summary and conclusions

A number of strategy implementation problems do seem to occur on a regular basis. In fact, 10 of the 22 potential problems rated occurred to at least 50 per cent of the sampled firms. While problems do occur frequently, the vast majority of firms experience them as minor or moderate problems. However, when a firm encounters several implementation problems, rated at the substantial or major level, it can have a very adverse impact on the implementation process.

Surprisingly, some of the traditional strategy implementation factors mentioned in the literature were not judged as frequently to be problems. Rated among the least frequent of the 22 implementation problems were:

● rewards and incentives utilized to get employee conformance to program were not sufficient (cited as a problem by only 18 per cent of the respondents);
● support and backing by top management in this SBU and at the corporate level were not adequate (21 per cent);
● financial resources made available were not sufficient (27 per cent);
● organizational structural changes made were not effective (33 per cent); and
● changes in roles and responsibilities of key employees were not clearly defined (38 per cent).

It may be that firms do such a good job in these areas that problems are prevented. Or it may suggest that other implementation problems identified in this study are more important than the literature has led us to believe.
[. . .]
Successful implementation in part involves preventing various implementation problems from occurring in the first place. It also involves taking quick action of resolve and address problems that do occur. Obviously, the faster corrective action is initiated during implementation, the more likely it can be resolved before it impacts adversely on the firm.

Successful implementation also involves doing the things that help promote success rather than just preventing problems from occurring. Although the five suggestions presented here are not statistically significant, they do help reinforce the importance of satisfying basic managerial tasks to help bring about success.
[. . .]

CHAPTER 27

Strategic Control: an overview of the issues

DAVID ASCH

Introduction

There are a number of complex issues surrounding strategic control. In this chapter I attempt to outline some of the key aspects. We start by considering control as a generic concept and process. The main elements of measurement, evaluation and feedback are equally relevant to both the short and the long term. Nevertheless specific questions or issues can vary for strategic and operational controls and we then identify issues of particular relevance to strategic control.

Different types of strategic control are explored in a discussion of strategic momentum control and strategic leap control. The findings of some empirical research are discussed and barriers to strategic control identified. We conclude by briefly looking at the problems associated with the use of financial measures for strategic control.

The control process

A simple model of the control process is shown in Figure 27.1.

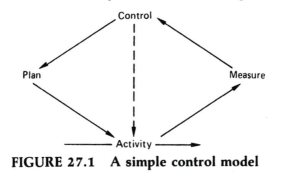

FIGURE 27.1   A simple control model

397

In essence this assumes that business activity is controlled by establishing plans, normally based on an assessment of the future, which are then implemented and measured. The actual results are compared to the plan – a process of either control through feedback which leads to reaction, or feedforward which leads to the amendment of plans in the light of experience. Three important points emerge from a consideration of this model:

1. Determining what to measure in terms of the business activity is crucial. Managers at all levels need to specify what will be monitored and evaluated. The processes and results must be capable of being measured in a reasonably objective and consistent manner with the focus on the most significant elements.
2. Leading on from (1) standards of performance need to be established. Such standards are detailed expressions of strategic objectives and represent measures of acceptable results. Actual performance is then measured and compared with the standard (Wheelen and Hunger, 1987, p. 234).
3. Action must be taken to correct the deviation where actual deviates from standard. Tricker and Boland (1982, pp. 109–11) observe that this control process presupposes that the manager responsible can bring performance into line and that they have the power to act. They identify three sources of power which should be considered in management control – position power, action power and knowledge power. Position power derives basically from the organization position in which authority is vested. Action power refers to the ability to manipulate essential resources where no substitute is available. Knowledge power stems from the ability to cope in a position of uncertainty. Tricker and Boland conclude that control cannot be established on the basis of positional power alone, but that it should be exercised in the context of both action and knowledge power.

Hrebiniak and Joyce (1984, pp. 198–203) identify five common control problems which in their view result in poor or unsuccessful strategy implementation:

● *Poor objectives*   Because objectives represent an output of the planning process and an input to the control system they represent the standards of performance for comparison with actual results. Note that this does not necessarily imply a separate process for planning and control, as it has been argued that planning and control systems are one process (see for example Anthony and Dearden, 1980). So, where objectives are not measurable a comparison of desired and actual performance is problematic. Where there are competing definitions or subjective measures of objectives a sound control system becomes improbable. Objectives should be measurable, realistic and challenging, consistent particularly between the long and the short term, and prioritized where necessary.

- *Insufficient or faulty information processing capabilities* It should be clear that for control to be exercised sufficient information should be available. Hrebiniak and Joyce note three factors which seek to explain why this may be a control problem. The first relates to the already expressed need for measurable objectives, without which the collection of information can become extremely difficult. The second factor refers to the needs of the organization's strategic control system. This is an issue which will be addressed in the next section, but it should be noted that strategic control is often more difficult than short-term operational control and probably creates some demands on the organization. Finally, a poor operating structure can lead to inaccurate or incomplete information due to inappropriate or insufficient reporting relationships, or insufficient communications.

- *Management by negative exception and poor evaluation of performance* The control model assumes that significant deviations from the plan deserve managerial attention. The absence of any aberrations implies that all is proceeding smoothly. Management by exception, then, focuses on significant deviations which may cause a problem if follow up only occurs when the deviation is negative. The underlying logic seems to be to concentrate only on poor performance. This could have a negative impact on control, evaluation, and the implementation process. Successful implementation depends upon a learning process premised on sound communication, confrontation of task related problems, and evaluation of the reasons underlying significant deviations from plan, both positive and negative.

- *Poor performance appraisal* The need here is to ensure that the formal appraisal or review process includes performance against objectives. Good performance and ensuring that sufficient attention is paid to the integration of short- and long-term organizational needs depend in part on the reinforcement of behaviour consistent with those ends.

- *Avoiding and embracing error* Control systems can have a major impact on the organizational climate. At one extreme the effects of control may include a strict avoidance of error. Managers become preoccupied with not making mistakes; mistakes carry an aura of failure or incompetence. At the other extreme control systems may embrace error. Here mistakes are a necessary consequence of a control system that encourages innovation and risk taking. Hrebiniak and Joyce suggest that top-down unilateral control is more often associated with avoiding errors than is self control or negotiation of control standards. Strict enforcement of rules under top-down control constrains behaviour and ensures formal accountability. This tends to result in a strong concern with defensibility of action and may even foster conservatism and rigidity of behaviour. In organizations that embrace error, defensibility is less important and the emphasis tends to be on innovation and assuming risk, even if this results in making mistakes.

Strategic control

The same general control elements, and the same problems surrounding them, will obtain for strategic control as under operational control. However, the relationship between means and ends is less precise, and the clarity or certainty of cause–effect relationships is likely to be lower under strategic control conditions. For example, Hurst (1982) argues that:

• Strategic control requires data from more sources, and more data from external sources, than does short-term control. In the latter case, the 'operation' itself generates the only data used for control purposes.
• Strategic control is less precise than is operational control, making analysis more difficult. The former aggregates approximations from a complex environment, while the latter focuses on more precise representations of a much smaller world.
• Alternative actions or decisions are more difficult to choose in advance under strategic control than in short-term operational control models. This has many consequences, including heightening the effect of errors of omission.
• Strategic control data are less accurate and their receipt more sporadic than those derived from operational monitoring.

A further dimension relates to the necessity of integrating long- and short-term objectives. Hrebiniak and Joyce (1984, pp. 205–6) argue that:

> short-term objectives or aims support and are critical to the achievement of long-term strategic ends. The problem is not the short- versus long-term concerns of management; it is the lack of integration of and consistency between long- and short-term plans and objectives in the control system that is vital to the successful implementation of strategy.

Due to the longer time scale associated with strategic control performance, evaluation should include an analysis of external conditions and the assumptions based upon them which might not normally be the case with short-term performance. This is because in the short term environmental or exogenous variables are likely to be relatively fixed.

It is often argued (for example, Bowman and Asch, 1987, pp. 195–205; Johnson and Scholes, 1988, pp. 248–51) that the budgeting process is a major component in implementing strategy. As a process it addresses issues of consistency and fit, areas of crucial concern to strategic development (Galbraith and Kazanjian, 1986, p. 109). As a strategic control process budgeting has its limitations. The fact that there will usually be a hierarchy of control systems with difficulties of linkage between them can lead to a decoupling of budgeting from control. Because it is a means of resource allocation and information dissemination budgeting identifies changes in emphasis across the organization. The whole process can become politically difficult due to the status attached to the size of budgets and the power struggles that can occur. The main measures are often financially based (though physical measures may also be used to measure output or efficiency levels) as well as being used for performance appraisal of managers through their ability to meet targets. Reed and Buckley (1988) believe that these features may render the budgeting process ineffective in communicating the importance of any of the more subtle benefits or risks of a strategy.

One way of overcoming some of the above problems would be to establish strategic budgets (Lorange *et al.*, 1986). This may also be a way of ensuring that strategic developments do not get subsumed in operating or short-term needs. Ansoff (1987, pp. 223–4) also advocates separation of operating and strategic budgets. He suggests that the operating budget should incorporate support of continued profit making by utilizing existing capacity of the firm, investment in capacity expansion and in increasing profits through cost reduction. The strategic budget would include investment in improvement of competitive position in the present strategic business areas (SBAs), plus the addition of related SBAs through geographic expansion and the addition of new SBAs.

Ansoff argues that this type of dual budgeting is relatively easy to install because it does not interfere with the existing organizational structure. The establishment of a strategic budget will not of itself ensure that managers will in fact devote sufficient of their time and energy to strategic rather than operational issues. In his discussion of strategic control Ansoff observes that the typical operating control philosophy, based on a comparison of actual to budget, may well be inappropriate. His point is that historic performance is much less relevant than future prospects, which can probably be better assessed now than when the venture started. Ansoff concludes that for effective strategic control the focus should be on ultimate cost benefits and not on tracking the budget. So it may be desirable to overspend the original budget if progress reveals very high net benefits (Ansoff, 1987, pp. 228–9).

Types of strategic control

The approach to strategic control will depend upon a series of wide ranging assumptions about the organization's internal and external environments. Perceived characteristics of the external environment, rather than objective reality, will influence strategy and control. Managers' perceptions of the environment will be influenced by a number of factors, including organization structure and management information systems.

Situations where the nature of environmental changes can be characterized as linear, that is the process of change is assumed to be continuous, will call for a different strategic control approach to one where changes are predominantly discontinuous. In the case of linear changes the strategic control process has been called momentum control (Lorange *et al.*, 1986, p. 16). This approach emphasizes the maintenance of a reasonably stable path by ameliorating problems and addressing deviations from normal development on a steady on-going basis. The process is all about maintaining momentum and modifying direction. Momentum control is concerned with facilitating a smooth evolution grounded in past strategic decisions. Where this mode of control is no longer adequate, because the environment is changing with a large degree of discontinuity, strategic leap control (Lorange *et al.*, 1986, p. 17) should be adopted.

Strategic momentum control involves knowing and understanding the underlying forces that effect and shape the development of the organization. It should allow managers to develop an awareness of critical environmental changes so that they are able to modify and strengthen the firm's strategy in anticipation of such changes. This will involve monitoring shifts in environmental assumptions and reassessing their potential impacts. The measurement package consists of both an assessment of critical external factors and measures of profits, costs, market share and so on. Three broad approaches to strategic momentum control are identified (Lorange *et al.*, 1986, pp. 62–93).

- Responsibility centre control is prevalent in most management control systems. The basic unit of analysis is the responsibility centre which is assumed to be both identifiable and under the supervision of a manager (or group of managers) who have discretion for impacting on performance. Responsibility centres would include cost, revenue, profit, discretionary cost and investment centres.
- Classic strategic planning offers an opportunity to re-examine basic strategic direction as well as the validity of the strategic implementation programmes being pursued. The systematic assessment of

environmental assumptions may provide early warning signals regarding the continued validity of current strategic objectives.

● Generic strategy: checking and testing involves checking the basic strategies being pursued to determine whether they seem to be reasonable. The test of reasonableness, or normality, relates to information collected from reviewing strategies in similar settings for other comparable organizations, or by reviewing the appropriateness of such strategies in a particular type of competitive environment.

These types of control systems are consistent with incrementalism. Logical incrementalism (Quinn, 1980) assumes a tension between the identified environment and organizational reality and argues that strategic change results, amongst other things, in a readjustment process. Consequently, as the environment changes gradually the organization's strategy develops incrementally in line with it.

However, we have already noted that the environment will not be viewed objectively. Johnson (1987, pp. 244–9) notes, in addition, that 'because marginal changes are taking place frequently, and are likely to be associated with some performance improvements, the view that change is in line with what is required to keep "in touch" with environmental change will be supported.' Johnson argues that for these two reasons strategic drift is likely to occur imperceptibly. Strategic drift refers to the notion that the organization's strategy fails to develop in line with environmental changes. Johnson goes on to argue that when strategic drift has become so marked that a decline in performance cannot be overcome by incremental/adaptive change, a more fundamental realignment becomes necessary.

Strategic leap control involves controlling strategic decisions in turbulent times. Decision situations involve unstructured problems and ambiguity, organizations may need to make discontinuous leaps. Lorange *et al.* (1986, pp. 101–23) focus on four approaches:

● Strategic issue management, where the organization identifies one or a few key issues which are believed to be crucial for achieving its objectives. The organization directs its collective energy towards understanding the impact of the issue and in overcoming the threats or exploiting the opportunities posed by the issue.
● Strategic field analysis is a method of directing attention to the nature and extent of synergies that exist between components of the organization. The two key aspects of strategic field analysis involve analysing the value chain in terms of the functional steps involved in providing a particular output, and examining the potential synergies between the various products, markets, or businesses.

- Systems modelling is a vehicle to address the feasibility of options for strategic change, given the internal reality of the organization. The emphasis is on ascertaining whether particular strategies are feasible and, if so, on identifying key dimensions for subsequent monitoring. The analysis involved in developing a model may help to avoid unrealistic strategies and facilitates better co-ordination across programmes, so avoiding internal inefficiencies. Systems modelling should be interactive and management and model should interface on a 'what if?' basis to understand better the interplay between the internal environment and various dynamic strategies.
- Scenario-based strategy development can provide insights into how major environmental changes might create new opportunities for refocusing strategy. It represents a way of controlling the organization's position relative to environmental developments. As a process it may help managers develop, at a relatively early stage, sensitivity to the opportunities that may arise from such environmental changes.

In considering types of strategic control the work of Goold and Campbell (1987) on the role of the centre in 16 large diversified corporations is very illuminating. They categorized the management styles into strategic planning, strategic control and financial control. Amongst other issues they examined the planning influence and control influence of the centre and business units. Planning influence refers to the centre's efforts to shape strategies as they emerge and before decisions are taken. Control influence refers to the way in which the centre reacts to results achieved.

Goold and Campbell (1987, pp. 47–85) observed that the emphasis in strategic planning companies is less heavily on control processes. Objectives are set in strategic planning reviews and the companies try to establish short- and long-term targets and to set financial and non-financial goals. 'But they find it difficult to identify non-financial targets or strategic milestones that are as precise, as objectively measurable and as widely accepted as financial objectives.' (1987, p. 65). All the strategic planning companies monitor financial results, monthly and quarterly, against the plan. Control tends to be less tightly enforced in these companies than in the strategic control or financial control companies.

The control processes in strategic control companies (Goold and Campbell, 1987, pp. 86–101) are closely linked to planning processes. Objectives emerge from the detailed discussion of plans proposed by the business units. Objectives exist for the short and the long term; they cover a variety of financial and non-financial aggregates; they cover different time periods. Strategic control companies have found difficulty in specifying non-financial strategic objectives that are as tangible and credible as financial objectives. All these companies have monthly and quarterly reporting systems to report actual against plan. Generally such systems are used on a management by exception basis.

Financial control companies (Goold and Campbell, 1987, pp. 111–31) appeared to exert little influence on the development of strategy. Unlike the strategic planning and strategic control companies, financial control companies do not have elaborate formal processes for reviewing strategies and budgets. They have only one regular formal planning process which is for reviewing and sanctioning the annual budget. Financial control companies focus on defining simple clear objectives and controlling against them. Results are monitored on a monthly and quarterly basis as the companies regard it as essential to catch variances from budget before they have gone too far. These companies appear to be quicker to replace managers, fiercer in applying pressure through the monitoring process and more effective at recognizing and acclaiming good performance than companies classified as strategic planning or strategic control.

Some problems with strategic control

A number of barriers to strategic control were identified by Lorange and Murphy (1984). Their research was based on a series of interviews with one corporate level planner and one corporate level controller in each of 25 Fortune 500 firms. They grouped the barriers into three classes:

- Systemic barriers stem from deficiencies in the design of the control system itself, or from an inability to manage the system. Several of their respondents appeared to be experiencing difficulty in defining adequate performance measures for strategic control. Another problem was excessive complexity of the control system. A further system design problem related to the cognitive capacity of managers to reconcile meaningfully a diversity of variables. Strategic control requires managers to reconcile several types of feedback information for each particular business or product, that is they have to carry out a multidimensional interpretation of performance.
- Behavioural barriers often appear to stem from an inability to dispense with the habit of thinking that a manager's background, education, training and corporate culture have created over many years. They may also stem from cognitive limits to managers' basic intellectual capacity. Vested interests and sunk costs typify the entrapments that can adversely affect the utility of strategic control. Closely related to this is the fear of losing face or being proved wrong. The difficulty involved in abandoning familiar thought patterns and acquired behaviours should not be underestimated.

- Political barriers relate to managements' ability to create a sufficiently broad sense of agreement regarding basic direction, as well as on their ability to allocate the resources needed to get there. A strategy must be 'politically' acceptable for the various power groups which exist in most organizations. The strategic control process may call for changes in the basic strategic agenda. Typically these will also affect internal power groups and may be viewed as potentially disruptive to the relative power of coalitions, leading to resistance. Another set of political barriers may result from the unwillingness of lower level managers to report unfavourable results to top management.

One of the most significant problems in strategic control relates to measuring performance. Throughout this chapter reference has been made to the difficulty in establishing objective measurable targets or goals. It was referred to by Hrebiniak and Joyce (1984), Lorange *et al.* (1986) and Goold and Campbell (1987). In general, these writers note the prevalence of financial measures of performance for strategic control purposes. This is not the place to enter into a prolonged discussion of the merits or otherwise of these particular methods (see Lorange *et al.*, 1986, pp. 64–77 for a more comprehensive view of the issues involved). However, it is worth noting that, although financial numbers appear to be objective, there are a number of issues which could affect their utility.

For example, return on investment (ROI) is a commonly used measure which raises the following questions:

- How should the asset base be measured? Should 'normal' accounting rules apply (i.e. book values) or should some other set of rules such as replacement value or current market value be used? Clearly the answer to this will help to determine the resulting ROI number. In general, the lower the asset base the higher the ROI, so it may be in the interests of business unit managers not to replace plant and equipment for example as this would tend to increase the asset base and hence lower the return.
- Profit measurement is also problematic in that unless the unit operates only in an open market the resulting revenues and costs may be subject to distortion due to imperfect or fixed internal markets. Even where such problems do not exist it is still possible for managers to influence results in the short term by postponing or cancelling altogether discretionary costs such as research and development and maintenance.

Despite these difficulties, and in spite of the fact that they tend to measure outputs only rather than inputs, financial measures based on accounting numbers are widely used, for example by the financial control companies in Goold and Campbell's research.

Summary and conclusions

In this chapter we have endeavoured to identify some of the main concerns in the exercise of strategic control. We have considered control as a generic concept and developed a discussion of a range of issues relevant to strategic control. Different types of strategic control were introduced as were some of the barriers and problems of strategic control.

On the basis of the issues raised here it would be inappropriate to attempt to formulate any common prescription of a normative view of strategic control. Nevertheless, Lorange and Murphy (1984) appear to have developed some ideas worthy of further consideration in the development of strategic control systems:

- keep the strategic control process as simple as the external environment will permit;
- create a broader and more explicit awareness of strategic control issues, for example by making the process explicit;
- interorganizational trust is crucial to the development of a viable control atmosphere, so strategic control may benefit from a shared perception that it can safeguard the long-term viability of the firm and also of its employees.

References

Ansoff, H. I. (1987) *Corporate Strategy*, revised edn (assisted by McDonnell, E. J.) (Harmondsworth: Penguin).

Anthony, R. N. and Dearden, J. (1980) *Management Control Systems: Text and Cases* (Homewood, Illinois: Irwin).

Bowman, C. and Asch, D. (1987) *Strategic Management* (London: Macmillan).

Galbraith, J. K. and Kazanjian, R. K. (1986) *Strategy Implementation: Structure, Systems and Process* (St Paul, MN: West) 2nd edn.

Goold, M. and Campbell, A. (1987) *Strategies and Styles* (Oxford: Basil Blackwell).

Hrebiniak, L. G. and Joyce, W. F. (1984) *Implementing Strategy* (New York: Macmillan).

Hurst, E. G. (1982) 'Controlling strategic plans', in *Implementation of Strategic Planning* (edited by Lorange, P.) (Englewood Cliffs, NJ: Prentice Hall) pp. 114–123.

Johnson, G. (1987) *Strategic Change and the Management Process* (Oxford: Basil Blackwell).

Johnson, G. and Scholes, K. (1988) *Exploring Corporate Strategy* (Hemel Hempstead: Prentice Hall).

Lorange, P. and Murphy, D. (1984) 'Considerations in implementing strategic control', *Journal of Business Strategy*, 4 (4) pp. 27–35.

Lorange, P., Scott Morton, M. F. and Ghoshal, S. (1986) *Strategic Control* (St Paul, MN: West).

Quinn, J. B. (1980) *Strategies for Change: Logical Incrementalism* (Homewood, Illinois: Irwin).

Reed, R. and Buckley, M. R. (1988) 'Strategy in action – techniques for implementing strategy', *Long Range Planning*, **21**, no. 3, pp. 67–74.

Tricker, R. I. and Boland, R. J. (1982) *Management Information and Control Systems* (Chichester: John Wiley).

Wheelen, T. L. and Hunger, D. J (1987) *Strategic Management* (Reading, Mass.: Addison-Wesley).

CHAPTER 28

The Nature and Use of Formal Control Systems for Management Control and Strategy Implementation

RICHARD L. DAFT and NORMAN B. MACINTOSH

Introduction

How do managers control organizations? When managers develop new organizational goals and strategies, how do they evaluate the organization's subsequent behavior and performance? How do they know whether plans are used and goals are achieved? These questions lie at the heart of management control. Managers need a way to assess whether top level decisions are incorporated into departmental activities and to determine whether strategies are influencing organizational performance (Christensen, Andrews, Bower, Hamermesh and Porter, 1982).

As recently as 10 years ago, organization and management scholars could not answer these questions. In the scholarly literature, control was studied as the amount of influence or participation employees had in organizational activities (Tannenbaum, 1968). Control theory of this period recognized control as an essential management function but consisted mostly of common sense principles such as 'Control should be kept simple' and 'Controls should measure only meaningful events' (Koontz, 1959; Sihler, 1971). These principles have some prescriptive value, but they do not provide a theoretical paradigm based on the organization's needs or contingencies.

In the last few years, concepts and models in the organizational control literature have come a long way (Kerr and Slocum, 1981). Control issues differ according to hierarchical level (Anthony and Dearden, 1980; Daft, 1983). Top managers are concerned with institutional control, midlevel managers with managerial control, and lower level managers and supervisors with operational control. In addition, concepts such as market control, bureaucratic control, output control, and behavioral control provide new tools for understanding and modeling organizational control processes (Ouchi, 1979; Ouchi & Maguire, 1975). Yet another development is new research into organizational control from the fields of accounting and business policy. Organizational control represents a point of convergence between these fields and management theory.

This chapter reports exploratory research findings about one poorly understood aspect of organizational control: the nature and use of formal management control systems. Our goal was to define the scope and characteristics of formal control systems actually used by managers and to define the role of formal systems in the organizational control and strategy implementation process. Our research investigates how middle and upper-middle managers control major organizational departments in order to implement business strategy.

Research background

Organizational control includes the activities used to achieve desired organizational goals and outcomes. Control activities include planning, motivation of employees, and co-ordination across departments (Barrett and Fraser, 1977). More specifically, organizational control can be conceptualized as a three stage cycle: (a) planning a target or standard of performance, (b) monitoring or measuring activities designed to reach that target, and (c) implementing corrections if targets or standards are not being achieved (Dunbar, 1981; Giglioni and Bedeian, 1974; Lorange and Scott Morton, 1974; Ouchi, 1977; Todd, 1977). The idea that control is used to achieve organizational goals and outcomes, and that the control process consists of a three stage cycle, is shared across the fields of organization theory, accounting, and business policy. Beyond this general definition, however, the conceptual and research base from each discipline offers a distinct contribution to our understanding of management control.
[...]

Theoretical focus

Several threads in the [...] literature provide a basis for the research undertaken here. First, we focus on formal management control systems used in organizations: an interesting and relatively unstudied aspect of organizational design. Control systems are a subcomponent of bureaucratic structure and represent impersonal mechanisms of control that have not been extensively studied in organization theory. Second, we focus on control at the middle management level, which Anthony (1965) called management control. Control at this level accomplishes organizational objectives through the activities of major departments.

The combination of formal control systems and a middle management perspective represents something of an unknown quantity. Market control and bureaucratic control, for example, explain how top managers can control the entire firm. At the bottom, operational level of organizations control can be accomplished through personal leadership and surveillance or through output data and records (Ouchi and Maguire, 1975). Moreover, the organization's technology may serve to standardize and regularize employee behavior (Perrow, 1978; Reeves and Woodward, 1970).

Middle managers are responsible for major departments and functions. Market control is ineffective because departmental outputs cannot be readily priced by the marketplace. Behavioral control is a tenuous method because middle managers may be located two or three management levels above first level activities, and behavioral control is difficult to transmit through the hierarchy (Ouchi, 1978). Middle managers are in the murky middle ground of the organization where control processes are not defined or well understood. The use of management information and control systems may allow middle managers to direct and control major departments to be consistent with overall organizational goals.

Third, we focus on management control because at that level business strategy is implemented. If an organization's strategy is a coherent series of decisions to achieve goals, how does the strategy translate into the activities of major departments and facilitate co-ordination across departments? Formal management control systems may be an important mechanism through which business strategy influences departmental activity; hence they may be an essential link in the strategy implementation process.

Fourth, control is a dynamic process. Control involves target-setting, activity-monitoring, and deficiency-correcting activities. Control also involves the provision of rewards and incentives to managers, and the co-ordination of activities to accomplish goals. Thus we link control systems to the ongoing control cycle. Our study is specifically directed at learning how formal management control systems are used at the middle management level to execute each step in the control cycle.

Finally, we focus on management control systems actually used by managers to determine whether these systems fit into a core control package. We propose to ground the study in the real world of organizations by asking middle managers which control systems they personally use. We seek also to determine whether the control systems complement one another to implement strategy and facilitate the control cycle. Thus, the operational base of this study is what managers actually do with respect to formal control systems.

Research method

The qualitative technique used to learn about formal management control systems is what Mintzberg (1979) called direct research. The study was not designed to test hypotheses; we were simply trying to learn. [...] The first stage was completely open-ended, defining the composition of management control systems and gathering ideas about their use. The second stage involved systematic interviews with departmental managers, gathering more systematic data about the scope and role of control systems across a larger number of departments and organizations. [...]

Research findings

The nature of management control

Initial interviews with controllers and upper level managers in stage one identified six components or subsystems that comprised the management control paradigm in nine firms. The management control system had a somewhat different form and scope in each organization, but there were clear similarities across corporations with respect to the appearance and use of these six subsystems. Two of these subsystems were used primarily for strategy formulation at the senior management level, and four subsystems comprised the management control system used by midlevel managers to implement strategy and evaluate performance. These six subsystems follow:

1. *Strategic plan*   The strategic plan typically consisted of an in-depth research analysis of the organization's position in the industry and included perceived opportunities in the environment and organizational strengths. This report might contain a few financial figures, such as projected profit opportunities, but was in written form and qualitative for the most part. The plan discussed products, competition, economic trends, ideas for exploiting new business opportunities, and other factors relevant to strategic decisions by top management.

2. *Long-range plan*   The long-range plan typically consisted of a five-year projection based on financial data. This report was often number based and included the details of departmental expenditures. These figures were projected up to five years in the future. Projected income statements and balance sheets typically were included. This plan was the financial and numeric counterpart to the strategic plan, which was non-financial and qualitative; both plans were detailed and voluminous.

3. *Annual operating budget*   This budget consisted of estimated profit, expenses, assets, and related financial figures for the coming year. Budget expenses typically fell into three categories: salaries, noncapital equipment, and other operating expenses. Budget reports were issued monthly or quarterly and included comparisons with budget targets and expenditures for the same period during the preceding year. Budget reports typically were developed for all cost centers, including small departments.

4. *Periodic statistical reports*   These reports were composed of statistical data, such as personnel complements, number of new customer contracts, volume of orders received, delinquent account ratios, and other statistics relevant to the department or business. Four to six separate reports might be used in a given department. The specific content of these reports differed for each department, but statistical reports existed in almost every firm. Most statistical data were nonfinancial and were issued in weekly, monthly, or quarterly reports.

5. *Performance appraisal*   This system was the formal method of evaluating and recording the performance of managers and employees. It typically included standardized forms that provided ratings scales and blank spaces for writing in individual goals for the next year. The appraisal system required an annual meeting between subordinate and manager to complete the forms and review performance, although more frequent meetings, sometimes informal, were not unusual. Management by objectives (MBO) was often part of the performance appraisal system.

6. *Policies and procedures*   These materials included all policies and standard operating procedures (SOPs) for the department and organization. Managers had general policy guidelines available in written form, as well as rules and procedures, to provide guidance for specific activities, such as dismissing an employee or handling a grievance. These materials also included job descriptions and other specifications for handling particular situations.

The managers sampled in our first stage described each of these six control subsystems as a distinct entity. Policies and procedures usually sat on a shelf and were used as a reference. The budget report typically arrived monthly and was kept in a desk drawer. Performance appraisals were kept in a personnel file. The strategic plan and long-range plan were not located in the office of department managers, but managers were aware of these reports and had access to them. The periodic statistical reports did not come in a single bound volume. Each report might pertain to a different aspect of departmental activities, but the managers thought of these reports as a distinct control subsystem.
[. . .]
    The strategic plan and long-range plan were part of the formulation stage of the strategic management process. These reports contained the information and forecasts used by senior managers to make decisions with respect to organizational goals and the strategies for achieving those goals. The four management control subsystems – budget, statistical reports, policies and procedures, and performance appraisal system – reflect the implementation stage of the strategic management process. The firm's resources were allocated through the budget. Policies, procedures, and performance appraisals could be used to guide human resources and technical activities. Statistical reports monitor various quantifiable outcomes. These four subsystems comprised the MCS package through which upper management enacted and monitored strategy and the control process.
    Another aspect of the MCS components [. . .] is that they originate in different departments; these reports converge on middle managers from different sources. Strategic plans were developed by a small, specialized strategic planning staff group. The five-year plan and the operating budget were the responsibility of the controller's office. The statistical reports were typically handled through an MIS department since most of the data were computer based. Performance appraisal systems were designed and maintained by the personnel department, and policies and procedures were the responsibility of either a subgroup in personnel or a separate systems and procedures group.
    The management control package was not a co-ordinated whole under the aegis of one department. Vertical links did exist between the strategic plan, the long-range plan, and the budget; but we did not detect any formal effort in these organizations to co-ordinate information laterally across the budget, statistical reports, policies and procedures, and performance appraisal system. Each source department was concerned only with the content of the report for which it was responsible.

Scope of management control systems

Our initial exploratory interviews helped us define the four management control system components and learn something about their source and use. In the second stage our survey of 86 departments in 20 corporations provided evidence of the presence and use of these four control systems in a larger sample of organizations.

Table 28.1 indicates the percentage of departmental managers reporting each of the four subsystems as a means of management control. Our criterion for determining the system's presence was whether the middle manager actually received and used reports from the system. As can be seen, the most widely used management control device was the budget, followed by statistical reports, policies and standard operating procedures, and finally the performance appraisal system.

Table 28.1 also indicates the average size of typical reports and the planning and measurement cycles. The budget report, averaging almost 9 pages, was typically a single report per month, while the 48 pages of statistical data were spread over five or six reports. Policies and procedures were lengthy and averaged about 1500 pages. Managers typically had four or five policy and procedure books for reference. The performance appraisal averaged less than three pages, including instructions and the forms to be completed during the personal interview.

Targets typically were established on an annual basis. The budget and statistical reports reported actual performance monthly; performance appraisals were reviewed annually. Policies and procedures, as standing directives, did not have planning cycles.

TABLE 28.1   Management control system frequency size and cycles
(N = 86)

Management control subsystem	Departments using (%)	Average pages	Typical planning cycle	Typical measurement period
Budget	94.1	8.9	Yearly	Monthly
Statistical reports	91.8	47.9	Yearly	Monthly
Policies/procedures	84.9	1,528	None	None
Performance appraisal	75.6	2.77	Yearly	Yearly

MCS utilization

The three stages in the organizational control cycle are target setting, measuring and monitoring, and corrective action to overcome a performance deficiency. From a strategic perspective, control may also entail management rewards and co-ordination across departments to facilitate business level outcomes. Thus, we sought to identify the role of each component in the MCS within the control cycle. In the second stage of the research we asked managers the extent to which they used the budget, the statistical reports, and the performance evaluation system to (a) help think ahead and plan specific activities for the department, (b) measure and monitor current departmental activities, (c) help people in the department do things correctly, (d) make promotion and salary decisions, and (e) co-ordinate departmental activities with other parts of the organization. Policies and procedures were not included in this question since they are static and do not follow a cycle of planning, measuring, and feedback.

Our findings of middle management's use of the MCS components are in Figure 28.1. The budget was used primarily for planning and thinking ahead, while statistical reports were used primarily for measuring and monitoring departmental activities. Each of the three control subsystems was used in the planning and monitoring stages of the control cycle; however, managers relied more on the budget for planning and more on statistical reports for monitoring. Policy books often suggest that budgets are used to monitor activities and evaluate managers (Pearce and

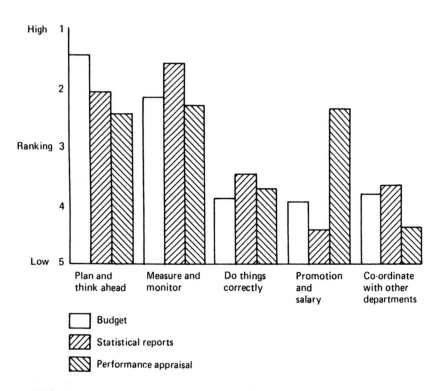

FIGURE 28.1   Average managerial ranking of management control subsystem use for five control functions (*N* = 86)

Robinson, 1982; Steiner, Miner and Gray, 1982), but the data in Figure 28.1 indicate that middle managers use budgets first as a planning device. The explanation is that the budget is used for the allocation of resources. The budget process told managers what resources they had for the next year. Once they knew their budget allocations, they did not need to refer to the budget reports very often. Statistical reports, in contrast, were tailored to specific departmental activities providing continuous information on output performance (production, absenteeism, scrap, etc.). Thus the two reports focused on different control activities: planning and measuring.

The reported use of control systems to 'do things correctly' within departments is puzzling. None of the three control subsystems were rated highly on that control function. Possibly, policies and procedures (not in Figure 28.1) played that role. Also, performance appraisals may have been instrumental for correcting the behavior of managers, although corrections would not always be timely with annual reviews. The awareness of performance appraisals, however, may have conveyed more corrective influence than did budgets and statistical reports.

The managers reported very little use of the MCS for co-ordination. This finding is also puzzling because we assumed that budget activities would reflect interdepartmental considerations. Possibly, control systems co-ordinate unobtrusively (Perrow, 1967). The middle managers we interviewed did not consciously use their budgets, statistical reports, or performance appraisals to co-ordinate with other departments. Interdepartmental issues may have been evaluated during strategy formulation and included in the original budget allocations and output targets set at the beginning of the year. Co-ordination decisions may have been made by top managers and the controller, based on competing demands from major departments. Department managers thus were more aware of their own needs and allocations than of interdepartmental co-ordination.

Written procedures were perceived to cover 54.9% of work activities and must be followed 53.9% of the time to do a good job. These percentages are not especially high, but they do indicate that SOPs had a definite role in doing things correctly. Managers further indicated the important role of policies and procedures in directing the behavior of employees; the use of SOPs in the prevention of 'trouble' exceeded their use in the evaluation of performance.
[...]

Budget versus statistical reports

The remaining data provide a closer look at budget and statistical reports because both entailed monthly reports at the departmental level. We asked managers which of three comparisons – comparison of actual performance to targets, to previous performance (previous month or year-to-date), or to the performance of other units – were made in budget and statistical reports. [...] 98% of budget data were compared to planned targets, which is consistent with the emphasis on planning and target setting associated with the budget in Figure 28.1. Budget figures were infrequently used for comparisons across departments and were compared to some extent to past performance; the budget focuses on the relationship of current to planned expenditures.

Statistical data, in contrast, were compared most frequently (81%) to past performance. They were also compared to performance targets and were much more likely than the budget to be used for comparisons across departments. Comparisons to past performance and across units are consistent with the measuring and monitoring function of statistical reports suggested in Figure 28.1. Departmental outcomes could best be evaluated by looking at a combination of indicators including previous output, the output of other units, and targeted outputs.

[...]

Managers named the two key items (actual numbers) they preferred to use on each report to evaluate departmental performance. Each response was classified as an input to the department (e.g. number of people), an output of the department (e.g. number of phones installed), or an indicator of departmental efficiency (e.g. number of phones installed per person per day).

The budget key indicators most often measured input items, providing information for planning and resource allocation. Key indicators on statistical reports frequently measured outputs, for measuring and monitoring departmental activities. [...] Budgets were important for planning and resource allocation; statistical reports were important for measuring and evaluating output performance. Policies and procedures and the performance appraisal system tended to be used in the corrective action stage.

Discussion

Our research probed the nature of formal management controls to understand middle management control and to learn how business strategies could be implemented and evaluated in major departments within organizations. The research has not provided definitive answers, yet it does provide a basis for preliminary suggestions about the accomplishment of implementation and the control process. The findings are summarized in five inferences:

1. *The business level control process in most organizations uses six control components*   The strategic plan and long-range plan were used by top

managers for strategy formulation. The budget, statistical reports, performance appraisal system, and policies and procedures were used by middle managers for departmental control and strategy implementation. [. . .] The managers in our study clearly defined the MCSs available to them. In the initial interviews, middle managers identified each of the four implementation subsystems as helping them manage and control the departments under their supervision. These organizations had other control systems, such as capital budgeting and inventory control, but these other systems were not as important to middle management for control of their departments and functional activities.

2. The four formal control systems used by departmental managers complement one another to help managers execute the control cycle, but the formal systems are not designed as a package   The budget dealt with resource allocation. Its primary use was during the planning and target setting stage of the control cycle. Statistical reports pertained to the volume of outputs from the department, and outputs were compared to previous performance and to other departments. Performance appraisal systems were used to reward lower level managers. While performance appraisals were used to determine salaries and promotions, we think they also helped managers enact corrections in the control cycle. Finally, policies and procedures helped departmental employees do things correctly. The role of policies and procedures was limited because they are a standing body of knowledge and are not renewed on an annual cycle. New policies and procedures were developed only as new situations arose for which managers need specific guidance.

The concept of a co-ordinated control package or a core control system (Flamholtz, 1983) was not supported, on two counts. First, control system elements were not discrete; one was not used exclusively for planning, nor one for measuring, nor one for correction. Although a division of labor was evident, the systems overlapped and served two or three functions. Second, budget and accounting information served more as a planning aid than as the measuring device envisioned in the core control system. Budgets reduce uncertainty for managers about resource inputs for the next year. Once plans are laid, managers turn to other systems, especially statistical reports, to monitor performance.

3. The first two stages in the control cycle – target setting and measuring – receive primary emphasis in formal management control systems   Formal control system elements place more emphasis on planning and measurement – the control of inputs and outputs – than on corrective action or co-ordination. Although the management control system components did complement one another, they apparently did not perform all three stages of the control cycle to the same extent.

One explanation for the lesser emphasis on feedback and corrective action is that these activities require other control devices, especially personal involvement. Budgets and statistical reports contain universal, impersonal information. These indicators are not particular, nor are statistics tailored to the unique problems confronting each manager. Moreover, corrective action and co-ordination across departments involve many exceptions. Thompson (1967) and Van de Ven, Delbecq and Koenig (1976) argued that rules and procedures could be used for simple tasks; but if co-ordination was difficult and departmental tasks uncertain, then face-to-face and other complex forms of co-ordination were required. In this respect, efforts of middle managers to change the behavior of lower level managers depend on networking and personal communications transmitted outside formal control systems. Corrective influence would occur through discussions and meetings and would include the evaluation of unusual circumstances not reported in routine control reports. Thus we infer that an informal, personal, face-to-face control process complements and enriches the formal, impersonal management control systems observed in this study. The personal control mechanism is based on leadership and direct involvement along the management hierarchy, providing a mechanism through which to accomplish feedback and corrective action.

4. *Management control systems are both financial and non-financial*   Financial information (ROI, profits, earnings per share) may be dominant at the business or corporate level where financial performance is paramount, but it is not dominant at the middle management level. Relying on financial figures, the budget was used to plan and allocate resources into departments. The other three control systems were based on nonfinancial data, although occasional figures were expressed in dollars. Statistical reports, performance appraisal systems, and policies and procedures provided a rich variety of technical, personal, and output data allowing managers to understand and guide activities within their responsibility centers. In terms of control system scope, financial data comprise a modest proportion of total control information at the department level in contrast to the emphasis given monetary information in the accounting and strategy implementation literatures.

5. *Management control relies heavily on the control of both departmental inputs and outputs*   Budgets and statistical reports were important control systems. Budgets focused on inputs, and statistical reports on outputs. This finding contrasts somewhat with Ouchi's assertion (Ouchi and Maguire, 1975) that control within organizations is either behavioral control or output control.
[. . .]

Toward a model of management control

[...]
The findings provide the basis for explaining how organizations resolve two control questions: (a) how is business strategy linked to departmental plans and activities, and (b) how does the formal MCS enable middle managers to enact each stage of the control cycle for their responsibility centers? The following discussion proposes two models that suggest how management control systems help organizations resolve these issues.

Linking strategy formulation to departmental activities through the MCS

Each department in an organization is part of a transformation process involving raw material inputs, actions by employees that change those inputs, and outputs that go to other departments or organizations. Inputs include people, equipment, and material. The transformation process includes the technology, knowledge, and work activities used to change input materials. Outputs are the finished product of the department (Daft and Macintosh, 1981; Perrow, 1967; Van de Ven and Delbecq, 1976). Each organization has several departmental technologies and transformation processes.

One role of management control systems is to implement organizational strategy downward to the departmental level. The transformation activities within departments should reflect business level strategic choices. The management control systems accomplish strategy implementation by directing and controlling resource inputs, influencing the transformation process, and monitoring departmental outputs. An ideal model describing how business strategy and departmental activities tie together is in Figure 28.2.

Figure 28.2 illustrates that the strategic plan is formulated at the organizational level and is used to formulate a long-range financial plan for the next 5 years. These two plans at the organizational level provide baseline information: targets and goals to determine short-range (1 year or less) plans and activities encompassed by the formal management control subsystems.

Organizational strategy can be directly implemented in two ways. First, by allocating resources to departments based on top management's strategic priorities. [...] Second, top managers can ask for departmental outputs that reflect strategic priorities (increased new products, greater market penetration, etc.). The outputs can be monitored through statistical reports; both inputs and outputs can be controlled to reflect business strategy.

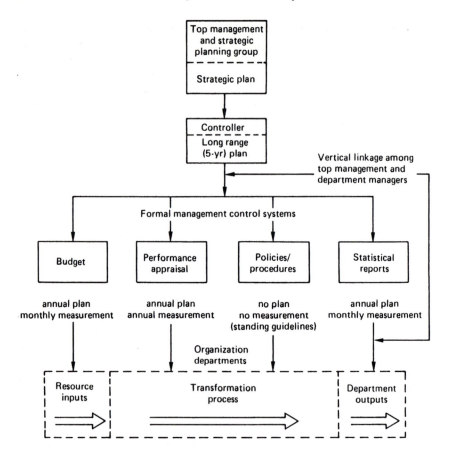

FIGURE 28.2   Model of vertical linkage among control systems for strategy implementation

Control of the transformation process is somewhat more complicated. A few budget or statistical indicators may reflect efficiency criteria and therefore provide one method for evaluating the transformation process. The performance appraisal system and standard operating procedures are auxiliary control devices for the transformation process.

[. . .]

The key to using the MCS for the implementation and evaluation of organizational strategy is linkage. Upper managers and department level managers must discuss and be aware of the relationship between organizational strategies and departmental activities. In order to implement strategic plans, the strategic and 5-year plans must be communicated to managers during the process of formulating budgets, developing performance appraisal systems, and compiling statistical reports. Managers who use formal systems to control departmental activities must be informed of company strategic plans and their department's strategic role; input and output targets and monitoring devices can guide departmental work. If the vertical links between strategy formulation and management control systems illustrated in Figure 28.2 is attained, then departmental activities will be co-ordinated with organizational goals, and business strategy can be implemented at the departmental level.

Using the MCS to enact the management control cycle

The second issue in this research is how middle and upper-middle level managers can use management control systems to direct and evaluate departmental activities. The answer lies in the division of labor among management control system components; the control system package provides each manager with a set of control tools to manage each stage in the control cycle.

Table 28.2 illustrates the relationships between each stage in the management control cycle and each management control subsystem. The planning or target setting stage is accomplished through the budget. The budget lets each manager know the resources available for the coming year and reduces uncertainty with respect to what can be accomplished. Statistical reporting and the performance appraisal systems are also used for planning to some extent, but they are not resource-based and play a secondary planning role.

Measuring and monitoring of departmental outcomes is accomplished through statistical reports. Statistical reports can be tailored to the specific output of the department, providing excellent data on a weekly or monthly basis about performance. The budget and performance appraisal systems provide additional data on performance. The budget report pertains to expenditure performance and the performance appraisal provides annual data on the performance of individual employees. The statistical reports, however, are the critical devices for measuring and monitoring departmental outcomes.

Feedback and corrective action are partially accomplished through the performance appraisal system and policies and procedures. Our interpretation from the study is that an additional and important means to achieve target performance is personal leadership conveyed through the management hierarchy; change is implemented through face-to-face discussion and personal communications. Management control systems are excellent for communicating plans and activities which can be quantified and reported through formal, impersonal systems. Corrective action to overcome failures, however, is an exception. The failure may involve unique circumstances not reported in the formal data; managers

TABLE 28.2 Relationship of management control cycle to MCS and personal control

Management control cycle	Budget	Statistical reports	Performance appraisal	Policies/procedures	Non-MCS: personal influence and leadership
1. Planning and Target Setting	Primary	Secondary	Secondary		Secondary
2. Measuring and Monitoring	Secondary	Primary	Secondary		
3. Feedback and Correction			Secondary	Secondary	Primary

will have to discuss these issues and develop alternatives for corrective action. The primary vehicle for these actions will be the management hierarchy. The performance appraisal system gives management a method of ensuring compliance with corrective action, and standard operating procedures prescribe correct behavior for a variety of situations. These control subsystems alone, however, would not always provide effective or timely corrective action. Formal control systems are augmented by personal management control processes.

Conclusion

Initially, we asked: 'How do managers control organizations?' [...] Our research was undertaken to provide a more complete answer to the question of strategy implementation and control at the departmental level. We found that middle managers use four management control systems to control their departments, using the control cycle.

Our findings both reinforce and build upon previous work. The assumption that MCSs provide an explicit tool for strategy implementation was supported (Hrebiniak and Joyce, 1984; Pearce and Robinson, 1982). Upper level managers develop a strategic plan, providing information for control subsystems, which act as short-term planning and monitoring devices.

The management control system also relates to bureaucratic control. The MCS is an impersonal (Reimann and Neghandi, 1975) means of control, using output control (Ouchi, 1977) and regulating inputs. The impersonal MCS was complemented by personal control through leadership and the management hierarchy (Kerr and Slocum, 1981). The control process at the departmental level is thus accomplished through a mix of personal and impersonal mechanisms, although only the impersonal were studied here.

Further, the MCS consists of a package, although not explicitly designed and co-ordinated by the organization (Flamholtz, 1983; Otley, 1980). Each MCS component had a different source, but they complemented one another in their application to different parts of the control process. The package controls both inputs and outputs, and it contains both financial and nonfinancial data. Indeed, nonfinancial data may be more prominent in formal management control than previously realized (Anthony and Dearden, 1980).
[...]
The design and use of budgets, statistical reports, performance appraisals, and policies and procedures may be influenced by the type of strategy, by the rate of change in the environment, by competitive issues in the industry, or by the nature of the organization's technology. All of these

factors may influence control outcomes for planning, measuring, or correcting departmental activities. We presented an initial glimpse into the process of middle management control. Additional research will help develop a better understanding of strategy implementation and answer more detailed questions about formal MCS design applications.

References

Anthony, R. N. (1965) *Planning and Control Systems: A Framework for Analysis* (Boston: Graduate School of Business Administration, Harvard University).

Anthony, R. N. and Dearden, J. (1980) *Management Control Systems* (Homewood, IL: Irwin).

Barrett, M. E., and Fraser, L. B., III. (1977) 'Conflicting roles in budgeting for operations', *Harvard Business Review*, **55** (4) pp. 137–46.

Christensen, C. R., Andrews, A. R., Bower, J. L., Hamermesh, R. G. and Porter, M. E. (1982) *Business Policy: Text and Cases* (Homewood, IL: Irwin).

Daft, R. L. (1983) *Organization Theory and Design* (St. Paul: West).

Daft, R. L. and Macintosh, N. B. (1981) 'A tentative exploration into the amount and equivocality of information processing in organizational work units', *Administrative Science Quarterly*, **26**, pp. 207–24.

Dunbar, R. L. M. (1981) 'Designs for organizational control', in P. C. Nystrom and W. H. Starbuck (eds) *Handbook of Organi. ational Design* (vol. 2, pp. 85–115) (Oxford: Oxford University Press).

Flamholtz, E. G. (1983) 'Accounting, budgeting and control systems in their organizational context: Theoretical and empirical perspectives', *Accounting, Organizations and Society*, **8**, pp. 153–69.

Giglioni, G. B. and Bedeian, A. G. (1974) 'A conspectus of management control theory: 1900–1972', *Academy of Management Journal*, **17**, pp. 292–305.

Hrebiniak, L. G. and Joyce, W. F. (1984) *Implementing Strategy* (New York: Macmillan).

Kerr, S. and Slocum, J. W., Jr. (1981) 'Controlling the performances of people in organizations', in P. C. Nystrom and W. H. Starbuck (eds) *Handbook of Organizational Design* (vol. 2, pp. 116–34) (Oxford: Oxford University Press).

Koontz, H. (1959) 'Management control: A suggested formulation of principles', *California Management Review*, **2**, pp. 50–5.

Lorange, P. and Scott Morton, M. S. (1974) 'A framework for management control systems', *Sloan Management Review*, **16** (1) pp. 41–56.

Mintzberg, H. (1979) 'An emerging strategy of "direct" research', *Administrative Science Quarterly*, **24**, pp. 582–9.

Otley, D. T. (1980) 'The contingency theory of management accounting: Achievement and prognosis', *Accounting, Organizations and Society*, **5**, 413–28.

Ouchi, W. G. (1977) 'The relationship between organizational structure and organizational control', *Administrative Science Quarterly*, **22**, pp. 95–112.

Ouchi, W. G. (1978) 'The transmission of control to organizational hierarchy', *Academy of Management Journal*, **21**, pp. 173–92.

Ouchi, W. G. (1979) 'A conceptual framework for the design of organizational control mechanisms', *Management Science*, **25**, pp. 833–48.

Ouchi, W. G. and Maguire, M. A. (1975) 'Organizational control: Two functions', *Administrative Science Quarterly*, **20**, pp. 559–69.

Pearce, J. A., II and Robinson, R. B., Jr. (1982) *Strategic Management* (Homewood, IL: Irwin).

Perrow, C. (1967) 'A framework for the comparative analysis of organization', *American Sociological Review*, **32**, pp. 194–208.

Perrow, C. (1979) *Complex Organizations: A Critical Essay* (Glenview, IL: Scott Foresman).

Reeves, T. K. and Woodward, J. (1970) 'The study of managerial control', in J. Woodward (ed.) *Industrial Organizations: Behavior and Control* (Oxford: Oxford University Press).

Reimann, B. C. and Neghandi, A. R. (1975) 'Strategies of administrative control and organizational effectiveness', *Human Relations*, **28**, pp. 475–86.

Sihler, W. H. (1971) 'Toward better management control systems', *California Management Review*, **14** (2), pp. 33–9.

Steiner, G. A., Miner, J. B. and Gray, E. R. (1982) *Management Policy and Strategy* (New York: Macmillan).

Tannenbaum, A. S. (1968) *Control and Organizations* (New York: McGraw-Hill).

Thompson, J. D. (1967) *Organizations in Action* (New York: McGraw-Hill).

Todd, J. (1977, Spring) 'Management control systems: A key link between strategy, structure and employee performance', *Organizational Dynamics*, pp. 65–78.

Van de Ven, A. H. and Delbecq, A. L. (1974) 'A task contingent model of work-unit structure', *Administrative Science Quarterly*, **19**, pp. 183–97.

Van de Ven, A. H., Delbecq, A. L. and Koenig, R., Jr. (1976) 'Determinants of coordination modes within organizations', *American Sociological Review*, **41**, pp. 322–38.

Index

Aaker, D. A.   206
Abelson, R.   41
Abranavel, H.   41
accounting, creative   277–9
Acito, F.   308
acquisition   238–9, 240–1, 251, 255
action planning   331
action power   398
activists   26
'adaptive' model   40
adhocracy   340, 344–5, 349–50
   strategy and   362–3, 364, 367–8
administration
   drive for efficiency   60–1
   portfolio planning   151–3, 154, 159
affinities, breakdowns in   211
age of organization   338–9, 375, 376
Aggarwal, R.   261
agreements
   breaking   273–4
   negotiated   299, 302
Air Canada   7, 14
Al-Bazzaz, S.   96, 97
ALCO Standard   235
Aldrich, H. E.   354
Alexander, G. J.   216
Allison, G. T.   40
Alpha process   103–4, 108–11 passim
Alutto, J. A.   308
American Hospital Supply   239
American Viscose   228
Amey, L. R.   211
analytical techniques, misapplication
   of   61–3
Andrews, A. R.   409
Ang, J.   96, 97, 260, 262
Ansoff, H. I.   87, 89, 90, 130, 401
Anthony, R. N.   398, 410, 411, 425
approval systems   110

Argyris, C.   318
Aristotle   271
Arthur D. Little Ltd   85, 144, 147,
   195, 266
Asch, D.   xiii, 400
asset parsimony   357, 359, 360
asset-swaps   203, 204, 213
assets
   declining industries   222–3, 225–7
   local authorities and fixed   277,
   278–9
Astley, W. G.   354, 356
AT&T   257
attractiveness of industry/
   sector   192–6, 237–8
attractiveness/mesh matrix   198–9
Audit Commission   278, 279
audits of planning process   68–9
automation   339–40
autonomy, business unit   241
autonomy crisis   380
awareness   21–2, 22–3

baby food industry   219
Barrett, M. E.   410
Bartunek, J. M.   40, 41, 52
Baxter Travenol   239
Beatrice   235
Bedeian, A. G.   410
behaviour
   barriers to strategic control   405
   formalization   327–8, 338
   political   295, 314–15
Berg, P. O.   87
Beta process   104–5, 108–11 passim
better-off test   239–40
Beyer, J. M.   41
BIG   282
Biggart, N. W.   40

board members 66
Boje, D. M. 52
Boland, R. J. 398
Boston Consulting Group 12, 61–2, 144, 147, 266
Boudreaux, K. J. 215
Bower, J. L. 40, 409
Bowman, C. xiii, 400
brand identification 135–6
Brightman, H. J. 259, 260, 265
British Airways 277
Brown, G. 289
Brown, R. H. 43
Brown, S. J. 215
Brunet, J. P. 4
BTR 245, 280, 281, 283–4, 288
Buchanan, B. 307, 308
Buckley, M. R. 401
budgeting
  and control 400–1, 413–20 *passim*, 422, 423, 424
  World Wildlife Fund 75
buffers 26
building share 183, 184, 189–90
Burch, J. G. 266
bureaucracies 327–8, 339–40, 343–8, 382
  see also machine bureaucracy
Burgelman, R. A. 204, 209
Burns, M. R. 215
Burns, T. 353, 354, 356, 365, 367, 368
Business in the Community 283
business ethics *see* ethics
business unit strategy *see* competitive strategy
buyers, powerful 138–9
buy-outs 202–4, 209, 210
Buzzell, R. D. 358, 359

Camillus, J. C. 97
Campbell, A. 404–5, 406
capacity 140, 211
capital
  investment 154, 155, 156, 160
  requirements for entry 136
Casson, M. 205
causal maps 318
Caves, R. E. 205
CBS 236, 254
centralization 335, 336, 337, 341–2
  see also decentralization
Chacko, G. K. 266

Chaffee, E. E. 40
champions 29, 127–8
Chandler, A. D. 51, 369, 374–5
change
  choice of strategy 301–5
  configurations and 355–6
  exploiting industry 141, 142–3
  incrementalism 37–53
  management of strategic 20–33
  need and divestment 205–11
  resistance to 157, 292, 294–301, 311, 312–14
chief executive officers (CEOs) 109, 157
  excessive rationality 63–4
  strategy implementation 393–5
Channon, D. 369
Chiplin, B. 204, 210
Christensen, C. R. 409
Chua, J. 96, 97, 260, 262
coalitions 28–9, 31–2, 35, 36, 314–15
  see also political behaviour
coercion 301, 302, 319–20
cognitive maps 41, 42–3
Cohen, M. D. 37
collaboration 382–3
commitment
  creation 21–2, 27, 35, 36; from participation 298
  environmental analysis 129
  formalization 29
  implementation and 307–8, 394–5; chief executive officers 157; middle managers 315
  managing low/negative 317–20
communication 297, 302, 394
Community of St Helens' Trust 282
Companies Acts 277
competing events 392
competition 133–43, 236
  contending forces 134–41
  declining industries 221–7
  judging strengths and weaknesses 172–3
  multifaceted 143
competitive strategy 234
  formulation 141–3
  performance and 214–16
compliance 36
computers, personal 266–7
conditioning process 35
configurations 342–52, 354–60

conglomerates   12, 149
    strategy and structure   359, 362–3,
        364–5, 368–70
    see also divisionalization
consensus, erosion of   29–30
consensus strategy   2, 13, 16
Consolidated Foods   244
constructive tension   52
consultants, modelling   260
consumers   139
contention teams   31
contracting-out   202, 203
control   397–400
    formal systems for
        management   409–26
    planning and   331
    strategic   293, 400–7
control crisis   381
Cook, J.   307, 308
co-optation   300, 302
co-ordination   381–2, 417, 419–20
    mechanisms   324–6, 330–1
core businesses   252
corporate moral obligations   272
corporate planners   64–5, 109
corporate planning models   85, 256–
    68
corporate strategy   234–54
    concepts   240–50
    premises   236–7
    selection   250–4
    small firms and   78–81
corporate theme   254
corporate ventures   85, 178–90
corrective action   419–20, 423–5
cost leadership   15, 357, 358, 360
    conglomerates   370
    machine bureaucracy   363, 366
costs
    competition and   136, 140
    diversification   236
    entry   238–9
    exit barrier   223
    modelling   259–60
    sharing activities   249
counter effort   310
Coyne, J.   210
Crampon, W. J.   307
creative accounting   277–9
creative evolution   379
credibility   23–4
creditors, able and willing   274–5

crises   21, 22, 34, 207, 208
    see also revolution
Crozier, H.   43
cultural web   45–6
culture
    corporate   126–7, 129
    planning   67
Cyert, R. M.   315

Daft, R. L.   46, 410, 421
Dandridge, T. C.   46
Data Decisions   267
Davis, P.   356, 357
Davis, S. M.   47
Day, D.   359
Deal, T.   52
Dearden, J.   398, 410, 425
debts, delayed payment of   273–6
decentralization   335–8, 340–1
    see also centralization
decision support systems (DSS)   266
decision trees   34–5
declining industries   85, 219–32
defensive strategy   141–2
Delbecq, A. L.   420, 421
delegation   380–1
deliberate strategies   2, 4–6, 17–18
Delta process   106–7, 108–11 *passim*
demand, conditions of   221–2, 226
demergers   *see* spin-offs
design parameters   326–38, 344–5
Dess, G.   356, 357
'devil's advocates'   31
Dialog   266
differentiation   357–8, 360, 361–5
direct research   412
direct supervision   324, 325, 330,
        336, 337
direction   380
distribution   136
diversification   85, 177–90
    assessing opportunities for   143,
        191–200
    corporate strategies and   235–6
    divisionalization and   341, 369
    management of   146–8; portfolio
        planning   149, 161
divestment   85, 201–16, 235
    declining industries   225, 229,
        230–1
    spectrum   202–4
    stages of   211–14

dividends, paying 254
divisionalization 205, 208, 344–5, 348–9
  diversification and 341, 369
  see also conglomerates
donor list, World Wildlife Fund and 74, 77
Dow Chemical 257
Dow Jones 266
Drucker, P. F. 296
Du Pont 220, 229, 235, 250
Dugger, W. M. 208
Dunbar, R. L. M. 410
Dyson, R. G. 86, 100

economies of scale 135
education 297, 302
efficiency, administrative 60–1
Ellert, J. C. 215
emergent strategies 2, 5, 6, 17–18
end-game strategies 227–32
Engledow, J. L. 114
entrepreneurial strategies 7–9, 16
entreneurship, subsidiary 209
entry, threat of 135–7
entry barriers 135–6, 239
entry costs 238–9
entry scale 186–8, 189
environment 14–15
  implementation and 392–3
  signals and incremental change 47–51
  strategic planning and 97–8, 99
  structure and 340–1, 354–5
environmental analysis 84–5, 113–30, 131–2
equifinality 316
errors, control and 399–400
ethics, business 85, 270–9
  strategy and 280–9
evaluation
  environmental analysis 129
  performance and control 399
  plans 67–8
evolution 374, 375, 376, 378
  phases 379, 380, 380–1, 381–2, 382–3
executive champions 127
exit barriers 140, 222–7
expectancy theory 308–10, 311, 317
experts 12–13
Exxon 235

Fahey, L. 37, 131
family philanthropy 289
Fedor, D. B. 52
feedback learning 175
Ferris, D. 266
finance, divestment and 209–10
financial attributes 165, 166, 170, 171
financial control 404, 405, 406, 420
financial markets, access to 224
financial performance 179–83, 183–4, 185–6
financial planning models 256, 258, 263–4, 266
Financial Times 283–4
Finn, R. 96, 260–1
Flamholtz, E. G. 419, 425
flexibility 9, 25–6
  environmental analysis 130
focus 357, 358–9, 360
focusing the organization 28, 35
forecasting 31, 264–5
formal-analytical techniques 31
formalization of behaviour 327–8, 338
formulation of strategies 41–4, 102–12, 394
  competition and 141–3
  control and 421–3
  processes 84, 103–7
Fortune '500' 144, 178, 377, 388
Fortune '1000' 144, 145, 149
Foster, M. J. 86, 100
franchising 202, 203
Franco, L. G. 205
Frank, R. H. 209
Fraser, L. B. 410
Frederickson, J. W. 40
Freeman, J. 354
Friedlander, F. 52
Friesen, P. 37, 51, 355–8 *passim*
Fulmer, R. M. 87, 89, 92, 94
funds, World Wildlife net 73, 75–6

Galai, D. 215
Galbraith, J. K. 7, 354, 367, 401
Gale, B. 358, 359
Gamma process 105–6, 108–11 *passim*
Garvin, D. A. 204
gasoline industry 219–20
General Cinema 245

General Electric   144, 147, 228, 232
  corporate strategy   235, 248–9
General Mills   236
General Motors (GM)   245–6
General, Municipal and Boilermakers'
  Union   284
generalization   316
generic strategy   403
Gershefski, G. W.   87, 89, 90, 258,
  259
Giglioni, G. B.   410
Ginter, P. M.   266
Glueck, W. F.   xiii
goals   79–80
  budgeting and   75
  control and   398–9, 400
  differing and implementation   319–
  20
Godiwalla, Y. M.   95
Goold, M.   404–5, 406
government policy   136
Gray, E. R.   417
Green, B.   284
Greenley, G. E.   86, 100
Greiner, L. E.   51
Griffiths, I.   277
Grinyer, P. H.   7
  corporate modelling   259, 260, 261
  incrementalism   37, 51, 52
  paradigm   47
  strategic planning   87, 89, 92, 96,
  97
grouping, unit   329–30
growth of organizations   204–5, 293,
  373–86
  attractiveness and   238
  key forces   374–7
  phases   378–83
  small firms   81
GTE Sylvania   220, 228
Gulf & Western   244
Guth, W. D.   311, 314

Hakansson, N. H.   214
Hambrick, D. C.   43, 353, 354, 361,
  366
  strategic configurations   356, 357,
  359, 368
Hamermesh, R. B.   409
Hammond, J. S.   257, 264, 265
Hannan, M.   354
Harrigan, K. R.   210
Harris, S. E.   259, 260, 265

harvest strategy   220, 228–9, 230–1,
  232
Hausler, J.   95
Heany, D. F.   359
Hedberg, B.   37
Henderson, B.   353, 358
Herold, D. M.   87, 89, 91
Heroux, R. L.   86
Hickson, D. J.   xiii–xiv, 43, 361, 365
Higgins, J. C.   96, 260–1
higher-order issues   316
Hinings, C. R.   354, 361, 365
historical judgement criteria   172–3
Hite, G. L.   214, 215
Hofer, C.   353
horizontal mechanisms   250, 253
House, R. J.   87, 89, 90–1
Hrebiniak, L. G.   307, 406, 425
  control problems   398–400
Huff, A. S.   37, 40
Hughes Aircraft   245–6
Hume, D.   271
Hunger, D. J.   398
Hurst, E. G.   400

IBM   235, 250, 251, 257
ideological strategy   9–10, 16
ideology   52, 323, 324
implementation   293, 388–96
  control problems   398–400
  management control systems   421–
  3
  middle management self-interest
  and   307–20
  organizational action   43–4
  problems   389–93, 396
imposed strategies   14–15, 16
incrementalism   37–53, 403
  logical *see* logical incrementalism
indoctrination   328–9
inducement   319
industry
  attractiveness   238
  exploitation of change in   141,
  142–3
  growth rate   375, 377
information   22, 107–8, 224, 399
innovating differentiators   357, 358,
  360
  adhocracies   363, 364, 367–8
integrated model of process   47–9
integration   142, 211, 224
integrating managers   332

intended strategies 45
internalization of transactions 205
International Union for the
    Conservation of Nature and
    Natural Resources (IUCN) 73
'interpretative' model 40–1
interrelationships 245–6, 252, 253
    see also sharing activities; skills
    transfer
intrapreneurship 209
investment
    portfolio planning 154, 155, 156
    security of 98
involvement 298, 302, 394–5
Irving, P. 96
Issues Management Association 113
ITT 244

Jain, S. 117
Janis, I. L. 41, 47
Jauch, L. R. xiii
job specialization 327, 338
Johnson, G. xiii, 41, 400, 403
Johnson & Johnson 251
joint ventures 251
Jonsson, S. 37
Joyce, W. F. 46, 406
    control 398, 399, 400, 425
judgements, disagreements
    between 317–19

Kahn, R. 315
Kant, I. 271
Kanter, M. 47, 52
Karger, D. W. 87, 88, 89, 91
Katz, D. 315
Kazanjian, R. K. 401
Kennedy, A. 52
Kennedy, J. 267
Kerr, S. 410, 425
Khera, I. 261
Kiesler, C. H. 9
King, W. 131
Kingston, P. L. 256, 264
Klein, B. 208
Klein, R. 258, 259, 260, 261
knowledge power 398
Koenig, R. 420
Koontz, H. 409
Kotler, P. 86
Kotter, J. P. 52
Kudla, R. J. 87, 88, 89, 92–3, 215

Lawler, E. E. 308
Lawrence, P. R. 354, 356, 361, 365,
    367, 368
leadership crisis 379–80
leadership strategy 227–8, 230–1
leap control 402, 403–4
Learned, E. P. *et al.* 163
learning 17–18, 175
legitimization of new options 24
Lenz, R. T. 114
Leontiades, M. 87, 89, 93
leverage 109
leverage buy-outs 202–4
Levitt, T. 143
Lewis, T. R. 211
liaison devices 331–5
liaison positions 332
licensing, Pilkington and 280–1
Lindblom, C. E. 37
line managers 65–6, 158
'linear' model 40
linkages
    control systems 421–3
    environmental analysis 124–5, 129
Little, A. D. *see* Arthur D. Little Ltd
Loasby, B. J. 95
local authorities 277, 278–9
Loew's 245, 253
logical incrementalism 2, 20, 37, 42
    environment and 49–50, 403
long-range plans 413, 414, 421–3
Lorange, P. 401, 410
    control 402, 403–4, 405, 406, 407
Lorsch, J. W. 354, 356, 361, 365,
    367, 368
Lyles, M. A. 37

machine bureaucracy 343–7, 355,
    362–3, 364, 365–6
Macintosh, N. B. 421
MacMillan, I. C. 357, 359, 361, 368
    middle managers and
    implementation 311, 314, 319
Maguire, M. A. 410, 411, 420
Malik, Z. A. 87, 88, 89, 91
management buy-outs 202–4, 209,
    210
management by exception 399
management by objectives
    (MBO) 157
    see also goals
management control systems
    (MCS) 409–26

management information systems
  (MIS)   264–5, 266–7
managers
  corporate strengths and
    weaknesses   163–76
  and diversity   146–8, 161
  formulation   111–12
  intentions and corporate
    ventures   188–9
  modelling   259, 261, 262–3
  opportunism   208–9
  personal computers   266–7
  portfolio management   241–4
  portfolio planning: impact   154–6;
    time for review   159
  resistance as exit barrier   224–5
  rewards   108–9
  small firms   79–80
  style and organization
    growth   378–83, 384
  see also line managers; middle
    managers; top managers
manipulation   300–1, 302
Mansfield, M. J.   263–4
March, J. C.   37
March, J. G.   315
market performance   183–4, 185, 186
market scale   186–7
market share   183–90, 227–8
marketing attributes   165, 166, 167,
  168, 170, 171
marketing differentiators   357, 358,
  360, 361–5
markets
  planning and   98–9, 160
  small firms' choice   80
Marris, R.   201
Martin, J.   52
Mason, R. O.   52
Masulis, R. W.   215
matrix structures   332–3, 334
maturity, sector   194, 195–6
McColough, P.   23
McHugh, A.   4
McIntosh, R. S.   215
McKelvey, W.   354
McKesson   248
McKinsey   144, 147, 266
McLean, E. R.   258, 259
Mead   144
Meeks, G.   201
Meinhart, W. A.   95
mergers   235, 254

mesh   196–8
  attractiveness/mesh matrix   198–9
Meyer, A. D.   41, 52
Meyer, J. W.   41
microcomputers   266–7
middle managers   323, 324
  control   411–20
  self-interest and
    implementation   292, 295, 310,
    311–14
Miles, J. A.   215
Miles, R.   15, 47, 354, 356, 358, 359
Mill, J. S.   271
Miller, D.   37, 51, 208
  configurations   354–8 passim
Miller, J. L.   267
Miner, J. B.   417
Mintzberg, H.   40, 354, 412
  ideological heterogeneity   52
  incrementalism   37, 39
  learning   18
  strategic drift   51
  strategy   4, 45; planned   7, 12
  structure   355, 360, 365, 367, 368,
    369
missionary   344–5, 350–2
misunderstanding   295–6
Mitroff, I.   46, 52
models
  corporate planning   85, 256–68
  excessive rationality   61–3
  integrated process   47–9
  strategic management   40–1
Mohrman, S. A.   308
Molière   149
momentum control   402–3
Monopolies Commission   282
moral philosophy   270–2
Morris, J. H.   307
Mueller, D. C.   201
multiple debts   276
Murphy, D.   405, 407
mutual adjustment   324, 325, 330–1,
  336–7

NASA weather satellite program   334
Naylor, T. H.   256, 258–61 passim,
  263–4, 266, 267
Neale, G. L.   258, 259
NEC Corporation   254
need-sensing   22
Neghandi, A. R.   425
negotiated agreements   299, 302

Nelson, R. R.   37
niche strategy   228, 230–1, 361–5
'no lose' situations   25
Norburn, D.   87, 89, 92
Norman, Sir A.   71
normative judgment criteria   172–3
norms, standardization of   325, 326, 337–8

objectives   *see* goals
objectivity, decline and   232
obligation   320
obligations, corporate moral   272
O'Brien, D. P.   201
offensive strategy   141, 142
Olin   144
Olsen, J. P.   37
operating core   323, 324
opportunism   208–9
opposition, overcoming   25
optimization models   257, 260, 261
organic structure   *see* adhocracy
organigrams   329
organizational action   42–4
organizational attributes   165, 166, 168, 170–1, 173
Otley, D. T.   425
Ouchi, W. G.   47, 410, 411, 420, 425
outputs, standardization of   325, 336, 337
Owen, D.   284
Owers, J. E.   214, 215
ownership, small firms'   79–80

packages, planning   265–6, 267
paradigms   2, 41, 43, 45–9
partial solutions   24
participation   298, 302
Patterson, F. S.   264, 265
payment of debts, delayed   273–6
Pearce, J. A.   416, 425
Pepsico   248
Per Cent Club   283
performance
   commitment and   308
   control and   399, 406; appraisal
      system   413–17 *passim*, 419, 422, 423–5
   corporate ventures   179–88
   diversification and   236
   divestment and   214–16
   portfolio planning   156–7
   strategic planning   84, 86–100

performance control   331
Perrow, C.   356, 361, 367, 411, 417, 421
personal computers (PCs)   266–7
personal control processes   420, 424, 425
personnel
   managers' judgment of
      attributes   165, 166, 169–70, 171
   strategic planning and   96, 99
persuasion   319
Peters, T. J.   40, 47, 52
petrol industry   219–20
Pettigrew, A. M.   37, 40, 47, 52
Pfeffer, J.   41, 43
Pfiffner, J. M.   30
philanthropy   *see* social responsibility
Philip Morris   239
philosophy, moral   270–2
Pilkington, Lord   280
Pilkington PLC   280–9
PIMS (profit impact of market
   strategy)   178, 181, 189, 266, 353
   configurations   356
   over-rationalization   61, 62, 63
planned strategy   6–7, 16
planners, corporate   64–5, 109
planning   3
   control and   331, 402–3, 404
   environmental analysis and   124
   excessive rationality   57–69
   models   256–68
   performance and   84, 86–100
   portfolio   85, 144–61
   World Wildlife Fund   71–7
planning and modelling languages
   (PMLs)   265
planning process audits   68–9
plans
   evaluation of   67–8
   implementation   395
   long-range   413, 414, 421–3
   strategic   412, 414, 421–3
Plato   271
policies, control and   413, 414, 415, 419, 422, 424
political access   308, 316–17
political barriers to control   406
political behaviour   295, 314–15
   see also coalitions
political support   25
political tools   315–17

Pondy, L. R.   37, 40
Porras, J. I.   87
Porter, L. W.   307
Porter, M.   15, 84–5, 353, 354, 409
  configurations   355, 356, 358, 359
  divestment   210
  portfolio management   240–4
  portfolio models   61–2, 220, 265–6,
    267
  portfolio planning   85, 144–61
position, taking a   310, 311, 312–14
position power   398
Power, P. D.   257, 261
power   31–2, 43–4, 46–7, 341–2, 398
Powers, M. E.   52
present value method   62
process advantages of strategic
    planning   95
process strategy   11–12, 16
Procter & Gamble   248, 249, 251
Proctor-Silex   228
product differentiation   135–6
product portfolio concept   177
production scale   186–7
productivity, World Wildlife Fund
    and   76–7
products, markets and   80
professional bureaucracy   344–5,
    347–8
professionalization of planning   58–60
profitability   142, 192
  corporate ventures   179, 181, 184
Pugh, D. S.   361, 365

quantification   60
Quinn, J. B.   xiv, 47
  environmental analysis   127
  logical incrementalism   37, 42, 49,
    403

raiders, corporate   234
Raisinghani, O.   37
Rapoport, A.   318
rationality   41–2
  excessive   57–69
Rawls, J.   271
rayon industry   220
Raytheon   220, 229, 232
RCA   229
realized strategies   45
Reed, R.   401
Reeves, T. K.   411
Reimann, B. C.   425

resistance to change   157, 292, 294–
    301, 311, 312–14
resources
  budget and   417
  implementation   395
  portfolio planning   154, 155–6,
    157, 159–60
  small firms   80
responsibility, social   281–9
responsibility centre control   402
restructuring   242–3, 244–5, 253
retailers   139
review process   154, 159
revolution   374, 375, 377, 378
  phases of growth and   378–9, 379–
    80, 380, 381, 382, 383
  see also crises
reward system   108–9, 111
Rhenman, E.   47
Rimmer, M.   283–4, 288–9
risk   319
  diversification and   177–90
rivalry   *see* competition
Robinson, R. B.   417, 425
Rohm & Haas   228
Romanelli, E.   354, 356
Rosenfield, J. D.   215
Rowan, B.   41
Rowland, K. M.   52
Rowntree   283
Royal Dutch Shell   238
Rucks, A. C.   266
Rue, L. W.   87, 89, 92, 94
Rumelt, R. P.   211, 358

Salancik, G. R.   43
Sara Lee   235, 244
Sathe, V.   41, 52
satisficing   316
scenario techniques   31, 404
Schauland, H.   258, 259
Schein, E. H.   41, 52
Schendel, D.   353
Scherer, F.   356, 359, 367
Schipper, K.   215
Schoeffler, S.   359
Scholes, K.   xiii, 400
Schrank, R.   41
Scott Morton, M. S.   410
sectors, assessment for
    diversification   191–200
security of investment   98
self-esteem, building   317

self-interest
  firms' 284–8
  managers' 292, 295, 310, 311–14
sell-offs 202, 203, 208, 210, 213
  performance and 214
Seven-Up Company 239
shareholder returns 235–6
shareholder wealth
  diversification and 214–16, 237–40, 250–1
  social responsibility and 285–7
  see also wealth
shareholders
  dividends 254
  self-diversification 236–7
sharing activities 242–3, 246, 248–50, 251, 253
Sheldon, A. 41
Shell 147
Sherwood, D. 260
Sihler, W. H. 409
Simon, L. S. et al. 262
simple structure 343, 344–5, 346, 361–5
simulation models 257, 260
situational factors
  choice of strategy 303–4
  structure and 338–42, 344–5
size
  organizations 338–9, 375, 376
  units 330–1
skills
  standardization of 325–6, 336, 337
  transfer 242–3, 245–8, 251, 253
slacks 26
Slocum, J. W. 410, 425
small firms 3, 78–81
Smircich, L. 47
Smith, A. 215
Smith, F. J. 307
Snow, C. 15, 47, 354, 356, 358, 359
social exit barriers 225
social responsibility 281–9
software, modelling 265–6, 267
Source, The 266
specialized assets 223
specialization, job 327, 338
Spence, M. A. 211
Spender, J. C. 7, 37, 47, 51, 52
spin-offs 203, 204, 208, 209, 213
  performance and 214–16
St Helens 282

Stalker, G. 353, 354, 356, 365, 367, 368
standard operating procedures (SOPs) 413
  control 414, 415, 417, 419, 422, 423–5
standardization 109, 324–6, 327–8, 330, 355
  decentralization and 336, 337
standing committees 332
Starbuck, W. H. 318
start-ups 251
statistical reports 413, 414–20 passim, 422, 423, 424
Steers, R. M. 307
Steiner, G. A. 417
Stern, M. E. 95
strategic apex 323, 324
strategic business units (SBUs) 147, 149–53, 158–9
  implementation 388–96
strategic control 293, 400–7
strategic drift 3, 49–51, 403
strategic field analysis 403
strategic issue management 403
strategic learning 17–18
strategic planning see planning
Strategic Planning Institute 266
strategic plans 412, 414, 421–3
strategic trades 203, 204
strategies
  choosing 301–5
  competitive 356–60; structure and 361–70
  deliberate and emergent 4–18
  formulation of see formulation
  implementation of see implementation
  paradigms and 45
Strater, F. R. 266
strengths
  assessment for diversification 196–8
  corporate 85, 162–76
structure, organizational 81, 292–3, 322–52
  strategy and 361–70
subsidiary entrepreneurship 209
substitute products 134–5, 139–40
Sultan, R. 358
Sun Oil 257
supervision, direct 324, 325, 330, 336, 337

suppliers   99, 137–8, 139
support   298–9, 302
support staff   323, 324
symbolic actions   23–4
symbolic mechanisms   52–3
synergy   196–8, 245–6, 248
systems modelling   404

tactical adjustments   24
Tannenbaum, A. S.   409
Tapon, F.   267
task forces   332
Taylor, B.   96
technical attributes   165, 166, 170, 171
technical system   339–40
technologies   160
technostructure   323, 324
Teece, D. J.   205
tension, constructive   52
Terpstra, D. E.   87–8
Tezel, A.   87, 89, 93
Théorët, A.   37
Thompson, J. D.   354, 367, 420
threat of entry   135–7
3M   235, 248
Thune, S. S.   87, 89, 90–1
Tiessen, P.   206
time-horizons   109–10
timeshare services, computing   266
Timex   136
Todd, J.   410
tolerance for change, low   296–7
top managers
  advocacy   24, 34
  control   414, 425
  environmental analysis   126–7
  modelling   259, 261
trades, strategic   203, 204
training   328
transactions, internalization of   205
transferring skills   242–3, 245–8, 251, 253
transistor effect   219
Trice, H. M.   41
Tricker, R. I.   398
Triplex   281, 282
trust, lack of   295–6
TRW   251
Tushman, M. L.   354, 356

umbrella strategies   2, 10–11, 16

unconnected strategies   12–13, 16
understanding   22–3, 318–19
United Nations Environmental Programme (UNEP)   73
United Technologies   251
units   329–31
  see also strategic business units
utilitarianism   271, 274
Utton, M. A.   201

vacuum tube industry   219, 220
value chain   246
Van de Ven, A. H.   420, 421
Vancil, R. F.   97
ventures, corporate   85, 178–90
verbal synopses   68
vertical integration   142, 224

waiting, systematic   26
Walker, K. R.   95
Wall, T.   307, 308
Walter, J. D.   264, 265
Warde, W. A.   95
Warner, J. B.   215
wars of attrition   227, 232
watchdogs   36
Waterhouse, J. H.   206
Waterman, R. H.   40, 47, 52
Waters, J. A.   4, 7, 18, 40
weaknesses   85, 162–76
wealth, altruism and   285–6, 286–7
  see also shareholder wealth
Weick, K. E.   37, 40–1, 126
well-being   287–8
Wells Fargo Bank   257
Westinghouse Electric   229
Wheelen, T. L.   398
Wiener, N.   175
Wilkins, A. L.   41, 46, 47
Williamson, O. E.   205
Wilson, I. H.   97
Wilson, R. M. S.   95
Winter, S. G.   37
Woodward, J.   354, 356, 361, 365, 411
Wooller, J.   259, 260, 261
work constellations   341
work processes, standardization of   325, 336, 337
working champions   127–8
working relationships   287–8
World of Glass, The   285

World Wildlife Fund   71–7
Wrapp, H. E.   28
Wright, M.   208, 210

Xerox   23, 252

Young, R. C. D.   266

'zones of indifference'   25, 35